Origins of the
African American
Jeremiad

Origins of the African American Jeremiad

The Rhetorical Strategies of Social Protest and Activism, 1760–1861

WILLIE J. HARRELL, JR.

McFarland & Company, Inc., Publishers
Jefferson, North Carolina, and London

Materials from Chapter 8 appeared as "'Thanks be to God that I am Elected to Canada': The Formulation of the Black Canadian Jeremiad, 1830–1861," *Journal of Canadian Studies* 42.3 (2008): 55–79, reprinted with permission from the *Journal of Canadian Studies*. Materials from Chapter 5 appeared as "A Call to Social and Political Activism: The Jeremiadic Discourse of Maria Miller Stewart, 1831–1833," *Journal of International Women's Studies* 9.3 (2008): 300–319, reprinted with permission from the *Journal of International Women's Studies*. Materials from Chapter 2 appeared as "A Call to Consciousness and Action: Mapping the African American Jeremiad," *Canadian Review of American Studies* 36.2 (2006): 149–180, reprinted with the permission from the University of Toronto Press Incorporated (www.utpjournals.com). Materials from Chapter 3 appeared as "'We Hold These Truths to Be Self-Evident': Characteristics of African American Jeremiadic Discourse, 1770–1850," *CLA Journal* 50.4 (2007): 395–417, reprinted with the permission from the College Language Association.

LIBRARY OF CONGRESS CATALOGUING-IN-PUBLICATION DATA

Harrell, Willie J., Jr.
 Origins of the African American jeremiad : the rhetorical strategies of social protest and activism, 1760–1861 / Willie J. Harrell, Jr.
 p.   cm.
 Includes bibliographical references and index.

 ISBN 978-0-7864-6689-4
 softcover : 50# alkaline paper ∞

 1. African Americans—History—To 1863. 2. African American messianism—History. 3. Jeremiads—United States—History and criticism. 4. African Americans—Race identity. 5. American prose literature—African American authors—History and criticism. 6. Slaves' writings, American—History and criticism. 7. Civil religion—United States—History. 8. United States—Race relations—History. I. Title.
  E185.18.H37 2011   323.1196'073—dc23   2011036508

BRITISH LIBRARY CATALOGUING DATA ARE AVAILABLE

© 2011 Willie J. Harrell, Jr. All rights reserved

No part of this book may be reproduced or transmitted in any form or by any means, electronic or mechanical, including photocopying or recording, or by any information storage and retrieval system, without permission in writing from the publisher.

Front cover image © 2011 clipart.com

Manufactured in the United States of America

McFarland & Company, Inc., Publishers
 Box 611, Jefferson, North Carolina 28640
 www.mcfarlandpub.com

For my mother

Table of Contents

Preface   1

Introduction: Mapping the African American Jeremiad   5

1. The Great Tradition of Black Protest: Characteristics of the African American Jeremiad   13
2. Early Development   36
3. The African American Jeremiad, the Constitution and the Declaration of Independence   60
4. Black Nationalism in the Early Republic   73
5. Black Women Jeremiahs   93
6. The Age of Abolitionism   115
7. The Transatlantic African American Jeremiad   160
8. The Black Canadian Jeremiad   177

Conclusion: The Great Tradition of Black Protest Continues   196

Chapter Notes   199

Works Cited   207

Index   227

Preface

This work is a major revision of my dissertation and represents the culmination of more than ten years of research, growth and change. Like many graduate students, I found myself struggling to find a focus that would not only establish for me a research interest but also help me begin building a professional reputation. After reading Wilson Jeremiah Moses' *Black Messiahs and Uncle Toms: Social and Literary Manipulations of a Religious Myth* (University Park: Pennsylvania State University Press, 1982), the search was over. I wanted to know more about the "Black Jeremiad" Moses identified in Chapter 3. I then searched the internet for any mention of the "Black Jeremiad" and discovered the only full-length manuscript devoted to the subject was David Howard-Pitney's *The Afro-American Jeremiad: Appeals for Justice in America* (Philadelphia: Temple University Press, 1990), and little else. After reading both Moses' and Howard-Pitney's provocative and stimulating works, I realized that I had to focus my research on an area that had not received much critical attention. This book, then, builds upon Moses' and Howard-Pitney's important works. Overall, my aim is to shed light on the complex interrelationship between African American jeremiadic discourse and its American predecessor.

In its present form, this work examines the first 100 years (more or less) of the development of this distinctive discourse. I was fortunate not to have to do any archival research. Since most of the speeches, editorials and essays I discuss in this work are out of print, the following were invaluable resources: *The Black Abolitionist Papers, Vols. I–V* (University of North Carolina Press, 1986, 1987, 1991, 1992), *The Frederick Douglass Papers* (Yale University Press, 1979, 1982, 1985), various anthologies (i.e., Robert S. Levine's *Martin Delany: A Documentary Reader*; John C. Shields' *The Collected Works of Phillis Wheatley*; Richard Newman, Patrick Rael, and Phillip Lapsansky's *Pamphlets of Protest: An Anthology of Early African American Protest Literature, 1790–1860*; Philip S. Foner and Robert James Branhan's *Lift Every Voice: African American Oratory, 1787–1900*; Dorothy Porter's *Early Negro Writing, 1760–1837*; and Martha Simmons and Frank A. Thomas' *Preaching with Sacred Fire: An Anthology of African Americans Sermons, 1750–Present* and others) and two digital archives, *The*

Black Abolitionist Archives (University of Detroit–Mercy Libraries) and *Documenting the American South* (University of North Carolina Libraries).

The chapters in this work seek to articulate African Americans' courses of action while utilizing jeremiadic discourse and to recognize the major influences that either aided or hindered the rise of the distinctive rhetorical strategies of the African American jeremiad. Chapter 1, "The Great Tradition of Black Protest: Characteristics of the African American Jeremiad," lays the foundation for the emergence of the African American jeremiad, discusses the differences from its American predecessor, and identifies three types of jeremiadic discourse: religious, political and economic. Chapter 2, "Early Development," identifies the African American jeremiad's rhetorical structure during the period of the Great Awakenings, from the poetic prose of Phyllis Wheatley and Jupiter Hammon to the narrative forms of early slave narrators like Ukawsaw Gronniosaw and Olaudah Equiano. Chapter 3, "The African American Jeremiad, the Constitution and the Declaration of Independence," explores how African Americans utilized the jeremiad to critique the founding fathers' conviction that "all men are created equal" and ends with a discussion on the rhetoric of the anti–Constitution jeremiad of Charles Lenox Remond. Chapter 4, "Black Nationalism in the Early Republic," investigates the growth and development of the jeremiad and Black Nationalism. Using Maria Miller Stewart as the focal point, Chapter 5, "Black Women Jeremiahs," examines the important role black women Jeremiahs played in the development of African American jeremiadic discourse. Chapter 6, "The Age of Abolitionism," explores jeremaidic discourse in the age of abolitionism. The next logical step, Chapter 7, "The Transatlantic African American Jeremiad," considers the rhetoric of the transatlantic African American jeremiad, which was created when activists crossed the Atlantic Ocean to expand the concept of the black abolitionist profession. Chapter 8, "The Black Canadian Jeremiad," uses Henry Bibb's Canadian rhetoric as the nucleus of the black Canadian jeremiad, and examines how blacks took the African American jeremiad and its polemics across the American-Canadian border to protest against both American and Canadian prejudices.

Serving as an introductory approach to examining the issues surrounding the growth and development of the African American jeremiad during America's antebellum years, my research has made it possible for me to probe several components of the African American jeremiad — the historical, political, social, religious, and economic. This book also serves as a response to early African Americans' call because it provides the much-needed correctives regarding the origin and development of the distinctiveness of the African American jeremiad. From my point of view, there are several reasons why an investigation into the origins of the African American jeremiad is important. First, this investigation examines the contributions of the American jeremiad to the antebellum social protest writings of African Americans at both practical and abstract levels. Second, it evaluates the role of the African American jeremiad in the development of an African American literary genre in antebellum America. Further, this book proposes that despite its rather unfavorable locale within a rather unreceptive environment, the African American jeremiad maintained its power as a rhetorical trope and influence in contemporary African American literary traditions.

I would like to thank my mentor, dissertation director, and friend, Professor Emeritus Henry L. Golemba, for his guidance over the years. I would also like to thank the anonymous reviewer who determinedly made suggestions on the organization, content and structure of this book when it was previously submitted for consideration to another academic press.

Finally, this work is by no means exhaustive or complete. No historical literary criticism is. There is still much work to be done. It is my hope that other scholars of the African American jeremiad will fill in the unintentional gaps.

I am pleased at long last to be able to present this book. I hope it will make meaningful contributions and advances in African American cultural studies.

Introduction
Mapping the African American Jeremiad

[Now] if I know anything about the history of this country, the 22nd day of December is the anniversary of the landing of the Pilgrims; the anniversary of the day when those ambassadors, those leaders in religion, came to the American shore; when they landed within the encircling arms of Cape Cod and Cape Ann, fleeing from political and religious tyranny, seeking political and religious freedom in the New World. The anniversary of that day is selected for selling an American mother and her four children.
— William Wells Brown, "A Lecture Delivered Before the Female Anti-Slavery Society of Salem," 14 November 1847

The history of the enslavement of people of African extraction in America has always been a tumultuous one, grounded in contradictions and paradoxes. In his 14 November 1847 "A Lecture Delivered before the Female Anti-Slavery Society of Salem," William Wells Brown reminded listeners that throughout American history, the subjugation of his people "has never been represented." By the time Brown had become a victim of America's "peculiar institution," slavery was part of a long-established system of labor exploitation for almost 200 years. Because of the "blighting influence of American Slavery," American prejudice, and issues surrounding politics and religion, "Slavery" Brown lamented, "never can be represented." Sharply comparing the incivility of American slaveholders with the present dishonorable disregard for black reform and uniformity, Brown took the time to reprimand the defenders of "democratic, Christian, republican America" for not adhering to their own credence that "all men are created equal." Lamenting the "system of slavery" that he represented as a "system that strikes at the foundation of society ... [and] strikes at the foundation of civil and political institutions," Brown's sole purpose was to express grief over the slave's condition: "[Slavery] is a system that takes man down from that lofty position which his God designed that he should occupy; that drags him down, places him upon a level with the beasts of the field, and there keeps him, that it may rob him of his liberty." In his derisive assault on the

American democratic system, Brown revealed the difference between what he called "the Slave-growing" and "the Slave-consuming States." The "Slave-growing" states were the southern slave holding states whose very existence depended upon the degradation of human beings for survival. The "Slave-consuming States," however, were the northern states that refused to offer the slave refuge from the South's growing peculiarity. Thousands of slaves, he believed, were consumed by, or because of southern prejudices, driven to the latter. Therefore, Brown positioned his rhetoric to assail the "morals of the people of the United States of America," both North and South. In his view, every Christian was to be held responsible for the sins of slavery. "The people of the North are connected with Slaveholding, they necessarily become contaminated by the evils that follow in the train of Slavery" (2–3, 4, 5).[1] Brown's moralizing employed the rhetoric of the developing African American jeremiad, a discourse that has undergone significant social, political, and intellectual changes since its initial conception and demonstrated an astounding literary authority by its architects.

Since this study is a discussion of the history of a rhetorical discourse, it is important to identify African American rhetoric. Since African American rhetoric "has been dislodged from our purview of what rhetoric is and how it gets defined" (Jackson and Richardson xv), the term "rhetoric" has been used to explore a wide variety of discourses. It has been identified as a vehicle of uplift, an instrument of language, while on the other hand, an art of deception (Ampadu 39). Dexter B. Gordon has defined rhetoric as "an ideological discourse in process, constantly responsive to the exigencies of the contingent situations in which it operates" (5). Because of its intricate evolution, then, analyses of the rhetoric of the African American[2] jeremiad have not been straightforward since rhetoric is, as Gordon suggested, continuously responding within and dependent upon circumstances in which it functions. The purpose of this book is to delve beneath the socio-religious and cultural exterior of the American jeremiadic tradition to unveil the complexities of African American jeremiadic rhetoric in antebellum America, which was given birth from an inhumane society and has developed a lasting effect on African American literary and cultural studies. This book also examines the varied ways that African Americans rationally adapted the elements of the American jeremiad to fit the needs of their communities during the early republic. The fundamental argument to be further developed is that the seeds for African American jeremiad to exist were planted as early as the 1760s and provided the organizational structure that gave rise to this distinct form of rhetorical discourse.

Jeremiadic discourse has always been a distinguishing construction that exchanged with cultures and governments to aid in the shaping of an idyllic society. In these moralistic texts, the authors acrimoniously lamented the condition of society and its morals in a stern tenor of sustained invective and utilized prophecy as a means of predicting society's ominous demise. In its simplest form, however, the term jeremiad is a result of scholars' understanding of the deeds of the Old Testament prophet Jeremiah. In the seventh century B.C., legend has it that Jeremiah prophesized the misfortunes of the Israelites as they abandoned the covenant God made with Abraham. Because of their dereliction to their duty, Jeremiah's lamentations revealed that their nation would be ruined, yet other nations would advance: "See, I have this day set thee over the nations and over the kingdoms, to root out, and to pull down, and to destroy, and to throw down, to build, and to plant" (Jer. 1:10, *New American Standard Bible*). Jeremiah's prophetic influence extended to all nations that the "Lord might choose for building up or for destroying" (Sharp 436). He held out hope, however, that Israel would progress. When Israel would rise again, according to Jeremiah's prophecies, the second Israel would be more remarkable than the first. According to scholars' exegesis, Jeremiah exhorted the people to a period of atonement and reformation so that God may be compelled to favor them again. Since Jeremiah's lamentations have transcended their originating cultural and historical meaning to modern socio-political needs and desires for communities around the world, today a jeremiad is loosely defined as a lament, or other work, that reflects the continuing calamities of a people as a moral punishment for their societal and moral evils as it maintains hope for a brighter future. Religion, then, takes on a political basis in this development. As they have evolved over time in American history, jeremiads today are visible in many forms of rhetorical modes, particularly the poetry, narratives, novels, music, and other forms of artistic creations of people who were historically oppressed.

Because of the impact of the revivalism of America's Great Awakenings (1730s–1740s; 1820s–1830s), religion was a mechanism employed to empower African Americans to transform their brutally disempowering reality in a language that was appropriate for the times. The African American jeremiad warranted credit in helping to forge and create this awareness concerning the oppression of blacks by challenging whites to take a stand on the issues surrounding black enslavement. A more in depth investigation of African American social protest of the early republic would suggest that the prototypical form of their rhetoric was not so much religious as it was political. Religion was not the only central ingredient in the evolution of the African American jeremiadic rhetoric. A consciousness among the African American community began to suggest that the rhetoric of evangelical Christianity granted blacks civil liberties but only to the point of delimiting them to "pagans," "savages," and "brutes." Blacks in the early republic used the ideology of Christianity to call for sociopolitical reformation; therefore, a consideration of their political activism during the early republic is fundamentally necessary for an all-encompassing view of the African American jeremiad and its polemics. Used as a vehicle to lament the social, religious, economic, and political conditions of blacks during the early republic, the African American jeremiad evaluated the racist status quo responsible for those very conditions.

The political culture which gave birth to the African American jeremiad was mainly an outcome of blacks seeking basic civil liberties which would comprise, for them, political participation. The building of separate communities (i.e., churches, schools) had political references. As Ronald W. Walters suggested, the definition of what is "political" must be broadened to include "most activities where race relations are involved" (146). Politically speaking, racism was the fundamental factor that led African Americans to adapt their white counterparts' rhetoric in their fight for justice and retribution. Political theorist John Rex identified several situations where political "conflict[s] between social strata or segments" can occur:

- A minority group is seeking to enter a stratification system from below.
- Two or more groups are in competitions for limited resources.
- Punitive policies are pursued by one group against another.
- One group seeks systematically to exploit the labor of another.
- There is a situation of virtual civil war [121].

In light of Rex's argument, the African American jeremiad called for radical changes in America's socio-political consciousness in several of the situations identified above. These political endeavors where manifested in numerous day-to-day situations used by blacks to gain political control in the early republic. As Steven Hahn has noted, "The rapid circulation of news and rumor, the complex ties of family and kinship, the contests over the deployment of labor, the accumulation of petty property, [and] the customs and institutions of internal authority and discipline" were means in which slaves amassed "social and political stability" (15). Religion, too, unquestionably forged political discourse in the early republic as it was one of the most important aspects affecting commitment to political parties. Religion, though not the sole ingredient of jeremiadic polemics, was transformed by the architects of the African American jeremiad into socio-political discourse and utilized to argue for basic civil liberties, making it one of the earliest forms of not only social, but more importantly, civil liberties protest utilized by black Americans.

As David Howard-Pitney argued, the African American jeremiad "protests injustices" (vii). Why, though, did African Americans employ jeremiadic discourse separate of their white counterparts? There are many reasons behind this phenomenon. Their appeal for social exchange, their demand for economic refuge, their need to necessitate moral and educational development, and their need for a political voice comprised the principal reasons. As with terms such as liberation, rhetoric and nationalism, the characteristics of the African American jeremiad will depend, however, on how one identifies its rhetorical structure: civil liberties, justice, retribution and empowerment, social progress, freedom and the call for social change. Therefore, the African American jeremiad can not be discussed properly unless we take into consideration the earliest contributors to the fight for justice and equality in the early republic.

Arguably, one can identify two apparently distinct characteristics of African American jeremiadic discourse. The first, and most widely accepted, sees the African American jeremiad as an interpretation of its American predecessor that is heavily centered on Christian values. But whose Christian values? Whites? Blacks? When blacks used the religion card, as personified in the rhetoric of Jupiter Hammon, Phyllis Wheatley, Absalom Jones and Richard Allen, Lemuel Haynes, and others, they did so to criticize traditional white Christian ethics. The other distinguishing character trait, however, not as widely accepted, sees African American jeremiadic discourse more fundamentally politically based, calling for social changes in lieu of social prophecy. The latter is the subject of this book. When looked at under this light, blacks' resistance to the injustices against them became classic examples of the African American jeremiadic tradition, as they sought to transform the entire socio-political structure of the early republic by attempting to illustrate to their white counterparts that they can be productive citizens.

Methodologies and Definitions of the African American Jeremiad

Scholars of the African American jeremiad have argued that as a rhetorical device it is an influential force in black protest. In his examination of the development of the black messianic tradition in African American history, Wilson Jeremiah Moses contended that the "Black Jeremiad" was "the constant warnings issued by blacks to whites, concerning the judgment that was to come for the sin of slavery." Moses declared that the "Black Jeremiad" was "mainly a pre–Civil War phenomenon and showed the traditional preoccupation with impending doom" (*Black Messiahs* 30–31). According to Moses' definition, blacks had a predetermined role to play and possessed a particular significance for the greater humanity. Building upon Moses' assertions, Keith Gilyard and Anissa Wardi interpreted the African American jeremiad as a "shrewd variation of the American one." Their analysis concluded that "blacks are cast as a chosen people *within* the parameters of the nation's archetypal civil myth — so, they are deemed to be a chosen people in the midst of a chosen people" (932; emphasis in original). Patrick Rael suggested that African American jeremiadic rhetoric attempted to connect the oppressors and the oppressed:

> Black jeremiads served to unite African Americans in the common cause of moral elevation, which was to say, in effective racial self-presentation. They set forth an imperative that corralled the non-elite into a community of the oppressed, defined by its struggle to find ways of compelling whites to grant the rights and liberty that they were due [*Black Identity & Black Protest* 175].

Blacks used the jeremiad, Rael continued, to demonstrate "the dangers of their recalcitrant stance toward slavery's abolition ... and to warn those loyal to the slaveholding country" (*Black Identity & Black Protest* 270). David Howard-Pitney concluded that the rhetoric of the American jeremiad ultimately developed into something distinctively "Afro-American" because of its call for social prophecy and criticism. He concluded that the rhetoric set out to warn white America that "the sin of slavery" is a "declension from the promise of a Christian America."[3] Howard-Pitney has identified three elements of the "Afro-American Jeremiad": "citing the *promise*, criticism of present *declension* or retrogression from the promise, resolving *prophecy* that society will shortly complete its mission and redeem the promise." These elements appear, somewhat intermittently, throughout African American social protest in the early republic. As Howard-Pitney argued, some blacks used this prototypical form of rhetoric in "its pure form" (12, 8, 15). To the architects of this rhetoric, the African American jeremiad served a threefold purpose: (1) to expose traditional white Christian convictions, (2) to emphasize the inhumanness of slavery and its effect on both the oppressed and the oppressors, and (3) to develop a socio-political consciousness among blacks that would be used to forge a unified black self.

Emory Elliott's discussion of the jeremiad takes on a more encompassing approach. According to Elliott, those who adapted jeremiadic rhetoric appropriated it in this manner:

> In current scholarship, the term "jeremiad" has expanded to include not only sermons but also other texts that rehearse the familiar tropes of the formula such as captivity narratives, letters, covenant renewals, as well as some histories and biographies [257].

Elliott's discussion on the jeremiad is important to this study because it looks beyond the prototypical sermonic rhetorical strategies of the jeremiad and suggests that its rhetorical pattern can be found in many modes of expression (i.e., "captivity narratives, letters, covenant renewals"). Perhaps Winthrop D. Jordan, however, offers the most comprehensive discussion on jeremiadic rhetoric. Jordan suggested that the jeremiad represented "a complex fusion of religious and political modes of thought strongly tinged with the less lofty quality of opportunism.... [The jeremiad] was a peculiarly introspective view; it focused not on the miseries of the victims of slavery but on the wickedness of the victimizers" (297). Jordan's discussion is of equal importance to this study because the previous definitions of the jeremiad avoided discussing issues of politics and its roles in the jeremiad's development. Given this, the African American jeremiad represented a deliberate fusion of rhetoric and social protest that represented a transformation from a religious to a socio-political evaluation of the ills of slavery while inspiring moral uplift and elevation in its black audience; it is concerned with the promotion of black consciousness while it involves a commitment to an unrelenting rational examination of selfhood and socio-political practices of blacks. Without question, the American jeremiad contributed to the socio-political and religious development of an emerging African American literary tradition, yet very little attempt, if any, has been made to progressively chronicle and explore the cultural syntheses of religion and politics in African Americans' social protest of the early republic. The ways in which African Americans utilized, or adapted, American jeremiadic rhetoric requires an inventive analytical approach.

Finally, it should be remembered how some black abolitionists, such as Frederick Douglass, viewed the reality of their existence in America. To a crowd in Paisley, Scotland, in April 1846, Douglass lamented:

> I am a man before I am an American. To be a man is above being an American. To be a human being is to have claims above all the claims of nationality. But I have no nation. America only welcomes me to her shores as a brute. She spurns the idea of treating me in any other way than as a brute — she would not receive me as a man ["British Influence on the Abolition Movement in America," 215].

Declarations like these, which were decidedly charged with passion and zeal, have been repeated throughout the developmental years of the African American jeremiad and were at the heart and soul of this distinguishing discourse.

1

The Great Tradition of Black Protest
Characteristics of the African American Jeremiad

> Every man might have need of others, and from hence they might be all knitt more nearly together in the Bonds of brotherly affection. From hence it appears plainly that noe man is made more honourable than another or more wealthy &c., out of any particular and singular respect to himselfe, but for the glory of his creator and the common good of the creature, man.
> — John Winthrop, "A Modell of Christian Charity," 1630

By the time John Winthrop delivered his opus "A Modell of Christian Charity" aboard the *Arbella,* the first 20 Africans to serve as a "Modell of Christian Charity"—the foundations of American slavery—had already arrived in Jamestown as indentured servants. In his sermon to his fellow expatriates on board the ship, Winthrop revealed that their purpose was to "shame the faces of many of God's worthy servants, and cause prayers to be turned into curses upon us till wee be consumed out of the good land whither wee are a goeing." Introducing their "errand into the wilderness," although not explicitly, Winthrop told them, "For wee must consider that wee shall be as a citty upon a hill. The eies of all people are uppon us" (48).[1] Scholars consider Winthrop's sermon to be the foundation for American jeremiadic discourse. Sacvan Bercovitch, for example, noted that "Winthrop's 'Model' of social cohesion derived from a doctrine of vocational calling which (by implication at least) undermined the tenets of feudal hierarchy by its appeal to self-discipline and self sufficiency." The American jeremiad, according to Bercovitch, matured as "an ancient formulaic refrain, a ritual form imported to Massachusetts in 1630 from the Old World.... The American jeremiad owes its uniqueness to this vision and mode of rhetoric." Conceptualizing the jeremiad as a "political sermon—what might be called the state-of-the-state-covenant address" (*The American Jeremiad* 20–2, 6, 4) that summoned its Puritan audience to acknowledge rather than question the basis of their present tribulations, Bercovitch continued:

> In Europe ... the jeremiad pertained exclusively to mundane, social matters, to the city of man rather than the city of God. It required not conversion but moral obedience and civic virtue. At best, it held out that prospect of temporal, worldly success. At worst, it threatened not hellfire but secular calamity (disease, destruction, death). The Puritans' concept of errand entailed a fusion of secular and sacred history. The purpose of their jeremiads was to direct an imperiled people of God toward salvation, and collectively toward the American city of God [*The American Jeremiad* 6, 9].

Bercovitch's analysis suggested that while the jeremiad foretold devastation, at the same time, it offered hope for a brighter future. To understand the structure of jeremiadic discourse, then, is to recognize that the jeremiad has been an evolving phenomenon throughout American history, exchanging with, and forging American culture. Puritan jeremiadic discourse, for example, "set out the sacred history of the New World; the eighteenth-century jeremiad established the typology of America's mission." Bercovitch suggested that the American jeremiad "was significantly concerned with a range of social and intellectual transformations. But through all change," he continued, "the persistence of the rhetoric attests to an astonishing cultural hegemony, one that the rhetoric itself reflected and shaped" (*The American Jeremiad* 93, 28). According to Bercovitch, "The sacred and profane [shapes] the American jeremiads."

> Their threats of doom, derived from Christian tradition, imply a distinction between the two realms; their language itself, expressing their special sense of mission, incorporates the threats within the broader framework of the absolute.... Drawing on the very precariousness of their experience, the American Puritans ... forged what was to become a framework of national identity [*The American Jeremiad* 29].

If the American jeremiad beseeched its audience to re-establish its community, as Bercovitch suggested, what role, then, would blacks play in *shaping* the "framework of national identity"? Scholars of the African American jeremiad avoid unveiling the politics behind a purportedly religious text. To this end, there can be no discussion on national identities without a dialogue on the political framework of the early republic. The moral values of the Puritan rhetoric, it seemed, were regarding the attainment of power and wealth, as it appeared to them that these interpretations pleased God, and therefore, He would bestow upon them His kindness. When blacks in the early republic employed the jeremiad, some did so under their understanding that they had to develop independent organizations in order to establish their citizenship in a land that did not offer them the same opportunities as their white counterparts. At the same time, however, some blacks felt that assimilationism was the way to eliminate racial oppression. At any rate, their employment of the jeremiad both operated within the black community, while, at the same time, played a vital socio-political role in building that community. When African Americans adapted this rhetoric in their fight for recognition, its polemics began to modify drastically.

1. The Great Tradition of Black Protest   15

What, then, is the relationship between the characterizations of the African American jeremiad to its American predecessor? African American jeremiadic discourse became a form of communication attempting to alter its audience's perspective on race relations. In its underlying form, the African American jeremiad varied from its American predecessor in a number of ways:

- The use of racial bias to argue for basic civil liberties for blacks.
- The appropriation of the vagueness of the republic's founding fathers' documents (i.e., Constitution and Declaration of Independence).
- The development of separate organization and communities void not of British influence but of Euro-American involvement.
- The call for black self-determination and equality (although at times, African American jeremiadic discourse appears to call for inclusion into mainstream).
- The recognition in the political arena of the developing consciousness of the oppressed.

An innovative approach to examining the African American jeremiad, then, would have to determine what makes it uniquely African American in the first place. A straightforward answer would be that it involved a racially compelled set of practices that structure the language, discourse, and models of behavior. These characteristics surfaced intermittently throughout the initial years of African American jeremiadic discourse and helped to shape the moral fabric of its rhetoric. William Whipper, an African American businessman and abolitionist who was born to a white Pennsylvania businessman and his black woman servant, put it this way:

> [The man of color] stands alone on his own merits, clothed, it is true, in the badge of complexional degradation — without the title of citizenship — without the enjoyment of a participation in the affairs of his government — without any share in the administration of its laws — without the hope of earthly reward or future fame; yet, under all these disadvantages, his virtues are seen embellishing his character, and encircling his name. He lives a model for the world — an honor to this country, but slave to its laws ["Speech by William Whipper Delivered before the Colored Temperance Society of Philadelphia" 126–127].

Whipper's statement suggested a major distinction between the Puritan use of jeremiadic rhetoric and the African American jeremiadic rhetoric, which lies in each discourse's philosophies. Whipper's invective also pointed to reasoning behind sorting Americans of divergent ethnicities into groups. During the early republic, the need to sort citizens into groups materialized as a societal imperative for two reasons: exceptional numbers of Africans were being brought to the country who were unfamiliar with the country's philosophies of egalitarianism and who often needed to acquire competence in the dominant language, and the growth of America's "peculiar institution" introduced the need for the large numbers of slaves to toil the lands. This sorting was strengthened and fueled by the formulation of white America's belief in racial and ethic supremacy.

There are, however, numerous components of any jeremiadic discourse. Every ethnic group that has been victimized by colonization, imperialism and despotism has devised a way to deal with the realities of its oppression and, at the same time, confront the domineering ideologies of the oppressors. The rhetoric that emerged as a means to protest this subjugation was, in fact, a jeremiad and became a form of deconstructing the dominate culture's values. American jeremiadic tradition, as James Darsey suggested, demonstrated a long "practical understanding of the principle" of crisis (69). In America, ethnic groups have developed jeremiadic discourse for the expressed purpose of bringing attention to their duress. William Apess' 1831 *A Son of the Forest: The Experience of William Apess, a Native of the Forest* became an eloquent example of Native American jeremiadic rhetoric because in it readers find "issues of identity and the formulation" (O'Connell 2) that were customary to this kind of discourse. Furthermore, the title of Apess' narrative appeared to be in response to the Puritan's "errand into the wilderness." Conceivably, what Apess proclaimed was that when the Puritans trampled into their metaphorical "wilderness," they found his people: "son[s] of the forest," the true "worm[s] of the earth" (*A Son of the Forest* 4). Apess, born in Massachusetts in 1798, was ordained a Methodist minister in 1829. Of Pequot descent, Apess took part in the Mashpee Revolt of 1833. On 21 May 1833, the Mashpee of Cape Cod signed what they called a Native American Declaration of Independence. The Mashpee reiterated to Boston bureaucrats that "all men are born free and Equal, as says the constitution of the country." In their document, the Mashpee indicated the particulars of what they considered an insufferable condition — whites' selfish behaviors, and the misappropriation of their woodlots, hay fields and pastures. The Mashpee acknowledged that they would oppose additional infringement by white colonists. A group of farmers resolved to test the Mashpee's steadfastness. When the farmers came to cut wood on Mashpee land, they were met with resistance. A violent conflict ensued; the Mashpee saw themselves as warriors battling an oppressive foreign government. Fearing an insurrection, the government approved the Mashpee's right of self-government in 1834.[2]

The fundamental thematic concern in Apess' *A Son of the Forest*, however, was the failure of white America to confront the paradox of their oppressive ideologies and their hypocrisy in refusing Native Americans the civil liberties assured "all men" by their own Declaration of Independence by labeling them as "heathens" and regarding them as savages. At the onset of his narrative, the earliest of Native American autobiographies, Apess attempted to unite all humanity— Native Americans, Africans, and Euro-Americans— under one blood:

> My grandmother was, if I am not misinformed, the king's [of the Pequot tribe] granddaughter and a fair and beautiful woman. This statement is given not with a view of appearing great in the estimation of others— what, I would ask, is *royal*

blood?—the blood of a king is no better than that of the subject. We are in fact but one family; we are all the descendants of one great progenitor—Adam. I would not boast of my extraction, as I consider myself nothing more than a worm of the earth [*A Son of the Forest* 4].

Apess positioned his rhetoric in his narrative in a similar revolutionary tone that some African American activists, such as David Walker, and later Henry Highland Garnet, utilized in order to deconstruct the Euro-American ideology that oppression was justified. As was customary in the maturing African American jeremiadic discourse, Apess attempted to place the oppressors in the light of the oppressed as a way to forge social change:

Not doubt there are many good people in the United States who would not trample upon the rights of the poor, but there are many others who are willing to roll in their coaches upon the tears and blood of the poor and unoffending natives—those who are ready at all times to speculate on the Indians and defraud them out of their rightful possessions. It has been considered as a trifling thing for the whites to make war on the Indians for the purpose of driving them from their country and taking possession thereof.... But let the thing be changed. Suppose an overwhelming army should march into the United States for the purpose of subduing it and enslaving the citizens; how quick would they fly to arms, gather in multitudes around the tree of liberty, and contend for their rights with the last drop of their blood. And should the enemy succeed, would they not eventually rise and endeavor to regain liberty? And who would blame them for it? [*A Son of the Forest* 31].

African Americans and Native Americans, according to Bercovitch, "could learn to be true Americans, when in the fullness of time they would adopt the tenets of black and red capitalism" (*The American Jeremiad* 160). This endeavor to forge social change in lieu of prophecy materialized throughout ethnic communities: their jeremiads force the oppressors to come to terms with issues that surround the subjugation of ethnic groups. It is important, then, to discuss the growth and development patterns of the African American jeremiad as a means of achieving civil liberties and equality for its constituents in America.

The racial attitudes of whites in the early republic certainly affected the content of the African American jeremiad. Peter Williams, in his 4 July 1830 speech celebrating America's independence, made it clear that blacks' lowly position in society was a direct result of white prejudice, and that blacks have little reason to celebrate:

But although this anniversary affords occasion of rejoicing, to the mass of the people of the United States, there is a class, a numerous class, consisting of nearly three millions, who participate but little in its joys, and are deprived of their unalienable rights, by the very men who so loudly rejoice in this declaration, that "all men are born free and equal."

The festivities of this day serve but to impress upon the mind of reflecting men of colour a deeper sense of the cruelty, the injustice, and oppression of which they have been the victims. While others rejoice in their deliverance from a foreign yoke, they mourn that a yoke a thousandfold more grievous is fastened upon them. Alas, they are slaves in the midst of freemen; they are slaves to those who boast that freedom is the unalienable right to all; and the clanking of their fetters, and the voice of their wrongs make a horrid discord in the songs of freedom which resound through the land ["A Discourse Delivered in St. Phillip's Church" 295].

The central problem, then, for early African American jeremiadic discourse was the construction of an elevated black consciousness against the racial stereotypes that had been formulated by whites. When black slaves were brought to the New World, colonists felt no need to change the "routine of their perceived manifest destiny" (Lincoln 11). The ideological concept of "manifest destiny" greatly influenced America's political structure. Believing that they were bringing enlightenment in the form of civilization to an inferior culture, Americans used "the empire-building slogan" (*BAP IV* 146; see Chap. 3, n. 4) "manifest destiny" to justify their deceitful, malicious, and racist treatment of the natives who occupied America. A similar ideological strain goaded their treatment of blacks, who they saw as ignorant and savage. As some blacks saw it, white America's "manifest destiny" was not a reasonable reality. "Those who regard slavery as at once our blessing and our 'manifest destiny' and who believe we can flourish in no other condition, are, of course, beneath the reach of any argument," mourned Samuel Ringgold Ward, "They will only be convinced [of their wrongdoings] when they wake up *as* Dives did, *where* Dives did" ("Modern Negro No. 1" 413; emphasis in original).[3]

However, race relations were heightened at the end of the Seven Years' War in 1763 and this instability would produce a continuing effect on black consciousness (Bruce 39). In view of the fact that African Americans were slaves when the country was established, the legislature refused them constitutional rights in 1787. These acts and the "unsettled political condition" of the colonists (Bruce 39) that led up to the American Revolution manifested a period of political, economic, religious, and social upheaval against African Americans. As they responded, the meaning of freedom was being actively challenged. As early as 1808, blacks revealed their unrest concerning the superficial freedoms espoused by many white Americans:

> Did not America think it was a privilege truly desirable to be enjoyed, when her mother nation was about to invade her land, and bring her under their dominion; did she not greatly regret the thought of a deprivation of her freedom when she asked the assistance of her sister nation, France, to vindicate her cause against Britain with her? If desirable, I say, to America under such circumstances, why not to any or all the nations of the earth? I answer, equally desirable to all. Well, if so desirable to Americans as that they exerted all their powers to obtain it, why then are they not willing to have it universal? [Anonymous, "The Sons of Africans" 18].

Oftentimes slaves' refusal to work and what was seen as other forms of plantation stubbornness were movements to further the process of basic civil liberties. Even though on a smaller scale than the movements of the 1960s, their actions gave the architects of the African American jeremiad the fuel they needed to advance liberation and black solidarity. Opposition to racial injustices and discrimination marked a remarkable awareness in blacks' consciousnesses concerning the philosophies of white oppression, while they acknowledged the struggle to end racial inequality.

As African American activists in the early republic began to conceive varying degrees of socio-political tactics to eliminate white oppression, their ideologies of freedom and citizenship fostered resistance in some blacks' consciousnesses. For example, while recounting the events that led to the founding of the African Methodist Episcopal Church, Richard Allen, America's "black founding father" (Nash 332), told readers that he, too, was "met with opposition." Allen wrote that there were only "three colored brethren that united ... in erecting a place of worship.... The Rev. C — B — opposed the plan, and would not submit to any argument we could raise" (*The Life, Experience and Gospel* 12). Other black activists were met with antagonism from the black community as well. After Henry Highland Garnet delivered his "Address to the Slaves of the United States of America" at the 1843 convention in Buffalo, New York, Frederick Douglass, "not concurring with certain points in the address, nor with the sentiments advanced" by Garnet, commented that his speech contained "too much physical force" (Garnet, "Debate over Garnet's 'Address'" 157). Douglass did not advocate Garnet's notions. Later, in an 1848 speech, Douglass would seemingly forfeit his conviction and maintain, "I say to you, get out of this position of body-guard to slavery! Cease from any longer rendering aid and comfort to the tyrant-master!" ("The Slaves' Right to Revolt" 131). In his 25 March 1850 speech delivered at Faneuil Hall in Boston, Samuel Ringgold Ward, however, seemed to concede with Garnet forthright. In reference to the Fugitive Slave Act of 1850, Ward recommended that the racial injustices against African Americans called for "the Right to Revolution." He maintained that "at whatever cost," this right will "most sacredly maintain" ("Speech by Samuel Ringgold Ward, Delivered at Faneuil Hall" 51). However, what some activists realized was that contradictory interests and differences of opinions over approaches and procedures often hindered community building efforts. James McCune Smith lamented that the vast barrier to the progression of the "free colored people [was] the want of unity in action." In order to overcome these and other hindrances, Smith could not imagine "no possibility beyond our power to compass." "The grand secret of lack" of black unity, Smith believed, was because all blacks were not "equally oppressed." Smith advocated that the "various grades of oppression inflicted on our people," some "two thousand distinct forms," would only strengthen. Therefore, he advocated revolution, "'up boys and at them.'"[4] In other words, "*do something*" to alleviate this "reproach of imbecility" he avowed ("James McCune Smith to Frederick Douglass" 220, 221, 223; emphasis in original).

Enhanced by lack of humanitarianism in the republic, African American jeremiadic discourse was further shaped by institutions, such as various secret societies—Prince Hall's society of Masonry—and the establishment of black churches—Allen's African Methodist Episcopal Church. Architects of the

African American jeremiad thus aligned their forces with these establishments to advocate the mobilization of the black community to provide enlightenment, guidance, and organizational structures that served as a site of resistance, and a place to critically assess and challenge the power of the early republic's white supremacy. Thus over 100 years prior to Martin Luther King, Jr.'s arrival on the scene in the 1960s, the ingredients for a civil rights movement had already been in the making. King and others helped to further attack the augmented laws of white supremacy in their language of liberation theology through their nonviolent sit-ins, demonstrations, marches, and jeremiads. African American jeremiadic discourse thus became a tool that amassed a large scale attack on the country's oppressive philosophies which would in turn position it as a movement to acquire civil rights for African Americans in America.

Slavery and Its Racial Oppression: The Call

What was American slavery? Countless scholars and historians have conceived descriptions over the years. However, the victims of its tyranny were the ones who were accurately able to define the parasitic organism through various agencies. Charles W. Gardner, a Presbyterian clergyman of Philadelphia, put it this way:

> [American slavery] consists in this: in making men chattels; in brutalizing the image of God, the purchase of the blood of Jesus Christ; impressing its seal on childhood, and wresting from the hand of the rightful owner that exercise of the judgment for which he is accountable only to God. It denies to the slave, and in many parts of the country to the free colored people also, access to that heavenly chart, which is laid down by Jehovah as the only safe rule of faith and practice, the liberty of reading and understanding how he may serve God acceptably. It withholds from him all the proceeds of his labor, except a scanty subsistence, and two suits of clothing in a year, of the coarsest description. Is it morally right and politically safe to abolish such a system immediately? ["Speech by Charles W. Gardner" 206].

The institution of American slavery adversely affected the religious and political philosophy formulated by the idea of democracy set forth by the country's founding fathers. Enslavement of blacks, therefore, was sanctioned by a far-reaching corpus of laws that grew from white supremacy. From its beginning as "a colonial institution" (Olwell 5), slavery and its immediate evils were shrouded in the early republic's political, religious, and economic arenas. During the republic's developmental years, the subject of slavery was centered on African slave trafficking (Franklin 65). Both a blueprint and representation of the most excessive modes of "exploitation, otherness, and even social death" (Berlin 2), slavery thrived sporadically throughout the North, mainly in the undeveloped, farming sections of New York and New Jersey. The first Africans to be exploited for their labor arrived in 1619 as indentured servants; a Dutch slave trader bartered his cargo of 20 Africans for food and other supplies. This tremendously important exchange between the Dutchman and the colonists altered the face of the preexisting New World indentured servitude. The markings of degradation and humiliation were surfacing as the settlements began to move toward the establishment of African-based slavery (Bruce 4). Many complex issues led to the progression of this African-based institutionalization of slavery; however, the creation of racial oppression did not begin with the African slave trade: Native Americans were an insecure choice for the rigorousness of labor and agricultural practices of the Europeans because of their vulnerability to European diseases; Native Americans were more familiar with the land and used that knowledge for avenues of escape. Because of these issues, the mounting fascination on the part of the "plantation bourgeoisie" in degrading Africans to a perpetual servitude (Allen, *The Invention of the White Race*, 24) traded off Native Americans as the objectification of perpetual enslavement. However, the most important issue concerning the substitution of Africans for Native Americans was the lucrative nature of the African slave trade.

By the time the newly found republic was beginning to take shape, however, slavery was slowly dissipating in the North. Because of the contradiction of the American revolutionaries' rhetoric that "all men are created equal," slaves were not merely the passive subjects of the slave society, they were considered valuable for their manual labor. As early at 1797, blacks began to communicate that America's disregard and conduct toward them was a learned behavior and that their "national identity" would never be achieved if they did not, first, recognize and accept their own past, and, second, change their attitude towards blacks. Abraham Johnstone illustrated this ideology in his "The Address of Abraham Johnstone, A Black Man, Who Was Hanged at Woodbury in the County of Glocester, and State of New Jersey, on Saturday the 8th day of July last; to the People of Colour." Johnstone, who was born a slave, manumitted and convicted of the murder of Thomas Read, another black man, reminded Americans that their heritage lay in bondage as well:

> But to bring it more closely home to these our enemies. I will ask them; if they would think it just or equitable for the Moors in Algiers to deny a salvation or a recompence in an [*sic*] hereafter to those of this country who are there kept in slavery; and whose colour is white? No, they surely would not, they would laugh at the absurdity of the idea, and treat it with all the ridicule it justly deserved ["The Address of Abraham Johnstone"18–19].[5]

Johnstone utilized his knowledge of an era following the American Revolution (1775–1783) when American ships were wrecked in the Mediterranean Sea and Americans were taken captive by the North African states of Tripoli, Tunis, Morocco, and Algiers (the Barbary Coast) to deride those who seemingly had forgotten that they were once seen as the inferior class.[6] He suggested, then, that America's behavior towards blacks was not entirely their fault. However, in Americans' "childishly prejudiced imaginations" Johnstone noted, there existed the "foolishly frivolous arguments" that "because we are black, we are not to enjoy a future state, not to be admitted to inherit the kingdom of God, and that our Saviour did not die for us, therefore we cannot hope a redemption" ("The Address of Abraham Johnstone"14). What Johnstone suggested is that white America's "national identity" was characterized by their refusal to acknowledge their own past and how that past had affected the nation's humanity. Johnstone's speech was an intricate part of the growing body of the great tradition of black social protest which accompanied the antislavery movement of the early republic.

By 1750, the numbers of free blacks began to intensify as African Americans were gaining their freedoms through various measures. Although free, they could not, however, escape slavery's shadows. Andrew Harris, who succeeded Daniel A. Payne as the pastor of the Liberty Street Presbyterian Church, lamented, "[Slavery] presses down upon the free people of color. Its deadly poison is disseminated from the torrid regions of the South to the frigid North. We feel it here." Even in the North, the black man was persecuted "because he has *the complexion which God has given him*" ("Speech by Andrew Harris" 295; emphasis in original). As they emerged as leaders and political activists in their communities, their rhetoric began to echo their socio-political and socio-economic conditions. Their voices began to transform the early republic's political arena significantly by 1780: Pennsylvania passed the Emancipation Act which would slowly abolish slavery. By the end of the American Revolution, the North and South were divided on the issue of abolishing slavery: in the North, the "peculiar institution" was in its last days; the South, however, with the majority slaveholders, saw no need to change their ways of life. At the first Constitutional Convention held in 1787, the South protected its right to slaveholding by arguing for the masses that advocated freedom, but still exerted their supremacy over others. Just six years later, the Fugitive Slave Act of 1793 would acknowledge the rights of slaveholders to recover their losses by reclaiming their escapees from any territory in the newly forming union. And by 1857, the U.S. Supreme Court furthered the partition of racial oppression by placing a white man, regardless of status, superior to any black man (Allen, *The Invention of the White Race*, 33). These nefarious designs assured African slaves and free people of African extraction would live in a society that regarded them as nonhuman. Holding their right to slave trafficking in high regard, slaveholders demonstrated that African slaves could have no sure expectation of maintaining even the deepest, most fundamental of their human bonds and familial connections. Families were torn apart — or lived with the constant threat of separation — in the ordinary course of the social, economic, religious, and political systems that promoted their inhumane treatment. Racially motivated and economically based, American slavery sought to identify the entire African American community with the bane of inferiority while, at the same time, profiting from their appalling labor. If blacks could become productive under slavery's yoke and despotism, why could they not achieve the same goals as free citizens? Charles W. Gardner called into question this very issue:

> If, under the oppressions of slavery, [blacks] can become skilful mechanics, trusty housekeepers, and safe nurses, would they be less so, if made fully free.... If they sustain so much moral worth while crowded within the small circle which slavery allows, what would they not exhibit, if placed in circumstances to develop all the powers with which they are endowed by a beneficent Creator? ["Speech by Charles W. Gardner" 207].

Slavery cultivated not just enslavement of Africans, but it promoted and sustained the principles and attitudes of white supremacy. Despite the oppression they suffered, African Americans' voices, resistance, and concerns did find their places in their social protest (Olwell 8–9). As Frances Ellen Harper suggested, American "slavery is mean, because it tramples on the feeble and weak" ("Liberty for Slaves" 307). In his speech celebrating the abolition of slavery in New York state, Nathaniel Paul, the founder of First African Baptist Church in Albany, New York, in 1822, painstakingly revealed that slavery was against the natural law of God:

> Slavery, with it concomitants and consequences, in the best attire in which it can possibly be presented, is but a hateful monster, the very demon of avarice and oppression, from its first introduction to the present time; it has been among all nations the scourge of heaven, and the curse of the earth. It is so contrary to the laws which the God of nature has laid down as the rule of action by which the conduct of man is to be regulated towards his fellow man, which binds him to love his neighbor as himself, that it ever has, and ever will meet the decided disapprobation of heaven ["An Address" 184].

How, then, did African Americans navigate and survive American slavery? The answer rests in their formulized strength which found its way in their perseverance and organizing of communities, churches, fraternal organizations, civil rights groups and schools.

As slaveholders were convinced that they were superior, enlightened Christians, in actuality, they were a parasitical class that survived in America only because of their overbearing and inhumane treatments of those who they felt were inferior to them. Samuel Ringgold Ward lamented, "Those who justify slavery from *their* Bible, on the authority of *their* God, intend to say that they read a Bible and worship a God of their own views and feelings on the question of negro inferiority" ("Modern Negro No. 1" 413; emphasis in original). Slaveholders' rationalization led them to justify their depravity with racism, religion, and excessive ignorance. The entire American slavery system was a political organization built upon fear which was indoctrinated in slaves and strained on slaveholders (for example, slave insurrections planted fear in slaveholders' consciousnesses). To this end, it becomes even more feasible that the African American jeremiad, in response to the political incorrectness of American slavery, would be steeped in socio-political rhetoric. It is because of these and other racial inequalities, however, that the African American jeremiad was born, and it is precisely this aspect of the story of the evils of slavery that goads this book.

The Birth of the African American Jeremiad: The Response

This study of African American jeremiadic discourse was conceived with an understanding that the African American jeremiad was historically feasible only if there were African American principles and values distinctive of American ideologies. Although the seeds of the jeremiad existed in the poetry and prose of Phyllis Wheatley and Jupiter Hammon, it was not until after the American Revolution that African American jeremiadic discourse became more direct. This was because African Americans insisted on their own freedom from the newly acquired sovereign and the basic civil liberties ordained to all. These philosophies gave African Americans a sense of self-determination, self-reliance, and personal growth as the architects of the African American jeremiad challenged and took on the task of condemning the perpetuation of white racial supremacist ideas, forging their rhetoric into a radical driving force that attacked the misrepresentations and hypocrisies of the attitudes of white oppressors in the early republic.

In his discussion of the evolution of the Puritan jeremiad, Perry Miller suggested that there was "one technical problem inherent in the convention" of the jeremiad:

> The jeremiad could make sense out of existence as long as adversity was to be overcome, but in the moment of victory it was confused. It had always to say that now the day of trouble may be ended, that God has thus far "answered us by terrible things in righteousness"—if our sins do not again undo us. It flourished in dread of success; were reality every to come up to its expectations, a new convention would be required, and this would presuppose a revolution in mind and in society [*The New England Mind* 33].

The dichotomy between white politics and white Christianity perplexed slaveholder and politician. White Christianity avoided assertively taking a position outside the realm of the church on "secular issues, such as human rights of blacks" (Marable 321). In his 1798 sermon, "The Influence of Civil Government on Religion," Lemuel Haynes, the preeminent black Jeremiah of his time and very likely the first African American to be ordained by a white Protestant Church, suggested that there were "many *sedition acts* in the Bible"[7] that caused "religion and good government" to be "nearly connected" (72). Haynes continued:

> May we not as well cry out, *Aristocracy!*—*Tryanny!*—and *Oppression!* Because we cannot commit the most daring outrage on the person, character and property of our neighbor, without being plagued with the molesting hand of civil authority? For

such kind of liberty, good Lord deliver us! ["The Influence of Civil Government on Religion" 72].

Haynes' concept of God was determined to aid in the reinforcement of the social renewal of the republic. He believed that God established government; however, what became cumbersome to him was the influence of government on religion. Government, he suggested, helped to further polarize the nation's religious principles; instead, government should have enforced religious life since "those general laws that prohibit *bearing false witness against our neighbor*, and that enjoin decent behavior toward all mankind" are an "insult cast upon the political body, tending to enervate the bands of government. These types of laws were set up to support the government's 'dignity and importance'" ("The Influence of Civil Government on Religion" 72, 73; emphasis in original). Politics, on the other hand, could not speak out for the rights of slaves, since slaveholders did not want a government that would free their property and most politicians who were slaveholders wore "a cloak of benign neutrality" (Hirschfeld 6). Years later, however, Frances Ellen Harper would connect government and religion differently. On 13 May 1857 at the New York Anti-Slavery Society, Harper told her audience that "the law of liberty is the law of God" and that it was the "antecedent to all human legislation." The "law of liberty," Harper continued, "existed in the mind of Deity when He hung the first world upon its orbit and gave it liberty to gather light from the central sun" ("Liberty for Slaves" 306). Although when blacks came to America they appeared to have differing outlooks "and varying approaches to the American conditions," which helped to create some of their situations (Bruce 3), the architects of the African American jeremiad, as illustrated in Haynes' and Harper's rhetoric, aided in resolving this conflict of interests through their pursuit of African American jeremiadic discourse.

Purposes of African American Jeremiadic Rhetoric

No doubt the groundwork that Perry Miller, Sacvan Bercovitch, and others cited has been fundamentally important in positioning the jeremiad in its rightful place in American historical and cultural studies. As these scholars have suggested, the progression of the jeremiad as a historical movement can be seen as such: the European jeremiad portrayed a society that was predestined to fall from its ideological destiny as it thrashed its public with a flood of shame and remorse; the American jeremiad, on the other hand, took its European predecessor's wailing a step further by including the possibility that society can advance and return to its state of stagnation. Although the African American jeremiad and its American predecessor vary in a topological sense, the same principles that operated in the American jeremiadic rhetoric held truth in the African American jeremiadic discourse: warnings were issued to lapse believers, and architects of both discourses depended on the reality of their oppression — imagined or otherwise — as a means to elevate themselves in society. The African American jeremiad, however, added its own flavor to the ingredients: it called for basic civil liberties for the oppressed. A major difference between the American and African American jeremiadic rhetoric can be seen not only in their purposes, then, but also in their strategies. These differences are the by-products of conflicting cultural experiences that were generated from the debauchery of slavery in America.

Another difference rests in both jeremiadic structures' motives. A strategy proposes the long-term actions and procedures exploited in progressing in the direction of the purpose, the philosophical end result for which something occurs. In their "errand into the wilderness," Miller suggested that the initial purpose of the Puritans' mission was to establish in America "the due form of government ... the aim behind that aim was to vindicate the most rigorous ideal of the Reformation," and the final outcome would be that "Europe would imitate New England" (*Errand Into the Wilderness* 12) instead of New England being a by-product of Europe. Bercovitch, however, did not believe that Miller's discussion of the jeremiad fully encompassed its true purpose. Bercovitch suggested that the aim of the American jeremiad was "to direct an imperiled people of God toward the fulfillment of their destiny, to guide them individually toward salvation, and collectively toward the American city of God." To a degree, Bercovitch continued, Miller established "this sense of purpose," but not fully. Bercovitch pointed out that Miller did consider the paradoxical reasoning behind his reading of the jeremiad's rhetoric because they included "both threat and hope" (9). At any rate, Miller's and Bercovitch's analyses of the American jeremiad was acceptable as far as early American religious thought was involved. It was not, however, entirely applicable to African American jeremiadic discourse. In order to appreciate the origins of African American jeremiadic rhetoric, then, we need to look beyond its American predecessor's influence.

What role did race play in the development of an American jeremiadic discourse? Saidiya V. Hartman argued that "the dominion and domination of slavery were fundamentally defined by black subjection"; therefore, "race appositely framed questions of sovereignty, right and power" (115). Given Hartman's argument, the main historical development of the African American jeremiad was spawned from the unjust treatment of blacks. As Richard L. Wright suggested:

> For African Americans, given their history of struggle against the individual and institutional forces/structures of exploitation, marginalization, isolation, degradation, and annihilation, one might conclude that the primary work of the rhetoric produced by African Americans has been essentially in protest against such conditions, thereby utilizing all of the verbal skills at their command to mount a verbal assault upon such conditions in the hope of challenging, persuading, cajoling, frustrating, exhausting, and so on in order to prepare the ground for the seeds of black liberation ["The Word at Work" 85–86].

Miller contended that beneath the expressions of increasing "wail of sinfulness," the purpose of the early Puritan jeremiad was to establish a foundation within "the process of Americanization." While engaged in this process, Miller suggested that the Puritans thought of themselves as "God's saints" who were "at best inferiors, dispatched by their Superior upon particular assignments." The Puritans sought, according to Miller, not just to simply flee from Europe, but they deliberately sought to "redeem it" (*The New England Mind* 9, 10, 15) in the New World. African Americans, who were not fleeing from their homeland, but rather were coerced from it, to a degree were not seeking to establish "the process of Americanization" in the same manner — that Miller suggested of their white counterparts — within the system that was responsible for their oppression. By employing the jeremiad, blacks sought to dispel many of the myths that oppressed them and sought to uplift the race. Furthermore, establishing a unified African American government within the development of an American one was not their aim either. The "wilderness" which Miller defined was, subsequently, not the same metaphorical wilderness African Americans perceived of their enslavement. Figuratively speaking, then, blacks' "wilderness" was the dark, unknown territory of American slavery and racism. Hosea Easton, born free in 1798, sternly criticized white America for its treatment of his "brethren," who he felt were "under the immediate scourge of avarice" ("An Address" 48). In his 1828 Thanksgiving Day address delivered to his "brethren" in Providence, Rhode Island, he lamented:

> [The] awful situation, doubtless, many [of you] have experience, who compose this respectable auditory — while other of you have been eyewitnesses to the bloody scenes of cruelty and murder. Brethren, what was the sensation of your mind, when you beheld many of the female sex, pregnant with their young, tied to a tree or stake, and whipt [*sic*] by their masters, until nature gave way, and both mother and infant yielded up the ghost, while bearing the hellish scourge of these candidates for hell? ... The dreary night of darkness, which our fathers passed through, is about to disperse. And notwithstanding we are a divided people, tossed to and fro, and hunted like the partridge upon the mountain, yet the glorious rays of rational intelligence and literary acquirements, are beginning to backen the chaos darkness, which has so long pervaded the minds of our population ... and we may rationally entertain the hope, that God, in wise Providence, will cause this glorious sun to arise to it meridian, and burst those fetters with which we are bound, and unlock the prison doors of prejudice; granting use Liberty to enjoy the blessing of life like other men ["An Address" 48–49, 53–54].

Despite their "dreary night of darkness" (or "wilderness"), Easton maintained, however, that blacks had a special role to play in their own uplift. As it was, African Americans were attempting to develop a sense of community building that would either be acknowledged by whites or — as they realized — denounced entirely. The varying ways in which blacks sought to develop black communities suggests that they were attempting to coalesce for the intent of identifying solidarity within the context of group recognition. Either way, every line of African

American social protest in the early republic — whether poetry, slave narrative, pamphlet, speech, sermon, or broadside — bemoaned white oppression and was constructed to serve as a form of radical jeremiadic discourse.

Race, furthermore, was not an influential force behind Puritan rhetoric. Selfhood, uplift and protest against oppression were major thematic concerns for African Americans during the colonial and antebellum periods. For example, in their 1835 "Address by William Whipper, Alfred Niger, and Augustus Price," Whipper, Niger, and Price utilized the jeremiad to "make our people, in theory and practice, thoroughly acquainted with [Education, Temperance, Economy, and Universal Liberty], as a method of future action." To aid in achieving this task, they "shall endeavour to enlist the sympathies and benevolence of the Christian, moral and political world" by first appealing "to the Christian churches to take the lead in establishing the principles of supreme love to God, and universal love to man." In hoping to "unite the colored populations in those principles of Moral Reform," they proposed appointing "agents to disseminate these truths among" blacks and establishing "auxiliaries wherever practicable, that the same leaven of righteousness and justice may animate the body politic." Their aim in seeking "Moral Reform" was to eliminate racial divisions, "those hateful and unnecessary distinctions by which the human family has hitherto been recognized, and only desire that they may be distinguished by their virtues and vices" (147, 148). In his 1837 pamphlet "New York Committee of Vigilance for the Year 1837, together with Important Facts Relative to Their Proceedings," David Ruggles stated that his purpose was "to effect a mighty revolution" (149), "to shield" blacks "from the deadly influence of slavery, even in a land of boasted liberty [the state of Pennsylvania], where perpetual watchfulness, prudence, and firmness is required to protect the peaceful citizen from falling a prey to the ruthless grasp of southern tyranny" (147).

In his *Interesting Narrative of the Life of Olaudah Equiano, or Gustavus Vassa, the African, Written by Himself*, Olaudah Equiano, who — as he told readers in his preface — was "actuated by the hope of becoming an instrument towards the relief of his suffering countrymen," revealed his purpose: to "melt the pride" of white supremacy and to force whites "to acknowledge, that understanding is not confined to feature of colour" (iv, 43). A major purpose of David Walker's *Appeal in Four Articles, Together With a Preamble, to the Colored Citizens of the World, But in Particular, and Very Expressly to those of the United States of America* was altogether different: to beseech white Americans to atonement. "O Americans! Americans!! I call God — I call angels — I call men, to witness that your DESTRUCTION *is at hand*, and will speedily consummated unless you REPENT" (56; emphasis in original). Sarah M. Douglass utilized the jeremiad "to stir up in the bosom" of her audience "gratitude to God for his increasing goodness, and feeling of deep sympathy" for the unfortunate souls "in this land of Christian light and liberty held in bondage the most cruel and degrading" ways in the South ("Speech by Sarah M. Douglass" 116). In his

Twelve Years a Slave: Narrative of Solomon Northup, a Citizen of New-York, Kidnapped in Washington City in 1841, and Rescued in 1853, Solomon Northup's purpose was to "speak of Slavery only so far as it came under my own observation." Northup revealed to readers that his rationale for recalling his story in bondage was "to give a candid and truthful statement of facts: to repeat the story of my life, without exaggeration, leaving it for others to determine, whether even the pages of fiction present a picture of more cruel wrong or a severer bondage" (18). For Denmark Vesey, the rhetoric of the emergent African American jeremiad became a way to surpass the impediments to racial unity in the African American community. While planning his 1822 conspiracy, Vesey reportedly told cohorts that a critical social change was inevitable. "He said, we were deprived of our rights and privileges by the white people," confessed Jesse, one of Vesey's lieutenants. Jesse continued, "'And that it was high time for us to seek our rights, and that we were fully able to conquer the whites, if we were only unanimous and courageous, as the St. Domingo people were'" (qtd. in Starobin 29).

The foremost distinction between the African American jeremiad and its American predecessor, then, lay in African Americans' degree of refusal to accept racial degradation and dehumanization. Were white Americans also victims of this racial degradation and dehumanization? Or were they the protectors of it? This difference was furthered when blacks realized that the Europeans who settled North America did so in what they believed to be the responsibility of seeking liberty and opportunity. Did blacks' arrival in North America mirror the same? In actuality, the Puritans "errand into the wilderness" became a search for power and control over those who they felt were subhuman. And as William Loren Katz suggested, Europeans "imported" with them "bigotry and the appetite" for an "unending conquest and agonizing slavery" (12). Other than David Walker's call to whites to atonement, however, there is very little evidence that blacks saw their white counterparts as "imperiled." To the architects of the African American jeremiad, whites were the creators of the racism that subjected them and their "brethren"; whites were the protectors of oppression; and whites' actions toward blacks represented the very essence of black degradation. Very few blacks, even those who worked alongside white abolitionists, designed their rhetoric to *save* whites from the confines of purgatory. Consider Henry Highland Garnet's "Call to Rebellion" to his "brethren" to shed blood or live as a slave; consider the purpose of Frederick Douglass' "What to the Slave is the Fourth of July?" speech where he lamented "This Fourth of July is *yours*, not *mine*. *You* may rejoice, *I* must mourn" (emphasis in original); consider Denmark Vesey's, Gabriel Prosser's, Charles Deslondes' and Nat Turner's measures to eliminate black oppression. If Turner, for example, was attempting to save whites from danger, killing them was not the answer. And he very well knew that. As a matter of fact, when it was time to shed blood, it was Will, Turner's lieutenant, who struck the first blow of death and who decided that even children had to be executed because if given enough time, they would grow up to be protectors of the "peculiar institution" from which Turner sought refuge.

"Liberty Further Extended": The Jeremiad as Religious, Political, and Economic Discourse

African American jeremiadic discourse had a profound effect on the social fabric of the newly evolving democracy as it criticized the America's democracy on three fronts: religion, political doctrines, and economic principles. Therefore, African American jeremiadic rhetoric of the early republic can be fundamentally categorized into three types: religious, political, and economic. In all three of these types of jeremiadic rhetoric, the architects sought to create a dichotomy between professed social life, its materialization, and the perceived destiny of the early republic. The most obvious of the three types, the religious jeremiad, was utilized while employing rhetoric based on its architect's biblical exegesis while exposing prejudiced white Christian values. It was the rhetoric of the preachers and exhorters that would have most likely had a profound outcome on African Americans of this period since some blacks were being influenced by the religious revivals that were sweeping the country.

In his 1776 antislavery manuscript, "Liberty Further Extended,"[8] considered "the first major black protest against slavery" (Newman, *Lemuel Haynes* 3), Lemuel Haynes suggested that every opportunity from which man benefits was made possible by the benevolence of a higher being. However, the wrongful exploitation of others was not welcomed in God's "Earthly court." Haynes continued to argue that the same "liberty" extended to whites by the Declaration of Independence should be "extended" to blacks as well. Haynes believed that "every privilege that mankind Enjoy have their Origen from god; and whatever acts are passed in any Earthly court, which are Derogatory to those Edict that are passed in the Court of Heaven, the act is *void*." Haynes juxtaposed the African captives' oppression with the oppression of the oppressors in order to show the early republic's backsliding: "We shall find that subsisting in the midst of us, that may with propriety be stiled *Opression*, nay, much greater opression, than that which Englishmen seem so much to spurn at. I mean an oppression which they, themselves, impose upon others." He then told readers that the "main proposition" of his argument was to recognize the slave's right to fight for what was naturally owned him: "*A Negro may Justly Chalenge, and has an undeniable right to his* ["freed(om)" is blotted out] *Liberty: Consequently, the practise of Slave-keeping, which so much abounds in this Land is illicit*" ("Liberty Further Extended" 95). Haynes suggested that if slaves were to be "*obedient*," they should use their obedience to seek enlightenment and freedom:

Slave-keeping was practised Even under the Gospel, for we find *paul*, and the other apostels Exhorting *Servants to be obedient to their masters.* to which I reply, that it mite be they were Speaking to Servants in *minority* in General; But Doubtless it was practised in the Days of the Apostles from what *St. paul* Says, I *Corin.* 7:21. *art thou called being a servant? care not for it; but if though mayest Be made free, use it rather* ["Liberty Further Extended" 101].

Serving as his argument against the depiction of slaves' obedience to their earthly master in Ephesians 6:5–9, Haynes' jeremiadic discourse dismantled the foundation of slaveholders' position that the Bible condoned slavery and that blacks were destined to be slaves. In his extremely political doctrine, Haynes found a dichotomy that was inherent in the gospel, and he positioned his argument in such a way as to unveil it. The onset of Ephesians 6 suggested that *all* should obey righteousness: children should obey their parents; likewise, fathers should not exasperate their children but teach them in the ways of the Lord; servants should obey those who they serve; and finally, masters should treat their servants with respect and dignity since *all* struggle "not against flesh and blood, but against principalities, against powers, against the rulers of the darkness of this world, against spiritual wickedness in high places" (Ephesians 6:12). Haynes used his biblical exegesis to further his argument:

> Again *Rev.* 16:6, *for they have Shed the Blood of Saints and prophets, and though has given them Blood to Drink; for they are worthy.* And *chap.* 18:6. *Reward her Even as She rewarded you.* I say this is often God's way of Dealing, by retaliating Back upon men the Same Evils that they unjustly Bring upon others ["Liberty Further Extended" 103].

His reading of the book of Revelations suggested that "*Oppression*" was not the "Judgement that God is pleas'd to Bring upon this Land," but he believed it was "the greatest reason to think that this is not one of the Least." Haynes' jeremiadic rhetoric, then, intertwined religious, political, and economic discourse while arguing for the basic civilities and "Liberty & freedom" of the African captives. Viewing the yearning for independence as "an innate principle" that was an unyielding aspiration for every man, white and black, since "Even an affrican, has Equally as good a right to his Liberty in common with Englishmen," Haynes further contended that freedom was a "Jewel which was handed Down to man from the cabinet of heaven, and is Coaeval with his Existance" ("Liberty Further Extended" 103, 94). His entire manuscript was a jeremiad: his exegesis of biblical text and other abolitionist texts helped him to produce one of the most provocative antislavery arguments of the early republic.

Moreover, the political rhetoric of liberty and justice for all which had been previously laid by the founding fathers began to shape the African American jeremiad. The political jeremiad materialized through the polemics that exposed issues concerning America's democratic ideologies and were based on African Americans' analysis of the language of the Constitution and Declaration of Independence. Rhetoric(s) have constantly been more than arguments and authority, and specific rhetoric(s), such as jeremadic discourse, had been connected with language and its architect's use of the domineering language. James Forten, Sr.'s "Series of Letters by a Man of Colour" best represented this manifestation. In Letter I, Forten, an African American businessman, drew upon the founding fathers most cherished ideals: "We hold this truth to be self-evident, that GOD created all men equal, and is one of the most prominent features in the Declaration of Independence, and in that glorious fabric of collected wisdom, our noble Constitution" ("Series of Letters by a Man of Colour" 67). By appropriating passages from the Declaration of Independence, Forten posited an essential aspect of African American jeremiadic discourse by suggesting that the document disagreed with the early republic's democratic principles. The irony was that Forten understood that the Declaration of Independence, the worst misinterpretations on equality and justice, was composed and supported by those claiming to believe in liberty and justice for all. Forten believed, as did countless other blacks, that his people were true sufferers from racism and racial prejudice developed from the Declaration of Independence.

The pledge to seek economic independence was in large part initiated by political self-determination. The economic jeremiad manifested amidst the socio-political rhetoric that attacked the monetary issues surrounding the African diaspora transatlantic slave trade. As an economic jeremiad, Haynes' manuscript adroitly criticized these issues by insisting that "those that are concerned in the Slave-trade, Do pretend to Bring arguments in vindication of their practise; yet if we give them a candid Examination, we shall find them (Even those of the most cogent kind) to be Essencially Deficient." Haynes further suggested that "Liberty is Equally as pre[c]ious to a *black man*, as it is to a *white one*" ("Liberty Further Extended" 94, 95). He believed that whites enjoyed sufficient civil liberties and that blacks were entitled to the same constitutional rights and should be legally guaranteed the same privileges. Philip Gould defined this type of jeremiad as the "commercial jeremiad," one that was spawned from

> the long-standing use by antislavery writers of Protestant discourses about human sin, Christian morality, and divine judgment. The commercial jeremiad represents the gradual process of secularization of these Protestant discourses in antislavery writing—the use of traditional languages and rhetorical conventions in formulating modern commercial ideologies [13–14].

Not only did those who utilized Gould's "commercial jeremiad" argue against the commerce of the African diaspora transatlantic slave trade, but they also "imbricated in larger questions about the nature of trade, manners, and consumption" (14). The best example of this kind of jeremiadic rhetoric is present in Quobna Ottobah Cugoano's 1787 *Narrative of the Enslavement of Ottobah Cugoano, a Native of Africa; Published by Himself.* Throughout his jeremiadic discourse, Cugoano made comparisons to African slavery and European slavery to illustrate how far Europeans had transgressed from God's covenant:

It is therefore manifest, that something else ought yet to be done; and what is required, is evidently the incumbent duty of all men of enlightened understanding, and of every man that has any claim or affinity to the name of Christian, that the base treatment which the African Slaves undergo, ought to be abolished; and it is moreover evident, that the whole, or any part of that iniquitous traffic of slavery, can no where, or in any degree, be admitted, but among those who must eventually resign their own claim to any degree of sensibility and humanity, for that of barbarians and ruffians [*Narrative* 10].

In his comparison of African and European slavery, Cugoano maintained the particular premise of the jeremiad when he lamented that Africans did "keep slaves," which were obtained through "war, or for debt." He further asserted that those enslaved where "well fed ... and treated well," unlike his "miserable companions and countrymen in this pitiful, distressed and horrible situation, with all the brutish baseness and barbarity." As he loathed the oppressive reality of slavery, Cugoano held that "every man in Great-Britain responsible, in some degree ... unless he speedily riseth up with abhorrence of it in his own judgement, and, to avert evil, declare himself against it." Believing that it was "not strange to think" that those "who ought to be considered as the most learned and civilized people in the world ... should carry on a traffic of the most barbarous cruelty and injustice," Cugoano used the economic jeremiad to argue that liberation of African slaves was a conscientious decision for Britons because it would permit Africans to obtain an affluent system of commerce which "would soon bring more revenue in a righteous way to the British nation, than ten times its share in all the profits that slavery can produce" (*Narrative* 16, 103, 121–22, 133–35). Believing that European slavery was a form of degradation and humiliation of it subjects, Cugoano aligned his jeremiadic discourse in a way that attempted to provide an all-encompassing ground for the creation of a black social identity.

William Watkins, Jacob M. Moore, and Jacob C. White, Sr., however, would later apply Gould's "commercial jeremiad" differently in their "To the Colored Churches in the Free States," a resolution adopted at a meeting of the American Moral Reform Society. Watkins, Moore and White advocated self-preservation by calling the American people "against using the products of slavery labor, both as a moral and Christian duty and as a means by which the slave system may be successfully abrogated" (189). These kinds of boycotts against slave labor would continue throughout the developmental years of the African American jeremiad.

Liberalism and the Construction of the African American Jeremiad

Brian Barry defined liberalism as "a doctrine about the way in which states should treat people" (123). During the early republic, liberalism made a travesty of the ideology that blacks could participate in the process of Americanization.

Some blacks sought to establish their own communities, the black self, while others used the rhetoric of the African American jeremiad to seek opportunity for coalition with their white counterparts. Likewise, it would be illogical to suggest that the numerous laws set in motion were not to ensure blacks remain outside of the process of forging the new government of the early republic. As previously stated, the Fugitive Slave Act of 1793 guaranteed that runaway slaves could be returned into slavery. Although the term "slave" did not appear anywhere within the walls of the document, a "person held to service or labor," however it is interpreted, was actually cloaked in its stead. Infringements like these were fundamental to guarantying that the standards of equality were rendered nonoperative and invalid in essential areas of blacks' social lives such as the right to marry, own property, or become educated, for example. Undoubtedly, many whites of the early republic would have been inclined to say that, other things being equivalent, the early republic was an advanced and enlightened society. The more widely diffused among its citizens was the temperament that their beliefs and practices toward blacks were biblically justified. The evidence lies in the founding fathers' declarations in the documents that are meant to govern chaos and disorganization. Nathaniel Paul refuted the argument that slavery was biblically justified:

> The power of the tyrant is subdued, the heart of the oppressed is cheered, liberty is proclaimed to the captive, and the opening of the prison to those who were bound, and he who had long been this miserable victim of cruelty and degradation, is elevated to the common rank in which our benevolent Creator first designed, that man should move — all of which have been effect by means that most simple, yet perfectly efficient ["An Address" 183].

The African American jeremiad, then, modeled to forge blacks' perceived liberalism of the day, has two distinct phases. In the first phase, African Americans in the early republic attempted to expose the oppressive reality of their enslavement. Through their actions, they committed themselves to eradicating this oppression. The alteration of consciousness was an important aspect of this stage. The second phase is where the reality of their oppression has already been confronted. For blacks, the jeremiad became not just a form of liberation for them, but for all oppressed, even those who are not the victims of slavery but who are welding its control over others.

With this in mind, there are three recognizable stages of development of African Americans' jeremiadic rhetoric of the colonial and antebellum periods: the first wave, 1760–1830, identifies the rhetoric as deeply rooted in religious exegesis of the Great Awakenings; in the second, 1830–1845, the discourse sought to obtain elevation for blacks through the use of moral reform and suasion; and the final stage, 1845–1861, represents the movement of the rhetoric as it became increasingly radical in its call to consciousness and its political discourse is more readily identifiable. Still feeling the effects of the First Great Awakening (1730s–1740s) and forging the Second Awakening (1820s–1830s),

American politics, economics, and social culture found some similarities in the transformation of American religion. For those of African extraction, religion was not only a leading focus in their social environment, but also played a vital role in their political beliefs. The establishment of the black church, for example, became the center of African American social and political life. Some Americans, such as Daniel A. Payne, one of nineteenth-century America's most profound African American Jeremiahs and one of the first blacks to be ordained by the Lutheran Church in 1837, suggested that those who

> have formed an idea that the Church must assume the same democratic or Republican form as the state, and consequently be governed by similar rules; so, conceiving the resultant idea that the discipline gives the ministry too much power, they will commence a scheme of revolution, nor will they cease until the Church is rent in twain ["First Annual Address of the Philadelphia Annual Conference" 16].

Therefore, religion, as exemplified in Payne's opine, would also introduce into socio-political discourse hordes of important moral concerns, such as the establishment of the black church and the paradox of Christian slaveholding. As a socio-political statement, then, the African American jeremiad advocated self-determination, self-reliance, and uplift in the African American community.

Conclusion: The Evolution of Jeremiadic Discourse

The African American jeremiad was haphazardly carved from a convergence of African American arts and letters (poetry, slave narratives, pamphlets, sermons, and speeches) and the oppression blacks experienced within the borders of America. In this regard, race was not the only determining factor in which early African American jeremiadic rhetoric constructed socio-political awareness. Historically, the evolutions of any jeremiadic rhetoric are convoluted. Such questions that may arise when searching for the origins of jeremiadic discourse are who first employed the rhetoric and what led to its development? Since a great deal of African American social protest of the early republic was not preserved (i.e. speeches, sermons, letters, oral tradition), there is no possible way to determine the true precursors to this discourse. Where, then, does one start? As the African American jeremiad progressed through the antebellum period, it began to converge with a powerful stream of confluence that began with, no doubt, the oral tradition and joined with new understandings of the aptitude of its architects and the impact of American culture, religion, politics, and economics. Through socio-political participation, the African American jeremiad made available the achievement of forging nationalistic civil rights opportunities, elevated black consciousness and racial uplift, and contributed to the transformation of an American socio-political and cultural life in the following decades of the nineteenth and twentieth centuries.

2

Early Development

> O Thou bright jewel in my aim I strive
> To comprehend thee. Thine own words declare
> Wisdom is higher than a fool can reach.
> I cease to wonder, and no more attempt
> Thine height t' explore, or fathom thy profound.
> But, O my soul, sink not into despair,
> *Virtue* is near thee, and with gentle hand
> Would now embrace thee, hovers o'er thine head.
> Fain would the heav'n-born soul with her converse,
> Then seek, then court her for her promis'd bliss.
> — Phyllis Wheatley, "On Virtue," 1773

> Remember youth the time is short,
> Improve the present day.
> And pray that God may guide your thoughts,
> And teach your lips to pray.
> To pray unto the most high God,
> And beg restraining grace.
> Then by the power of his word,
> You'll see the Savior's face.
> — Jupiter Hammon, "A Poem for Children with Thoughts on Death," 1782

There are countless complexities that arise when searching for the beginnings of a literary tradition or political movement such as the jeremiadic discourse. Who was the first to employ the rhetoric? How was it manifested within the discourse or movement? What factors led its employment? The hunt for the origin for the African American jeremiad takes us to the latter part of the eighteenth century, when the dissenting New World colonists were surmounting opposition against the British sovereignty. As the founders of the new republic saw it, they were enslaved, or subjects of their own government. To justify their freedom from the British, the New World colonists argued the Enlightenment ideology that all men were created equal, and that they had the birthright to liberty and justice. The rhetoric of these insurgent colonists was soon adapted by African Americans in their fight for personal freedom and equality, but from the colonists themselves. As they began to appropriate this rhetoric, African

Americans felt a communal calling: to abolish the oppressive reality of their enslavement. The poetry of Phyllis Wheatley and Jupiter Hammon began to represent the socio-political invectives of early African Americans as Wheatley and Hammon saw a way to utilize this rhetoric in their fight for freedom and basic civil liberties. The jeremiad, although usually associated with prose works, was poetically suitable for Wheatley's and Hammon's era (Carretta, *Phyllis Wheatley* xxiii). As the above poems emphasize, through their usage and understanding of the jeremiad, both poets, in their conscientious poetic verse, offered their audience — both black and white — hope that their status would change with God's intervention. Wheatley's discourse in "On Virtue" encouraged her audience to seek wisdom, which was "higher than a fool can reach," instead of prayer as a way to further their conditions. "*Virtue*," she implied, will soon follow through proper religious instruction. On the other hand, Hammon's "A Poem for Children with Thoughts on Death" informed his young audience — captive Africans as well as disadvantaged whites — that in order to "improve" their "present day," or any socio-political condition that has befallen them, they should adopt the art of praying. Then, and only then, Hammon suggested, would God's grace become visible. For Hammon, it was clear that "youth" must comprehend that they also have to believe in God — that "youth is a fleeting opportunity best used if consecrated to God, and filled with responsibilities if they would accept them" (James 48). Wheatley's and Hammon's poetic forms, obviously influenced by the sermonizing tradition of the times, represent the basis for considering the jeremiad as a literary formulation in African American literature of the early republic. Both Hammon's and Wheatley's poetry was used by abolitionists throughout the antebellum period to rally for the "humanity, equality, and literary talents of African Americans" (Carretta, *Phyllis Wheatley*, xxxvii).

The earliest African American jeremiadic structure was consistent with the principles of the jeremiad: it mourned humanity's declension from the covenant and it criticized public advocacy of racial subjugation, thus making the jeremiadic form distinctively African American. Because the jeremiad embodied the tenets of justice and retribution, Wheatley and Hammon realized that they were composing their verse in an era when questions concerning blacks' social and political status were eminently important. As such, they employed the jeremiad to speak to African American torment and dehumanization with an authoritative voice. There is insufficient evidence that other architects before them employed the jeremiad. However, because of their separate experiences as victims of American slavery, Wheatley and Hammon did not represent the full essence of the warnings and precepts of the jeremiad; subsequent generations who would feel the crack of the whip from dusk to dawn would pick up where they left off. Unlike their followers, then, Wheatley's and Hammon's jeremiadic rhetoric did not hurl down condemnation upon an audience of sinners. Instead, they chose to cloak their ideologies on reform in ways they thought were appropriate in eighteenth-century America. They cleverly blended rationale with their sentiments to make their pleas against the victimization of their brethren. In general, their literary works showed their skill and knowledge to their audience.

What role did their verse play in developing a sense of community among the African captives? Were the seeds for revolution planted beneath the veil of their verse? Because of their insistent use of biblically-based language, the jeremiad was a "response to increasing opposition, defenders of slavery and the slave trade sought to justify their actions with religious and economic arguments" (Carretta, *Phyllis Wheatley*, xxiii). The religious enthusiasm of the time had been heightened by the first Great Awakening, which taught that redemption was available to all and that every human being had an equal chance at obtaining God's grace. This revivalism of religious fervor, which left colonists further divided along religious and socio-political lines, helped to further shape the African American jeremiad. Amid this cloud of uncertainty, Wheatley and Hammon employed artistic and spiritual approaches to address these issues and created a consciousness that initiated literary voices that called blacks to demand equal rights for themselves and others like them.

The Sermonizing Tradition and the Jeremiad: From the Wilderness to the Land of Freedom

Wheatley's and Hammon's jeremiadic discourse was initially influenced by the sermonizing tradition of Great Awakenings exhorters such as George Whitefield and Samson Occom. The Great Awakenings surfaced throughout the country when the rhetoric of social change began to represent traditional religious practices and when the colonists could not find answers to questions established by the existing social life. With this in mind, a particular discord transpired among religion, politics, and social life. When this manifestation materialized, new social ideas struggled to bridge the differences in socio-religious and political opinions. One of the major purposes of the Great Awakenings was to unify colonists to accept the Christian faith and life. When the Great Awakenings swept the country, however, blacks were not excluded in the spread of religious enthusiasm (Raboteau 128), although they had been previously excluded from the forming of the country's "national identity." It was this period, the era from the 1760s to the early 1830s, the age of religious piety, that was recognized as laying the foundations of African American jeremiadic discourse. Arguably, as previously stated, the essence of any jeremiadic discourse was religion. The kind of religion that occupied African American jeremiadic rhetoric of this period, however, was that of refined virtue and morality as exemplified in Wheatley's and Hammon's works. During this period, blacks' idea of religion grew from their social situations. This representation was significant because African Americans lamented their dehumanization and degradation cloaked in their biblical exegesis, some more radical than others. Such piety engrossed the lamentations of Phyllis Wheatley.

Stolen from Africa and brought to America around the age of seven, Wheatley lamented her "being brought from AFRICA to AMERICA." The implication of Wheatley's composition was that hope was imperative; redemption, she believed, provided hope. Russell Reising argued that in the religious context, redemption indicated "that glorious moment of the soul's salvation and the certainty of its spending eternity in heaven. Wheatley's admission of neither knowing about it nor seeking it prior to her enslavement" could suggest her approval of the "religious culture imposed on her new existence as a slave" (88). What emerged from Reising's argument was that Wheatley believed that some sort of liberating or redemptive value must be interwoven into every aspect of black life; in essence, redemption should play a role, she believed, in the African American community's passage from the wilderness to the land of freedom. In Wheatley's "On being brought from AFRICA to AMERICA," she brought to the forefront some of the trepidations African Americans had concerning the contradictions she believed existed between the way slaves were treated and the Enlightenment principles of America's fight for its own freedom from the British (Lowance 25). She wrote:

> "TWAS mercy brought me from my *Pagan* land,
> Taught my benighted soul to understand
> That there's God, that there's a Saviour too;
> Once I redemption neither sought nor knew,
> Some view our sable race with scornful eye.
> 'Their color is a diabolical die.'
> Remember, Christians, Negroes, black as Cain,
> May be refined, and join th' angelic train" [*CW* 18; emphasis in original].[1]

In the last two lines of the poem, Wheatley's denunciation of the Euro-American ideology that the *barbarous pagans* of Africa knew nothing of salvation surfaced along with her declaration of the "socially, culturally, biologically, and certainly theologically" (Lowance 26) impartiality of the races. Calling for the deculturization of both "*Christians*" and "*Negroes*"—who are, consequently, "black as *Cain*"—Wheatley suggested, "'May be refined,' or enlightened, and have the privilege to 'join the' angelic train.'" Wheatley saw it as the present duty of all men of "refine(ment)," of every man who maintained affinity to the "*Christians*" name to rally for the abolishment of the abasement of the African captives. Wheatley's coded jeremiads could not have come at a worse time for the developing republic. African Americans who utilized the jeremiad labored in a society that did not allow the black voice recognition and, furthermore, was not readily accepting of blacks as capable leaders of either their own communities or in the mainstream republic. The major influence on African American jeremiadic discourse during this period was the harsh reality of racist ideologies and African Americans' perceived inferiority. This type of racism, the crucial source of conflict of their jeremiadic discourse, was the most persuasive element that forged African American empowerment and self-determination.

"Glory be to the Most High": To Disclose the Evils of Slavery

Even today, there exists an immense misinterpretation of Wheatley's poetic creations. Elisabeth James suggested that Wheatley's "literary perspective is now purely of historical note and serves only as folio proofs of her existence and accomplishments" (viii). In "On being brought from AFRICA to AMERICA," Wheatley mourned that her understanding of salvation taught her "benighted soul to understand/That there's a God, that there's a *Saviour* too." It is effortless to understand how this can be seen as Wheatley's indoctrination to a Christian God. However, a more exhaustive reading of Wheatley's poem would suggest that the poem was structured to answer some implicit questions about Africans' supposedly inferior status: How did Africans in the New World come to be where they were? And who was responsible for their status? Wheatley must have accepted that their fate was in God's hand, and she organized her poem to address issues of their suffering. She believed her unsullied soul *further* understood her confinement, which she believed was an act of God, not man's act of enslavement. She also believed that God would deliver *all* from the clutches of slavery, blacks who are victims of its tyranny, and whites who depend on its labor for commerce.

"Once I redemption neither sought nor knew," she continued in the fourth line of the poem. Having thus implied that redemption was not an Afrocentric term, Wheatley suggested that blacks were willing to learn about this Eurocentric ideology, and she appeared to advocate the embracing of American values and customs in the process. If, as Stephen Henderson noted, within literary texts the existence of "such commodity as 'blackness'" was readily identifiable in poetic creations, "since poetry is the most concentrated and the most allusive of the verbal arts" (3),[2] what did Wheatley's jeremiadic rhetoric overtly suggest? Although she illustrated to her audience that she understood the misfortune of her socio-political predicament, it did not mean that she accepted it. There would come a time, one can infer, that Wheatley would deal with her own freedom within the margins of the socio-political atmosphere that surrounded her, but it was of the utmost importance to amass a consciousness among the captives first. Wheatley assured the African captives that God understood their rejection and disenfranchisement, and would accept them on the "angelic train." This poem more than any of her other works showed that she understood that whites sensed the wounds of their bondage, yet did nothing to better Africans' lot. If the captives could understood that God heard their pleas, they could find gratification in knowing that the end to their enslavement would come (James 28). Wheatley saw that the first step of amassing socio-political and socio-economic empowerment was for the captive Africans to accept Christ as their personal Savior. She believed that through such spiritual enlightenment their unconventional status in society would be uplifted (James 28), thus creating a viable solution from which freedom could be obtained.

In *All Black Voices Count*, Elisabeth James argued that most of Wheatley's poems were written to suit prominent white figures of her day, and her works were published largely at their request. Despite this influence, however, Wheatley's views became masked under the veil. In "On being brought from AFRICA to AMERICA" there existed a rebelliousness in her message that was not at first discernible. As Wheatley asserted that salvation would come to those who were prepared to accept God's benevolence, she urgently called the African captives to social action: "Remember, *Christians, Negroes*, black as *Cain*, / May be refin'd, and join th' angelic train" (*CW* 18).

While her white audience's reading created a self-serving rationalization that Wheatley accepted their ideology that people of African descent were inferior, beneath the veil, Wheatley directly pronounced African Americans' socio-religious and socio-political liberation by informing her black audience that they, too, were worthy of God's grace, a message that would probably have the most impact coming from a fellow captive. The first line of the poem helped to reveal Wheatley's mournful critique. "'Twas mercy brought me from my Pagan land" was dual, intricate, and it articulated the Calvinistic theology of divine determination ubiquitousduring the era of the Great Awakenings as well as the partiality that God used the evil imprudence of men to achieve His moral and virtuous will. This complexity continued throughout the short piece as Wheatley posited a jeremiadic vision of redemption after having been brought from Africa to American under the circumstances of slavery. Still, however, Wheatley realized that being a slave made the entire process of redemption incomplete — one must be free in soul and body if he or she was indeed to be free.

Of course the poem may be read in many ways. Two sets of reservations emerge from this examination. First, Wheatley's poem was meant to arouse whites' conscience and ignite remorse and embarrassment of their transgressions. The vagueness of "Remember, *Christians, Negroes*, black as *Cain*" introduced several components of Wheatley's racial consciousness: it indicated that Wheatley was aware of the racist insinuation of the curse of Ham and its connection to people of African extraction (Jamison 412), and it indicated that Wheatley was aware of America's paradoxical involvement in the enslavement of her people.

One of the reasons why Wheatley's poetry was acceptable to both black and white audiences, however, was because her "poetic closures would quite easily and naturally be missed by her readership." This usage of a double voice was important for Wheatley because the popularity of her work largely depended on her readers' interpretation (Reising 114). Her white audience's reading of "On being brought from AFRICA to AMERICA" was somewhat mundane because it aroused their guilt as Wheatley accused them of disobeying their own egalitarian system and Christian values by denying the African captives basic civil liberties. Dickson D. Bruce, Jr., suggested that Wheatley asserted "her own identity" while she saw "the failure in others" (44). The way in which Africans were seen in whites' eyes, Wheatley inferred, was because of their so-called primitive behavior, their "*Pagan* land." A colorful expression for certain modernist religious convictions of the time, the term pagan was, at any rate, Eurocentric and multifarious, and even today complex to define.[3] Secondly, what was it about African culture that constituted paganistic qualities? Why would whites see Africa as such and what were the standards by which they defined "*Pagan*"? What, then, was Wheatley's message? Wheatley understood that by her oppressors calling her homeland "*Pagan*," they were attempting to control the destiny of all mankind by discrediting Wheatley's race and their contribution to Western civilization. Their interpretation of Wheatley's Africa was seen through their Eurocentric lenses, as Europeans sought to tell the story of Africa but lacked the linguistic and cultural background to do so effectively.

Wheatley's usage of terms such as "*Pagan*," "benighted soul," "sable race," "scornful eye," and "diabolic die" in relation to her people was a product of her early instruction, not necessarily her beliefs. Wheatley was aware of the "existing attitudes of Whites toward Blacks" (Jamison 412), and the use of the aforementioned terms helped to illustrate this point. Such wording may also demonstrate an embedded denunciation against the oppression of her fellow captives.

The poem revealed more than a remarkable aptitude and precociousness at word dexterity; it also uncovered the complicated role Wheatley was to assume as she took on her voice in the poem. Wheatley, therefore, used the jeremiad to warn her fellow captives of such cultural predicaments. She implored them to become a part of the American mainstream to erase the "diabolical die" imposed on them by whites, and to obtain civil liberties they were denied. It is not clear whether or not Wheatley believed that these rights would come all at once, or rather through time. What was evident, however, was that she did believe that through a steadfast belief in God, African Americans would "join th' angelic train"—but only void of their so-called paganism—which equated to obtaining political and economic rights and other basic civil liberties.

"We'll follow saints and angels all": Hammon's Jeremiadic Discourse

Wheatley and Hammon applied a similar rhetorical strategy while employing the social fabric rhetoric of the jeremiad; however, as scholars have argued, Hammon used a liberation theology as an opportunity to discuss racial inequality whereas Wheatley saw the ideology of deliverance as an opportunity to question slavery. This was largely because their audiences and situations were so different. Hammon, for example, "championed education for blacks" by making the Bible less complex to them. The rationalization Hammon offered "for a slave committing service to his or her earthly master was that it might enable them to better their lot through moral suasion based on biblical precedents" (Baker 5). This "moral suasion" equated into social, political and economic uplift and empowerment for the African captives. In the first two stanzas of "A Dialogue, Entitled, The Kind Master and Dutiful Servant," Hammon wrote:

1
Master.
Come my Servant, follow me,
According to thy place;
And surely God will be with thee,
And send thee heav'nly grace.
2
Servant.
Dear Master, I will follow thee,
According to thy word,
And pray that God may be with me,
And save thee in the Lord [JH 205–206].[4]

What was not clear in his caricature of a racist slaveholder and a subservient slave was whether the slaveholder was challenging the slave's salvation to either the slaveholder himself, or the slave's true salvation to God. An essential element of jeremiadic discourse for Hammon in this poem included the demonstration of the inhumanity of the cruelties brought on by the institution of slavery practiced by Christian slaveholders who, as Hammon's dirge insinuated, defied every Christian concept. For Hammon, this exchange between slaveholder and slave also revealed the spiritual and psychological journey he undertook to define himself as a black man in the early republic. Hammon, then, believed that the search for self-reconciliation had to be created in the socio-political rhetoric of his verse.

Hammon's poetry echoed the resiliency of Methodism and the religious revival that swept the country during the early republic. Methodism taught converters that their "profession of religion was not worth a rush unless their sins were forgiven and they had the witness of God's spirit with theirs, that they were the children of God" (*200 Years of United Methodism: An Illustrated History*). For Hammon, this religion became a socio-political force that acculturated him to the world's immorality. Because of this, he was forced to "spend his own hours reading the Bible and contemplating heavenly things" (Baker 6); he then seemed be filled with "penitential cries" (Barksdale and Kinnamon 46). When he developed jeremiadic discourse in "An Evening Thought, Salvation by Christ, with Penitential Cries," Hammon declared that for those who love God, "Redemption [was] now to every one." To further illustrate this, Hammon's poem can be read as a message that the day of liberation can not be thwarted by white masters. Hammon wrote:

13

Master.
Ten thousand Angels cry to Thee
Yea louder than the Ocean
Thou art the Lord, we plainly see;
Thou art the true salvation.

14

Servant.
Now is the Day, excepted Time:
The Day of Salvation;
Increase your Faith, do not repine;
Awake ye every nation [*JH* 61].

Alluding to the suffering servant motif that linked unjust anguish and oppression with liberation, Hammon's jeremiad criticized the condescending religion that was given to him as a way of asserting his independence from the white authorities since "the Day of Salvation," according to Hammon, was nigh.

As he filled the role of a Jeremiah, then, Hammon apprised "his brethren" with even more zeal that God would deliver them from their present wilderness in his jeremiadic dissertation "A Winter Piece." Hammon alluded to Moses' deliverance of the children of Israel from Egypt:

> My brethren, many of us are seeking a temporal freedom and I wish you may obtain it; remember that all power in heaven and on earth belongs to God. If we are slaves, it is by the permission of God; if we are free, it must be by the power of the Most High God. Stand still and the salvation of God. Cannot that same power that divided the waters from the waters for the children of Israel to pass through make way for your freedom? [*JH* 101, 105].

Hammon saw liberation in the contradictions of slavery; therefore, he exhorted his brethren to "stand still."[5] Other free blacks during this time also believed that if slaves would wait on the Lord, they would see His work at hand. Cyrus Bustill, a former slave who became the first African American school teacher in Philadelphia (Foner and Branham 20), was one such activist. In his "I Speak to Those Who are in Slavery" address on 18 September 1787, Bustill told a group of slaves:

> My Bretherin Let us endevour to Learn to fear the Lord it is the beginning of wisdom and will to us [be] a Good understanding, if we will but Depart from Evil, you being in bondage in Particular, I would that [ye] take heed that afend not with your toungue, be ye wiss [wise] as Serpants and harmless as Doves, that hey may take with you, when you are wrong'd. other ways, you Cannon Exspect him to side with you nor to Soport your Cause, no not at any time or Place, I would my Bretherin that ye be faitful to your masters, at all times and on all occasions, too, for this is Praise worthy, be honst and true to their intrust [22].[6]

Declaring that slaves take no action against their oppressors, Bustill told them that in due time, God would work to ratify their wrongs (Foner and Branham 20). In his 1828 address, Hosea Easton cautioned blacks "against any revengeful or malignant passions" but urged them to "stand still and see the salvation of God." However, because of the "great labour and ardent zeal which involves upon" them, Hosea revealed that there "is no time to stand still." The time had come, he added, when blacks' "necessities calls aloud for our exertions, to prepare ourselves for the great events which are about heaving in view" ("An Address" 53). In the early nineteenth century, architects of African American jeremiadic discourse such as David Walker and Henry Highland Garnet would advocate rebellion as a way to eliminate oppression. Their interpretation of "stand still" meant only to hold one's grounding in the fight for liberation. Hammon, however, believed that slaves had been given what they needed to survive the journey out of the wilderness. Did Hammon's usage of the phrase "stand still" encourage slave obedience? If so, too whom? Earthly masters? Or a Heavenly Master? Or to no master but to one's own charge? What was apparent was that Hammon believed that a higher power would work wonders far beyond the slave's comprehension. Hammon lamented that the same God who delivered the Israelites can deliver the African captives from American slavery. He suggested, however, that this shall come to pass if they "Stand still and see the salvation of God." Politically speaking, Hammon's encouragement was meant to suggest that the day of deliverance from their socio-political constraints would come whether God worked through the oppressors, or through the oppressed. Hammon believed, however, that the African captives should have a hand in their own deliverance. He further advised his "brethren" to "avoid all bad company" and keep themselves "pure in heart":

> "Blessed are the pure in heart: for they shall see God" (Matt. 5:8). Now, in order to see God, we must have a saving change wrought in our hearts, which is the work of God's Holy Spirit, which we are to ask for. "Ask, and it shall be given you; seek, and ye shall find" (Mat. 7:7) [*JH* 98].

Again, Hammon's jeremiadic discourse offered his audience optimism that God would intervene if they only trusted in Him and asked Him for salvation. As he perceived the paradoxical difficulty of Christianity and slavery, Hammon still believed that by asking for salvation, the African captives were taking control of their own destiny which would assure recognition. Hammon insisted that salvation was available to all who would love and obey God's directives. Hammon's compositions began to represent the idea that blacks owned the right to control their destiny, their voice, and their pen, and that they would establish for themselves what kind of socio-political and economic systems that would best suit their communities.

More straightforwardly than Wheatley, Hammon wrote primarily for a black audience, and his works were constantly filled with evangelical rhetoric, providing many blacks with a strong sense of identity and community. Hammon's poems were layered with his biblical exegesis. Hammon enlisted his fellow blacks to become productive citizens by leaving their African traditions behind, and he delicately pleaded with them to conform to the conservatism of the early republic (O'Neale 191). What impact would this have on blacks? Socio-politically, it would give them more leverage toward equal rights, citizenship, and economic empowerment. For example, in "A Dialogue, Entitled, The Kind Master and Dutiful Servant," Hammon illustrated a possibly realistic proselytization of slaveholder to servant. A surface reading of this dramatic dialogue was meant to illustrate blacks' subordination to their white masters; meanwhile, to the African captives it fueled their subversive needs to gain control over their destiny. Hammon wrote:

5
Master.
My Servant, grace proceeds from God,
And truth should be with thee;
Whence e'er you find it in his word,
Thus far come follow me.

6
Servant.
Dear Master, now without control,
I quickly follow thee;
And pray that God would bless thy soul,
His heav'nly place to see.

* * *

13
Master.
My Servant, we must all appear,
And follow then our King;
For sure he'll stand where sinners are,
To take true converts in.

14
Servant.
Dear Master, now if Jesus calls,
And sends his summons in;
We'll follow saints and angels all,
And come unto our King [*JH* 206, 207–08].

Hammon developed a style of religious catechism that he must have witnessed at some point. This religious catechism was later practiced in the realm of antislavery politics from pulpit to other religious gatherings to lecture halls and other forms of reprimand and later adopted by others such as William Wells Brown in *Clotel*.[7] Stanza 14 of Hammon's poem, however, exemplified his perseverance to a public pursuit, a self-conscious investigation he accepted, and hope that his brethren would also find solace. Hammon's use of language to build up a dramatic exchange between slaveholder and slave was actually reinforced when at the onset of the poem he suggested that the "Servant," of his own accord, will "quickly follow" the master's command: "Come my servant, follow me, / According to thy place," a place that whites have defined for blacks. The master in Hammon's poem, on the other hand, characterized the conventional "interests and beliefs" of his aristocracy. Both — slave and master — profess Christianity, but their religiosity differs vastly (O'Neale 191). This was important to Hammon's development as a jeremiadic poet because he offered his audience — both black and white — an illuminating critique of the master–slave caste system of the early republic that was meant to create a conflict of ideologies between idyllic social life and its materialization. A close reading of the poem suggested that Hammon insinuated that black men of the early republic, regardless of class or educational background, shared a similar predicament: white oppression. Therefore, Hammon's style of social protest reflected his search for racial identity: he opposed slavery based upon his experiences in the early republic as a black man who had a strong belief in God.

It can be inferred that within his coded messages, blacks could find the fuel needed to attack slavery straightforwardly. Hammon repeatedly refers to blacks as "my brethren" in "A Winter Piece," informing them that he suffered the same plight that they did, but through salvation and a fervent belief in God, he triumphed over the injustices of his enslavement. He also sought to create a new image of his fellow "brethren." In his "Address to the Negroes of the State of New York," Hammon plainly lamented his views on slavery. He told his "brethren":

> I think you will be more likely to listen to what is said, when you know it comes from a negro, one your own nation and colour, and therefore can have no interest in deceiving you, or in saying any thing to you, but what he really thinks is your interest and duty to comply with. My age, I think, gives me some right to speak to you, and reason to expect you will hearken to my advice ["Address to the Negroes of the State of New York" 6].

By claiming that he did "not wish to be free, yet I should be glad," he continued "if others, especially the young negroes were to be free," Hammon seemingly played on the "happy darkie" myth. He maintained, however, that his age and many years of servitude had claimed the best of his character and that he "must soon go the way of all the earth" ("Address to the Negroes of the State of New York" 13, 6–7). Given his awareness of the role age would play in his invectives, one could only speculate why he would have written his address. American slavery was still, he continued, an unjust system and ought to be eradicated. It was up to the "young negroes," Hammon believed, to take such actions into their own hands.

A Poetic Appeal for Social Change

There were some instances of the African American jeremiad where an appeal was made to whites to plead with them to take control of the privileges that had been given to them. While employing the jeremiad in one of her earlier works, Wheatley's "To the University of Cambridge, in New-England" offered an example of how some blacks during the early republic suggested to whites that they had abandoned God's directive, and they, too, were in need of salvation. In the second stanza of the poem, Wheatley addressed her audience, the students of the University of Cambridge, New England, young white males, the future politicians and leaders of the country, who had been given the opportunity to study and learn of worldly things and to have received the news from God's "messengers from heav'n" of the redeeming power that flows from the blood of Jesus, "How *Jesus*' blood for your redemption flows." In the final stanza of the poem, Wheatley urged her white audience to appreciate and make good of the sacrifice that Jesus made while they were living and make an effective change in their lives: "Improve your privileges while they stay" (*CW* 176), she suggested. How did this relate to the rhetoric of the African American jeremiad? It gave Wheatley a voice to not only critique whites in their own socio-religious and cultural arguments, but also it enabled her to offer them enlightenment. It became evident that Wheatley hoped that the students' newly found enlightenment would help gain more respect for the African captives. In "An Address to the Deist," Wheatley offered the same encouragement to "the vilest prodigal" to "Seek the Eternal while he is so near" (*CW* 132).

Wheatley's and Hammon's employment of the jeremiad pointed to their beliefs that salvation depended on a new mode of thinking and new forms of expression. Every line of their prose and poetry became a protest of some sort — either against slavery, "*Various Subjects, Religious and Moral*," the "Salvation of Christ," or for black moral and collective independence. Wheatley and Hammon made it clear that initiative for such change would have to come from the African captives. What role would whites play in this movement? It was their jobs to act morally and allow them to take their rightfully place in American society. When Wheatley beckoned for whites' attention, she addressed the existing systems of dominant oppressions in their own socio-religious discourse. While doing so, she fostered a new consciousness and advanced revolution. In her letter to the "Reverend and Honoured Sir [Samson Occom]," she divulged her attitude on the republic's institution of slavery and treatment of blacks (Lauter 1112). It is important to note that this letter was written after Wheatley obtained her freedom. Although not treated like the typical house slave, Wheatley realized that she was a slave in every sense of the word. During her first few months of freedom, she gained a new self-determination; she was reborn into a society where she could now further immerse herself in developing an acceptable voice. Wheatley wrote:

2. Early Development

> For in every human Breast, God has implanted a Principle, which we call Love of Freedom; it is impatient of Oppression, and pants for Deliverance; and by the leave of our modern Egyptians I will assert, that the same Principle lives in us. God grant Deliverance in his own way and Time, and get him honor upon all those whose Avarice impels them to countenance and help forward the Calamities of their Fellow Creatures. This I desire not for their Hurt, but to convince them of the strange Absurdity of their Conduct, whose Words and Actions are so diametrically opposite. How well the Cry for Liberty, and the reverse Disposition for the Exercise of oppressive Power over others agree,—I humbly think it does not require the Penetration of a Philosopher to determine [CW 176].

The most important benefit that Wheatley's freedom afforded her was the development of her social and political voice. As she forged a new role for herself in the public sphere, this letter illustrated a significant transformation in Whealey's jeremiadic discourse because it directly called for a just treatment of blacks. After a visit to London in 1774, Wheatley "transformed her literary identity," and she gained the "opportunity to transform her legal, social, and political identities as well" (Carretta xxii). Even though the socio-political inference of her works has been "widely ignored" (Shields 232), Wheatley's many compositions suggested that she intentionally used her voice as a vehicle to lament the world around her and the jeremiad as a coping mechanism.

The idea of equality was further illustrated in Wheatley's jeremiadic discourse when she generated a discussion between religious and political leaders by adopting a similar rhetoric they had employed when they defined a "place" for people of African descent in the early republic. This was illustrated in her poems "On the Death of the Rev. Mr. GEORGE WHITEFIELD. 1770" and in "To the Right Honorable William, Earl of Dartmouth, His Majesty's Principal Secretary of State for North America, Etc." While Whitefield's usage of social protest did not explicitly campaign against slavery, he insisted that people of all colors, economic statuses, and educational backgrounds were equally deserving of God's grace. Of Whitefield, Wheatley wrote:

> Behold the prophet in his tow'ring flight!
> He leaves the earth for heav'n's unmeasur'd height,
> And worlds unknown receive him from our fight.
> There *Whitefield* wings with rapid course his way,
> And sails to *Zion* through vast seas of day.
> Thy pray'rs, great saint, and thine incessant cries
> Have pierc'd the bosom of thy native skies.
>
> * * *
>
> Take him my dear *Americans*, he said,
> Be your complaints on his kind bosom laid:
> Take him, ye *Africans*, he longs for you,
> *Impartial Saviour* is his title due:
> Wash'd in the fountain of redeeming blood,
> You shall be sons and kings, and priests to God [CW 23].

The idea of white men enslaving blacks was sinful, according to Whitefield, since Africans also had immortal souls. Whitefield's poignant sermons "did more perhaps, than anything else to encourage the slave along the road of mental escape from his conditions ... and it stimulated him to assert himself as a human being" (Pipes 68). When looked at under this light, Wheatley's recognition of Whitefield as a "prophet" and an *"Impartial Saviour"* who "longs for" "ye *Africans*" to come and accept Christ so that they "shall be sons and kings, and priests to God," was important to her socio-political development as a poet and her jeremiadic discourse because, again, it gave her an authoritative voice which she now used to criticize whites in a manner that was acceptable to both black and white society. Wheatley promptly gained influence in the mainstream republic. In "To the Right Honorable William, Earl of Dartmouth, His Majesty's Principal Secretary of State for North America, Etc." Wheatley congratulated Dartmouth on his appointment as Secretary of State for the colonies. Seeing new political hope and possible changes for Africans in America, she wrote:

> HAIL, happy day, when, smiling like the morn,
> Fair Freedom rose New-England to adorn:
> The northern clime beneath her genial ray,
> Dartmouth, congratulates thy blissful sway:
> Elate with hope her race no longer mourns,
> Each soul expands, each grateful bosom burns,
> While in thine hand with pleasure we behold
> The silken reins, and Freedom's charms unfold.
> Long lost to realms beneath the northern skies [*CW* 114].

There was an apparent binary connection of Wheatley's attitude and way of thinking about slavery between the occasion to Dartmouth and the much earlier poem, "On Being Brought from Africa to America." In order to understand this connection and her use of the jeremiad, one must give significant and equal thought to her conditions as a woman, "the slave, and as the writer, the slave" (James 31).

Critics have argued that Wheatley was influenced by the religious fervor and neoclassicism of the times.[8] Wheatley would amalgamate these influences in her writings to articulate the theme of freedom for her and those like her. In one of her most politicized works, "To the King's Most Excellent Majesty. 1768," Wheatley suggested that King George III had the power to grant the captives their freedom while she alluded to political comments supporting America's freedom from Britain:

> But how shall we the *British* king reward!
> Rule thou in peace, our father, and our lord!
> Midst the remembrance of thy favours past,
> The meanest peasants most admire the last*

---

*The Repeal of the Stamp Act in 1766.

> May *George,* beloved by all the nations round,
> Live with heav'ns choicest constant blessings crown'd!
> Great God, direct, and guard him from on high,
> And from his head let e'ry evil fly!
> And may each clime with equal gladness see
> A monarch's smile can set his subjects free! [*CW* 17].

Because America's freedom rests in his hands, she pleaded with God to protect King George; therefore, George's religiosity and political power and status were of utmost importance to Wheatley. The implication was that once the republic received its freedom from the British, the African captives' deliverance would soon follow, if not instantaneously.

An invariable element of Wheatley's jeremiadic discourse was optimism. In very few instances, however, did she step from behind the veil in protest of the perceived injustice of the social nature surrounding the African captives. In most all of Wheatley's poems, her race was not a factor driving her to compose, but the treatment of her race seemingly was, since Wheatley's efforts showed that blacks can be educated and produce artistic creations. The very fact that Wheatley had to "defend" her first collection of poetry proves this point.[9] In his "Address to the New York African Society," William Hamilton argued that although Wheatley's poems "may not possess the requisitions necessary to stand the test of nice criticism, and she may be denied a stand in the rank of poets, yet does she possess some original ideas that would not disgrace the pen of the best poets" (82). Wheatley adopted, as an unwavering stance in any given poem, a tone that ranged from restrained irony and/or indignation to biblical exegesis and/or revolutionary ideas about injustices. This became more evident in Wheatley's "To S.M., a young *African* Painter."[10] While seeking wisdom and enlightenment for herself, Wheatley's jeremiadic discourse would also arouse a need of the influential white men of her day to additionally seek enlightenment for themselves. Wheatley accomplished this by juxtaposing a black servant's artistic qualities with the qualities of some of the noblest of white males to aide in the elevation of the black servant's works. After observing his paintings, Wheatley composed the poem and went beyond "scripturally delivered affirmations of African freedom and equality to hail the dignity, artistic worth, and future immorality of Scipio Moorhead," a fellow slave (Zafar 19, 18–19). Wheatley wrote:

> Still, with the sweets of contemplation bless'd,
> May peace with balmy wings your soul invest!
> But when these shades of time are chas'd away,
> And darkness ends in everlasting day,
> On what seraphic pinions shall we move,
> And view the landscapes in the realms above?
> There shall thy tongue in heav'nly murmurs flow,
> And there my muse with heav'nly transport glow:
> No more to tell of Damon's tender sighs,

> Or rising radiance of Aurora's eyes,
> For nobler themes demand a nobler strain,
> And purer language on th' ethereal plain.
> Cease, gentle muse! the solemn gloom of night
> Now seals the fair creation from my sight [*CW* 114].

The poem was meant to heighten the "*African*" painter's social status to those of other prominent white individuals of her day (Zafar 19) and has an insinuation of self-assurance for blacks. By adding value to his works, Wheatley's lament was meant to persuade Africans to take their rightful place in society, since, as she expressed in the poem, "nobler themes" of black artistry "demand a nobler strain" or effort. It was up to the "purer language" of the "ethereal plain" of the American mainstream, Wheatley implied, to reinforce Moorhead's artistry. The implication was that for those whites who advocated Wheatley's verse, Moorhead's work could be included not only in conversation, but also in their presence, galleries, and homes. Wheatley's status as a "*black* Christian in a *white* world added ... a ... unique stress to her quest for enlightenment" (Zafar 22; emphasis in original). Within Wheatley's quest for truth, she afforded her black audience the means to seek cultural hegemony and the true roots of their gender and racial identity, as her poem dedicated to Moorhead's works indicated.

As Wheatley and Hammon realized that their invectives were a new experience for most, they accordingly created their compositions based on the peace they found in the biblical subjects of deliverance, uplift, freedom, and self-determination. These themes, however, would give way to larger social and political issues of the day as Wheatley and Hammon attacked the crucial issues of the brutality of human bondage. The growth and development of African American literature and jeremiadic discourse, then, were intricately linked. Both shared common intellectual interests concerning the effects of slavery on the enslaved. This connection was further intensified when early African American activists forged social protest instead of seeking literary endeavors. The earliest slave narrators would also find a place for the jeremiad in their invectives against slavery.

To "bear the slave's heavy cross": Early Slave Narrators Employed Jeremiadic Discourse

The revivalism of the Great Awakenings no doubt influenced the rhetoric of slave narrators. As the motion of the jeremiad cascaded throughout their works, early slave narrators used its polemics to lament the socio-religious dogmas of white Christianity. Employing their unique jeremiadic approach, early slave narrators attempted to persuade their readers to accept not only the candid truth of their messages, but also the necessity for the reformed individual to work against the institution of slavery. Christianity was central to their conception and presentation of the self. Their autobiographies functioned not merely as a recollection of their lives, but as "artifact[s], a construct in which experience is fictionalized and one framework prioritized over all others. For the slave, the climactic point of this prioritized framework, 'the moment of spiritual / cultural conversion' also acted as a moment of 'self-liberation in which the narrator[s] broke free from the shackles' of their oppressor 'and past cultural identity'" (Thomas 178), and emerged a newly redeemed self. Take, for example, Thomas Jones' conversion to Christianity in his *The Experience of Thomas H. Jones, Who Was A Slave for Forty-Three Years*. After accepting Christ as his personal Savior, Jones recalled:

> All was bright and joyous in my relations towards my precious Saviour. I felt certain that Jesus was my Saviour, and in this blessed assurance a flood of glory and joy filled my happy soul. But this sweet night passed away, and, as the morning came, I felt that I must go home, and bear the *slave's heavy* cross. I went, and told my mistress the blessed change in my feelings. She promised me what aid she could give me with my master, and enjoined upon me to be patient and very faithful to his interest, and, in this way, I should at length wear out his opposition to my praying and going to meeting [26; emphasis in original].

Although published in 1862, Jones' account provided excellent examples of conversion, religion and jeremiadic discourse in the slave narrative. Jones' text also showed that the second Great Awakenings—32 years after its revivalism reaches its apex—still had a profound affect on blacks who were included in its polemics. Readers familiar with Jones' account will note that he ignited a seemingly critical conclusion (nonreligious slaveholders could be worse than religious ones) and transformation (amalgamating the slaveholders' religion into his own social pantheon), by showing allusions of himself in his plight as a contemporary child of Israel and metaphorically aligning himself with Christ, who must, "bear the *slave's heavy* cross" (26; emphasis in original). The phrase became an implicit call to consciousness and action. To blacks of a similar plight, Jones showed that those who were *in* Christ were His children, not property of slaveholders, that they were no longer slaves to whites, but they were part of the family of God. After all, according to interpretation of his passage, Christ and slaves endured the burden of the *"heavy cross."* As the passage also suggested, it appeared to Jones that Christianity was masking the two certainties that were innate in the gospel: first, Christ gave himself for Jones' (and the slave's) sins, and second, Christ gave himself to deliver Jones (and the slave) from his present evil of slavery.

When looked at under this light, Jones' account became a classic example of a narrative that was influenced by the religious elements of African American jeremiadic tradition. The jeremiadic discourse of the slave narratives of the early republic relied heavily on the narrators' socio-political religiosity, as also personified in Jones' account, while calling for social change. In an earlier work,

A Narrative of the Most Remarkable Particulars in the Life of James Albert Ukawsaw Gronniosaw, An African Prince, As Related By Himself, James Albert Ukawsaw Gronniosaw told readers that "GOD is pleased to incline the hearts of his People at times to yield us their charitable assistance" (39). Gronniosaw's short narrative in its entirety was a lamentation of the "adventures in the realm of religious experience" (Starling 59). To those who have been touched by the evil hands of slavery, Gronniosaw's narrative helped to justify an earlier case concerning Phyllis Wheatley's and Jupiter Hammon's beliefs that blacks should not give up hope that "the LORD shall deliver us out of the evils of this present world and bring us to the EVERLASTING GLORIES of the world to come" (39). After their deliverance from slavery's tyrannical clutches, a new sociopoliticized African American would emerge demanding all the rights promised to him. As Walter Shirley told readers in the preface to Gronniosaw's narrative, "Faith did not fail him; he put his Trust in the Lord, and he was delivered" (iv). Although not much else is known of Gronniosaw after his narrative appeared on the scene, his trials and tribulations during and after his enslavement depicted an ideological struggle of accepting the dishonorable Christianity. Jarena Lee, the first woman to be certified to preach by Richard Allen, founder of the African Methodist Episcopal Church, also illustrated this idea in her toils and tribulation. Toward the end of "My Call to Preach The Gospel" in her *Religious Experience and Journal of Mrs. Jarena Lee, Giving An Account of Her Call to Preach the Gospel*, Lee revealed that God would make known His goodness and power: "I have not even doubted the power of goodness of God to keep me from falling, through the sanctification of the spirit and belief of the truth" (13). Since she did not lose hope that God would keep her in her most troubled time of need, her people should not doubt it either. Later in her narrative, she invited the "backslider" to hear the word of God: "'Repent ye and be converted, for God hath called all men everywhere to repent. Without reserve give Christ your heart / Let him his [sic] righteousness impart — then / then all things else he'll freely give / With him you all things shall receive'" (32).

The sermonizing tradition of the Great Awakenings found its place in Olaudah Equiano's appeal to the British in his *The Interesting Narrative of the Life of Olaudah Equiano, or Gustavus Vassa, the African*. Although there is little evidence that Equiano was in the American colonies during the revivalism of the awakenings (1730s–1740s; 1820s–1830s), Equiano did hear well-known evangelist George Whitefield sermonize in Savannah in 1765. His socio-political reform against slavery became poignant in his comparisons with the two forms of slavery in the New World and Great Britain. In his *Narrative*, Equiano noted that his treatment as a slave begat a sharp contrast between how slaves were treated in Africa as opposed to his treatment on a British slave ship:

> I now saw myself deprived of all chance of returning to my native country, or even the least glimpse of hope of gaining the shore, which I now considered as friendly; and I even wished for my former slavery in preference to my present situation, which

was filled with horrors of every kind, still heightened by my ignorance of what I was to undergo. I was not long suffered to indulge my grief; I was soon put down under the decks, and there I received such a salutation in my nostrils as I had never experienced in my life: so that, with the loathsomeness of the stench, and crying together, I became so sick and low that I was not able to eat, nor had I the least desire to taste any thing. I now wished for the last friend, death, to relieve me; but soon, to my grief, two of the white men offered me eatables; and, on my refusing to eat, one of them held me fast by the hands, and laid me across I think the windlass, and tied my feet, while the other flogged me severely. I had never experienced any thing of this kind before; and although, not being used to the water, I naturally feared that element the first time I saw it, yet nevertheless, could I have got over the nettings, I would have jumped over the side, but I could not; and, besides, the crew used to watch us very closely who were not chained down to the decks, lest we should leap into the water: and I have seen some of these poor African prisoners most severely cut for attempting to do so, and hourly whipped for not eating. This indeed was often the case with myself [*Narrative* 73–74].

Equiano's lamentation stemmed from his belief in and acceptance of Jesus Christ's gift of salvation, and from his belief that He died for everyone's sins on the cross. To demonstrate his argument more concretely, Equiano questioned the morality of slave owners:

O, ye nominal Christians! Might not an African ask you, learned you this from your God? Who says unto you, do unto all men as you would men should do unto you? Is it not enough that we are torn from our country and friends to toil for your luxury and lust of gain? Must every tender feeling be likewise sacrificed to your avarice? Are the dearest friends and relations ... still to be parted from each other, and thus prevented from cheering the gloom of slavery.... Why are parents to lose their children, brothers their sisters, or husbands their wives? Surely this is a new refinement in cruelty, which, while it has no advantage to atone for it, thus aggravates distress, and adds fresh horrors even to the wretchedness of slavery [*Narrative* 33–34].

Labeling slaveholders as "nominal Christians," Equiano evaluated the violence of the slave traders against Christianity in order to further argue for a sociopolitical opposition to slavery. As he devalued and deconstructed their perceived notions about *true* Christianity, Equiano's expression of grief of the slave trafficking system develops at the conclusion of his work when he posited:

When you make men slaves you deprive them of half their virtue, you set them in your own conduct an example of fraud, rapine, and cruelty, and compel them to live with you in a state of war; and yet you complain that they are not honest or faithful! You stupify them with stripes, and think it necessary to keep them in a state of ignorance; and yet you assert that they are incapable of learning; that their minds are such a barren soil or moor, that culture would be lost on them; and that they come from a climate, where nature, though prodigal of her bounties in a degree unknown to yourselves, has left man alone scant and unfinished, and incapable of enjoying the treasures she has poured out for him!— An assertion at once impious and absurd. Why do you use those instruments of torture? Are they fit to be applied by one rational being to another; And are ye not struck with shame and mortification, to see the partakers of your nature reduced so low? But, above all, are there no dangers attending this mode of treatment? Are you not hourly in dread of an insurrection? Nor would it be surprising: for when

> — No peace is given
> To us enslav'd, but custody severe;
> And stripes and arbitrary punishment
> Inflicted — What peace can we return?
> But to our power, hostility and hate;
> Untam'd reluctance, and revenge, though slow,
> Yet ever plotting how the conqueror least
> May reap his conquest, and may least rejoice
> In doing what we most in suffering feel.
>
> But by changing your conduct, and treating your slaves as men, every cause of fear would be banished. They would be faithful, honest, intelligent and vigorous; and peace, prosperity, and happiness, would attend you [*Narrative* 224–26].

The political importance of Equiano's narrative surfaced more as he beseeched his white audience to amend "your conduct" and treatment of black men. Equiano's narrative instituted a "conscious effort to ascribe spiritual enlightenment" to the political discourse of abolitionists by establishing "the importance of the relationship between spiritual intervention, the 'mysterious ways of Providence' and parliamentary decisions concerning the abolition of the slave trade" (Thomas 228). Equiano informed the assembly of "the chief design of which is to excite in your august assemblies a sense of compassion for the miseries which the Slave-Trade...." He believed that such injustices have

> torn away from all the tender connexions that were naturally dear to my heart; but these, through the mysterious ways of Providence, I ought to regard as infinitely more than compensated by the introduction I have thence obtained to the knowledge of the Christian religion, and of a nation which, by its liberal sentiments, its humanity, the glorious freedom of its government, and its proficiency in arts and sciences, has exalted the dignity of human nature [*Narrative* iii–iv].

Early in his narrative, Equiano divulged his purpose: to draw a political opposition to slavery by pressing Parliament to become involved in his mission. If "the polished and haughty European disclose his history," Equiano wrote, "he will discover that his "ancestors were once, like the Africans, uncivilized, and even barbarous" (*Narrative* 43).

Before Equiano published *The Interesting Narrative*, his jeremiadic rhetoric seemingly manifested in the work of his noble friend, Quobna Ottobah Cugoano. When Cugoano's *Narrative of the Enslavement of Ottobah Cugoano, a Native of Africa; Published by Himself, in the Year 1787* arrived on the antislavery scene, there was great reason for the abolitionist community in both Great Britain and America to suspect that the appearance of this horrific story of the baleful carnage and violence of human bondage would help solidify the beginning of black jeremiadic discourse. The first of its kind to enter antislavery polemics by criticizing "European imperialism in the Americas" (Carretta, preface), Cugoano's narrative opened the doors for the antislavery institution to further its cause. Though there appears to be no evidence in his narrative that Cugoano made his way to North America as a slave, one of his owners, Alexander Campbell, Esq., reportedly lived in Virginia from 1753–1759 (Carretta x). Conversely, Cugoano possibly only witnessed North American slavery in Grenada in the Caribbean Islands at an early age. His influence, however, on African American jeremiadic rhetoric was immeasurable, because he offered blacks hope that freedom could be obtained through "God" and "providence." Likewise, his narrative gave later slave narrators the fuel, language, and determination they needed to attack assimilation of white American mainstream values. Cugoano's lament presented abolitionists with the vehicle needed to beseech slaveholders to cease the nefarious slave trafficking. Thus Cugoano can be considered the first former slave to demonstrate his polemic in his narrative that "to be a slave is to be under the brutal power and authority of another" (Hartman 3). In his *Thoughts and Sentiments on the Evil and Wicked Traffic of the Commerce of the Human Species*, Cugoano wrote:

> Among other observations, one great duty I owe to Almighty God, (the thankful acknowledgement I would not omit for any consideration) that, although I have been brought away from my native country, in the torrent of robbery and wickedness, thanks be to God for his good providence towards me; I have both obtained liberty, and acquired the great advantages of some little learning, in being able to read and write, and, what is still infinitely of greater advantage, I trust, to know something of HIM *who is that God whose providence rules over all, and who is the only Potent One that rules in the nations over the children of men. It is unto Him, who is the Prince of the Kings of the earth, that I will give all thanks* [*Thoughts and Sentiments* 17; emphasis in original].

Cugoano prophesized that "the time of our deliverance is fast drawing nigh, and when the great Babylon of iniquity will fall" (*Thoughts and Sentiments* 98). Then, Cugoano "pleads with God to place in the hearts of the British the notion that justice and righteousness are compatible, and Africans are deserving of these rights as well" (Adams and Sanders, *Three Black Writers in Eighteenth Century England* 98). A plan might be implemented, Cugoano suggested, to diminish the oppression of Africans:

> And as we look for our help and sure deliverance to come from God Most High, should it not come in an apparent way from Great-Britain, whom we consider as the Queen of nations, let her not thinks to escape more than others, if she continues to carry on oppression and injustice, and such pre-eminent wickedness against us: for we are only seeking that justice may be done to us, and what every righteous nations ought to do; and if it be not done, it will be adding iniquity to iniquity against themselves [*Thoughts and Sentiments* 97].

Since the "purpose of the Black Jeremiad was not simply to provide a verbal outlet for hostilities; it was a means of demonstrating loyalty — both to the principles of egalitarian liberalism and to the Anglo-Christian code of values" (Moses, *Black Messiahs* and *Uncle Toms* 38), Cugoano, therefore, further proposed "that a total abolition of slavery should be made and proclaimed; and that an universal emancipation of slaves should begin from the date thereof" and "that a fleet of some ships of war should be immediately sent to the coast of Africa" in order to stop the bringing of Africans "from the coast of Africa." If Great Britain acknowledged this, he prophesized, "it would meet with the general approbation and assistance of other Christian nations" (*Thoughts and Sentiments* 98, 100). Cugoano's argument was simple: "Every man must live as a Christian" (Adams and Sanders 102). However, Cugoano's tone seemed to suggest that he was disappointed by the lack of good judgment and sincerity in men; he grieved over the lack of true Christian philosophy in the world. What should Cugoano expect? After all, the line between religion and philosophy in the Christian tradition was bleak because Christians have supposedly always had a distinctive approach to philosophy. What seemed cumbersome to Cugoano was the existence of evil in the Christian ways to philosophy. Morality, the concepts of right, wrong, and punishment, he believed, were replaced with wickedness. Therefore, Cugoano condemned Christians who "either do not speak or dare not speak the truth" (Adams and Sanders 106) against the evils of slave trafficking. Becoming an activist in the Afro-Britain community, Cugoano represented one of the first to promote the moral right and duty of slaves to resist slavery.

Latter black orators of jeremiadic discourse such as Frederick Douglass and Martin Delany would chastise blacks for not taking the necessary steps to liberate themselves. Douglass, for example, believed that most blacks did not "deserve respect" if they did nothing to elevate themselves (Howard-Pitney 22). When slave narrators employed the jeremiad, they structured it to act as a reminder to its Christian audience of their impudent transgression of God's directive. This task was graphically expressed through the use of concrete language, description, and detail. William Wells Brown, for example, took the time to remind his reading audience that "They call themselves a Christian nation; they rob three millions of their countrymen of their liberties, and then talk of their piety, their democracy, and their love of liberty" (*Narrative* 137). The condemnation of the treatment of blacks, slavery and the slave trade were major areas to criticize as they argued in detail that "the tendency of the spirit of slaveholding is, to kill in the soul whatever it touches. It [slaveholding] has no eyes to see, nor ears to hear, nor mind to understand, nor heart to feel for its victims as *human beings*" (Watson 43).[11]

Conclusion

The revivalism of the Great Awakenings not only affected the religious fervor of the times, but it had an adverse affect on political thought as well: it forced Americans, both black and white, to deal with their religious zealousness more politically by introducing important questions that concerned slaveholding and Christianity. During the early republic, African American jeremiadic discourse could be read as expressing grief on the dehumanization blacks endured while searching for truth and self-determination, a fact that reflects its marginalization in American letters. This neglect, however, is not the only reason why further studies on African American social protest of the early republic as jeremiadic rhetoric is important. Although the works of Phyllis Wheatley and Jupiter Hammon laid the foundation for not only the African American literary tradition but also for the African American literary tradition as social protest, the jeremiad played a vital role in the successes of building this foundation.

3

The African American Jeremiad, the Constitution and the Declaration of Independence

> We the people of the United States, in order to form a more perfect union, establish justice, insure domestic tranquility, provide for the common defense, promote the general welfare, and secure the blessings of liberty to ourselves and our posterity, do ordain and establish this Constitution for the United States of America.
> — *Constitution of the United States*,
> Adopted by convention of States, 17 September 1787;
> Ratification completed, 21 June 1788

> We hold these truths to be self-evident, that all men are created equal, that they are endowed by their Creator with certain unalienable Rights, that among these are Life, Liberty and the pursuit of Happiness.
> — *Declaration of Independence*, 4 July 1776

As the above quotes from the country's founding fathers suggested, America was founded on the principles of liberty, equality, and justice for *all men*. Was oppression, however, an ingredient in the founding fathers' discourse to construct a national identity? Before the 1787 Constitutional Convention convened in Philadelphia to begin the task of establishing the country's new democracy, blacks in America had already endured white supremacy. When blacks criticized America's democratic ideas declared in the Declaration of Independence and Constitution, they placed emphasis on what they considered the founders' failed legislative efforts. Frederick Douglass, one of America's most laudable African American Jeremiahs who felt that all men were not treated equally, read the founders' Constitution as "inhuman, unjust, and affronting to God and man" (qtd. in Adams and Sanders, *Alienable Rights* 51). According to Douglass, the Constitution was "a most foul and bloody conspiracy against rights of three millions of enslaved and imbruted men" ("Comments on Gerrit Smith's Address" 141). As Douglass' reading suggested, blacks in antebellum America understood the reality of oppression and its effects on the oppressed.

3. The Constitution and the Declaration of Independence

Their interpretation of the founding fathers' documents denied them citizenship. William J. Watkins criticized American patriotism as the cause of blacks' oppression in America:

> I stand before you to-day ... a victim of American patriotism — a patriotism that stands by the Union — a patriotism that is truly *American*.... I stand before you to-day ostracized — the victim of a spirit the most merciless and unrelenting — a spirit that would drive me from the land of my birth. Why is it that we colored people are this treated? ["Anti-Slavery Celebration at Abington"; emphasis in original].

Watkins insightfully pointed out that the United States must live up to its sentiments that "all men were created equal." Granville B. Blanks concluded that under the present Constitution and discriminations, it was "impracticable, not to say impossible, for the whites and blacks to live together, and upon terms of social and civil equality, under the same government" ("Granville B. Blanks to Editor" 131–132). Because of their understanding of civil liberties for their people, African American Jeremiahs demanded a new social order, a new consciousness among the dehumanized and exploited. They utilized the language of the Constitution and Declaration of Independence to stimulate the conscience of the nation. While traveling to Manchester, England in 1854, William Wells Brown told his audience that the founding fathers' documents were so ingrained into America's way of life, that they supported the "infamous system" at every turn.

> No one can read ... the declaration of American independence, and compare that document with the history of the legislation of the federal government of the United States, without being struck with the marked inconsistency of the theory of the people and their acts; the one declaring that all men are created equally, endowed by their Creator with certain inalienable rights, among which are life, liberty, and the pursuit of happiness, and the other is the history of the encroachment of slavery upon liberty, or legislation in favour of slavery in that country against the cause of freedom ... slavery was introduced into the constitution by allowing the African slave trade to be continued for twenty years, making it lawful and constitutional, which had never been before; and then the slave-owner was allowed representation for this slave property, and every man that would go to the Coast of Africa, and steal five negroes and bring them to the United States, was allowed by the constitution, then, three votes for the five slaves ["Speech by William Wells Brown, Delivered at the Town Hall, Manchester, England" 399].

One of the most visible characteristics of the African American jeremiad, then, stems from the development of civil liberties set forth by the founding fathers in their fight to free themselves of British control. Their protest helped to characterize the pervasive force of the African American jeremiad as the *promise* made by the Declaration of Independence declared that "all men are created equal, that they are endowed by their Creator with certain unalienable Rights, that among these are Life, Liberty and the pursuit of Happiness." Initially, to African Americans, these sound ideologies set forth by the founding fathers promised they would also benefit from the country's independence; it gave them hope. However, African Americans quickly realized that the documents offered rather abstract truths when their own liberation was in question. Peter Paul Simons made this clear when he lamented, "If our forefathers held the truths of immortality of the soul before their eyes, there would have been no such thing as African slavery" ("Speech by Peter Paul Simons" 292). As they began to directly attack the causes of their disenfranchisement through their usage of the jeremiad, African Americans were able to map out inconsistencies in the construction of what their white counterparts called the republic in which all would acquire civil liberties: (1) the decentralization of their culture, with respect to the main construction of the republic, was a major concern; and (2) the republic was poorly organized in terms of economic, social, political, and religious affairs. These contradictions in the development of the republic and their minimal level of application to African American concerns of equality represented — as blacks saw it — an impediment in the creation of a *true* democracy.

Encouraging perspectives that placed their discourse into social, cultural, religious, economic, and political contexts, African American Jeremiahs attacked the very essence of white hegemony and criticized the nation for not fulfilling its credence that "all men are created equal." As William Wells Brown lamented:

> A great mistake was made by the fathers of this country when they incorporated the slave trade in the Constitution of the country, allowed the slave representation in Congress,[1] and gave to the slaveholders the right to hunt his victims in the free States. It was believed that Christianity and Republicanism would wipe out the foul blot, but such has not been the result ["Speech by William Wells Brown, Delivered at the Horticultural Hall" 245–247].

African American Jeremiahs' positions toward race relations of their times were beached in a social representational structure, which recognized that oppression was above all forms of institutional, cultural, and individual discrimination and group exclusion rather than a product of differences between blacks and whites. The aim of their rhetoric was to secure the status of equal citizenship in American democracy since they felt that American democratic ideologies were a cover for placing people into classes. To this end, the aim of "The Sons of Africans: An Essay on Freedom. With Observations on the Origin of Slavery," published in 1808 by "A Member of the African Society in Boston," was to initiate a dialogue with readers concerning slaves' experiences:

> Freedom.... Although none can rightly estimate its worth, but those who have been deprived of that invaluable blessing, and through the interposition of Divine Providence have been brought to the enjoyment of the same, yet we may all have a faint idea concerning its worth, if we would contrast our present circumstances with many which we might mention.... But we will for a moment collect our ideas to contemplate bondage, oppression, or slavery, as they are the reverse from freedom, as we are at the present time to suggest the idea of freedom's being valuable. This we cannot have so consistent ideas of, unless we refer back to some of the earliest periods of time,

or rove from our present situation into foreign climes, by way of contemplations, and see how sin hath introduced those various abominations in the world; amongst which slavery is the capital that we shall mention at the present time ["The Sons of Africans" 13, 15].

Brian Barry has suggested that within the American democracy, there existed particular "rights against oppression, exploitation, and injury, to which every single human being is entitled to lay claim" (132). African American Jeremiahs realized, then, that the certain rights endowed to most men in the founding fathers' documents did not apply to *all* men, and that they were not reaping the benefits of equality for all men.

Many poverty-stricken white citizens, conversely, felt that they too were not reaping the benefits of the founding fathers' democratic philosophy and felt that they were being enslaved by their own government. There was no evidence, however, that this influenced African American jeremiadic rhetoric. Nevertheless, in their ratification of the Constitution, many of the founding fathers felt that their rights to form a new government void of British influence ought to be protected. "It was not asserted by America that the people of *the Island of Great Britain* were slaves," wrote "An American Citizen" in the *Independent Gazetteer* on 26 September 1787, "but that *we*, though possessed absolutely of the same rights, were not admitted to enjoy *an equal degree of freedom*." The Constitution, the anonymous writer felt, was "*inadequate to the preservation of liberty, property, and the union*" ("An American Citizen" 21; emphasis in original). According to African Americans, whites were the tormenters of the oppressed. The differences of opinions between white and black Americans did not surface so much from oppositions to the structure of government as from discrepancies concerning certain essential rights resulting from the fundamental principles of liberty, which the founding fathers' Constitution had previously sealed to all the persons inhabiting the country. General Charles Cotesworth Pinckney, while discussing the importance the Constitution, told the South Carolina House of Representatives: "In short, considering all circumstances, we have made the best terms for the security of this species of property it was in our power to make. We would have made better if we could; but on the whole, I do not think them bad" (286). The architects of the African American jeremiad navigated the debate of the self-worth of the Constitution. At the same time, they remained steadfast to their own constructivist principles which led toward a shared purpose of abating every edifice of slavery and racial discrimination. Not accepting the conviction that the founding fathers' did their best to ensure equality for the country's citizens of African extraction, James Forten, Sr., lamented that when the founding fathers "adopted the glorious fabric of our liberties, and declaring 'all men' free, they did not particularize white and black, because they never supposed it would be made a question whether we were men or not" ("Series of Letters by a Man of Colour" 69).

The constructivist philosophy of the African American jeremiad called blacks to voice their beliefs so the fabric of racial harmony would be strengthened rather than weakened, and so that the structure had political, social, and economic value for their constituents. After all, the Constitution worked out the voting rules relative to issues concerning slavery by suggesting that the solution was to count slaves as three-fifths of a human being for representation purposes. Historian Jack N. Rakove, however, maintained that the three-fifths clause was "neither a coefficient of racial hierarchy nor a portent of the racialist thinking of the next century." Rakove continued:

> [The clause] was rather the closest approximation in the Constitution to the principle of one person, one vote — even if in its origins it was only a formula for apportioning representation *among*, as opposed to *within*, states and even if it violated the principle of equality by overvaluing the suffrage of the free male population of the slave states [74].

Given the mounting black social protest of the early republic, it was neither feasible nor realistic, however, to corroborate Rakove's inference that the three-fifths clause was not a common factor of racial motivation, yet, it overestimated the "suffrage of the free male population" (74). Could blacks — slave or free — be otherwise represented in the new budding political process? Hosea Easton, who "offered the most searing and comprehensive rebuttal of popular racism in the early republic" (Sinha 27), reminded his brethren of this fact when he lamented:

> The first enquiry is, Are we eligible to an office? No. — Are we considered subjects of the government? No. — Are we initiated into free schools for mental improvement? No. — Are we patronised as salaried men in any public business whatever? No. — Are we taken into social compact with Society at large? No. — Are we patronised in any branch of business which is sufficiently lucrative to raise us to any material state of honour and respectability among men, and thus, qualify us to demand respect from the higher order of Society? No. — But to the contrary. Everything is withheld from us that is calculated to promote the aggrandizement and popularity of that part of the community who are said to be the descendants of Africa ["An Address" 49].

Other blacks furthered Easton's philosophy. Charles Lenox Remond lamented, "Where ... are the colored people of the United States? ... Where do they stand? ... So far as the masses of the American people are concerned, they have no place in their regard, they have no place in their esteem" ("Speech by Charles Lenox Remond Delivered at Mozart Hall" 385). There was little opposition, however, to ratifying the Constitution: the North apathetically approved because they understood that the South would not agree to the document otherwise. In 1780, just seven years after the Constitutional Convention's deliberations, Paul Cuffee and "Several Negroes & Molattors" of Darmouth, Massachusetts, lamented black distress on issues concerning their right to participate in the political process of the country's democratic ideologies: "We are not allowed the Privilage of freemen of the State having no note or Influence in the Election of those that Tax us ... we are not allowed in voating in the town meating ... nur to chuse an officer ... & we have not an Equal Chance with white people" [qtd. in Kaplan and Kaplan 152].[2]

Other blacks began to bemoan the misleading notions inherent in the founding fathers' documents. William Hamilton, in a speech delivered 4 July 1827 at the African Zion Church that celebrated the abolition of the slavery in the state of New York, lamented:

> Victory obtained by the principles of liberty, such as are broadly and indelibly laid down by the glorious sons of '76; and are contained in the ever memorable words prefixed to the *Declaration of Independence* of these United States: viz. "We hold these truths to be self-evident, that all men are created equal, that they are endowed by their Creator with certain unalienable rights, that among these are life, liberty and the pursuit of happiness." A victory obtained by these principles over prejudice, injustice, and foul oppression ["An Oration Delivered in the African Zion Church" 97].

Since New York had been "cleansed of the most foul, poisonous and damnable stain" ("An Oration Delivered in the African Zion Church" 97), Hamilton hoped that blacks would obtain equality from whites.[3]

William Watkins, writing under the pseudonym "A Colored Baltimorean" in a letter to William Lloyd Garrison praising Garrison for his efforts in *The Liberator* ("William Watkins to Lloyd Garrison," 92),[4] explicitly revealed that the rights and privileges given to the creators of the Constitution were denied to blacks:

> When we say, however, that we are, as a boy, blind to our interests, we would not be understood as meaning, we are ignorant of our condition, and unconscious of our rights: this cannot be in America. The *self-evident* principles, "that all men are created *equal*, and endowed by their Creator with certain *unalienable* rights, that among these are life, liberty, and the pursuit of happiness," are as indelibly stamped upon out original faculties, as upon those of the lords of the land ["William Watkins to William Lloyd Garrison" 93; emphasis in original].

As he bemoaned the Constitution as "pro-slavery," H. Ford Douglas suggested that "no colored man can consistently vote under the United States Constitution." At the 16 January 1851 convention in Columbus, Ohio, Douglas revealed that the Constitution was used to justify the most atrocious and inhuman acts of the country's history: the continued degradation of blacks. After Douglas' resolution, William Howard Day agreed that the Constitution was pro-slavery; but dismissed, however, what he believed to be the misleading attitudes of "mistaken men in regard to it." Day believed in the Constitution and supposed that it was "framed to 'establish justice'" ("Exchanged Between H. Ford Douglas and William Howard Day" 73, 75). Day concluded:

> [the document] was made to foster and uphold the abominable, vampirish and bloody system of American slavery. The highest judicial tribunals of the country have so decided.... Slavery was one of the interests sought to be protected by the *Constitution* ... whether the *Constitution* is pro-slavery, and whether colored men "can consistently vote under that *Constitution*," are two very distinct questions.... I

would vote under the United States *Constitution* on the same principle ["Exchange Between H. Ford Douglas and William Howard Day" 75].

Day saw redemptive value in the Constitution and used it to glorify the achievements of the country's founding fathers. After Day's rebuttal to Douglas' resolution, the committee dismissed Douglas' resolution by a 28–2 vote (*BAP IV* 73). These types of resolutions, however, did not deter leaders, such as Douglas others, as they continued to create strategies for socio-political and socio-economic development through a separate public realm. As Brian Barry has noted, "appeals to 'cultural diversity' and pluralism under no circumstances trump the value of basic liberal rights" (132–33). In 1853, for example, Frederick Douglass wrote "we plead for our rights in the name of the immortal Declaration of Independence and of the Constitution, and we are answered by our countrymen with imprecations and curses" ("A Nation in the Midst of the Nation" 424). Four years later in reference to the Dred Scot Decision, Douglass further appropriated the founding fathers' language to show how it further stripped blacks of basic civil liberties:

> Your fathers have said that man's right to liberty is self-evident. There is no need to argument to make it clear. The voices of nature, of conscience, of reason, and of revelation, proclaim it as the right of all rights, the foundation of all trust, and of all responsibility. Man was born with it. It was his before he comprehended it. The *deed* conveying it to him is written more palpable to the sight than man's right to liberty is to the moral vision ["The Dred Scott Decision" 164; emphasis in original].

As the dominant culture looked at African Americans with contempt and created the racial stereotypes that would force activists to begin to argue for inclusion into the political, economic and social life of the mainstream republic, other black activist revealed the misleading dogmas of the Constitution. Martin Delany, born in Charlestown, Virginia to a slave father and a free black woman — which legally made him a free person — and raised in Pittsburgh after being taken there by his mother in 1822, oftentimes used the jeremiad as a vehicle of moralizing opinions about issues concerning the elevation of his race. In 1847, Delany lamented that the Constitution was a "pro slavery instrument," and that "no consistent antislavery person should either vote or hold office under it." Delany believed:

> More is asked of us, than ever was asked of any other people, and if it is expected that with all the disadvantages with which we are surrounded, that we should still equal the other citizens, it is giving us more than we claim; it is a tacit acknowledgement, that we are naturally superior to the rest of mankind, and, therefore, are much more susceptible than they ["Not Fair" 33].

As blacks personified the essence of black struggle and consciousness denied them by these documents—at the same time serving as the catalysts to black empowerment — early African American Jeremiahs felt that the rights of African Americans ought to be protected.

Some blacks seemingly believed in the essence of the Declaration of Independence and Constitution. At their First Annual Convention, held in Philadelphia 6–11 June 1831, conventioneers did not surrender their beliefs that these documents should protect the rights of all men. Believing that the documents should be read at the beginning of each annual meeting, they believed that the "truths contained in the former [documents] are incontrovertible, and that the latter guarantees in the letter and spirit to every freeman born in this country, all the rights and immunities of citizenship." They lamented, nevertheless, "the many oppressive, unjust and unconstitutional laws" "against the free people of color" (qtd. in Horton). They illustrated their awareness that their cultural exclusion from the mainstream republic was built on white consciousness and white politics. Therefore, their employment of the jeremiad at times was in opposition to antisocial legislation that they felt was responsible for their cultural exclusion. In his 1837 pamphlet *An Appeal to Forty Thousand Citizens, Threatened with Disfranchisement, to the People of Pennsylvania*, Robert Purvis' mourning was in opposition to the exclusion of "a distinct class of the community" who have experienced "sufficiently the objects of prejudice ... and are for ever, disfranchised and excluded." "When you have taken from an individual his right to vote," Purvis lamented, "you have made the government, in regard to him, a mere despotism; and you have taken a step towards making it a despotism to all" (135).

The Democratic Mission of James Forten, Sr., and the Anti-Constitution Jeremiad of Charles Lenox Remond

Born free in 1766 in Philadelphia, James Forten, Sr., influenced the growth and development of the African American jeremiad when he suggested that if documents like the Declaration of Independence and Constitution were realistic, there would neither be divisions based on race, nor the racial discriminations forced by the separate states' constitutions. Forten brought these ideologies to the forefront at the onset of his "Series of Letters by a Man of Colour" in which he urged free blacks to claim their rights to live as free citizens in America. "Series of Letters by a Man of Colour" condemned a bill that was put before the Pennsylvania legislature that would require all black emigrants to Pennsylvania to register in that state. In the Pennsylvania's 1838 constitution, African Americans who resided in the state lost the right to vote. With slave catchers from the South terrorizing free blacks, their rights were being additionally dishonored. According to Forten's assessment, the "bill of unalienable rights belonging to black men" ("Series of Letters by a Man of Colour" 70) would have further violated the rights of any free African American who chose to enter the state. It would also strengthen the wide-ranging opinions that blacks were inferior. Forten viewed the bill as a step toward regression for black Pennsylvanians. In retaliation, he lamented that the ideas of liberty should mean that all men receive the benefits of the founders' doctrines:

> This idea embraces the Indian and the European, the Savage and the Saint, the Peruvian and the Laplander, the white Man and the African, and whatever measures are adopted subversive of this inestimable privilege, are in direct violation of the letter and spirit of our Constitution, and become subject to the animadversion of all, particularly those who are deeply interested in the measure ["Series of Letters by a Man of Colour" 67].

Forten's understanding of the language utilized by the country's founding fathers actually opposed the language of the manuscript to show that the documents reinforced blacks' subjugation and further refused blacks the basic civil liberties enjoyed by white men of their time. If "language skills are said to be mastered and masterable," as Judith Butler (116) asserted, Forten's words, then, epitomized the intellectual anguish that blacks in the early republic experienced when they tried to find meaning amid the founding fathers' language: "We hold this truth to be self-evident, that GOD created all men equal." Although the bill did not pass (Newman, Rael and Lapsansky 66), it would, Forten suggested, "prevent the emigration to people of colour into" the state of Pennsylvania. Looking toward whites as "our protectors," Forten hoped that before the next Senate held session, white men would "have become convinced of the inhumanity and impolicy of such a measure, and forbear to deprive us of those inestimable treasures, Liberty and Independence." Forten's appeal to those who he saw as guardians, the "descendants of the immortal Penn," proposed that "the same power which protects the white man, should protect the black." As blacks sought to reside in "a State where Civil Liberty, and sacred Justice were administered alike to all" ("Series of Letters by a Man of Colour" 67, 69, 72), Forten argued for social respect, self-assurance, and well-being for blacks:

> Those patriotic citizens, who, after resting from the toils of an arduous war, which achieved our independence and laid the foundation of the only reasonable Republic upon earth, associate together, and for the protection of those inestimable rights for the establishment of which they had exhausted their blood and treasure, framed the constitution of Pennsylvania, have by the ninth article declared, that "all men are born equally free and independent, and have certain inherent and indefeasible rights among which are those of enjoying life and liberty." Under the restraint of wise and well administered laws, we cordially unite in the above glorious sentiment, but by the bill upon which we have been remarking, it appears as if the committee who drew it up mistook the sentiments expressed in this article, and do not consider us as men, or that those enlightened statesmen who formed the constitution upon the basis of experience, intended to exclude us from its blessings and protections. If the former, why are we not to be considered as men? Has God who made the white man and the black left any record declaring us a different species? Are we not sustained by the same power, supported by the same wrongs, pleased with the same delights, and propagated by the same means? And should we not then enjoy the same liberty, and be protected by the same laws? ["Series of Letters by a Man of Colour" 68].

Forten's ideologies concerning God transcended religious meaning to sociopolitical when he became critical of the undeniable limitations of African Americans created by this bill.

As he personified the American Revolution's ethics of equality and opportunity, Forten's convictions suggested that the objective of the African American jeremiad echoed social change rather than accommodation to the mainstream republic. Were white Americans seeking social change? Were they seeking to assimilate into the established social stratosphere of the oppressor? Or, moreover, were they seeking to establish a community void of an oppressive reality of slavery? In his appeal to his "protectors," Forten's purpose was "an appeal to the heart" ("Series of Letters by a Man of Colour" 72). Forten began, however, to seemingly argue for inclusion into the political, economic and social life of the mainstream republic. Since he felt that the founding fathers did not consider African Americans as men, he lamented that they formed the country "upon the basis of experience intended to exclude us from its blessings and protection." He further expressed his grief:

> It cannot be that the authors of our Constitution intended to exclude us from its benefits, for just emerging from unjust and cruel emancipation, their souls were too much affected with their own deprivations to commence the reign of terrour over others ["Series of Letters by a Man of Colour" 68–69].

Forten concluded "Series of Letters by a Man of Colour" with his prophecy, while pursuing his final fulfillment in America's democratic mission. He trusted that "the eloquence of nature will succeed, and the law-givers of this happy Commonwealth will yet remain the Black's friend, and the advocates of Freemen, is the sincere wish of every freeman" ("Series of Letters by a Man of Colour" 72).

African Americans soon discovered that their place in the white man's world was not within the realm of his politics, or social inclusion. David Walker was well aware of the common belief that blacks' perceived racial inferiority was the cause of enslavement: he informed his brethren, whites want blacks "for their slaves, and think nothing of murdering us in order to subject us to that wretched condition" (*Appeal* 37). Since African American Jeremiahs criticized America's own credence that "all men are created equal," their disapproval of all ideas, religious and profane, that America was founded on the principles of liberty, justice, and freedom surfaced. Sacvan Bercovitch interpreted this phenomenon as the "anti-jeremiad," which evoked the "ubiquity of the national symbol" by "reading into America the futility and the fraud of hope itself" (191). The "anti-jeremiad," was not "so much a rejection of the culture as it is a variation on the central cultural theme" (194). The differences between the jeremiad and the "anti-jeremiad" was that the jeremiad absorbed the optimism of Americans into the meaning of the idea of democracy that evoked the country's spirit, while the latter called America to be accountable for its senseless treatment of its countrymen. African American Jeremiahs were interested with making use of power, particularly language, to affect their own objectives and their own communities. Some African American Jeremiahs, such as Charles Lenox Remond, utilized Bercovitch's "anti-jeremiad" as they appropriated white America's rhetoric of identity to make their case that their degradation was not ordained by God.

By the early 1840s, moral suasionists had concluded that the founding fathers' documents were proslavery. They believed that by dissolving any political unification between the North and South would eventually result in the eradication of slavery (*BAP III* 442). Remond, born in Salem, Massachusetts in 1810 to free parents, originally believed in the moral suasionists philosophy. The "Union," according to Remond, was "one that ought to be dissolved" ("Speech by Charles Lenox Remond, Delivered at Marlboro Chapel" 443). In his emotional lament delivered at Marlboro Chapel 29 May 1844, Remond revealed his convictions concerning the enslavement of his brethren under the Union flag:

> Look as they are falling, generation after generation beneath the sway of the Union, sinking into their ignominious graves unwept, uncared for, unprayed for, enslaved, and say what has the Union been to them that they should look upon it with filial reverence! ["Speech by Charles Lenox Remond" 443].

Remond called for the "dissolution of the union between Freedom and Slavery" because he believed that if the Union had been "formed upon the supposition that a colored man was a *man*, a man he would be considered, whether in New Hampshire or Kentucky." Instead, however, Remond lamented the black man was "kicked, stoned, insulted, enslaved, and the public sentiment that does it, falls back upon the Constitution for support" ("Speech by Charles Lenox Remond," 444; emphasis in original). Believing that the wording of the Constitution included provisions for slavery, Remond, in his anti–Constitution jeremiad, questioned its doctrines in resilient language calculated for effect:

> What if the word "slave" is not in [the *Constitution*]? It does not matter to me nor mine. Slavery was in the understanding that framed it — Slavery is in the will that administers it. If there were nothing but Liberty in it, would there be two and a half millions ground to the dust beneath it this day? ["Speech by Charles Lenox Remond," 443].

Remond believed that the Constitution was not the "glorious means to a glorious end," ("Speech by Charles Lenox Remond," 443) and he unwaveringly denounced it. His message was simple: he argued for his brethren's citizenship.

Defending the right to protest against the injustices imposed on his brethren, Remond compared their struggle with that of the founding fathers who fought for their freedom from Great Britain. Remond argued that when African Americans fought for civil rights and proposed "'IMMEDIATE EMANCIPATION' — to the Government and to the South," it appeared to whites that "'niggers' are of no consequence" ("Wednesday Afternoon — Fifth Session";

3. The Constitution and the Declaration of Independence 71

emphasis is original). Utilizing the language of America's freedom movement, he pleaded:

> If it was well for our fathers to lay down the principles of Liberty — if it was well for them to sunder their connection with oppression, for the principles, I humbly opine that we are not to be censured for walking in the path they struck out. I humbly conceive that the principles of Freedom know nothing of color ["Wednesday Afternoon — Fifth Session"].

However, the Constitution itself, Remond argued, not those who protected it, upheld slavery. He believed the Constitution protected the rights of slaveholders by securing their right to own slaves: "What ground would [those who support the document] have us take with regard to the Constitution? Does it not secure the slaveholder a slave?" Because he felt it did, Remond argued that government needed to be freed from its own "debasing alloy" ("Wednesday Afternoon — Fifth Session"). By 1847, however, Remond became increasingly radical in his anti–Constitution jeremiads: "Let any man lay hands upon me, and attempt to enslave me," he heatedly protested, "and that fact would soon become public." Since government did not protect his rights, Remond proclaimed that he would "not support such a Government. Show me a Constitution which protects the rights of all men," he announced, "and I'll sustain it." According to Remond, those who supported the document "made no distinction between our natural relations and responsibili[ties] and voluntary associations in wrong doing, and the [guilt] which attached itself to every individual that associates himself with evil-doers." Remond refused to "yield to no man in loyalty to the Constitution.... What must be its necessary character," he bemoaned, "to afford no protection to the coloured man" ("Cazenovia Anti-Slavery Convention").

Remond would increasingly grow aggravated over the injustice of color discrimination that he felt the Constitution sustained. Examining 50 years of antislavery activity to an audience at Mozart Hall 13 May 1858, he used his anti–Constitution jeremiad to critique the failure of the American government, not its progress (*BAP IV* 382):

> The question of anti-slavery and pro-slavery in the United States is not the black man's question; ... the question of slavery and anti-slavery is patricianly an American question — all the way American, from beginning to end — and especially with every *decent* American ["Speech by Charles Lenox Remond Delivered at Mozart Hall" 385; emphasis in original].

Remond believed that the friends of the slave did not expect that emancipation would ever occur. "The pressure of this failure," he lamented, "that all attempts form the old gradual Abolition Society ... down to the last phase of anti-slavery have proven vain." Because of this, Remond ended his dirge with his prophetic vision. "If justice was done in this country" concerning the antislavery question, he prophesized, "we should have a class of criminals arraigned before the gaze of the world such as a few of us have presumed to anticipate" ("Speech By Charles Lenox Remond Delivered at Mozart Hall" 384, 385).

Conclusion

Throughout antebellum America, African American Jeremiahs drew heavily upon the cherished and honored ideals of the Constitution and Declaration of Independence in their struggle against the injustices of slavery and their demand for civil liberties. They appropriated the language of the founding fathers' documents as means of devaluating those American ideologies that were the cause of their disenfranchisement and breaking down whites' barriers of hegemonic rule, while at the same time, forging a new consciousness among the black community to insist that their representation was felt and their voice heard. They understood the basic ideologies inherent in inclusion in the discourse of American democracy: acknowledgment, acceptance, and representation. They understood that their culturally sanctioned exclusion, as it were, was built on their similarities with whites, *not* their differences. Forten believed that whites "felt that they had no more authority to enslave us, than England had to tyrannize over them" ("Series of Letters by a Man of Colour" 69). Was this cultural exclusion fabricated on race? The effects of their differences resulted in blacks' devaluation, and banning and banishment in the public sphere, which would give them a sense of cultural alienation or detachment from the world of politics and economics. Therefore, blacks in antebellum America were not able to amass a sense of social capital — the collective value of communal networks and the proclivity that would arise from these networks to do things for the good of others — with their white counterparts. They employed the language of revolution and the structure of democracy in their social protest against democratic principles they felt mired their citizenship.

4

Black Nationalism in the Early Republic

> Let us not be cast down under these and many other abuses we at present labour under: for the darkest is before the break of day.... Nothing but the snap of the whip was heard from morning to evening; hanging, broken on the wheel, burning, and all manner of tortures inflicted on those unhappy people for nothing else but to gratify their masters pride, wantonness, and cruelty: but blessed be God, the scene is changed; they now confess that God hath no respect of persons, and therefore receive them as their friends, and treat them as brothers.
> — Prince Hall, "A Charge," 1797

In 1797, Prince Hall, one of America's most prominent African American activists and founder of the African Lodge of the Honorable Society of Free and Accepted Masons of Boston,[1] charged his "brethren" to reject the present atrocities of their degradation. Using his position as "Worshipful Master" of his lodge to speak out against slavery and the denial of black basic civil liberties, Hall sought to convey that they had recognized that their oppression and dehumanization was the cause of their inferior status in society. Blacks, he urged, had to oppose — both independently and collectively — white oppression in order to reestablish their communities and self-respect in a foreign land. In his rhetoric, Hall made an effort to grapple with black identity by maintaining that his "brethren" would rise "from a sink of slavery to freedom and equality" ("A Charge," 47). His intricate structure in his "charge" propelled and guided two modes of rhetorical strategies operating simultaneously: the African American jeremiad and Black Nationalism. Which mode of rhetoric would have the lasting effect would largely depend upon the architect's intended audience. However, black nationalists, such as Hall, used the African American jeremiad to lament African Americans' lack of identity as a collective group of oppressed people in the New World as they found ways to align their rhetoric with similar philosophies of jeremiadic discourse. African American Jeremiahs, such as Hall, coupled the African American jeremiad with nationalistic rhetoric to aide in the restoration of black communities and to forge social change and new political, religious, and economic ideologies in lieu of prophecy concerning equality for blacks during the early republic. With this in mind, when both modes of rhetoric were coupled together, each sought to promote racial uplift and establish group recognition among its constituents.

When the African American jeremiad sought to establish group recognition, however, it became a successful tool only when blacks came to the realization that they were communally oppressed by white hegemony. To this end, both Black Nationalism and the African American jeremiad sought to unify an entire race of people who were victims of European colonialism, expansionism, and imperialism, either in America or abroad. As Wilson Jeremiah Moses noted, "slavery was ... the cause of black nationalism. It destroyed the ethnic loyalties of those whom it enslaved; it disastrously eroded traditional culture within a generation or two" (*The Golden Age of Black Nationalism* 16). Politically speaking, then, how does one separate jeremiadic discourse from nationalist rhetoric? Whether one forges the other is a complex issue. To conceptualize the African American jeremiadic tradition grounded in black nationalistic discourse is to suggest that both forms of rhetoric had related backgrounds and were persistently attempting to create viable solutions for oppression. A similar approach of Black Nationalism goads the African American jeremiad: the principles that highlight what Dexter B. Gordon noted as "black self-definition and self-determination in contrast to the continuing efforts of white Anglo-America to define blacks and determine their role in the debate about race" (1). The arena of social protest during the early republic was the crucial battlefront for both forms of expression to exist and fight for a common cause.

Suggesting that the jeremiad "threatened lapsed believers with the consequences of apostasy," Patrick Rael identified the jeremiad's most important aspect as building a "community by offering believers a shared history endowed with divine meaning" (*Black Identity* 241). This nationalistic approach to discussing African American jeremiadic rhetoric, then, suggested that the jeremiad increasingly influenced black nationalistic discourse and vice versa. Rael continued:

> In the early nineteenth century, they [African-American Jeremiahs] fused with the discourse of nationalism, which posited nationality as the sole legitimate means of representing the interest of the individual in the court of national and international politics, to serve as the conceptual framework through which a great many Americans understood their world and the events unfolding in it [*Black Identity* 241].

The connections of Black Nationalism to the purposes and aims of the African American jeremiad, however, revealed that the most important goal of each discourse of the early republic was to employ continuous improvement ideologies in order to amass social change or to substantiate the existing oppressive philosophies. Whereas the methods and techniques of both discourses were similar, the strategy necessary for both discourses to be consistently successful equaled to the differences. Scholars, such as Moses,[2] have suggested that Black Nationalism was the oldest form of social protest rhetoric utilized by African

Americans. If looked at under the socio-political, religious, and economic conditions that created it, it was very possible that the rhetoric of the jeremiad forged a nationalistic consciousness among blacks; thus making the jeremiad the oldest form of social protest employed by African Americans. Therefore, to further solidify the connection between the two for purposes of this chapter, Black Nationalism became a module of the African American jeremiad's fight against white oppression. To understand how and when this fusion took place, we need to juxtapose the historical growth and development of the Black Nationalism.

The Search for a Shared Communal Identity: Diverse Characteristics of Nationalism

Black Nationalism has been a subject of scholarly research for some time. Like the African American jeremiad, Black Nationalism was adapted from white ideologies and aided in forging a black consciousness into public sphere. Recently, however, Black Nationalism has superseded its white predecessor with a corpus of research and characterizations. The varied definitions of Black Nationalism have conceptualized the term beyond its categorical significance. Therefore, before delving into a discussion on Black Nationalism and its relationship to African American jeremiadic discourse, it is necessary to explore some of the major characteristics of nationalism in general in order or contextualize an acceptable rationalization. One common element inherent in scholars' dialogues concerning nationalism, whether black or white, is the search for a shared communal identity.

Wilson Jeremiah Moses suggested that the ways in which Black Nationalism was defined depended on how scholars defined "the concept of Nationalism in general, and there is no universally accepted definition of Nationalism" (*Black Messiahs and Uncle Toms* 3). Martha L. Cottman and Richard W. Cottman defined the categorical term "nationalism" as a "behavioral manifestation of identity [to] community attachments," such as "religious, racial, and ethnic communities" that, in large part, are responsible for creating said communities (2). David Brown's discussion on nationalism suggested that the concept involved thoroughly sorting out "the uncertainties of national identity and the restructuring of multicultural nations." Brown believed that by separating and investigating the components of nationalism, "we can more clearly understand the resultant changes — the ethnic conflicts, the emergence of new nation-states" (1). The "emergence" of these "new nation-states," William L. Van Deburg implied, was articulated through "demands for territorial cession, political empowerment, or increased cultural autonomy." Black nationalists believed that "the ethnic, religious, or linguistic group to which they are most intimately attached is undervalued and oppressed by 'outsiders'" (2). Because the "outsiders" had previously controlled the ethnic communities' destiny, Mattias

Gardell saw nationalism as involved in the construction of a "national awareness and national identity by references to a perceived origin" conceptualized due to "a nostalgic projection of the nation back into a legendary time, a shared history, and an envisioned destiny" (8). James G. Kellas defined nationalism an ideology that "builds on people's awareness of a nation to give a set of attitudes and a programme [sic] of action" while seeking to "defend and promote the interests" of its architects. As a form of political behavior, nationalism "is closely linked to ethnocentrism and patriotism" (3, 5). One can see Kellas' "ethnocentrism"—which he defined as a "psychological term" that focused "strictly on the individual's relationship with an ethnic group rather than with a 'nation' or a 'race'" (5)—surfacing in Maulana Karenga's discussion of Black Nationalism as "a social theory and practice organized around the concept and conviction that blacks are a distinct historical personality and they should therefore 'unite in order to gain the structural capacity to define, defend and develop their interests'" (334). According to Fred Lee Hord, black nationalistic rhetoric encompassed "a feeling of racial solidarity, whether from positive or negative experiences, and a desire to organize around that solidarity" (65). Since racial solidarity has no other position than to call blacks to seek the foundation of their universal oppressive condition and move in some way to eliminate their situation (Bracey xxvi), organization was the key component for Black Nationalism to exist. During the early republic, Black Nationalism not only sought to connect its architects to racial solidarity, but also to engaged blacks in the processes of creating sites for contextualizing common grounds about oppression. This could occur either in America or aboard, even Canada; it could be the building of separate institutions (such as schools, churches); it could be the development of communities (such as the establishment of black newspapers and social organizations).

Meanwhile, the jeremiad lamented the need to establish such communities. Blacks' employment of the jeremiad, thus, became intricately linked with nationalism as both became viable solutions to fight racial oppression and a voice to lead blacks from perpetual servitude to united communities. Consider, for example, an 1831 anonymous editorial published in the *Liberator*, in which the author suggested:

> The men who have been foremost, in withholding from us our dearest and most sacred rights, have always held out false colors to the community at large, (such as, inferiority, degradation, nuisance, pest, slaves, species of monkey, apes, &c.) to justify their inhuman and unchristian acts towards us, and to deaden the severe pangs of conscience that harass them. They would wish to appear innocent before the world; as doing unto all men as they would do unto them. Do they base their objects, in full, upon such frivolous excuses as these? No. The truth is, actions speak louder than words ["Editorial"].

The jeremiad as nationalistic rhetoric, then, encompassed African Americans' fight for equality and their pursuit to distinguish their differences from mainstream white America. Black Nationalism was rooted in the long-lasting debate over rights for African Americans and their struggle for equality. Early in its developmental stages, Black Nationalism "claimed its place as a legitimate Nationalism at a time when only national status conferred the right of political self-determination" (Rael, *Black Identity and Black Protest* 221). Advocating black empowerment and race consciousness, while aligning its forces with jeremiadic rhetoric, a black Jeremiah Nationalist discourse materialized into a feasible channel for group representation. black Jeremiah Nationalists stressed a shared commitment to unity and dolefully pleaded with white America to acknowledge their need for selfhood, citizenship, and recognition.

The Oppressor Representing the Oppressed

This chapter seeks to explore the relationship between African American jeremiadic rhetoric and Black Nationalism — two discourses that were forged from the same dehumanization and degradation of blacks in the New World. As previously stated, Black Nationalism and the African American jeremiad have a shared birth: they both grew from their American predecessors' ideologies. White American Nationalism created attitudes that the New World belonged to the white man (Robinson 9). This ideology was derived from white America's attitudes concerning their "manifest destiny," "national identity," and their supposed superiority. As Hans Kohn noted, White Nationalism, was "not a movement of romantic protest against the Western equalitarian and rational attitude ... but the consummation of this western attitude." White Nationalism was not a "voice crying out of the depth of the dark past," but was "proudly a product of the enlightened present, setting its face resolutely towards the future" (291). Black Nationalism differed from White Nationalism in America in that the former required that its architects possess a common language and a geographical confinement to a certain area. Kohn indicated that "loyalty to America meant therefore loyalty to that idea, and as the idea was universal, everyone could be included and, if he were of good will, assimilated" (324). Kohn's argument suggested that Americans of African extraction could partake in nationhood. In reality, however, that was hardly the case. Like the American jeremiad, White Nationalism's origin in America reached across the Atlantic to a time of European expansionism. The predecessor to White Nationalism in America arose in Europe in the middle eighteenth century amidst ideologies that Europeans needed to create a separate nation as a means of defending themselves from their oppression. When blacks began to appropriate these ideologies in the early republic, Black Nationalism, however, sought "to override the numerous differences among" people of African extraction before "the age of European expansionism." As it attempted to unify all black people, regardless of locale, Black Nationalism sought to create an autonomous "black nation in the Americas" (Moses, *The Golden Age of Black Nationalism* 17, 19), and was in opposition to whites' categorization of blacks into groups. African Americans realized that their culture, religion, politics, and economics were not being represented, or as Joseph C. Holly lamented in 1848, blacks came to the realization that "the oppressor [was] representing the oppressed" ("American Slavery" 19). Holly sought, as did other black Jeremiah Nationalists, to represent African Americans positively in contrast to the whites' stereotypical images.

The argument here, however, does not suggest that Black Nationalism and the African American jeremiad are the same, but that there are similarities between the two that can not be overlooked. Both responded to each other. Relying on the ideologies of the American Revolution and the reasoning of uplift and elevation, black Jeremiah Nationalists responded to declarations of their inherent inferiority, maintaining instead an essential national identity. At times when the African American jeremiad coupled its strategies with the principles of Black Nationalism, it fostered resistance to accepting the customs of mainstream America. When he delivered his 1843 speech at the National Convention in Buffalo, New York, Henry Highland Garnet told his "brethren":

> Many of you are bound to us, not only by the ties of a common humanity, but we are connected by the more tender relations of parents, wives, husbands, children, brothers, and sisters, and friends. As such we most affectionately address you. Slavery has fixed a deep gulf between you and us, and while it shuts out from you the relief and consolation which your friends would willingly render, it affects and persecutes you with a fierceness which we might not expect to see in the fiends of hell.... Brethren, it is as wrong for your lordly oppressors to keep you in slavery as it was for the man thief to steal our ancestors from the coast of Africa. You should therefore now use the same manner of resistance, as would have been just in our ancestors when the bloody foot-prints of the first remorseless soul-thief was placed upon the shores of our fatherland ["Address" 90, 93].

Elements of both jeremiadic and nationalistic discourse were present in Garnet's address. In his antagonism to white American standards, Garnet first lamented and connected the plight of slaves to those of free blacks, and second, offered them alternative methods to their enslavement by suggesting that they resist as their forefathers in Africa had done. By resisting white supremacy, what else could blacks hope but to form a community void of white American interaction? Garnet's discourse was anything but assimilationist. The jeremiad surfaced in Garnet's rhetoric through his critique of white support of slavery: slavery "persecutes you with a fierceness which we might not expect to see in the fiends of hell." The extremist incentives of Garnet's nationalism, however, were spawned from advocates and institutions— such as Prince Hall's African Masonic Lodge and the African Methodist Church — which, as expected, lost assurance in attaining civil liberties for blacks under white supremacy.

Black Nationalism in its earliest stages sought to employ the entire black community (Rael, "Black Theodicy") in its radical call for social change; some of this initial rhetoric can be seen as early as 1789 when the Free African Society of Newport, Rhode Island, suggested to its sister group in Philadelphia a return-to-Africa movement. The Free African Society's plan was further implemented by 1815, when Paul Cuffee began transporting blacks to Sierra Leone by sponsoring 38 settlers on his ship, *Traveller*. "Back-to-Africa" movements, however, were not the only ways in which Black Nationalism was manifested. Community building and social cohesiveness were important aspects of the rhetoric; this consciousness had to be manifested in some ideological form. John N. Still, in an 1854 letter to *Frederick Douglass' Paper*, encouraged blacks to build communities and organize associations for the express "purpose of placing yourselves in a responsible relation to the National and State Council,[3] or their officers." Still believed that if such displays among blacks were not made, thousands "will know more about our movements five years hence, than they did five years ago" (214–215). When black Jeremiah Nationalists began to appropriate the language of American jeremiadic and white nationalist rhetoric,[4] however, they began to envision the potentiality of developing a nation in an ideological sense which would result in the building of black communities autonomous of the preexisting white sovereigns. An institution of worship, for instance, was a good place to start.

Richard Allen, cofounder of the Free African Society (FAS), later known as the African Church of Philadelphia, which laid the foundation for the establishment of African American churches (Wesley 61), lamented "the necessity of erecting a place of worship for the colored people." Although met with some trepidation from both the black and white communities, Allen and his cohorts "succeed[ed] in building the house of the Lord." Blacks "were considered as a nuisance," and according to Allen "were destitute of a place of worship" (Allen, *The Life, Experience,* and *Gospel Labours* 13). The very establishment of a separate place of worship had jeremiadic undertones because it called for black self-discipline and fortitude. Likewise, the act of erecting a place of worship was attuned to nationalism in that it illustrated that blacks were seeking to control their politics by implementing their self-determination. Allen, however, would continue to support the construction of black communities when he supported the predominantly white American Colonization Society (ACS), a society founded in 1817 that encouraged free black colonies in Africa. Allen would later show support for the Haitian Emigration Society, which was founded in 1824 to help African Americans colonize in Haiti. Allen's nationalistic actions were further developed when he established FAS, his "self-improvement society" (Wesley 60).[5] E. Curtis Alexander suggested that FAS, a "mutual aid" organization, represented the "first evidence" in American history where "an organization for social cooperation and economic development among Africans in the New World" (22) was constructed.

The End Result of the Communal Conscience of Blacks in the Early Republic

The division between the African American jeremiad and Black Nationalism cannot be sufficiently rationalized in terms of just differences between two types of communities they represent: the real community (American mainstream republic) and the imagined community (blacks' ideological construction of a community). Black Nationalism transpired within a generated process of the real community, and functioned to legitimate, rather than to change, as the jeremiad sought to do, the preexisting set of governing directives. The jeremiad perceived these changes when the oppressed unite in the path of their own liberation, when the oppressed refuse to remain a submissive participant to the oppressor's brutality.

To African Americans in the early republic, Americanism symbolized the very essence of black oppression. Joseph C. Holly concluded that the document that creates American democracy, the Constitution, was "another proof of the futility of any attempt at compromise between liberty and slavery, right and wrong; they are incompatible, incongruous, and wrong must ever strengthen at the expense of right" ("American Slavery" 22). As Holly personified, American political philosophies and religious doctrines were rejected by those who were able to envision socio-political, socio-religious, and socio-economic independence. Black Nationalism was a way in which its constituents represent a "militant rejection of things American and European" (Robinson 1). The principal characteristic of Black Nationalism was

> its apparent inability to diverge from what could be considered the "normal" politics of its day. By accepting the notion that black people constitute an organic unit, and by focusing on the goal of national building or separate political and economic development, Black Nationalism *inadvertently* helps to reproduce some of the thinking and practices that created black disadvantage in the first place [*Black Nationalism* 1–2; emphasis in original].

The radical consciousness of nationalism within the African American community was engaged in the gradual elevation of blacks and forged within them a collective awareness of their destiny. How did this differ from jeremiadic discourse? It didn't. The foundations of self-consciousness were usually a product of some form of oppression. According to Paulo Freire:

> To surmount the situation of oppression, people much first critically recognize its causes, so that through transforming action they can create a new situation, one which makes possible the pursuit of a fuller humanity.... Although the situation of oppression is a dehumanized and dehumanizing totality affecting both the oppressors and those whom they oppress, it is the latter who must, for their stifled humanity, wage for both the struggle for a fuller humanity; the oppressor, who is himself dehumanized because he dehumanizes others, is unable to lead this struggle [29].

African American acknowledgement of what Freire called "the struggle for a fuller humanity" begat the materialization of the African American jeremiad and Black Nationalism in the early republic. Freire continued, "Only as [the oppressed] discover themselves to be 'hosts' of the oppressor can they contribute to the midwifery of their liberating pedagogy" (30). What African Americans also came to understand during antebellum America was that their consciousness afforded them more than just accepting their "liberating pedagogy"; it demanded them to take action. When he delivered his didactic speech, "An Address to the Slaves of the United States," at the 1843 National Negro Convention in Buffalo, New York," Henry Highland Garnet urged his "brethren" to take their liberation into their own hands: "Brethren, arise, arise. Strike for your lives and liberties. Now is the day and hour." Garnet's aim was not just to mobilize blacks to a collective body, but to organize their individual oppressions so as to promote the attainment of such mobilization. By undercutting those conventional representations of blacks, Garnet insisted that the oppressed would have to liberate themselves or they would never be truly free: "Let every slave throughout the land" take matters into his own hands, Garnet assured them, "and the days of slavery are numbered" (96). Garnet's rhetoric may have alarmed some of the more liberal black activists, but Garnet guaranteed blacks that their freedom would not come without bloodshed. Writing under the pseudonym "Sidney," Garnet's convictions were furthered in his letters, which provided a forum of exchange between Garnet and William Whipper (Ripley et al. 356) and began appearing in the late 1830s. Taking on his perceived voice of young activists, Garnet fiercely defended racial consciousness and called attention to the need for black agency and direction in the antislavery movement (*BAP III* 356):

> The oppressed are ever their best representatives ... it is one of the most malignant features of slavery, that it leads the oppressor to stigmatize his victim with inferiority of nature, after he himself has almost brutalized him. This is a universal fact. Hence the oppressed must vindicate their character. No abstract disquisitions from sympathizing friends, can effectually do this. The oppressed themselves must manifest energy of character and elevation of soul. Oppression never quails until it sees that the downtrodden and outraged "know their rights, and knowing, dare maintain." *This* is a radical assurance, a resistless evidence both of worth and manliness, and of earnest intention and deep determination...
>
> Yet our condition will remain the same, our sufferings will be unmitigated, until we awaken to a consciousness of a momentous responsibility, with we shall manifest by giving it actuality. We occupy a position, and sustain relations which they cannot possibly assume...
>
> In coming forth as colored Americans, and pleading for our rights, we neither preclude the necessity, nor forbid the action of our friends, no more than the Americans forbade the help of their French allies.... The Americans received the aid and co-operation of their French allies; but they kept the idea of *American* resistance to oppression distinct and prominent ["Essay by 'Sidney'" 357–58; emphasis in original].

Stokley Carmichael and Charles V. Hamilton suggested that the emergence of such a consciousness that Garnet exemplified against oppression would occur "only when black people fully develop [this] sense of community, of themselves,

[can] they begin to deal effectively with the problems of racism in *this* country ... this is the vital first step" (39; emphasis in original). Taking the "vital first step," black Jeremiah Nationalists became aware of the immeasurable oppressive consciousnesses that existed around them. And their racial realization was in response to their being surrounded by these predominate consciousnesses in a foreign society. Second, they realized that there was no escaping their duty: they must respond to these outside forces. The Fugitive Slave Act of 1850 helped to solidify their responses and furthered some black Jeremiah Nationalists' argument that refuge void of white hegemonic rule was necessary. Granville B. Blanks lamented that because of the FSA, blacks "must have a country and laws and privileges of their own, in order to take that rank among the people of the earth to which they are entitled to aspire" (134). Thus the African American jeremiad and Black Nationalism became an end result of the communal conscience of blacks in the early republic as its appeal called to black people to persuade them to take charge of the struggle for racial uplift, self-determination, self-reliance, and independence on a nationalized level.

Sacvan Bercovitch suggested that the American jeremiad "posits a movement from promise to experience — from the ideal of community to the shortcomings of community life — and thence forward, with prophetic assurance, toward the resolution that incorporates (as it transforms) both the promise and the condemnation." In a sense, Bercovitch's analysis also seemed to be a critique of Puritan Nationalism rather than jeremiadic discourse. The American jeremiad, according to his interpretation, sought to establish community by visualizing the "dynamic of the errand" as progress towards an end (16, 17). Conversely, in their emerging voice against oppression, early black Jeremiah Nationalists built a concept of a community through their employment of nationalistic discourse and helped to rally equal rights and thus forged African American jeremiadic rhetoric into the sphere of public interest. Hosea Easton believed that blacks' liberation belonged in their own hands. Respecting their "oppresst [sic] community," it was evident to Easton that blacks had to turn their "attention to moral improvement" ("An Address" 54). He maintained, "The first thing necessary, is, to cultivate the principles of concord and unanimity among ourselves, that we may become aids to each other; for the prosecution of which, we ought to introduce operations that is accordant with the object in pursuit." Easton imminently pointed out that if this occured, uplift was inevitable:

> It will open a field of labour for the reception of our youth, who are coming upon the state of action, and give them an opportunity of displaying their intellectual talents; which will give a character to our community, and take away our reproach. When our operations become united, that the voice of our community, may be heard as the voice of one man; then shall we be able to control the principles of indolence and immorality of every species, and inculcate those of industry and virtue, with all qualifications necessary to enable us to control the effects of our own labour, and make it subservient to the benefit of our own community. We may look abroad and see sufficient to induce us to become active in our own interest ["An Address" 54].

As African American jeremiadic rhetoric manifested in the latter part of the eighteenth century from the socio-political and religious concerns that surrounded their enslavement, African Americans realized that eradicating slavery's particular evils was justifiable, and as such, the jeremiad and nationalism offered a useful counter attack. The intricate relationship between the African American jeremiad and Black Nationalism became ever more apparent when David Walker's *Appeal* appeared on the antislavery lineup. Walker lamented that blacks should be involved in establishing the black community:

> Men of colour, who are also of sense, for you particularly is my APPEAL designed. Our more ignorant brethren are not able to penetrate its value. I call upon you therefore to cast your eyes upon the wretchedness of your brethren, and to do your utmost to enlighten them —*go to work and enlighten your brethren!*—Let the Lord see you doing what you can to rescue them and yourselves from degradation.... They are of the very lowest kind — they are the very *dregs!*— they are the most servile and abject kind, that ever a people was in possession of! ... I advance it therefore to you, not as a *problematical,* but as an unshaken and for ever immoveable *fact,* that your full glory and happiness, as well as all other coloured people under Heaven, shall never be fully consummated, but with the *entire emancipation of your enslaved brethren all over the world.* You may therefore, go to work and do what you can to rescue, or join in with tyrants to oppress them and yourselves [40; emphasis in original].

Walker's jeremiadic nationalism suggested that the "great work" to be done is "as trifling as some of you may think of it. You have to prove to the Americans and the world, that we are MEN, and not *brutes,* as we have been represented, and by millions treated. Remember," he called to them, "let the aim of your labours among your brethren, and particularly the youths, be the dissemination of education and religion" (42; emphasis in original). Walker felt responsible for initiating this call to consciousness and action because, as he suggested, the "more ignorant brethren" will not mentally understand the insults placed on them daily.

The Jeremiadic Nationalism of Prince Hall and James Forten, Sr.

Black Jeremiah Nationalists persevered in combating every indication of racism. Prince Hall was one of the earliest blacks who noticeably personified both the African American jeremiad and black nationalistic discourses. Throughout his career, Hall became well-known in the circles of black protest (Newman, Rael and Lapsansky 44). A former slave himself, Hall challenged the white supremacy laws in Boston. With the founding of one the first and most recognized African American social organizations, the African Masonic Lodge, Hall was considered America's "first organizer ... of a black society for social, political, and economic improvement" (Kaplan 202). Dedicating itself to "community-building efforts, education, racial uplift — and protest," Hall's African Masonic Lodge became a driving force in Boston's black community as it became a vehicle for counterattacking "racism because it encourages mutual protection and community action" (Newman, Rael and Lapsansky 44). In Hall's invectives both elements of the jeremiad and nationalism existed.

With the success of his lodge, Hall, the preeminent black Jeremiah Nationalist, made several petitions to the Massachusetts government in favor of African American nationalistic ideologies (Newman, Rael and Lapsansky 44). First, through his jeremiad, Hall called for the abolishment of slavery in the state of Massachusetts; second, while employing nationalistic discourse, he petitioned the legislature to willingly endorse black emigration to Africa; finally, he petitioned the government to open a school for blacks in the Boston area, which was both jeremiadic and nationalistic. Hall's nationalism offered his "brethren" hope in "A Charge" by celebrating the victory of Toussaint l'Ouverture's fight in the Haitian Revolution which began on 22 August 1791, and ended on 1 January 1804. "My brethren, let us remember what a dark day it was with our African brethren six years ago, in the French West-Indies" (47). Hall continued to emphasize racial uplift through his nationalistic rhetoric encouraging his "brethren" to remember the plight of the Haitians. In his persuasive pamphlet, "A Charge," Hall ensured his "brethren" that God would deliver them from the "unhappy condition" (45) that plagued them.

> I shall just mention the good deeds of the Samaritan, though at that time they were looked upon as unworthy to eat, drink or trade with their fellowmen, at least by the Jews; see the pity and compassion he had on a poor distrest and half dead stranger, see Luke x. from 30 to 37. See that you endeavour to do so likewise. — But when we consider the amazing condescending love and pity our blessed Lord had on such poor worms as we are, as not only to call us his friends, but his brothers, we are lost and can go no further in holy writ for examples to excite us to the love of our fellowmen. — But I am aware of an objection that may arise (for some men will catch at any thing) that is that they were not all Masons; we allow it, and I say that they were not all Christians, and their benevolence to strangers ought to shame us both, that there is so little, so very little of it to be seen in these enlightened days ["A Charge" 45].

Hall continued, "Thus doth Ethiopia begin to stretch forth her hand, from a sink of slavery to freedom and equality" ("A Charge" 45). Hall's nationalistic discourse suggested that the black community should reach across the Atlantic Ocean to the continent of Africa to draw strength via generations who have toiled and spilled their blood. Furthermore, his jeremiadic discourse lamented that blacks have an obligation to receive the same rights as their white counterparts.

Another black Jeremiah Nationalist who was passionately involved in the realm of black politics while promoting basic civil liberties for African Americans was James Forten, Sr. Through his jeremiadic discourse, he beseeched the Pennsylvania legislature to emancipate the African captives. As previously discussed in Chapter 3, Forten reprimanded Congress for its proposed law to prevent emigration into the state of Pennsylvania by mandatory registration. He lamented:

> Shall colonial inhumanity that has marked many of us with shameful stripes become the practice of the people of Pennsylvania, while Mercy stands weeping at the miserable spectacle? People of Pennsylvania, descendants of the immortal Penn, doom us not to the unhappy fate of thousands of our countrymen in the Southern States and the West Indies; despise the traffic in blood, and the blessing of the African will forever be around you ["Series of Letters by a Man of Colour" 67].[6]

In his nationalistic discourse, Forten sought safe havens for blacks to build communities void of white oppression. An avid reader of the recent Haitian Revolution, Forten, like Hall, was intrigued by the Saint Dominguians willingness to overcome French imperialism, and he advocated emigration to the newly independent country (Winch 209–210). Africa was also a viable solution for emigration. Some years later, however, Forten would conclude that blacks felt that emigration was risky business. In his 1817 letter to Paul Cuffee, Forten wrote that black Philadelphians were "very much frightened" about the ideology of emigration. According to Forten, blacks "were afraid that all the free people would be compelled" to leave the country, "particularly in the southern states." Nearly 3,000 attended the recent meeting at Richard Allen's church, Forten wrote to Cuffee, and "not one soul was in favor of going to Africa." Although Forten informed Cuffee that the resolution was agreed upon "to remain silent" as a people — both black and white — he concluded that blacks "will never become a people until they come out from amongst the white people" ("Letter to Paul Cuffee" 51). Forten's voice indicated that he spoke for the consciousness of the entire African American community. His radical call to consciousness within the African American community was engaged in the gradual elevation of blacks and in the forging within them a collective awareness of their destiny. The intricate makeup of Forten's call to socio-political and socio-economic consciousness voiced a communal commitment to forging African Americans' humanity.

"I would not be taken to Africa": The Pros and Cons of Black Emigration

By the early 1800s, emigration was a major topic of debate for Black Nationalist Jeremiahs. Advocating emigration to Canada, Haiti, Guiana, Demerara, Trinidad, Texas, or other nations abroad (Porter 249), they substantiated their arguments through the economic and social conditions blacks suffered in both the North and South. George Lawrence, Jr., advocated emigration from the "demonized States." He wrote, "If we are not prepared to act upon the ideas that 'man must be free, if not within the law, then above the law,' in these demonized States, then let us prepare to go where we can be free, and untrammeled live out our lives" ("A Carbonari Wanted" 111). The American Colonization Society (ACS) fostered gradual liberation of slaves and aided in the formulations of laws that would facilitate this endeavor. Afraid that the emancipation of blacks would not set well with many northern and southern white slaveholders, ACS advocated emigration to Liberia for those freed or born free blacks in America. Some Black Nationalist Jeremiahs supported ACS; some did not.

In an 1817 speech delivered in Philadelphia, James Forten, Sr., and Russell Parrott rejected the colonization plan of ACS:

> If the plan of colonizing [by ACS] is intended for our benefit, and those who now promote it will never seek our injury, we humbly and respectfully urge that it is not asked for by us: nor will it be required by any circumstances, in our present or future condition, as long as we shall be permitted to share the protection of the excellent laws and just government which we now enjoy, in common with every individual of the community.
>
> We, therefore, a portion of those who are the objects of this plan, and among those whose happiness, with that of others of our color, it is intended to promote, which humble and grateful acknowledgement to those who have devised it, renounce and disclaim every connexion with it; and respectfully but firmly declare our determination not to participate in any part of it ["To the Human and Benevolent Inhabitants" 265].

Forten and Parrott did not trust that white colonizationists had blacks' best interest at heart: "We are not desirous of increasing their prosperity but by honest efforts." When colonizing for the brethren would occur, Forten and Parrott believed it would "be attended with transportation to a distant land, and shall be granted on no other condition." They did not believe that white colonizationists were capable of uplifting the colonized. "Nor do we view the colonization of those who may become emancipated by its operation among our southern brethren, as capable of producing their happiness." They argued that colonization was no good without education and proper religious instruction. "Unprepared by education and knowledge of the truths of our blessed religion for their new situations, those who will thus become colonists will themselves be surrounded by every suffering which can afflict the members of the human family." Forten and Parrott furthered believed that white colonizationists were not qualified to transport their brethren to their new home. If the colonization plan of ACS was to be implemented, "to emancipate and transport to Africa will be held forth by slaveholders as the worst and heaviest of punishments; and they will be threatened and successfully used to enforce increased submission of their wishes, and subjections to their commands." Therefore, Forten and Parrott "humbly, respectfully, and fervently" beseeched Philadelphia's denizens to reject "the plan of colonization now offered by 'the American Society for colonizing the free people of color of the United States'" ("To the Human and Benevolent Inhabitants" 266, 267). Others would add their voices to the anticolonization movement. To a crowd of "nearly five thousand abolitions at the Broadway Tabernacle in New York City" (*BAP III* 294), Andrew

Harris lamented the ills of colonization. "I ... would rather stand and endure it all [American prejudice], choosing rather to suffer affliction with my people, than to emigrate to a foreign shore" ("Speech by Andrew Harris" 296).

Haiti and Mexico were popular choices for emigration. Prince Saunders advocated emigration to Haiti because he believed that the "authorities of Hayti [sic] are themselves desirous of receiving emigrants" from the United States. According to Saunders, of the various colonization plans, "there are none which appear to many persons to wear so much the appearance of feasibility, and ultimate successful and practical operation, as the luxuriant, beautiful and extensive island of Hayti (or St. Domingo)." Saunders outlined the various reasons why Haiti was the most viable solution to the emigration problem, but the one of most importance was the fact that "at present, there are but very few, if any, European, or whites of any description, even in [that section] which is nominally, and in fact, in allegiance to old Spain" ("A Memoir" 272, 273, 275). Mexico was also a practical solution. "A Colored Female of Philadelphia" lamented that sending blacks to Africa, or establishing nationhood "as a distance people anywhere, but to attach ... to a nation already established" (like the United States) would be detrimental to the cause. The American government, she lamented, was "not the only one in this hemisphere that offers equal rights to men." Other governments offered safety "under whose protection we may safely reside." No doubt she struck discord with some Black Nationalist Jeremiahs when she chastised them for "sitting still and sighing for that liberty our white brethren tell us we never shall obtain, or in hoping that in some fifty or a hundred years hence, our children's children will be made free." She revealed that in Mexico, there existed "an independent nation, where indeed 'all men are born free and equal' possessing those inalienable rights which our constitution guarantees." In Mexico, she maintained, blacks "may become a people of worth and respectability; whereas in this country [they] are kept poor, and of course, cannot aspire to anything more than what [they] always have been" ("Emigration to Mexico" 292, 293). Although it appeared that she did not advocate nationalism, she nonetheless supported "cultivating the spirit of enterprise as well as the whites":

> I would not be taken to Africa, were the Society to make me queen of the country; and were I to move to Canada, I would not settle in the colony, but take up my abode in some of the cities where a distinction is not known; for I do not approve of our drawing off into a separate body anywhere ["Emigration to Mexico" 293].

Some Black Nationalist Jeremiahs, however, denounced colonization of any kind. Peter Williams was one such activist who felt that colonization would not have been an issue if American society was not "warped by prejudice." "If we are as vile and degraded as [white colonizationists] represent us," he lamented, "and they wish the Africans to be rendered a virtuous, enlightened and happy people, they should not think of sending us among them, lest we should make them worse instead of better." Williams argued that colonization would not improve the lives of blacks. Colonizationists' argument about sending blacks to Africa was "inconsistent." He posited, "We are to be improved by being sent far from civilized society." Williams prophesied that blacks' social status would improve if the colonizationists would "lay aside their own prejudices" ("A Discourse Delivered at St. Phillip's Church" 296, 297, 298):

> Much of the burden would be at once removed; and their example (especially if they were as anxious to have justice done us here, as to send us to Africa) would have such an influence upon the community at large, as would soon cause prejudice to hide its deformed head ["A Discourse Delivered at St. Phillip's Church" 298].

By the early 1830s, ACS had successfully transplanted over 1,000 blacks to Liberia. This small success rate, however, beckoned for more drastic measures. The black Abolitionist Jeremiahs of the 1830s answered the call. Because Black Nationalist Jeremiahs, who served as the "racial conscience of the antislavery movement" (*BAP IV* 189), believed the cause of their deprivation was racial motivated, they, more so than their white counterparts, pursued a more radical assessment of the society that they felt caused their degradation.

Martin Delany's Emigration, Self-Elevation, and Uplift

Martin Delany used his jeremiadic nationalistic rhetoric to persuade his audiences to look for retribution and conduct "great work" in a more wide-ranging way than his predecessors. Blacks' only hope, Delany perceived just prior to the Civil War, was the building of a prevailing black nation elsewhere — either in North America or Africa — that would succeed in gaining admiration for blacks who chose to continue building efforts in America. His nationalist discourse differed from Hall's and Forten's in that Delany advocated black emigration to the republic of Liberia; "Canada West, formerly called Upper Canada," which he believed was "equal to any portion of the Northern States"; or "Central and South America" which he saw as "evidently the ultimate destination and future home of the colored race on this continent" (*The Condition* 189, 193) as means of elevation and uplift among the African American community. In *The Condition, Elevation, Emigration and Destin of the Colored People of the United States*, Delany sought to support a consciousness among African Americans by informing them that certain conditions for which "emigration is absolutely necessary" to blacks' "political elevation, cannot be disputed" (175). Drawing analogies to several great migrations, Delany lamented that emigration helped to improve the lot of oppressed people globally:

> This we see in the Exodus of the Jews from Egypt to the land of Judea; in the expedition of Dido and her followers from Tyre to Mauritania; and not to dwell upon hundreds of modern European examples, also in the ever memorable emigration of the Puritans in 1620 from Great Britain, the land of their birth, to the wilderness of

4. Black Nationalism in the Early Republic 89

the New World, at which may be fixed the beginning of emigration to this continent as a permanent residence [*The Condition* 175].

When Delany's lamentation advocated emigration to Canada, he concluded that "disfranchisement" and "degradation" were the lot for blacks if they remained in America:

> This we forewarn the colored people, in time, is the inevitable and not far distant destiny of the Canadas. And let them come into the American Republic when they may, the fate of the colored man, however free before, is doomed, doomed, forever doomed. Disfranchisement, degradation, and a delivery up to slave catchers and kidnappers are their only fate [*The Condition* 190].

One of the foremost black Jeremiah Nationalists of nineteenth-century America, Delany questioned blacks' state of affairs in his rhetoric. Believing that emigration was a vital solution to place African Americans in their God-ordained places as leaders of their own destiny, Delany's jeremiadic nationalism was based on his liberation theodicy. He called it, however, "self elevation." Delany believed that blacks were leaders and that they should lead their own communities. In an 1846 edition of *The Mystery*,[7] Delany revealed his thoughts on establishing his Self-Elevation Tract Society, which was meant to establish "claim to civil and decent respect":

> Situated as we are, as mere nonentities in the midst of others—the most deserving, respectable, and praiseworthy among us, in the eye of the law and its consequent enactments, being placed far beneath the most vile vagabond while being denied privileges granted to the pauper and vagrant—those by the laws, declared to be nuisance—while privileges are being enjoyed by other men, privileges which from their nature necessarily elevate the female, the wife, mother, sister and daughter, and stimulate the tender youth; we colored male citizens are made the degraded vassals of the most insufferable servility, more intolerable than death itself ["Self-Elevation Tract Society" 36].

Delany's jeremiadic nationalist vision imagined a "more perfect union" for blacks. This would require, he believed, more than just education. It would involve a "collective commitment to strive for all that white America preached and failed to achieve" (Ullman 22). Delany fervently believed that the oppressed should free themselves from their oppressors as "the Irish and Dutch, the Hungarians, and others who forever turned their backs on their native land because it denied them that liberty which was the birthright of man" ("Martin R. Delany in Liberia" 334). Encouraging black self-determination and elevation, Delany posited "Have we no other destiny—no other social and political relations in prospect as an inheritance for our children?" ("Letter to James McCune Smith" 371). In an 1852 letter to Frederick Douglass, Delany declared that his desire was that blacks "have light and information upon the available means of bettering their condition; this," he wrote, "they must and shall have." Delany further lamented, "We never have, as heretofore, had any settled and established policy of our own—we have always adopted the policies that white men established for themselves without considering their applicability or adaptedness to us." Believing that no race of people can rise above racial oppression this way, Delany sought to encourage black independence to "white men as nations." Growing disillusioned of blacks' socio-political situation in America, Delany became "heartily sick of whimpering, whining and sniveling at the feet of white men, begging for their refuse and offals [sic] existing by mere sufferance" ("Martin R. Delany to Frederick Douglass" 222–223). Saturated in Ethiopianism, Delany lamented blacks' position in America to suggest that elevation was needed to seek independent communities. He modified Ethiopianism to suggest that black power should be guided by black intelligentsia, "With the light of the age in which we live — with our advantages of educational attainments — with the Divine Promise that 'Princes' (Power) 'shall come out of Egypt' (from among the African race), 'and Ethiopia stretch forth' (from all parts of the world) 'her hands unto God'" ("Letter to James McCune Smith" 371). Delany's Ethiopianism appreciated Ethiopia's ancient civilization as well as its profound role in the Bible and world history. A common trope in the black community before the Civil War (Moses, *The Golden Age* 157), Ethiopianism manifested throughout blacks' jeremiadic rhetoric as a means to identify with the celebrated, virtuous, and conceivably the earliest of all human civilization. A similar dissemination of Ethiopianism appears in Abraham D. Shadd, Peter Spencer, and William S. Thomas' 1831 "Address of the Free People of Color of the Borough of Wilmington, Delaware." Suggesting that blacks deserve the same rights and privileges as whites, Shadd, Spencer, and Thomas revealed:

> We are natives of the United States; our ancestors were brought to this country by means over which they had no control; we have our attachments to the soil, and we feel that we have rights in common with other Americans; and although deprived through prejudice from entering into the full enjoyment of those rights, we anticipate a period, when.... "Ethiopia shall stretch forth her hands to God" [103].

At the 1854 National Emigration Convention of Colored Men held in Cleveland, Ohio, Delany evaluated America's "manifest destiny," a policy of imperialism rationalized as inevitable, to argue that:

> our oppressors are ever gratified at our manifest satisfaction, especially when that satisfaction is founded upon false premises; an assumption on our part, of the enjoyment of rights and privileges which never have been conceded, and which according to the present system of the United States policy, we never can enjoy ["Political Destiny of the Colored Race on the American Continent" 246].

Instead of advocating America's "manifest destiny," Delany supposed that blacks should advocate their own "political destiny." "The liberty of no man is secure," he believed, "who controls not his own political destiny" ("Political Destiny of the Colored Race on the American Continent" 247). He proposed that the only way to cure the disease of American racism was to leave the country:

> We have fully discovered and comprehended the great political disease with which we are affected, the cause of its origin and continuance; and what is now left for us to do is to discover and apply a sovereign remedy — a healing balm to a sorely diseased

body—a wrecked but not entirely shattered system. We propose for this disease a remedy. That remedy is Emigration. This Emigration should be well advised, and like remedies applied to remove that diseases from the physical system of man, skillfully and carefully applied, within the proper time, directed to operate on that part of the system, whose greatest tendency shall be, to benefit the whole ["Political Destiny of the Colored Race on the American Continent" 249].

Since, as Moses suggested, Black Nationalists' examination of "history is mystical, based on the prophecy that 'Ethiopia shall soon stretch forth her hands unto God,' that Africa's redemption will be accompanied by a decline of the West; that God would make a new covenant with black people" (*The Golden Age of Black Nationalism*, 10), Shadd, Spencer, and Thomas—as did Delany— realized that no all encompassing criterions existed by which their communities should be judged, or at the very least no such reasoning could rightfully form a foundation for the implementation of socio-political, socio-economic, and socio-religious restraints against their communities.

Conclusion

The development of the African American jeremiad and Black Nationalism clearly pointed to the materialization of a recognized black consciousness in the early republic. Sharing a strong sense of racial consciousness and racial pride, both discourses became not just philosophies but also manners of behavior. As stated in the beginning of this chapter, it becomes complex to separate the two when looked at as a force of black empowerment. This chapter suggests that both philosophies have been influenced by similar historical, philosophical, and cultural ideas. Although it is achievable to examine both discourses as thoughts and deeds not dependent on each other during the early republic, we can not disregard their interconnectedness. Both discourses would share similar principles when African American Jeremiahs shared their visions concerning the elevation and treatment of black America, and when Black Nationalists expressed a mood of distancing themselves from mainstream white America.

Conversely, the dismantling of British rule in postcolonial New World and the emerging dominancy of postcolonialism in the decades following the American Revolution marked a major developmental period for African American jeremiadic and nationalistic discourses. As the African American jeremiad began to retain language that conveyed not just blacks' present socio-political status but their pasts as well, it began to knit a social fabric with Black Nationalism that suggested that the essence of black struggle for civil liberties and social equality attacked the notion of blacks' perceived racial inferiority on two fronts: black empowerment and black consciousness. This convergence with historic political changes—the enactment of the Fugitive Slave Act in 1850, Nat Turner's insurrection in Virginia, America's "manifest destiny" philosophy, the widespread growth of the abolitionist movement to end slavery, the Amistad trial, the Dred Scott case, and many others—helped to build an arena where blacks could exercise their political, civil, economic, and social and cultural rights, which had subsequently been partially denied. "If we are not strong enough openly to *resist*," announced George Lawrence, Jr., "we are strong enough to *conspire*" ("A Carbonari Wanted" 111; emphasis is original). As blacks began to achieve these God-given rights, the African American jeremiad and Black Nationalism continued to unfold and shape the American political sphere.

5

Black Women Jeremiahs

> Why sit ye here and die? If we say we will go to a foreign land, the famine and the pestilence are there, and there we shall die. If we sit here, we shall die. Come let us plead our cause before the whites: if they save us alive, we shall live — and if they kill us, we shall but die ... unless with united hearts and souls you make some mighty efforts to raise your sons and daughters from the horrible state of servitude and degradation in which they are placed.
>
> — Maria Miller Stewart,
> "Lecture Delivered at the Franklin Hall," 1832

Anticipation surely filled the atmosphere as the attendees assembled at Boston's Franklin Hall No. 16, Friday, 21 September 1832 to discuss their antislavery concerns. Located on "Franklin Street," Franklin Hall was the "site of regular monthly meetings of the New England Anti-Slavery Society" (M. Richardson 45). Included in the roster of speakers was one of the first recognized African American women to deliver a public address. The lecturer, a native of Hartford, Connecticut, who moved to Boston in the 1820s, knew that her radical discourse would be ill supported by American society and by some of her Bostonian associates. "I hope my friends," she previously revealed in October 1831, would "not scrutinize" her message "with too severe an eye" (*Religion and the Pure Principles* 28). At the onset of her Franklin Hall homily, however, the novice revealed that two years prior to delivering her speech she experienced an "encounter with divinity" (Bassard 3), which she felt had called her to come forth and articulate the "miserable existence" of her brethren to Boston audiences. The "spiritual interrogation" which she encountered posited: "Who shall go forward, and take off the reproach that is cast upon the people of color? Shall it be a woman?" Her heart compassionately replied: "If it is thy will, be it even so, Lord Jesus!" Possessing, then, nothing but "moral capability — no teachings" but those of the "Holy Spirit," she answered the call to political and social activism. That evening at Franklin Hall, the speaker condemned America's so-called "democratic principles" that deprived black women of education and prohibited their occupational advancement. Emotionally, she revealed to the audience the "condition" her sisters suffered in the North was "but little better than" that of "southern slavery." She announced white America had "long and so loudly proclaimed the theme of equal rights and privileges, that our souls have caught the flame also, ragged as we are" ("Franklin Hall" 45, 47). When she sermonized from Boston's platform of abolitionism, Maria Miller Stewart[1] delivered her opinions to both black and white Bostonians during her short-lived career as a New England antislavery lecturer. Active in the sphere of black Boston's social reformation from 1831 until 1833, her moralizing employed the rhetoric of the African American jeremiad.[2] This chapter utilizes Stewart's Bostonian jeremiadic discourse as a foundation for discussing how African American women activists employed the tenets of the African American jeremiad to call attention to not only the threats facing black women, but the race as a whole.

Double-Edged Sword: The Advancement of Black Women Jeremiahs

It is important to discuss the growth and development patterns of the jeremiad as a means of achieving civil liberties and equality for its constituents when delivered by prominent black women. Black women Jeremiahs advanced the jeremiad in many ways. They utilized the rhetoric by delivering scornful jeremiads not only to racially mixed audiences, but also to audiences often times filled with men. It was not until the mid–1840s that the majority of black women Jeremiahs would be able amass a footing in the antislavery regime. This was partly because although women had a place in society, it was not, however, in the midst of affairs that were dominated by men abolitionist. The "dual forces of racism and sexism constituted unique constraints" on black women Jeremiahs (Bacon 165). In their protest, they participated in enhancing the voice of social change by opposing the slave trade, the growth of slavery into new regions, the admission of new slave states (Texas, for example) into the Union, the gag rule, and the continued existence of slavery in the nation's capital (*BAP III* 326). What would lead the black women to develop jeremiadic discourse separate from their male counterparts? Men shaped the direction of the societies and chaired the state and national organizations. It was expected that women were to structure their own individual, supporting organizations. The function of black women Jeremiahs was parallel to that of other female improvement organizations of the time, to be precise, to support the abolitionist's lecturers and its representative correspondents—men. To encourage women to get politically involved in the abolitionist movement, however, an anonymous black woman Jeremiah appealed to the "Free women of Connecticut" to "go to work *now*" to get involved in the mission. The writer reminded them that they were not far removed from servitude, "You are yourself almost qualified to be a slave. Ay, you *are a slave*—a slave to hardness of heart," she wrote in her 1839 essay published in the *Charter Oak*, a Hartford reform journal. After witnessing "the revenge of some lustful brute of an overseer," the anonymous writer lamented "our GREAT and WISE men (?) in the nation's BLACK LAW FACTORY have decided that *you have no right to ask for mercy* in their behalf." The writer ended her improvement address with one last call to consciousness, "Up, my sisters, speak while there is time. Millions are perishing, victims of your delay," and identified herself simply as "A Colored Woman" ("Essay by 'A Colored Woman'" 326–27; emphasis in original).

In the discourse of black women Jeremiahs, a number of universal themes materialized: the sexual mistreatment of slave women by white men and the effect slavery had on slave mothers; the optimism for constructing a coalition between black and white women; and the call for black community uplift (Yee, *Black Women Abolitionists* 122). An examination of their rhetoric uncovers the exacting contribution black women Jeremiahs made to the African American jeremiadic tradition. Gender would play an influential role. Black women Jeremiahs realized that their messages may not be well received because not only were they black, but also they were women, mothers of children seen as homemakers and caregivers, not a part of the growing defense force in the crusade against oppression. They came from all walks of life and most were either fugitives or working class who thrashed about to make wages and support themselves. Those who were married often found ways to help their husbands, who were possibly abolitionists, support their families (Yee, *Black Women Abolitionists* 122). Some black women Jeremiahs, however, became as popular as their male counterparts. Stewart's discourse of dissent blatantly attacked the moral fabric and effects of slavery and racism in America, making her America's preeminent black woman Jeremiah.

Gender in Stewart's Jeremiadic Discourse

Stewart's jeremiadic rhetoric called for the decline of American racism and sexism by arguing that "prejudice would gradually diminish" ("Franklin Hall" 46) while at the same time held out hope that blacks in America would ascend dehumanization of slavery and sexual and racial prejudice. When she violated the boundaries of womanism in nineteenth-century America, for example, Stewart illustrated that at the very nucleus of racial prejudice of American slavery was a domineering and tyrannical structure that impeded every stratum of black life. Opposition to slavery and its racial prejudice was an ongoing struggle. When Stewart joined that struggle, she advanced the social protest rhetoric of the African American jeremiad against slavery and its racial prejudices in several ways: a demand for improved educational opportunities, women's rights and civil liberties.

During the "short period" of her "Christian warfare" ("Farewell Address" 71), Stewart advanced onto Boston's platform of abolitionism and received hostilities from her "promiscuous audiences" (Sterling 154), meaning groups comprised of both men and women (Ryan 376). A significant challenge Stewart faced, however, was how to rise above the difficulty of, first, preserving the right to speak in public and, second, questioning the foundations of racial and sexual discrimination and the injustices that did not follow with America's democratic rights, without compromising her sense of solidarity with her community. Stewart was determined to demonstrate that she was a virtuous woman of "high moral character" (O'Connor 137). Born in 1803, she was orphaned at the age of five and sent to live with a minister and his family, where she was a servant until the age of 15. While living in the minister's home, Stewart did not have access to education. At the age of 20, she began attending a Sabbath School where she would receive formal education in literacy and religious instruction. These early teachings and religious trainings gravely affected the development of her jeremiadic discourse. Education, she felt, was a means in which the downtrodden could rise above the injustices of racial and sexual discrimination. Contrary to the prejudices and sexisms that plagued blacks in the early republic, Stewart declared that all African Americans deserved the opportunity to attain an education. The function of Stewart's jeremiads, she lamented in her first "track addressed to the people of color," was to stimulate them "to exertion" and to impress upon their psyches the "great necessity of turning" their "attention to knowledge and improvement" (*Religion and the Pure Principles of Morality* 28). Her purpose for raising her voice of dissent, she revealed, was because she had "discovered that religion is held in low repute among" some African Americans (Stewart 50).

Since many of her lectures showed immense evangelical aptitude, Stewart soon became known as an audacious and revolutionary Black woman Jeremiah. Mindful that she was disregarding the norm that forbade women to speak in the public sphere, Stewart's jeremiads called African Americans to develop resilient, self-sufficient educational and economic institutions within their communities, including businesses, schools, and churches. "Possess the spirit of independence," she beseeched them. "The Americans do, and why should not you? Possess the spirit of men, bold and enterprising, fearless and undaunted. Sue for your rights and privileges. Know the reason that you cannot attain them." When she voiced the rhetoric of resistance, Stewart was defiant toward the forces that silenced the voices of women and African Americans and the traditional hegemonic practices of white America; therefore, she demonstrated resistance when plagued by the ills of racism and prejudice. Yet, in order to envision an America where equality existed for all, Stewart had not only to undercut the dominant notions of race but also to overturn the dominant sexist prejudices that existed at the time. Her jeremiads frequently argued, then, that black women had an exceptional accountability for instilling intellectual consciousness in the minds of their children, "O ye mothers, what a responsibility rests on you! You have souls committed to your charge, and God will require a strict account of you" (*Religion and the Pure Principles* 38).

When she sowed the seeds of self-determination for black men and women, Stewart illustrated that women were the moral leaders (Waters 376). Men, she believed, also had great responsibility in this process. While Stewart's jeremiadic rhetoric condemned — and at the same time showed support of — the black man's dilemma of asserting manhood while dealing with the effects of slavery, she also advocated black self-determination and racial uplift. She lamented "our young men — smart, active, and energetic, with souls filled with ambitious fire" had no one from which to admire or gain self-respect because the older generation was oblivious and downtrodden, due to the influence of "prejudice, ignorance and poverty" ("Franklin Hall" 49). As she forced her audience to reflectively analyze themselves and consider the rationale for their lowliness, Stewart's jeremiad became even more critical of her "brethren" when she asked if they had "made a powerful effort" as the Britons had done when they first arrived to gain the power and control they wielded over their servants. "Have you," she beseeched them,

> prayed the Legislature for mercy's sake to grant you all the rights and privileges of free citizens, that your daughters may rise to that degree of respectability which true merit deserves, and your sons above the servile situations which most of them fill? ["Franklin Hall" 49].

Stewart's choice to engender a jeremiad in this fashion was clearly a calculated one. Instead of attacking the hegemonic structure that placed her "brethren" in their socio-political and economic conditions, Stewart sought to uplift "ye sons of Africa" when she vehemently criticized the essence of their manhood and condemned them for not following the fundamental Christian values of "thrift, sobriety, and hard work" (Yee, *Black Women Abolitionists* 115). "Most of our color have been taught to stand in free of white man from their earliest infancy," she argued, "to work as soon as they could walk, and to call 'master' before they scarce could lisp the name of *mother*." Their status would never change, she lamented, unless they let their resources be "appropriated for schools and seminaries of learning for our children and youth." While she reprimanded black men for not making themselves men of distinction, Stewart could not comprehend why black elevation and empowerment was such a difficult task. Had black men joined and assiduously turned their attention to "mental and moral improvement," she believed, there would be no need for audacious Black women Jeremiahs like herself ("Franklin Hall" 49; emphasis in original).

The Development of Stewart's Anti-Colonization Jeremiad

Stewart tenaciously disagreed with separatist schemes such as colonization. Her opposition toward proposals for colonization stemmed to some extent from her disdain for colonizationists' schemes and the methods they employed. During the 1820s and 1830s, the American Colonization Society (ACS) grew and established economic stability. By the late 1820s, however, African Americans believed colonization was as threatening to their prosperity as slavery and prejudice. When ACS received mixtures of "diverse interests," most ACS supporters were certain that the growing number of free blacks threatened the new, budding republic; they believed that blacks would "corrupt American society with their alleged immorality and their reputed inability to cope with freedom" (*BAP III* 3, 5). Many blacks believed that the ACS was a racist society, while others pointed to its compassionate origins and believed men with visions of an American empire in Africa would later control it.

Because of her dislike for immigration schemes, Stewart's anticolonization jeremiad developed and lamented the ills of the Colonization Movement, which proposed to send free blacks to Africa and to emancipate those who would agree to go. As a Black woman Jeremiah, Stewart was the forerunner in the impassioned anticolonization discourse. From the inauguration of her vocation amidst Boston's abolitionist movement, Stewart used her jeremiads to vehemently dispute colonization and urged African Americans to remain in America and demand the elimination of racial prejudice. She implored them to use their economic resources to appropriate "schools and seminaries of learning for our children and youth." Stewart filled the role of Jeremiah of her people when she further exhorted them to hold steadfast with the American covenant with its promise of social redemption. She argued, "African rights and liberty is a subject that ought to fire the breast of every free man of color in these United States, and excite in his bosom a lively, deep, decided and heart-felt interest." Stewart took the time to convey how whites initially drove Native Americans from their homeland and procured blacks from Africa to oppress them in America. Now, she argued, "whites sought to send blacks back to Africa" ("African Masonic Hall," 60, 63–64, 63). Stewart saw colonization as defeat against the power of collective progress. She expected decency to avail. Colonization, therefore, was unjust conduct in her eyes. In her lecture concerning "AFRICAN RIGHTS AND LIBERTY" delivered at Boston's Masonic Hall No. 28 on 27 February 1833, Stewart lamented:

> The unfriendly whites first drove the native American from his much loved home. Then they stole our fathers from their peaceful and quiet dwellings, and brought them hither, and made bond-men and bond-women of them and their little ones; they have obliged our brethren to labor, kept them in utter ignorance, nourished them in vice, and raised them in degradation; and now that we have enriched their soil, and filled their coffers, they say that we are not capable of becoming like white men, and that we never can rise to respectability in this country. They would drive us to a strange land ["African Masonic Hall" 63–64].

When activists adopt discourse of social protest, they do so for one of two reasons: they are inclined to follow the established format through a combination of interpretation and obligation or they may follow the form intentionally. In her anti-colonization jeremiad, Stewart employed the latter. In the above passage, Stewart infused her homily with nationalistic discourse that was influenced by David Walker. The pages of Walker's *Appeal* were laced with jeremiadic and nationalistic discourse. Walker was one of America's most prolific activists who inquired, "Have [whites] not to make their appearance before the tribunal of Heaven, to answer for the deeds done in the body, as well as we? Have we any other Master by Jesus Christ alone?" (*Appeal* 16). Walker lamented the social condition of blacks in America and sought to infuse pride in his African American audience by giving them hope that social change was inevitable. Walker's *Appeal* was against any plan that sought

> to get those of the coloured people, who are said to be free, away from among those of our brethren whom they unjustly hold in bondage, so that they may be enabled to keep them the more secure in ignorance and wretchedness, to support them and their children, and consequently they would have the more obedient slaves [*Appeal* 59].

As did Walker's jeremiadic rhetoric in his *Appeal*, Stewart's call through nationalistic discourse surfaced when she called black women to place themselves in the line of celestial sanction. She beseeched them, "O woman, woman! Upon you I call; for upon your exertions almost entirely depends whether the rising generation shall be any thing more than we have been or not" (Stewart 55). Walker's influence on Stewart's denunciation against colonization was palpable. "God had raised you up a Walker," she contended, "Though Walker sleeps, yet he lives, and his name shall be had in everlasting remembrance" (*Religion and the Pure Principles* 40). The "colonizationists," she lamented, asserted that "we were lazy and idle." Stewart painstakingly refuted this with a voice that echoed Black Nationalism. "We feel a common desire," she bemoaned, "to rise above the condition of servants and drudges" ("Franklin Hall" 46, 47).

Stewart launched her Anti-Colonization Jeremiad at America's hypocrisy when she continued to attack the "colonizationists," who she evaluated as "blind to their own interest." When she argued that colonization was a farcical design, Stewart proclaimed that if "the nations of the earth make war with America, they [the "colonizationists"] would find their forces much weakened by our absence." If the "colonizationists are the real friends of Africa," she lamented, "let them expend the money which they collect in erecting a college to educate her injured sons in this land of gospel, light, and liberty." An endeavor of such magnitude would be graciously received by blacks and convince them of the trustworthiness "of their profession." She believed, however, that whites' hearts were so harden towards blacks that "they had rather their money should be sunk in the ocean than to administer it to our relief" ("African Masonic Hall" 61).

Stewart's Prophetic Jeremiads Emerged from Her Biblical Exegesis

As customary in jeremiadic discourse, the prophecy element surfaced in Stewart's rhetoric and served as a forewarning to her African American audience of the righteousness to come. When she sought to convince America of blacks' greatness, she cautioned blacks that "our own efforts, however feeble" must avail. "Without these efforts," she bemoaned, "we shall never be a people, nor our descendants after us" (Stewart 53). In jeremiadic discourse taken as a whole, though, the prophetic was at once marginal, yet pervasive. Most prophets, as it were, never really recognize their role as a prophet, therefore, marginalizing their rhetoric (Darsey 24). However, often times the prophet's mission was overt and definite, sometimes so pervasive it became visible. The prophet, "accuser and judge," as James Darsey reminded us, was "called into being when the law has been violated ... the prophet announces both the charges and the verdict of God or nature against the transgressors of the law" (24). Although she declared that God put His words in her mouth, Stewart neither explicitly called herself a prophet nor did she understand why the "Almighty imparted unto" her "power of speaking" ("Farewell Address" 68). As her contact with the Spirit was "dialogical, a give-and-take" circumstance (Bassard 3), Stewart announced that since the call to political and social activism was imparted onto her, she would take on the role of prophet. When she advanced and made herself "a hissing and a reproach among the people" ("Franklin Hall" 48),[3] she indeed rationalized that she was doing God's work. Her spirituality, then, was at the very center of jeremiadic discourse. As Susan Roberson argued, her spiritual interrogations connected God's call to her "active and vocal engagement in racial and gender equality." Stewart's conversations with God aided in shifting political interests of social equality to sacred concerns, and connected "equality and freedom, self-improvement and social uplift ... in the secular world" (57). At a crucial moment in her choice to accept the call to political and social activism, Stewart lamented that with God's help society's disapproval would never discourage her from carrying out her avowed duty. Stewart believed she would "withstand the fiery darts of the devil" (Stewart 50), thus explicitly making herself the one chosen to deliver God's message. When she determined that religion was benevolent, that joy and peace existed when one believed, and that she was "commanded to come out from the world and be separate," Stewart felt that great work lay ahead and impulsively made a vocation of her "faith in Christ" ("Farewell Address" 66, 67).

In her jeremiadic fashion, Stewart's prophetic discourse also warned the "great and mighty men of America" of her prophecy. When judgment day arrives, she prophesized, white Americans would "call for the rocks and mountains to fall upon" them and conceal them "from the wrath of the Lamb," who would be steadfast on the throne. Stewart warned the nation of several issues, but united these warnings with a fundamentally hopeful message in which she confirmed her devotion to civil liberties for blacks. When she echoed the rhetoric of the book of Revelation 6:16,[4] for example, she prophesized that many of the "sable-skinned Africans" that white Americans abominate would excel in "the kingdom of heaven as the stars forever and ever." Stewart placed the main duty of reform on white America, though, whose deeds threatened true democracy. She portrayed blacks, however, as fulfilling their promised duty. For example, Stewart warned white America of the hardships of their consequence of racial oppression and issued a direct threat that if they did not change:

> You may kill, tyrannize, and oppress as much as you choose, until our cry shall come up before the throne of God; for I am firmly persuaded, that He will not suffer you to quell the proud fearless and undaunted spirits of the Africans forever [*Religion and the Pure Principles* 39–40].

She called her brethren to "stand still and know that the Lord He is God. Vengeance is His," she sermonized, "and He will repay. America has risen to her meridian." However, Stewart understood that her black audience could not idly stand too far away because it would illustrate a sign of ungratefulness toward others who have already articulated their voice amidst the growing abolitionist regime. Stewart cautioned her brethren to get close to each other and see God's work in progress. Therefore, she urged them to support each other and prophesized, "When you begin to thrive, [America] will begin to fall" (*Religion and the Pure Principles* 40). Stewart attempted to instill in her black audience that in order for change to occur, they had to believe that they were not intended to fill a second-rate place in society to which they had to adapt themselves.

Stewart's prophetic voice was also articulated in the midst of the racial and gender turbulence during the turmoil of nineteenth-century America (Roberson 57). Because the influence of prophetic rhetoric normally derived in large measure from its representation as coming from a divine encounter, Stewart's prophecy further lamented, "O, ye daughters of Africa, Awake! Awake! Arise! No longer sleep nor slumber, but distinguish yourselves." When she prophesized the rising of the "daughters of Africa," Stewart believed that they would become "fired with the truth of freedom" and "enlightened to distinguish themselves among other people." Stewart's discourse was tantamount with the prophetic rhetoric of the jeremiad as it simultaneously called her audience to consciousness about their oppression by implanting a sense of self-importance, which provided a source of inspiration important to the continuance of her jeremiads. "Many will suffer for pleading the cause of oppressed Africa," she lamented, "and I shall glory in being one of her martyrs" (*Religion and the Pure Principles* 26, 30, 31). Her prophecy envisioned a time when black oppression would "soon come to an end" ("Franklin Hall" 49). Stewart's jeremiad looked forward to the day when blacks "hearken unto the voice of the Lord," and walked in His ways and followed His decree. When this occurred, she believed, eminence, elegance and grace would combine with their virtues (*Religion and the Pure Principles* 29).

Stewart consistently described blacks' lowly temporal status by invoking the suffering servant image that associated unjustified torment and subjugation with redemption. For example, she reminded her audience, "As the prayers and tears of Christians will avail the finally impenitent nothing; neither will the prayers and tears of the friends of humanity avail us anything, unless we possess a spirit of virtuous emulation within our breasts" ("Franklin Hall" 49). Stewart's jeremiadic prophecy stood as unequivocal proof of the divine revelation she envisioned. The tenets above are apparent, but it should also be noted how this passage could have served for more than one function: it stood as an detailed declaration of what Stewart determined as the fundamental sequence of the prophetic discourse for blacks, namely a period of marginality on Earth because of the injustices of slavery, followed by a period of "virtuous emulation." Thus, her jeremiads included two segments. First, God would acknowledge black disenfranchisement and liberate them, and second, God would punish white America for its injustices. "For in his own time," she warned, "He is able to plead our cause against" the oppressors, and release upon them "the ten plagues of Egypt" (*Religion and the Pure Principles* 39–40).

Laced in biblical exegesis, Stewart's political sermon "An Address Delivered before the Afric-American Female Intelligence Society of America" was immersed with prophetic rhetoric and became the sort of "political sermon" that Sacvan Bercovitch discussed in *The American Jeremiad* (4). She drew from the books of Matthew and Romans to illustrate that God's judgment was His bond. Judgment day, she prophesized, "is coming." When this day would arrived, all the "secrets of all hearts shall be manifested before the saints and angels, men and devils." To the meek followers of Christ, this day would be a day of bliss and exultation; to the charlatans and nonbelievers, however, it would be a day of "terror and dismay." In her prophecy, though, Stewart admitted that "no man ... not even the angels of heaven" knew the day and hour of Christ's vehemence. When she reminded her audience of Christ's return, Stewart bemoaned:

> Christ shall descend in the clouds of heaven, surrounded by ten thousands of his saints and angels, and it shall be very tempestuous round about him, and before him shall be gathered all nations, and kindred, and tongues and people; and every knee shall bow, and every tongue confess; they also that pierced him shall look upon him, and mourn. Then shall the King separate the righteous from the wicked, as a shepherd divideth the sheep from the goats and shall place the righteous on his right hand, and the wicked upon his left. Then, says Christ, shall be weep and wailing, and gnashing of teeth, when ye shall see Abraham and the prophets, sitting in the kingdom of heaven, and ye yourselves thrust out. Then shall the righteous shine forth in the kingdom of their Father as the sun [Stewart 51].

In the above passage, Stewart encoded Romans 14:11 and Matthew 25:32–33. The roots of her prophetic vision, then, lie in the very structures of biblical text. Like the opening of many prophetic books of the Old Testament, Stewart's message began with her call to political and social activism. "I have enlisted in the holy warfare, and Jesus is my captain," she cried, "and the Lord's battle I mean to fight, until my voice expire in death." Stewart expected that some would hate and victimize her even unto her death (Stewart 52). This identification allowed Stewart to deliver her jeremiads in radical fashion because she put words in the Maker's mouth. The wicked, or whites would be "thrust out" of heaven, while the moral and virtuous, blacks, would "shine forth in the kingdom." As Marilyn Richardson noted, Stewart delivered God's message to "direct intervention in the affairs of nations and individuals, against the wicked and on behalf of the downtrodden"; God's wrath would only occur, however, "according to his own time" (16).

At the very nucleus of her prophetic jeremiads, Stewart's identification with God communicated a profound awareness of His presence and activity. As with prophets in their inspired state, Stewart was closer to the realm of the spirit than her audience. To blacks she illustrated optimism that they would finally receive the earthly rights promised to every man. She reassured them that if they continue to follow Christ, they would be carried by "angels into Abraham's bosom ... and the Lord God shall wipe away their tears." When this happened, Stewart exhorted, they would then be "convinced before assembled multitudes, whether they strove to promote the cause of Christ, or whether they sought for gain or applause (Stewart 51). Therefore, Stewart's prophetic jeremiads attempted to stimulate the urgency of "spiritual purification" she envisioned African Americans needed and to proclaim the moment of reckoning against corrupt America (Richardson 16). When she connected blacks' plight with the transcendent beliefs and values of the Bible, Stewart's jeremiadic prophecy sought to establish a nurturing foundation from which progress would develop. She dealt justly and practically with the problems facing African Americans, especially women, and offered them boundless optimism in the future.

Stewart's Jeremiadic Prophecy Materialized Masked in Ethiopianist Discourse

Stewart positioned Ethiopianist rhetoric within the walls of her jeremiads. Her employment of Ethiopianism contributed to the legacy of forerunners who had utilized it as a strategy to move African Americans to a consciousness concerning their historical and political unity. In the early republic, identification with Ethiopian traditions was a recurring thematic concern to black activists who spoke out against oppression. Perhaps the first to utilize the phrase was Prince Hall. Hall believed that when "Ethiopia begin to stretch forth her hand," blacks would ascend slavery and advance toward equality ("A Charge" 47).

Hall's Ethiopianist rhetoric suggested that people of African extraction would take their rightful place in the republic's democracy. The phrase, "Ethiopia begin to stretch forth her hand," however, was later employed by activist such as Richard Allen and Absalom Jones, Abraham D. Shadd, Peter Spencer, William S. Thomas, and Martin Delany. Their employment of Ethiopianism corresponded with Keith Gilyard and Anissa Wardi's declarations that African American Jeremiahs in the early republic saw themselves as the chosen ones among the perceived chosen nation (932). Moses suggested that this "Ethiopian tradition," then, stemmed from the Biblical verse "Princes shall come out of Egypt; Ethiopia shall soon stretch forth her hands unto God." A religious movement among sub–Saharan Africans during the colonial era, Ethiopianism became not just a "trans-Atlantic political movement" when employed by African Americans, "but a literary movement as well." It concerned an ever changing and recurring outlook of history, "the idea that the ascendancy of the white race was only temporary, and that the driving providence of history was working to elevate the African people" (*The Golden Age* 23–24). Stewart's interest in Ethiopianism blossomed in her jeremiadic discourse. As Lena Ampadu suggested, Stewart provoked, yet captivated her audience through her rich use of anaphora, a rhetorical device that used repetition to connect with its audience ("Modeling Orality" 139). Therefore, when Stewart expanded her prophetic discourse and simultaneously augmented the development of Ethiopianism, variations of the phrase appeared throughout her Boston antislavery speeches, sermons and essays.

While Stewart aligned her woes with the biblical prophet Jeremiah's, she lamented that her eyes were filled with a "fountain of tears," that she "might weep day and night" (*Religion and the Pure Principles* 30).[5] In her prophetic discourse, Stewart sincerely believed that "Ethiopia might stretch forth her hands unto God." The shackles of slavery and ignorance would not rupture, however, until blacks became unified as one and cultivated amongst themselves "the pure principles of piety, morality and virtue" (*Religion and the Pure Principles* 30). Her jeremiad would have been adequate to mobilize blacks to rise up against oppression. At the onset of *Religion and the Pure Principles*, Stewart skillfully attempted to accomplish this through a series of questions in which she sought to further reach her audience. "Where is the parent who is conscious of having faithfully discharged his duty," she asked, "and at the last awful day of account, shall be able to say, here, Lord, is they poor, unworthy servant?" (31).

The second time the phrase appeared in Stewart's jeremiadic discourse was in her essay "Cause for Encouragement." Written as a letter to William Lloyd Garrison, the editor of the *Liberator*, as response to Garrison's account of the "Second Annual Convention of the People of Color," Stewart urgently sought to call blacks to social action when she lamented "the day-star from on high is beginning to dawn upon us, and Ethiopia will soon stretch forth her hands unto God." Therefore, she believed that the work to "soon" start would rest on the shoulders of blacks. Again surfacing as her prophetic discourse, Stewart utilized the phrase to lament what she saw as divine intervention. "Holy religion" would ascend and advance blacks higher than their condition and cause their dreams and ambitions to align with antislavery advocates and become the final means of rupturing the "bands of oppression" (43). She exhibited both the hope and prophecy elements of the jeremiad when she lamented:

> O, America, America! Thou land of my birth! I love and admire thy virtues as much as I abhor and detest thy vices; and I am in hopes that thy stains will soon be wiped away, and thy cruelties forgotten. O, ye southern slaveholders! We will no longer curse you for your wrongs; but we will implore the Almighty to soften your hard hearts towards our brethren, and to send them a speedy deliverance [43].

Stewart suggested that blacks were the moral beings, since they are the ones that would "implore" God to show decadent white America the way to righteousness. She then prophesized that if free African Americans devote their interests more persistently to "moral worth and intellectual improvement," the result would be palpable, "prejudice would gradually diminish, and the whites would be compelled to say, unloose those fetters" ("Franklin Hall" 49).

When her Ethiopianist rhetoric appeared next in her Boston jeremiadic discourse, Stewart's anamnesis, a recalling intended to move her audience from the biblical past to the present, reminded her audience "God has said, that Ethiopia shall stretch forth her hands unto him." God, she sermonized, had different ways to "bring about his purposes." She further prophesized, unless the rising generation was discerning enough to display a distinctive disposition toward "each other from what we have manifested, the generation following will never be an enlightened people" (Stewart 53). Such reference assisted in an important role of Stewart's Ethiopianism, which was to fashion amidst the black community an awareness of unanimity and historical and political strength.

Subsequently, in her "An Address Delivered at the African Masonic Hall," Stewart's biblical exegesis played homage to God's promise to blacks. Stewart's mythic vision of Ethiopia was an account of its uniqueness, its destiny and its future. In her jeremiads, Ethiopia had been set apart for the noble purpose of universally affording justice to blacks. It was Stewart's hope that blacks would be able to triumph over all obstacles if they remained steadfast to the idea of political, social, and economic freedom. Because "God in wrath remembers mercy," she lamented, blacks would certainly despair. When Stewart revealed that they sprang from "one of the most learned nations of the whole earth" as the original people, yet remained marginalized in American, her prophesy interpreted "a promise is left us; 'Ethiopia shall again stretch forth her hands unto God.'" This time Stewart used the word Ethiopia to symbolize all descendants of Africa as she appealed to each person of African extraction to rise up and cast off the injustices they endured. Stewart's interpretation and employment of the phrase illustrated her frustration that blacks were denied advancement in the American democratic system and her irritation that racial prejudice was being encouraged in general.

Stewart further lamented that the condition blacks suffered "has been low for hundreds of years." This would continue to be the case, she argued, "unless by true piety and virtue" blacks endeavored to reclaim that which was originally given to them by the Almighty ("African Masonic Hall" 58). Stewart's repeated reference to the phrase "Ethiopia will stretch forth her hands unto God" also illustrated a remarkable attachment of antebellum strivings by blacks toward religious, social and political freedom in New England. Based on her Afrocentric exegesis of biblical text, Stewart's Ethiopianist rhetoric and imagery also represented her belief that blacks' dignity and place in divine favor would set the stage for blacks' future in America.

The Alpha and the Omega of Stewart's Boston Jeremiads

In her first Boston jeremiadic tract, *Religion and the Pure Principles of Morality, the Pure Foundation on Which We Must Build*, Stewart illustrated elements of jeremiadic discourse when she lamented "it is not the color of the skin that makes the man or the woman but the principle formed in the soul" (29). She spiked her jeremiads with two overriding principles. She believed blacks had to rely upon themselves for emancipation and civil rights, and that she was an instrument of God, called to represent her brethren in the fight against oppression. "And I believe," Stewart bemoaned, "that the glorious declaration was about to be made applicable to me, that was made to God's ancient covenant people by the prophet" ("Farewell Address" 74). Often times in her jeremiads, Stewart incorporated passages from the Books of Lamentations, Judges, Ester, Genesis, Psalms, Matthew, Isaiah, Revelation, and many others; scripture to her was an evocative instrument. She lamented:

> Every man has a right to express his opinion. Many think, because your skins are tinged with a sable hue, that you are an inferior race of beings; but God does not consider you as such. He hath formed and fashioned you in his own glorious image, and hath bestowed upon you reason and strong powers of intellect. He hath made you to have dominion over the beasts of the field, the fowls of the air, and the fish of the sea [Genesis 1:26]. He hath crowned you with glory and honor; hath made you but a little lower than the angels [Psalms 8:5]; and, according to the Constitution of these United States, he hath made all men free and equal [*Religion and the Pure Principles* 29].

Unquestionably, the recurrent biblical allusions in her jeremiadic rhetoric substantiated an understanding of the importance of the Bible as an essential model of discourse in the lives of New England blacks in the 1830s. In the above passage, Stewart made use of Genesis and Psalms to assert insurgence in the consciousness of her oppressed brethren. Warning as the message was and imperative as the manifesto from which it was delivered, Stewart lamented that the problem the African American community faced was that many blacks adhered to the racist philosophy of their inferiority; thus, she sought to insist that they attune their interest toward knowledge and development of the race. Stewart's message chimed with echoes of jeremiadic discourse. Her critique of social justice; her mourning for her people; and her optimism for a future where democracy in America was selected on a nationalized basis. Her rhetorical strategies distinguished her from those of her male counterparts, despite the significantly related subject matter. Since male activists sustained the role of Jeremiah within the community, the influence of social gender boundaries placed on African American women during the early republic propelled Stewart's adoption of jeremiadic discourse, thus feminizing her voice of elevating society's moral awareness. Stewart's focus on oppressions—especially racism, sexism, and class—that affected black women, was what most clearly distinguished her jeremiadic discourse from her male counterparts. The reactions to Stewart's speeches, however, were devastatingly pejorative. Outright condemned for having the courage to transgress the "hegemonic mechanisms of power through her discourses" (Roberson 59) and speak out in a public setting, Stewart met opposition even from some who supported her; therefore, she chose to leave Boston. She ended her *Religion and the Pure Principles* with a lasting prophetic revelation, "The Lord will raise us up, and enough to aid and befriend us, and we shall begin to flourish" (*Religion and the Pure Principles* 29).

Optimistic to the very end, however, Stewart refused to go quietly and connected her initial and final Boston discourses by repeating the phrase "it is not the color of the skin that makes the man or the woman but the principle formed in the soul" from *Religion and the Pure Principles* to get her final point across concerning civil liberties of black women. This time, however, Stewart's use of anaphora amended the phrase to include anamnesis of "a young lady of Bologne" who, in the thirteenth century obtained the Doctor of Laws degree and launched public redress "to expound the Institutions of Justinian."[6] Thus, Stewart suggested that when women activists rose to tackle issues of importance to their communities, they possessed celestial authority, and her message materialized that the power the "young lady of Bologne" possessed was that of persuasiveness and expression. When Stewart immortalized the "young lady of Bologne," she initiated a feminist tradition long before the women's movement was ever launched (Ampadu, "Maria W. Stewart," 41). While she emphasized the sex of her audience as well their solidarity to the abolitionist movement, Stewart further imagined what would happen if such a woman appeared among "our sable race." In her feminist prophecy, she responded, "Brilliant wit will shine come from whence it will; and genius and talent will not hide the brightness of its luster" ("Mrs. Stewart's Farewell Address" 70). Here Stewart's jeremiad became a feminist vehicle to empower black women to a consciousness about how they are perceived in society. When she spoke for black women, Stewart called upon them to establish their "individual and communal identity, their moral and political liberty." She achieved this when she articulated and acted out the terms of nineteenth-century black feminism (Roberson 57), which constituted possessing a feminist consciousness that dissected subjugation and worked to purge that oppression. Stewart extended the normative accepted roles and restrictions of female social action, thus adding a feminist perspective to the emerging African American jeremiadic discourse, a feat her male counterparts did not have the ability to achieve.

Stewart believed her individual attempt to make herself helpful among blacks in Boston and her calls to black Bostonians had "accomplished little" (Yee, *Black Women Abolitionists* 115). She, then, delivered her farewell jeremiad Saturday, 21 September 1833 to a crowed audience in a "School Room in Belknap St."[7] Throughout her exodus address, Stewart mourned immorality, foretold doom, and appeared to rise "at moments to a serene lyricism" (Richardson 65, 23). While she attempted to reason with her enemies of justice and judgment to come, Stewart quoted Isaiah 55:9: "For as the heavens are higher than the earth, so are his ways above our ways, and his thoughts above our thoughts." She believed that God had, for purposes only known to Him, loosened her tongue and placed His words into her mouth "in order to put all those to shame" who had risen against her ("Farewell Address" 67). The very walls of her farewell address loiters an intertext of anamnesis. "What if I am a woman; is not the God of ancient times the God of these modern days? Did he not raise up Deborah, to be a mother, and a judge in Israel [Judges 4:4]? Did not queen Esther save the lives of the Jews? And Mary Magdalene first declare the resurrection of Christ from the dead?" ("Farewell Address" 68). When she aligned her plight as a present day Black woman Jeremiah with the plight biblical women endured when answering the call to social activism, Stewart challenged her audience to consider new and changing dimensions of the role of black women in society. She shared a consciousness of how their sexual identities combined with their racial identities made their life situations and focus of their political struggles unique. Despite her aggressive tone, the audience would have understood the voice of feminist discourse in the context of equality and fairness for all women. At the same time, Stewart's jeremiadic anamnesis kept her audience rooted in the greater standard of biblical witness. She denounced St. Paul's declaration that it was a "shame for a woman to speak in public" and suggested that "our great High Priest and Advocate did not condemn the woman for a more notorious offence than this"; He will not, she predicted, condemn her ("Farewell Address" 68). Stewart beseeched her audience to cease talking of prejudice, until it has been eliminated in America. "For while these evils exist," she lamented, to talk of them is "like giving breath to the air, and labor to the wind" ("Farewell Address" 70–71). Stewart then ended her farewell address with one last lamentation, "Bless those who have hated me, and cheerfully pray for those who have despitefully used and persecuted me" ("Farewell Address" 74).

Stewart Concluded Her Boston Jeremiads

During her Boston years, Stewart never vacillated from her position that the principal cause of African American subjugation and affliction lay within the control of white society. Engrained in Stewart's call to political and social activism was a jeremiadic discourse that progressed into a highly structured and effective vehicle she utilized to implant a sense of self-importance and uplift. Stewart beckoned America to live up to its sacred principles. In doing so, she called her brethren, and sisters, to organize as a society of Christians. Stewart's jeremiads publicized her "celebratory vision of redemptive progress toward independence of body and spirit" (Richardson 16). As she lamented to her audience in her farewell address, "Let us follow after godliness, and the things which make for peace"; she bemoaned, "cultivate your own minds and morals; real merit will elevate you" ("Farewell Address" 72). Stewart's persuasive voice in Boston's arena of abolitionism challenged the American consciousness. Her jeremiads were passionately evangelical, astutely filled with criticism and an unyielding declaration of the credence of natural and divine rights for African Americans. Receptive of "Afric's woes," Stewart's jeremiadic discourse, then, played a pivotal role in shaping not only black Boston's social protest rhetoric, but also in forging an array of new political agendas that eventually were used to create a viable new nationalized place for African Americans. The structure of her jeremiads was prescribed by her pledge to oppose the racial oppression and subjugation blacks suffered. While she provided a significant voice to black Boston's resistance against the injustices of racial oppression, Stewart's career as a black woman Jeremiah was significant enough in laying the rhetorical influence for future black women Jeremiahs. Others, such as Sojourner Truth and Frances Ellen Watkins Harper, would carry on and utilize the struggle for freedom, self-respect, and civil liberties.

The Jeremiadic Discourse of Sojourner Truth and Frances Harper

Black women Jeremiahs also organized public speaking engagements and called for social change at a time when such activities were generally male dominated. Sojourner Truth made it exceptionally clear in her 1851 "Women's Rights Convention" speech at Akron, Ohio, that black women deserved the right to fight for equality because they, too, have suffered:

> I have ploughed and planted, and gathered into barns, and no man could head me! And ain't I a woman? I could work as much and eat as much as a man — when I could get it — and bear the lash as well! And ain't I a woman? I have borne thirteen children, and seen most all sold off to slavery, and when I cried out with my mother's grief, none but Jesus heard me! ["Women's Right Convention" 103].

Women especially had a difficult time persuading their audiences. Before Truth was allowed to speak, some who attended the convention felt that her message — "nigger's rights" they called it — would interfere with their cause — "women's rights." Truth, however, chose to unveil the unvarnished "truth" about slavery's practices. Her jeremiads were tailored to the audience that would receive women's oppression as unacceptable; her homilies also revealed the many attitudes of women — both black and white — in the nineteenth century. Obviously, some nineteenth-century audiences in America were credulous and easily persuaded. Truth, although illiterate and not a trained orator, had the power to turn a hostile crowd to a hushed silence with "streaming eyes and hearts bearing with gratitude" (qtd. in Fitch and Mandziuk 104). Before she delivered her renowned, revolutionary speech in Akron:

> The leaders of the movement trembled on seeing a tall gaunt black woman in a gray dress and white turban, surmounted with an uncouth bonnet, march deliberately into the church, walk with the air of a queen up the side, and take her seat upon the pulpit steps. A buzz of disapprobation was heard all over the house [Stanton 115–116].

After she delivered her address on women's rights to an audience mixed with well-to-do white men, ministers and women, Frances Gage, the presiding officer at the convention, pointed out that Truth's speech was "pointed and witty and solemn, eliciting at almost every sentence defeaning applause" (qtd. in Fitch and Mandziuk 104). Truth ended her speech by telling her white audience "If de fust woman God ever made was strong enough to turn de world upside down all alone, dese women togedder ought to be able to turn it back, and get it right side up again!" ("Women's Right Convention" 104). If all things in Christ were made anew, then Truth's declarations that the differences established on color and gender represented the essence of resistance. According to Gage, Truth had:

> Magical influence that subdued the mobbish spirit of the day, and turned the sneers and jeers of an excited crowd into notes of respect and admiration. Hundreds rushed up to shake hands with her, and congratulate the glorious old mother, and bid her God-speed on her mission of "testifyin'" agin concerning the wickedness of this 'ere people ["Women's Right Convention" 104].

Truth was able to employ the jeremiad to captivate her audience to such an extent that one of the audience participants admitted that in trying to describe her one might "as well attempt to report that apocalyptic thunders" (qtd. in Fitch and Mandziuk 104).

Truth used the jeremiad consistently throughout her protest to contest not only the inferior status of women, but also the perceived status of all blacks. Truth understood that since most women in the audience had never witnessed the degradation she would articulate, black women, she argued, should profit from the admiration of *all* women, "Nobody ever helps me into carriages, or over mud-puddles, or gives me any best place! And ain't I a woman?" ("Women's Right Convention" 104). Truth positioned her jeremiadic discourse to look toward a future where black women were granted the same rights as white women (Fitch and Mandziuk 5), or as she puts it in her 1843 "Specimens of Religious Talk to Second Adventists," "Nothing belonging to God can burn, any more than God himself." White America could be saved only by acknowledging this *truth*. Truth warned Americans that blacks were the ones who will walk with Christ when He "comes and burns" the "ashes of the wicked." Present in her message was Keith Gilyard and Anissa Wardi's convictions that the African American jeremiad depicted blacks as the chosen ones, who, as Truth suggested, would "have no need to go away to escape the fire" upon His return ("Specimens of Religious Talk to Second Adventists" 102).

Truth, a former slave in New York who gained her freedom when the state abolished slavery in 1827, quickly became one of the most prolific Black women Jeremiahs on the antislavery ticket. She used her understanding of biblical text to convey in her messages that she did not hold any anger against her oppressors. As she "bore pity rather than bitterness toward the slaveholders" (Quarles 121), Truth employed the African American jeremiad to further her convictions that slavery was the product of an oppressive white society. Truth's jeremiads assumed an apparently tolerant and sympathetic tone that "nonetheless invokes potentially violent themes" (Bacon 206). To her 1853 audience at the New York City Anti-Slavery Society, she disclosed how slavery corrupted slaves:

> My poor mother would weep and say, in Dutch, "Oh! mein Got, mein Got," which means in English my God. "My poor children will be sold into Slavery." I did not know what that meant then, but I have learned since. My mother cried bitterly, and I took the corner of her old apron, and wiped her eyes and asked her what she cried for. She said "my poor child we are going to be sold, and we shant see one another again...." I asked her who made them [slaveholders], and she told me God did, and that I must pray that he would make the bad people good. I did pray, but the people didn't get any better, and so I prayed that he would kill them, for they seemed to die quicker than they got good ["New York City Anti-Slavery Society" 109–110].

Even though Truth did not wish "God to kill them [slaveholders] anymore," she appeared optimistic that white America would take the necessary steps to "ameliorate the condition of her race" (Fitch and Mandziuk 110). In her 1853 "Address by a Slave Mother," Truth's potential aggression towards whites became more defined (Bacon 206):

> She used to say she wished God would kill all the white people.... Her mother had taught her to pray to make her master good, and she did so, but she was tied up and

whipped till the blood trickled down her back and she used to think if she was God she would have made them good, and if God were she, she would not allow it [qtd. in Bacon 206)].

Truth imagined America as a land of one people momentarily splintered by moral obstructions and corruptions built on race. Blacks would, as she prophesized, "*stand the fire.*" It would be "*absurd* to think they could not" ("Specimens of Religious Talk to Second Adventists" 102; emphasis in original). Truth's radical jeremiads took flight as other black women abolitionists found avenues to battle white supremacy and work to create a society that would give concrete hope to blacks irrespective of the hegemony of the overriding and prevailing culture, which had denied them democratic vision and involvement in the creation of the society that oppressed them.

When Frances Ellen Watkins Harper stepped to the podium, she shrewdly attacked American democracy with her jeremiads. Born of free parents 24 September 1825 and self-educated, Harper was one of the leading Black women Jeremiahs, poet and antislavery advocates, and a strong supporter of prohibition and woman's suffrage. Harper's jeremiads often assailed the government for its hypocrisy. On 23 May 1857, for example, Harper told her audience that the ills of slavery ought to be enough to eradicate it:

> A hundred thousand new-born babes are annually added to the victims of slavery; twenty thousand lives are annually sacrificed on the plantations of the South. Such a sight should send a thrill of horror through the nerves of civilization and impel the heart of humanity to lofty deeds. So it might, if men had not found out a fearful alchemy by which this blood can be transformed into gold. Instead of listening to the cry of agony, they listen to the ring of dollars and stoop down to pick up the coin ["New York City Anti-Slavery Society"].

Delivering her speech amid applause, Harper criticized the continuance of the system of slavery in the professedly Christian republic. She concluded her speech by informing her audience that the North was just as responsible for the continuation of slavery as was the South. "When you fail to catch the flying fugitive," she lamented, "the North is base enough to do your shameful service" ("New York City Anti-Slavery Society").

Racial progress through moral reform was a major element of Harper's jeremiadic rhetoric throughout the 1860s. As previously stated in Chapter 1, jeremiads were shaped by the political and economic conditions surfacing at the time. After the John Brown raid on Harper's Ferry, for example, many southern whites lived in fear of outright slave insurrections. Some called for exile or enslavement of free blacks. Arkansas was the first to act on this injustice. Appealing "to Christians throughout the world," Harper, and a group of twelve "exiles from Little Rock and the Mississippi River ports of Napoleon and Redfork" (*BAP V* 54), called their audience to action to protest against the enforced banishment from the state. Nowhere in America, Harper lamented, were free southern blacks welcome:

> From this terrible injustice, we appeal to the moral sentiment of the world. We turn to the free North, but even here oppression tracks our steps. Indiana shuts her doors upon us. Illinois denies us admission to her prairie homes. Oregon refuses us an abiding place for the soles of our weary feet. And even Minnesota[8] has our exclusion under consideration ["Circular" 55].

Harper lamented, however, that in Ohio free blacks did find "kind hearts." Because of this "terrible injustice," she appealed to the "heirs of the same heritage, and children of the same Father" and evoked the spirit of Americanism to protest against the "gross and inhuman outrage, which has been committed beneath the wing of the American Eagle, and in the shadow of the American Church." American churches were noticeably more distorted than American politics. Harper lamented that the American church was to blame for many of the worst traits that existed in regard to American slavery. Her jeremiads called for the entire community to unite their voices "against the outrage which disgraces our land and holds it up to shame before the nations of the earth" and to "*protest* against the inhumanity that has driven us from our homes and our kindred" ("Circular" 55; emphasis in original).

Fervently supporting the reformation movement, Harper later lamented, "We need some earnest and elevating influence among ourselves." Believing that moral reform was "the very best anti-slavery work" she could do, Harper took it upon herself to "elevate the character of the colored people, not merely by influencing the public *around* them but *among* them." Harper's feminist jeremiad beseeched "Christian mothers, by our plundered cradles and child bereft hearts, we appeal to you and ask your protest" ("Circular" 55, 81; emphasis in original). Harper took pride in representing her race. Although free, she still felt that the racial stereotypes of white America affected all African Americans, regardless of education, gender, or economic status. She lamented:

> Upon our alleged inferiority is based our social ostracism and political proscription, and so long as they are down, I belong to the downtrodden race. To teach our people how to build up a character for themselves—a character that will challenge respect in spite of opposition and prejudice; to develop their own souls, intellect and genius, and thus verify their credentials, is some of the best anti-slavery work that can be done in this country. I do not say that this is the whole work, but it should be an important department of reform effort ["Circular" 82].

Endorsing moral reform, Harper's jeremiads carried the broader tenet of the abolitionist movement: the concern for shattering all adherences of racial discrimination not only for the slave, but for all blacks. She lamented:

> Our fault, in a land of Bibles and Churches, of baptisms and prayers, is that in our veins flows the blood of an outcast race; a race oppressed by power and proscribed by prejudice, a race cradled in wrong and nurtured in oppression.... We were weak, our oppressors were strong. We were a feeble, scattered people; they, being powerful, placed before us slavery or banishment. We chose the latter. Poverty, trials, and all the cares incident to a life of freedom are better, far better, than slavery ["Circular" 54–55].

In her 1859 speech, "Our Greatest Want," Harper confronted her fellow blacks. "Our greatest need is not gold or silver, talent or genius, but true men and true women. We have millions of our race in the prison house of slavery, but have not yet a single Moses in freedom" (163). In those words, Harper summed up the challenge facing African Americans during her time.

Conclusion

Black women Jeremiahs like Stewart, Truth and Harper contributed to countless activities of the abolitionist movement, and their participation was profound. Those who were able to benefit the most from involvement in the social reformation of the jeremiad lived in mostly Northern urban areas. It was in those towns and locales that Black women Jeremiahs could amass the greatest effect and, therefore, have their voices disseminated more easily than in smaller locales. The continuation of racism and sexism collectively, while it endangered all black women in general, did not silence Black women Jeremiahs entirely. In fact, it only helped to fuel their need to further the quest of social reformation in America and strengthen their commitment to ending American prejudice based on race, sex, and gender (Yee, *Black Women Abolitionists* 120–121).

6

The Age of Abolitionism

> If a slave ran away and succeeded in getting clear, or if a slave killed his master, set fire to a barn, or did any thing very wrong in the mind of a slaveholder, it was spoken of as the fruit of *abolition*. Hearing the word in this connection very often, I set about learning what it meant. The dictionary afforded me little or no help. I found it was "the act of abolishing"; but then I did not know what was to be abolished. Here I was perplexed.... After a patient waiting, I got one of our city papers, containing an account of the number of petitions from the north, praying for the abolition of slavery in the District of Columbia, and of the slave trade between the States. From this time I understood the words *abolition* and *abolitionist*.
> — Frederick Douglass, *Narrative of the Life of Frederick Douglass, an American Slave. Written by Himself*, 1845

The Black abolitionist Jeremiah understood the critical role rhetoric and activism played in the antislavery movement. At an early age, Frederick Douglass began to conceptualize the disparities between slavery and freedom. Unexpectedly, the discerning, promising abolitionist heard his first antislavery speech — he retrogressively acknowledged — under the auspices of Hugh Auld. Douglass was so driven by the verbal communication that he "set out with high hope, and a fixed purpose, at whatever cost of trouble," to ensure that he obtained his freedom. After Auld discovered his wife, Sofia, teaching young Douglass letters, Auld chastised both Sofia and Douglass. "If you give a nigger an inch," Hugh told them, "he will take an ell":

> Learning would *spoil* the best nigger in the world ... "if you teach that nigger (speaking of myself) how to read, there would be no keeping him. It would forever unfit him to be a slave. He would at once become unmanageable, and of no value to his master. As to himself, it could do him no good, but a great deal of harm. It would make him discontented and unhappy" [*Narrative* 29; emphasis in original].

This "invaluable instruction" Douglass acquired "by the merest accident" sparked feelings "within that lay slumbering, and called into existence an entirely new train of thought" (*Narrative* 29). His experiences as a slave in Maryland would later lead Douglass to conclude that "a large portion of the slaves *know* that they have a right to their liberty" and that "emancipation ... is that cure for slavery and its evils" ("I Have Come to Tell You Something about Slavery" 4; emphasis in original). Douglass' reputation as one of America's most profound Black abolitionist Jeremiahs would depend upon the power of his words to scythe through mainstream white America's romanticism concerning black elevation. Douglass coupled the jeremiad and the rhetoric of the abolitionists' crusade and used them as a vehicle to achieve this feat during America's age of abolitionism.

Although historians agree that abolitionism in America reached its apex with the publication of William Lloyd Garrison's antislavery newspaper, *The Liberator*, on 1 January 1831, they neglect the fact that from the dawning of the New World's "peculiar institution," means to eradicate the establishment grew and flourished. Charles W. Gardner reminded white abolitionists that they were not progenitors of progressive movements meant to uplift blacks:

> Garrison has been branded as the individual who turned the people of color against the colonization scheme. But I can tell you, sir, that when William Lloyd Garrison was a schoolboy, the people of color in different parts of the country were holding extensive meetings, which always agreed in declaring that they regarded the scheme as visionary in itself, and calculated only to rivet the chains of those who remain in slavery.... How far it may act beneficially, in abolishing the slave trade, or in planting benevolence and civilization in Africa, I leave for time to disclose. But these facts show, that as to its bearing on ourselves, the people of color were not asleep. Long before William Lloyd Garrison was a man, we had fixed our *veto* on it. From its very commencement, we had washed our hands of all connection with it ["Speech by Charles W. Gardner" 210–211; emphasis in original].

Gardner's speech belied notions that blacks were the first abolitionists as well. He revealed a major rift between the moral suasionists, those who supported gradual adherence to the abolition of slavery, and the ultra-abolitionists, those who fervently believed in full civil rights for all blacks:

> We view slavery to be like the carnal mind, which is not subject to the law of God, neither indeed can be. And therefore it must be abolished, and not ameliorated. There is no such thing as ameliorating slavery. You might as well talk of having the love of God in a carnal mind ["Speech by Charles W. Gardner" 210].

With its growth, abolitionism became a driving force in tearing down the walls that slaveholders used to protect their justification of their insidious design. During colonial America, however, the chief abolitionists comprised the majority of those who were reapers of slavery's tyranny. This trend would continue throughout the history of slavery in America as black formulation of abolitionism was largely a direct response to freed blacks; consequently, it was detrimental, slaveholders felt, that their slaves be taunted by free black presence. Therefore, the dilemma that black abolitionists faced was how to negotiate and connect resistance to slavery with a call for civil rights for blacks, especially since racism was prominent in the republic's history. For black abolitionists, fighting racism was not only a troublesome dilemma, but also it became a "matter of self-definition" (Shortell 76). William Wells Brown, for example, grieved over "the system of Slavery" because he felt that it "not only robbed him of his liberty, but a portion of his colour." For Brown, the best way to persuade white Americans that the atrocities of slavery were unjustified and against the natural law of man was to appeal to their moral consciousness. Since white Americans went against the country's "national honour" ("Speech by William Wells Brown, Delivered at the Horticultural Hall" 249), Brown bemoaned:

> We are told by the colonizationists that we must be sent out of the country — that we are not citizens of it. If I am not a citizen of the United States, pray, are you? Did your fathers not come from another country? We were brought here by force, it is true (I speak not now as an Anglo-Saxon, as I have a right to speak, but as an Africa), but that fact does not alter our birthright.... But because I am a shade darker than you, you disfranchise me. I am ashamed when I hear men talking about the national honour of this country being insulted by the Spaniards, or the Cubans, just as if we had any national honour to be insulted! ["Speech by William Wells Brown, Delivered at the Horticultural Hall" 249].

Because Brown was a mulatto — the son of a white plantation owner, while his mother was a black slave — he felt that he had been deprived of a true black heritage. He also felt that he had the right "to speak of the shortcomings of the people of this country" ("Speech by William Wells Brown, Delivered at the Horticultural Hall" 248). Slavery, he felt, was responsible for his status as a mulatto.

Prejudice also played a role in Black abolitionist Jeremiahs' "self-definition" during the age of American abolitionism (1830–1861). Theodore S. Wright, a freeborn black who became a minister in the Presbyterian church and conductor of the New York Underground Railroad, lamented the influence of prejudice on blacks because he felt it "cuts us from every thing; it follows us up from childhood to manhood; it excludes us from all stations of profit, usefulness and honor; takes away from us all motive for pressing forward in enterprises, useful and important to the world and to ourselves" ("Prejudice Against the Colored Man"). Frederick Douglass expressed grief over "prejudice against color" as he believed it to be "stronger north than south; it hangs around my neck like a heavy weight. It presses me out," he believed, "from among my fellow men" ("I Have Come to Tell You Something about Slavery" 5). "In my opinion," William Whipper lamented, "the power that [this] prejudice *now* exerts in the few States is not dependent on the foetid [sic] breath of slavery." Whipper believed that prejudice was caused by the "people of the Commonwealths" who were "capable of perpetuating it after slavery is abolished" ("William Whipper to Frederick Douglass" 244). Whipper continued:

> Therefore, I am unable to comprehend the doctrine that this prejudice has its origin in "chattel slavery," or that it will be obliterated by its abolition. I think the discovery will yet be made that this prejudice is of very ancient birth, that it has pursued different nationalities down the long catalogue of ages, that it is older than American slavery and that the latter derived its existence from an organic action of the former ["William Whipper to Frederick Douglass" 244].

Therefore, as Wright, Douglass, and Whipper lamented, for the most part, the process of consciously evaluating and choosing from among their options on the basis of their perceived merits and values within the American democracy was problematic for most blacks.

During America's early republic years, black dissent to slavery manifested in the voices of whites as well. Sondra O'Neale noted that the abolitionists' movements first began to solidify as an interest group in The Society of Friends (SOF), one of the first social aid societies to speak out against the enslavement of blacks. Progressively, the movement developed in the rhetoric of the Methodist followers of John Wesley and George Whitefield. This endeavor began in the church, which held the interests of the colonizers from the arrival of the Great Awakening in the 1730s ("Challenge to Wheatley's Critics" 501). SOF, also known as the Quakers, declared that the inner light of God existed in all mankind, which lead them to be a peaceful, harmonic people. Slavery, degradation, and the dehumanization of Africans, they thought, was not apart of God's religious idealism. Their rhetoric found its way into the everyday voices of other abolitionists.

By the advent of the abolitionist movement of the 1830s, however, African Americans had drawn heavily from the regression rhetoric of the American jeremiad to illustrate that their enslavement was punishable through God's commandments. Some of their white sympathizers, such as the Quakers and William Lloyd Garrison and his legion of followers, represent some of the complexities in defining what was uniquely African American rhetoric. Where does one place white abolitionists like the Garrisonians? Although David Howard-Pitney noted that "the abolitionist jeremiad sometimes crossed the color line to appear in the reflections of prominent whites" (11), African Americans' struggle for basic civil liberties was unyieldingly based on the education and experience of black people. Samuel Ringgold Ward noted the differences between the divisions of abolitionists and rejected the respected assumption that abolitionism was the white man's work:

> Abolitionists differ and vary in their knowledge and estimate of the negro. Some think we are not to be encouraged to be anything more than a sort of half way set of equals. Others desire and claim for us a full recognition of our equal and inalienable rights. The former class, like the Yankee Quakers, desire that we should be free; but, as to our being regarded and treated as equals, *that* is another thing. This class are [sic] always desirous to keep up with the short frocks of childhood on. They assume the right to dictate to use about all matters; they dislike to see us assume or maintain manly and independent positions; they prefer that we should be a second-rate set of folks, in intellectual matters. A thousand times would they rather see us tied to some newspaper that represents us as being about mid way betwixt slaves and men, than to see us holding up a bold front, with a press worthy of entire freemen. Such will always doubt ... "whether it is best to encourage '*our dear colored brethren*' in going too far." Some people doubt and deny the abolitionism of this class. I simply call them a good sort of folk, who are not exactly up to the idea of human equality. They have been so long accustomed to inferior and degraded Blacks,

that they scarcely know how to regard us in any other light. Unfortunately, too many of these occupy leading positions. Happily, however, such are scarcer in Canada and in England, than in the United States.... Many who are not careful to call themselves abolitionists, will treat [abolitionist efforts] with much more practical, tangible favor ["Samuel Ringgold Ward to the Readers" 391–392; emphasis in original].

Ward vehemently attacked efforts of both Quakers and Garrisonians, believing that neither possessed the practical knowledge to shed light on the black experience. To further establish a bond between himself and his reading public, Ward attempted to disqualify all Quakers. According to his *ad personam*, Quakers "have yet to present the first iota of practical evidence of their regarding the negro as equal to themselves." Although Quakers did not join in the "low, vulgar ribald abuse of the negro," Ward believed that they "never do that which anyone can possible mistake for an absence of fashionable contempt for and disparagement of the negro." Ward justly argued that only a member of the race could be considered representative of race, not a member of the oppressors. His special authority as a former slave led him to further reveal that "no sect produces specimens of deeper, more determined, and what is no better, more religious negro-haters than does the sect of Friends of Quakers.... If nothing more is done for us than what Quakers in America do," he lamented, "God save us!" Turning his attention to the "Garrison Abolitionists," Ward believed that they "do not, except in words—mere words, believe in negro equality, nor is it a natural result of their movements to inspire negroes with any such idea, but rather to repress it." Blacks, he contended, put too much faith in both the Quakers and Garrisonians. "Just so far as that class of abolitionists have influence at all over our people," he bemoaned, "they repress rather than inspire the idea of equality" ["Modern Negro No. 2" 418, 420].

Some, such as Mary Ann Shadd Cary and William P. Powell, supported the efforts of white abolitionists. "They toiled in our cause when it cost something," Cary revealed in 1861 while living in Canada West, "and their noble sacrifices, crop out into a harvest of gratitude from the entire colored people" ("Mary Ann Shadd Cary to Robert Hamilton" 454). At the same time, though, Cary chastised the African American community for not taking control of their own destiny:

> Once upon a time brave men and women, with the bugle-blast of indignation, spoke out against wrong when it was perpetrated against black men, at the risk of the halter. I have a dim recollection of one noble man called William Lloyd Garrison in such peril. Why cannot there be a strong and manly voice now? ... why does not somebody speak OUT? Are not you recording the dead and buried? ["Mary Ann Shadd Cary to Robert Hamilton" 454].

Powell used metaphors to defend Garrison's antislavery sentiments. "When the abolition doctors disagree about prescribing medicine to cure the infectious *disease* of slavery," he lamented, "who shall we look to for a decision?" Praising Garrison's efforts (i.e., establishing a school in Boston; supporting women's involvement in the movement), Powell's metaphorical fusion advised abolitionists to support Garrison's efforts. "I warn all true-hearted abolitionists to buy and circulate the genuine medicine to cure the 'infectious disease of slavery'" ("William P. Powell to William Lloyd Garrison" 300; emphasis in original). Praises like these, however, were few.

Some Black abolitionist Jeremiahs, such as Peter Paul Simons, a black porter, declared war on what he considered "false philanthropy." On 23 April 1839, Simons challenged the significance of moral reformation. His speech delivered before the African Clarkson Association in New York included tenets of the jeremiad when he lamented "this moral elevation of our people is but a mere song, it is nothing but a conspicuous scarecrow designed expressly ... to hinder our people from acting collectively for themselves." Moral elevation, according to Simons, was "contrary to common sense or any plan of elevation laid down in record.... It is practised on our people as a means for to hinder them from acting in another way to obtain their rights." He fervently believed that the blacks did not fully realize the significance of the role they had to play in their own uplift. In this regard, he maintained that they could not afford to be permissive in the movement. "It is his time for us to act, for we must certainly see this deception, and all that is left for us to do is simply collective action, and we will profit our desires." Simons beckoned his brethren to utilize more aggressive approaches to combat racial discrimination. His prophecy illustrated the possible positive results of immediate emancipation, and how freed slaves will live in and contribute to society. He prophesied, "We must show ACTION! ACTION! *ACTION!* and our will to be, or not to be; this we study, this we much physically practice, and we will be in truth and independent people." His employment of prophecy was closely aligned with a particular vision of the future of blacks and of a particular political agenda designed to advance their plight. Moral elevation had done nothing to actually elevate blacks. Simons belittled the complexity between the relationship of slavery and true freedom. "This northern freedom is nothing but a nickname for northern slavery," he lamented. Blacks, according to Simons' assessment, had been deceived by abolitionists and colonizationists alike. He warned his brethren not to "domesticate yourself, do not be any man's servant, for it helps to degrade you" ("Speech by Peter Paul Simons" 289, 290, 292; emphasis in original). Simons argued that it was only through unity that the blacks could reach their human potential to become self-determined and autonomous.

Black abolitionist Jeremiahs' employment of the jeremiad not only spoke to their power to connect in a decisive and deliberate form of resistance but also represented the nature of social relations within the African American community. Therefore, white abolitionists such as Garrison, although they argued in favor of basic civil liberties for blacks, were still very much categorized as outsiders and could not fully employ the essence of the African American jeremiadic discourse. Houston A. Baker acknowledged the differences between

American and African American striving for selfhood. White America "could look to a Puritan ontology and sense of mission ... [to aide their] definition of self." Black America, Baker continued, did not have the ontological foundation because "white externality [offered] no ontological or ideological certainties" (29, 30). As with African American literature, then, the foremost ingredient of the African American jeremiad was that its architects must be African American.

"The rights of men are decided by the colour of their skin": Freedom, Retribution, and Civil Equality

The period of abolitionism that marked the end of the American revolutionary era and the beginning of the 1830s represented the commencement of a fundamental transformation in African American jeremiadic discourse precisely because America had won its independence from Great Britain. As they "elicited sympathy, tears, and increased interest in abolition" (Blassingame, *Slave Testimony* 123), Black abolitionist Jeremiahs viewed America's newfound freedoms as guarantees that their freedom from their oppressors was inevitable. The abolitionist movement gave them "a heightened sense of self-respect" (Quarles 41) and increased with astonishing momentum. What freedoms blacks were able to obtain were substandard. Peter Williams reminded his audience of this fact when he lamented:

> The freedom to which we have attained, is defective. Freedom and equality have been "put asunder." The rights of men are decided by the colour of their skin; and there is as much difference made between the rights of a free white man and a free coloured man, as there is between a free coloured man and a slave ["A Discourse Delivered in St. Phillip's Church" 296].

In an address delivered in Paisley, Scotland, on 17 April 1846, Frederick Douglass argued that the goal of abolitionism was to get white Americans to "speak about it, preach about it, and pray about it" because that was the only way to get them "heartily enlisted in the cause" ("British Influence on the Abolition" 220). Later in his career, however, Douglass expressed grief over white abolitionists' attitude concerning black elevation. They did not, he lamented, "like colored celebrations ... colored conventions ... colored antislavery fairs for the support of colored newspapers [or] any demonstrations whatever in which colored men take a leading part" ("If There Is No Struggle There Is No Progress" 309). Douglass felt that the best abolitionists were those who had felt, firsthand, slavery's tyranny. When he arrived in the North after his escape from Maryland's "peculiar institution," Douglass was amazed "to find that the abolitionists knew so much about [slavery]" and were so knowledgeable about:

[I]ts deadly effects as well as if they had lived in its midst. But though they can give you its history — though they can depict its horrors they cannot speak as I can from *experience*; they cannot refer you to a back covered with scars, as I can; for I have felt these wounds; I have suffered under the lash without the power of resisting. Yes, my blood has sprung out as the lash embedded itself in my flesh" ["I Have Come to Tell You Something about Slavery" 3; emphasis in original].

As their speeches were "filled with pathos and humor" (Blassingame, *Slave Testimony* 123), some Black Abolitionist Jeremiahs would use the jeremiad to further the paradoxical irony they faced. They realized that they had to identify and develop a consciousness concerning the evils of slavery, yet they could not find acceptable words to achieve this feat (Foner and Branham 80). On 1 January 1809, William Hamilton, a carpenter and president of the New York Society for Mutual Relief, raised these issues in his speech celebrating the abolition of the slave trade (Foner and Branham 80). The "man-stealing crew[s] ... sever [Africans] from all their enjoyments! ... who can recount half their sufferings, where is the artist that can delineate a full picture of their miseries? Their wretched situation baffles description," Hamilton lamented, "let us then withdraw from, and at once acknowledge our inability to the task" ("An Address to the New York African Society" 35). In his 10 February 1854 editorial published in the *Frederick Douglass' Paper*, William J. Watkins discussed how far the abolitionist movement had progressed. "The slave still mingles his groans with the soul-harrowing screams of the American Eagle," he lamented. Watkins suggested that the good intentions of abolitionists were sometimes more harmful. "Now, the accusation we make, in candor and sincerity, against the Abolitionists, as a class, is that they lack the moral courage to *actualize* their ideas." He lamented that defeating prejudice would pave the way to freedom. In order to achieve this, however, abolitionists had to first overcome their own prejudices. "If the Abolitionists wish to see this prejudice vanish like frost-work before the rising sun, they must begin the great work by 'conquering *their* prejudices.'" Even though the movement had, in Watkins' mind, made advancement by placing those who were "nominally free, upon the broad platform of Equality," Watkins still believed that blacks were "still the victims of the relentless ferocity of pro-slavery hate" ("One Thing Thou Lackest" 200, 203; emphasis in original).

During America's age of abolitionism, what had gracefully materialized in the works of Phyllis Wheatley and Jupiter Hammon as partial protest against the racial injustices of slavery during the postcolonial and pre–Revolutionary eras began to give birth to a form of social protest that was more militant and less cloaked. With the dawning of the abolitionists' movement in the early 1830s, the African American jeremiad, coupled with the religious fervor of the Second Great Awakening, began to impact the face of American abolitionism by transforming the "gradualist antislavery" notions of the latter 1700s to the "immediatist antislavery movement" which called for the immediate end of slavery (Ripley et al. 8). Ardent abolitionists, like Martin Delany, joined the antislavery regime because they thought that white abolitionists had withdrawn from pressing the instantaneous abolition of slavery to gradual emancipation. Delany believed that the first white antislavery society established begat this phenomena (Ullman 82). Delany mourned:

> [Whites] earnestly contended, and doubtless honestly meaning what they said, that they (the whites) had been our oppressors and injurers, they had obstructed our progress to the high positions of civilization, and now, it was their bounden duty to make full amends for the injuries thus inflicted on an unoffending people. They exhorted the Convention to cease; as they had laid on the burden, they would also take it off; as they had obstructed our pathway, they would remove the hindrance [qtd. in Ullman 82].

When Delany's jeremiad criticized American democracy, he no doubt furthered the divide between white and black abolitionist while declaring that he would "rather be a Heathen *freeman*, than a Christian *slave*" (*The Condition* 18; emphasis in original). In his 1852 *The Condition, Elevation, Emigration, and Destiny of the Colored People of the United States*, Delany furthered expressed his grief about white abolitionists' control over what he thought should have been a strong, unified black movement. "Politicians, religionists, conlonizationists, and abolitionists, have each and all, at different times, presumed to *think* for, dictate to, and *know* better what suited colored people, than they knew for themselves" (190; emphasis in original). Believing that the "*Anglo-Saxon* race, was the most inveterate enemy of the *colored races*, of whatever origin — whether African, Mongolian, Malayan, or Indian" ("Martin R. Delany to Frederick Douglass" 126; emphasis in original), Delany's conviction indicated that blacks must take the lead of their own elevation. For him, the African American jeremiad called for a black consciousness that rallied for a socio-politicized persona in the black community. Delany and other Black abolitionist Jeremiahs theorized that slavery obstructed the newly forming republic's "economic and social development" (Ripley et al. 8). Therefore, they sought means in which they could align their abolitionists' rhetoric with the principles of the jeremiad: freedom, retribution, and civil equality.

William Whipper argued:

> Therefore let us, like them, speaking of the abolitionists, obliterate from our minds the idea of revenge and from our hearts all wicked intentions toward each other and the world, and we shall be able through the blessings of Almighty God to do much to establish the principles of universal peace. Let us not think the world has no regard for our efforts — they are looking forward to them with intense interest and anxiety. The enemies of the abolitionists are exhibiting a regard for the power of their principles that they are unwilling to acknowledge ["Speech by William Whipper Delivered at the First African Presbyterian Church Philadelphia" 249].

Scattered throughout the abolitionist movement, the African American jeremiad, as illustrated in Whipper's speech, developed to support social reconstruction that was collective in scope. Although Whipper cultivated his pervasive ideas on a worldly horizon, he did not ignore the call for social changes that were needed for the African American community. Black abolitionist Jeremiahs sought to eradicate and modify in particular the socio-political and economic — and in some cases, the educational — conditions of blacks. Education for blacks was an important aspect of elevation for the race. Black activists endorsed a variety of training programs, including manual labor schools. When the National Council for the Colored People advocated a manual school, the American Industrial School, which was endorsed by activists such as Frederick Douglass, John Peck, and James McCune Smith, the school was approved by a seven to five vote (*BAP IV* 295). Some activists, however, such as Barbara Ann Steward, teacher and antislavery lecturer and daughter of black abolitionist Austin Steward, was disappointed by the seeming unwillingness of those who did not approve the school. "We are an unsettled, unstable people, destitute, in a great measure, of our homes that we call our own," she lamented. Blacks, according to Steward, were "looked down upon, by our more favored fellowmen, as ignorant and degraded." In her critique, Steward believed that slavery would not be an "all engrossing subject ... if there had been no [Frederick] Douglasses, [Samuel Ringgold] Wards, [Henry Highland] Garnets, bearing on their own persons the severity of the lash of slavery, and feeling perhaps too sensitively its degradation" ("Barbara Ann Steward to Frederick Douglass" 297).

Although many Black Jeremiah abolitionists did not fully trust their white counterparts, they realized, however, that the elimination and transformation of their particular socio- political and economic status would only come to pass if their ability to change the social associations with their white counterparts was improved. Some quickly came to realize that their white counterparts did not share the same urgency on issues of prejudice as they did (*BAP IV* 198). William J. Watkins, for example, charged his abolitionist brethren to "begin the great work" of "'conquering *their* prejudices'" and live out the doctrines they so publicize. Watkins' allegation toward white abolitionist who "sympathize[d] with" him but who were not willing to take any action was because "they lack the moral courage to *actualize* their ideas" ("One Thing Thou Lackest" 203; emphasis in original). At their 1835 Fifth Annual Convention for the Improvement of the Free People of Color in the United States, William Whipper, Alfred Niger, and Augustus Price, concluded:

> We will endeavour to establish in our people a correct knowledge of their own immortal worth, their high derivation as rational, moral and intelligent beings. We shall appeal to them to abandon their prejudices against all complexion and bury them in oblivion, and endeavour to live in the same country as children of one common father, and as brethren possessing the same holy, religious faith, and with a zeal determined on the promotion of great and glorious objects.... We will not stoop to contend with those who style us inferior beings.... We claim to be American citizens, and we will not waste our time by holding converse with those who deny us this privilege, unless they first prove that man is not a citizen of that country in which he was born and reared ["Address by William Whipper, Alfred Niger, and Augustus Price" 150–151].

Therefore, the pursuit of political recognition through jeremiadic discourse meant that blacks during antebellum America were not always confronting the essence of institutional hierarchy that was responsible for their conditions. Some Black Jeremiah abolitionists, like Watkins, Whipper, Niger, and Price, understood that their pursuit for political recognition would result in public redress.

David Walker and Nat Turner: The Jeremiadic Rhetoric of the "Militant Abolitionist Journalist" and the "Insurrectionary Commander"

Of the few blacks during the early republic who were able to take advantage of opportunities arising from the mounting political activism, David Walker, the "militant abolitionist journalist" (Howard-Pitney 13), was one of the most prolific activists who inquired, "Have [whites] not to make their appearance before the tribunal of Heaven, to answer for the deeds done in the body, as well as we? Have we any other Master by Jesus Christ alone?" (*Appeal* 16). Born in Wilmington, North Carolina, possibly in 1796 or 1797, Walker was the son of slave father and a free mother. Since the preexisting laws stipulated that a black child born to a free black mother was free, Walker did not feel the lash of the whip as others had. Although shielded, in a way, from slavery's clutches, Walker still witnessed its effects on the enslaved, perhaps even on his father. Thus Walker's voice in his *Appeal* took a more aggressive position than his white and black counterparts' who promoted moral suasion. Instead of offering a way to make white religion work for blacks in his intricate jeremiadic structure, Walker's jeremiad offered whites a way to be saved from God's wrath while offering hope for blacks. His radical pamphlet aggressively attacked slavery as well as the colonization movement. As he filled the role of a Messiah, encouraging blacks to take their liberation into their own hands, Walker's *Appeal* marked a transformation in African American jeremiadic discourse, not because it astonished abolitionist when it arrived on the antislavery ticket at the apex of abolitionist movement, but because more straightforwardly than any text prior, Walker's convictions condemned white Americans for their involvement in the degradation of black people. Nothing about Walker's text was cloaked as it had been in the creative verse of Phyllis Wheatley and Jupiter Hammon; Walker did not take the time to chastise ideologies of documents in the days of James Forten, Sr.; instead, Walker's prophetic vision vehemently enlightened white America of the judgment which he felt was to transpire for their insidious practice. Therefore, Walker's position expressed in his *Appeal* was an archetypal example of what African American jeremiadic discourse would propose at the onset of the abolition movement in the 1830s. Walker concluded Article III,

"Our Wretchedness in Consequence of the Preachers of the Religion of Jesus Christ," by informing his "brethren" that redemption was promised to them and that if white America repented for their sins, black trepidation would cease to exist:

> Will the Lord suffer this people to go on much longer, taking his holy name in vain? Will he not stop them, PREACHERS and all? O Americans! Americans!! I call God — I call angels—I call men to witness that your DESTRUCTION is at hand, and will be speedily consummated unless you REPENT [*Appeal* 55–56; emphasis in original].

Instead of calling for collective action against oppression in parts of his *Appeal*, Walker laced his plead with his philosophy that each individual black person had to use his/her own proficiencies in eliminating the degradation of multitudes of the race (Hinks 88). The goal of the *Appeal* was to encourage pride and give hope that change was inevitable. Early in the tract he revealed:

> And as the inhuman system of *slavery,* is the *source* from which most of our miseries proceed, I shall begin with that *curse to nations,* which has spread terror and devastation through so many nations of antiquity, and which is raging to such a pitch at the present day in Spain and in Portugal. It had one tug in England, in France, and in the United States of America; yet the inhabitants thereof, do not learn wisdom, and erase it entirely from their dwellings and from all with whom they have to do. The fact is, the labour of slaves comes so cheap to the avaricious usurpers, and is (as they think) of such great utility to the country where it exists, that those who are actuated by sordid avarice only, overlook the evils, which will as sure as the Lord lives, follow after the good. In fact, they are so happy to keep in ignorance and degradation, and to receive the homage and the labour of the slaves, they forget that God rules in the armies of heaven and among the inhabitants of the earth, having his ears continually open to the cries, tears and groans of his oppressed people; and being a just and holy Being will at one day appear fully in behalf of the oppressed, and arrest the progress of the avaricious oppressors; for although the destruction of the oppressors God may not effect by the oppressed, yet the Lord our God will bring other destructions upon them —for not unfrequently will he cause them to rise up one against another, to be split and divided, and to oppress each other, and sometimes to open hostilities with sword in hand. Some may ask, what is the matter with this united and happy people?— Some say it is the cause of political usurpers, tyrants, oppressors, &c. But has not the Lord an oppressed and suffering people among them? Does the Lord condescend to hear their cries and see their tears in consequence of oppression? Will he let the oppressors rest comfortably and happy always? Will he not cause the very children of the oppressors to rise up against them, and oftimes put them to death? "God works in many ways his wonders to perform" [*Appeal* 5–6; emphasis in original].

Walker's message was no doubt heard by many blacks, but hardly understood by them. African Americans had to deal with the obstacles of having no education and no ability to compete in the budding republic. His *Appeal* illustrated how involved he felt blacks were, or should have been, in their liberation. Walker straightforwardly "recognize[d] the judgements [*sic*] of God among the Spaniards" for having initiated the slave trade in the New World. Slavery was "*the principal*" of the "fierceness with which they cut each other's throats"

(*Appeal* 15; emphasis in original), and that should have served as a warning to their successors that the institution would become detrimental to societies to come. In his *Appeal*, Walker offered Americans a prophetic vision meant to bring about social change. The Almighty, which was in heaven, "will give you a Hannibal," who, as Walker suggested, was "one of the greatest generals of antiquity, who defeated and cut off so many thousands of the white Romans or murderers" (*Appeal* 30).

The onset of the 1830s gave birth to a more radical form of African American jeremaidic rhetoric. Although some of their moral suasion and moral reform was bleached in religious ideologies of the Second Great Awakening, it began to quickly and more ardently chastise white America for their treatment of blacks and continue the call for black political participation even to the means of insurrection. Slave revolutions were not remote, unique phenomena (Aptheker 11). As this chapter suggests, from the emergence of the institution in America, slaves lashed out in one way or another. In attempts to shrug off the restraints of the "social death"[1] of racial subjugation that white Americans imposed on them, the jeremiadic discourse of the revolutionaries was interesting in that much of it was not recorded or written down but the rhetoric called for immediate action. Jupiter Hammon had previously asked his brethren to "stand still" and see a higher power's salvation at hand which he believed would result in justice, civil liberties, and political participation. Seeking a common ground between enslavement and radical action toward enslavement, Hammon suggested that if his "brethren" waited for salvation, the day would come when the restraints of slavery would cease to exist. There was no reason to wait, however, as far as insurrectionists were concerned. There had to be, the commanders in chief believed, an immediate forged resolution to black enslavement. Religious zealousness of activist such as Hammon seemingly found refuge in the revolutionaries' rhetoric during the age of abolitionism. How, then, was it diverse and what constituted this variation?

Nat Turner, who William Wells Brown christened "the Spartacus of the Southampton revolt" ("The History of the Haitian Revolution" 248), — one of the bloodiest slave revolts in American history — decided to help mold a solution, or as Henry Highland Garnet would urge 13 years later, "die freemen than live to be slave[s]." Turner seemed to have profoundly absorbed "all the best elements of evangelical Southern white religion, all the proper anesthesia against the knowledge of who he had been, what he had lost, and what there was to regain" (Harding 77). The moral suasion and reformation discourse of popular abolitionists did not have a place in Turner's discourse. Likewise, Jupiter Hammon's "stand still" ideology transcended biblical meaning for Turner. His actions acknowledged that there was simply no easy solution to obtain a balance between the biblical justification and perpetuation of slavery and social change, thus politicizing his struggle. This transformation from Hammon's seemingly passive jeremiadic rhetoric to Turner's persuasive jeremiadic discourse was fueled by the countless statutes and edicts endorsed to control Southerners' rights to slaveholding. For example, in 1820, Washington DC issued a charter that duly authorized whites "to restrain and prohibit the nightly and other disorderly meetings of slaves, free Negroes, and mulattos, and to punish such slaves by whipping, not exceeding forty stripes, or by imprisonment not exceeding six calendar months, for any one offence."[2] The 1822 conspiracy of former slave Denmark Vesey, a carpenter who had won the lottery and purchased his freedom, was revealed; Vesey and his coconspirators were hung for their perceived treachery. One year later, Mississippi enacted a law that prohibited teaching reading and writing of more than five slaves or free blacks. Other "black codes," as they were later dubbed, found a place in the Southern traditions of subjugation. In 1830, hope for blacks was further manifested, however, when the first of what would be the annual Convention of the People of Colour convened in Philadelphia to coordinate African American resistance to slavery and discrimination in the free states. One year after the Convention assembled, Turner, the "faithful black exhorter and singer of spiritual songs [who] was of great value in the eyes of the white world" (Harding 78), forged his revolution, just seven months after William Lloyd Garrison's inaugural edition of *The Liberator*. There is no evidence in Turner's *Confessions*, however, that he was aware of, or acted accordingly to any of the aforementioned developments. Turner's actions, nonetheless, waged war against the Southern sovereign during the apex of the age of abolitionism. Turner's discourse would also differ from that of his counterpart abolitionists because he and his cohorts "lacked faith in a higher power than man" (Starling 100). What Turner's jeremiadic discourse did not lack, in contrast, was the ability to move the oppressed far beyond the scriptural acceptance of a higher power. The evidence lay in his affirmation of his so-called crimes.

Turner's 1831 *Confessions*, laced with jeremiadic discourse while recorded and written by lawyer Thomas Gray, provided an authoritative voice and political vehicle for both black and white abolitionists equally. The influence of Turner's rebellion / *Confessions* had a profound effect on the growth and development of the African American jeremiad. After receiving information about Turner's revolution, Garrison found ways to honor Turner's "first wailings of bereavement." Although, as stated earlier, Garrison could not represent the pure essence of African American jeremiadic discourse, he declared that "the first drops of blood, which are but the prelude to a deluge from the gathering clouds, have fallen." Believing that his "prophecy" published in the first edition of *The Liberator* in January of that year had become a reality, Garrison suggested that the spilling of blood, be it white or black, was the only way to achieve equality between the races. "The oppressor and the oppressed equal at last in death — what a spectacle!"[3] Henry Highland Garnet held that Turner "was goaded to desperation by wrong and [the] injustice[s]" of slavery ("An Address to the Slaves" 95). Charles Lenox Remond believed that Turner "had no place in life under [slavery's] protecting aegis." Because of his deeds, Remond mourned, whites thought that the commanding officer of the insurrection "is only Nat Turner, the miserable negro" ("Speech by Charles Lenox Remond, Delivered at Marlboro Chapel," 443). Frederick Douglass, too, eulogized Turner's actions. Douglass believed that since "abolition followed close on the heels of insurrection in the West Indies,[4] ... Virginia was" on no account closer to liberation "than when General Turner kindled the fires of insurrection at Southampton" ("The Significance of Emancipation in the West Indies" 190). Turner's fight for freedom in his *Confessions* substantiated his jeremiadic rhetoric to lead a movement for the freedom of his people since he believed that God had spoken to him on the subject of black liberation:

> Struck with that particular passage which says: "Seek ye the kingdom of Heaven and all things shall be added unto you." I reflected much on this passage, and prayed daily for light on this subject — As I was praying one day at my plough, the spirit spoke to me, saying "Seek ye the kingdom of Heaven and all things shall be added unto you" [*Confessions* 9].

The spirit that spoke to Turner was the same "Spirit that spoke to the prophets in former days" (*Confessions* 9). Through his message of liberation, Turner, "once harshened and honed in the burning river" (Harding 78), believed in, as it would seem, the power of his interpretation of God's message which differed vastly from what white Christians advocated. He felt that he had to respond to this urgent mission. In his orations to the slaves on his master's plantation, Turner positioned his jeremiadic rhetoric in a revolutionary tone that David Walker had employed two years earlier in his *Appeal*. Just before Turner and his "band of black avenging angels" (Harding 97) set out on their quest to slaughter, decapitate, and eviscerate approximately 60 whites, Turner assured his cohorts that their purpose was not to shed blood shamelessly as the oppressors had done:

> Friends and brothers, we are to commence a great work to-night! Our race is to be delivered from slavery, and God has appointed us as the men to do his bidding; and let us be worthy of our calling. I am told to slay all the whites we encounter, without regard to age or sex.... Remember, we do not go forth for the sake of blood and carnage; but it is necessary that, in the commencement of this revolution, all the whites we meet shall die, until we have an army strong enough to carry on the war upon a Christian basis. Remember that ours is not a war for robbery, nor to satisfy our passions; it is a *struggle for freedom*. Ours must be deeds, not words. Then let's away to the scene of action [qtd. in G. W. Williams 87–88; emphasis in original].

In his attempt to provide a viable solution to black enslavement, Turner's biblical exegesis sought to compel slaveholders to acknowledge and take full responsibility for their transgressions since "God has appointed us as the men to do his bidding." For Turner, the African American jeremiad became a new theodicy, a force of liberation language conveyed in his moralizing exhortations to his "friends and brothers." Through his adamant belief in retribution and liberation, Turner's jeremiad illustrated that liberty was a privilege every man should enjoy, making Turner's fight exceedingly political in nature.

Moral Suasionists or Militant Abolitionist Jeremiahs? Frederick Douglass and Henry Highland Garnet

As the African American jeremiad appeared in a variety of modes, from its scathing attacks on America's religious principles to its critical arguments on America's political ideologies, it took form in the protests of two of America's most profound Black abolitionist Jeremiahs. Frederick Douglass' career as the nineteenth century's "preeminent black Jeremiah" (Howard-Pitney 17) began shortly after he attended an August 1841 American Anti-Slavery Society convention held on Nantucket Island, just three years after his escape to freedom. Eagerly looking forward to the meeting, Douglass called it his "holiday" (qtd. in McFeely 86), his period of exemption from the burdens of work. Little did he know, however, his paradoxical "holiday" would be the turning point of his jeremiadic career and would be the day he worked the hardest to appeal to his audience for acceptance and, at the same time, raise a consciousness about black degradation. While he waited to deliver his address, Douglass anxiously sat calling up for the "courage to rise and speak" (McFeely 88). In the Preface to Douglass' *Narrative*, abolitionist William Lloyd Garrison, in an effort to characterize Douglass as a messiah, wrote that Douglass hesitantly approached the podium with the unease and anxiety that are "necessarily the attendants of the sensitive mind in such a novel position" (*Narrative* 5). During the speech, Douglass took the time to apologize for his lack of knowledge, but at the same time he took advantage of this moment to be honest and remind his audience that slavery "was a poor school for the human intellect and heart" (*Narrative* 5). After Douglass recounted his experiences with America's "peculiar institution," Garrison wrote:

> As soon as he had taken his seat ... I reminded the audience of the peril which surrounded this self-emancipated young man at the North, — even in Massachusetts, on the soil of the Pilgrim Fathers, among the descendants of revolutionary sires; and I appealed to them, whether they would ever allow him to be carried back into slavery, — law or no law, constitution or no constitution. Their response was unanimous and in the thunder-tones—"NO!" "Will you succor and protect him as a brother-man—a resident of the old Bay State?" "YES!" shouted the whole mass, with an energy so startling, that the ruthless tyrants south of Mason and Dixon's line might almost have heard the night burst of feeling [*Narrative* 5–6].

His audience, mostly Quakers; his story, that of a runaway slave; his abilities, those of a novice; his speech, the only one from which — Douglass retrospectively acknowledged — he could "'not remember a single connected sentence'" (qtd. in McFeely 88). After gaining the knowledge and wisdom that set him on the road to liberation, Douglass revealed that his "very discontentment" that had been "predicted would follow my learning to read had already come, to torment and sting my soul to unutterable anguish" (*Narrative* 40). Douglass concluded that learning to read appeared to be more of a punishment than a blessing:

> The silver trump of freedom had roused my soul to eternal wakefulness. Freedom now appeared, to disappear no more forever. It was heard in every sound, and seen in everything. It was ever present to torment me with a sense of my wretched condition. I saw nothing without seeing it, I heard nothing without hearing it, and felt nothing without feeling it. It looked from every star, it smiled in every calm, breathed in every wind, and moved in every storm [*Narrative* 40].

Douglass' form of liberation theology was inextricably linked with jeremiadic discourse: his lament served as a warning to his "fellow-slaves" regarding their plight if they chose the same path as he had done. Douglass did not, nor could he at this point in his career, offer them a viable solution to their oppression. What he could do, however, was offer them hope that their liberation must start within them, within their own consciousnesses.

First believing in Garrison's "moral suasion" tactics, Douglass would later adopt the philosophy that African Americans would never obtain the civil liberties that their white counterparts enjoy unless they took their emancipation into their own hands. Blacks had to be, Douglass felt, at the forefront of their own liberation movements. In his 1857 "If There Is No Struggle There Is No Progress" speech, Douglass told his audience:

> The general sentiment of mankind is that a man who will not fight for himself, when he has the means of doing so, is not worth being fought for by others, and this sentiment is just. For a man who does not value freedom for himself will never value it for others, or put himself to any inconvenience to gain it for others.... The poet was as true to common sense as to poetry when he said, *Who would be free, themselves must strike blow*[5] [308–09; emphasis in original].

Douglass received much criticism from the Garrisonians for going against their "moral suasion" philosophy. He lamented that the "struggle may be a moral one, or it may be a physical one, and it may be both moral and physical, but it must be a struggle." Acknowledging that "power concedes nothing without demand" ("If There Is No Struggle There Is No Progress" 310), Douglass totally washed his hands of the Garrisonians' moral suasionist views:

> Men may not get all they pay for in this world, but they must certainly pay for all they get. If we ever get free from the oppressions and wrongs heaped upon us, we must pay for their removal. We must do this by labor, by suffering, by sacrifice, and if needs be, by our lives and the lives of others ["If There Is No Struggle There Is No Progress" 310].

Either "with words or blows, or with both" ("If There Is No Struggle There Is No Progress" 310), Douglass maintained, blacks had to lead the fight rather than live under whites—abolitionists alike—as second-rate sympathizers (Foner 308).

Perhaps one of the best illustrations of the African American jeremiadic tradition, although radical in nature and positioned in political discourse, appears in the orations of Henry Highland Garnet, who, like Douglass, was a supporter of moral suasion but later urged more radical black political participation. Garnet believed that "earnest, Godly, men" were needed to "go forth *among the people*—to sympathise with [blacks], and teach [blacks] in divine things and to encourage [blacks] in everything that belongs to well ordered living" ("Letter to Simeon S. Jocelyn" 36; emphasis in original). In his unwavering jeremiadic fashion, Garnet advocated resistance to white oppression and offered slaves hope for a brighter future, but only if they took their liberation into their own hands. The jeremiad's position in Garnet's message to Americans at the 1843 Negro Convention illustrated that America was in dire need of social change. As the audience sat in excited anticipation, "knowing the speech they were about to hear would be controversial" (Johnson and Smith 383), Garnet startled America with what was probably the most militant and uncompromising idea of the entire antislavery campaign — a general slave revolt. Unnerving even white abolitionists, Garnet remained adamantly pessimistic about the needed manifestations in the America idea of democracy:

> The diabolical injustice by which your liberties are cloven down, NEITHER GOD, NOR ANGELS, OR JUST MEN, COMMAND YOU TO SUFFER FOR A SINGLE MOMENT. THEREFORE IT IS YOUR SOLEMN AND IMPERATIVE DUTY TO USE EVERY MEANS, BOTH MORAL, INTELLECTUAL, AND PHYSICAL THAT PROMISES SUCCESS. If a band of heathen men should attempt to enslave a race of Christians, and to place their children under the influence of some false religion, surely Heaven would frown upon the men who would not resist such aggression, even to death. If, on the other hand, a band of Christians should attempt to enslave a race of heathen men, and to entail slavery upon them, and to keep them in heathenism in the midst of Christianity, the God of heaven would smile upon every effort which the injured might make to disenthrall themselves ["An Address to the Slaves" 93; emphasis in original].

Unquestionably, Garnet's rhetoric was convincing. In his "An Address to the Slaves of the United States of America," Garnet reminded his black audience, "We have been contented in sitting and mourning over your sorrows, earnestly hoping that before this day your sacred liberty would have been restored. But we hoped in vain" ("An Address to the Slaves" 90). It is time, Garnet said, to stop "sitting still"—an argument that Martin Delany would also prefer—and "hoping and sympathizing." "The star of hope is slowly and steadily rising above the horizon" ("The Past and the Present" 28). Garnet took innovative perceptions about slavery and told his slave audience that liberation was impossible without the "shedding of blood." Said he:

> You had better all die —*die immediately* than live lives as slaves and entail wretchedness upon your posterity. If you are to be free in the generation, here is your only hope. However much you and all of us may desire it, there is not much hope of Redemption without the shedding of blood.... Where is the blood of your fathers? Has it run out of your veins? ... Awake, awake, millions of voices are calling you. Your dead fathers speak to you from their graves ["An Address to the Slaves" 94, 96; emphasis in original].

Garnet's jeremiadic rhetoric called for slaves willing to "*die immediately.*" For him, insurrection was inevitable; as Nat Turner had done 13 years before him,

Garnet saw active resistance to oppression as an element of the price to pay for freedom. "If it is our power to destroy the evils, and we do not," he argued, "then much of our own blood will be found on us" ("The Past and the Present" 18). Vehemently attacking the very institution that was responsible for black degradation, Garnet recommended that slaves avail themselves of every prospect to become politically involved in their liberation. Their political participation was essential in the pleading of their "own case." Garnet reminded his audience of this fact when he charged that life for them could not possibly get any worse:

> Brethren, the time has come when you must act for yourselves. It is an old and true saying, that "if hereditary bondmen would be free, they must themselves strike the blow." You can plead your own case, and do the work of emancipation better than any others.... Let every slave throughout the land do this, and the days of slavery are numbered. You cannot be more oppressed that you have been — You cannot suffer greater cruelties than you have already. RATHER DIE FREEMEN, THAN LIVE TO BE SLAVES. Remember that you are THREE MILLIONS.... It is in your power so to torment the God-cursed slaveholders, that they will be glad to let you go free.... Let your motto be RESISTANCE! RESISTANCE! RESISTANCE!— No oppressed people have ever secured their liberty without resistance [rptd. in *Walker's Appeal and Garnet's Address* 93, 95, 96; emphasis in original].

Garnet's pursuit of political redress through jeremiadic discourse attempted to challenge power relations between blacks and their oppressors. Garnet was convinced that if whites would not take the liberation of blacks more seriously, the battle for liberation belonged in the hands of the slaves. It was their essential duty to exercise this right, he suggested, as he reminded them that they were "THREE MILLIONS" strong and that, with those numbers, there was no possible way they could fail in their mission. Garnet felt that *"the principles of progress in the ways of truth, and resistance to tyranny should be the bases of all our public demonstrations, and numerical representations"* ("The Past and the Present" 20–21; emphasis in original).

In his "The Past and the Present Condition, and the Destiny, or The Colored Race: A Discourse Delivered at the Fifteenth Anniversary of the Female Benevolent Society of Troy," Garnet's jeremiadic discourse attacked black degradation on another front. He beckoned blacks to shed the unspeakable burden of the search for their identity because it further complicated the issues of freedom, liberation, and retribution:

> Let there be no strife between us, for we are brethren, and we must rise or fall together. How unprofitable it is for us to spend our golden moments in long and solemn debate upon the questions whether we shall be called *"Africans" "Colored Americans,"* or *"Africo Americans,"* or *"Blacks."* The question should be, my friends, *shall we arise and act like men, and cast off this terrible yoke*? ["The Past and the Present Condition" 19; emphasis in original].

Their searching for selfhood, Garnet suggested, was partly responsible for their degradation. Garnet saw the African American community "divided by party feuds" and "torn in pieces by dissensions" ("The Past and the Present Condition"

18). His jeremiadic rhetoric, however, caused debate among some abolitionists because it questioned the political foundation of whites' power. Therefore, he advocated that blacks become "acquainted with the arts and sciences and agricultural pursuits" as these will "elevate any people and sever any chain." Blacks should also uphold "a national and patriotic sentiment and attachment" to America. His "sentiment and attachment" to his "home," led him to "loathe her slavery," but "pray Heaven that ere long she may wash away her guilt in tears or repentance" ("The Past and the Present Condition" 29). Garnet concluded his speech drenched with his pro–Americanism:

> I love every inch of soil which my feet pressed in my youth, and I mourn because the accursed shade of slavery rests upon it. I love my country's flag, and I hope that soon it will be cleansed of its stains, and be hailed by all nations as the emblem of freedom and independence ["The Past and the Present Condition" 29].

Garnet's patriotism for his America, however, was not enough to keep him focused on remaining there. The very next year, 1849, Garnet encouraged emigration to Liberia, an African country that had declared its independence two years earlier and opened its doors to free blacks from America. Garnet's Ethiopianism surfaced during his second trip to Great Britain to gain support for the African Civilization Society. Honoring Africa as the progenitors of civilization and the debt England owed to Africa, Garnet revealed that "the cheering prophecy was to be fulfilled, 'Ethiopia shall quickly stretch forth her hands unto God'" ("Speech by Henry Highland Garnet, Delivered at the Music Hall" 516). Black abolitionist Jeremiahs called for the same respect and acknowledgment; they drew, however, some strength from the repressive reality of other oppressed groups. David Walker's jeremiad, in his *Appeal*, provided an excellent example of how blacks grew fuel from other oppressed groups. He wrote:

> The sufferings of the Helots among the Spartans, were somewhat severe, it is true, but to say that theirs, were as severe as ours among the Americans, I do most strenuously deny—for instance, can any man show me an article on a page of ancient history which specifies, that, the Spartans chained, and handcuffed the Helots, and dragged them from their wives and children, children from their parents, mothers from their suckling babes, wives from their husbands, driving them from one end of the country to the other? ... Have they [Christians] not made provisions for the Greeks, and Irish? Nations who have never done the least thing for them, while *we*, who have enriched their country with our blood and tears— have dug up gold and silver for them and their children, from generation to generation, and are in more miseries than any other people under heaven, are not seen, but by comparatively, a handful of the American people? [*Appeal* 23–24; emphasis in original].

In his attempt to unify blacks, Garnet argued that, instead of feuding, their time and efforts could be better spent by assembling in a similar manner that which "animated the Irish people," who "were led by that giant of freedom Daniel O'Connell, which should be, to use his own words, to 'agitate, and agitate, and agitate until the chains of the three million's are broken.'"[6] With his alluding to O'Connell, it seemed—five years after his didactic speech before the convention where he advocated bloodshed — that Garnet himself now had a more political agenda in mind than a revolutionary one. "The besetting sins of the Anglo-Saxon race are," Garnets lamented, "the love of gain and the love of power" ("The Past and the Present Condition" 20, 27). As personified in Garnet's speech, Black abolitionist Jeremiahs drew from a variety of sources when utilizing the jeremiad in their fight for retribution and justice. Given Daniel O'Connell's "record on the slavery question and his influence among Irish everywhere," it was expected that the American abolitionist would make use of his rhetorical appeals (Ignatiev 8). In his fight for justice in Ireland, O'Connell, as early as 1829 united his condemnation of slavery with assaults on American democracy (Ignatiev 7). O'Connell told his Irish brethren:

> Let America, in the fullness of her pride wave on high her banner of freedom and its blazing stars.... In the midst of their laughter and their pride, I point them to the negro children screaming for their mother from whose bosom they have been torn.... Let them hoist the flag of liberty, with the whip and rack on one side, and the start of freedom upon the other [qtd. in Ignatiev 7].

O'Connell had not visited America and witnessed her cruelty to her black populace and had no intentions of visiting as long as slavery existed. His sentiments, however, provoked antipathy by some Irish Americans who felt that O'Connell was not addressing the issues they faced in America on a daily basis. When Irish emigrates came to America, fleeing class subjugation, their conditions were "comparable to those of an American slave" (Ignatiev 7–8, 2).

Some Black abolitionist Jeremiahs, however, would help to fill in the gaps that Irish Americans felt O'Connell left untouched. In 1853, Douglass lamented the backsliding of American civility on Irish Americans. Upon arriving to American, "the Irish people, warm hearted, generous, and sympathizing with the oppressed everywhere," Douglass told his audience, "are instantly taught ... to hate and despise the colored people ... they are taught to believe that we eat the bread which of right belongs to them ... the Irish American ... will find that in assuming our avocation he also has assumed our degradation" ("A Nation in the Midst of the Nation" 433). However, the Irish had to develop their own jeremiads in their fight from British hegemony in Ireland, and in their fight for justice and acceptability in America. Douglass told his audience that "When O'Connell, with all Ireland at his back, was supposed to be contending for the just rights and liberties of Ireland, the sympathies of mankind were with him, and even his enemies were compelled to respect his patriotism" ("If There is no Struggle There is no Progress" 309).

The Infamous Laws of American Democracy

The African American jeremiad required its architects to use vivid portrayals and well-defined language. By the time the country was on the brink of civil war, William and Ellen Craft realized this and attacked American democracy from another angle: the laws that augmented the rights of slaveholders. For example, at the onset of their *Running a Thousand Miles for Freedom; or, the Escape of William and Ellen Craft from Slavery*, the Crafts reveal the laws of Louisiana, South Carolina, and the "Constitution of Georgia," in part to justify their quest for the abolishment of the institution of slavery:

> According to the law of Louisiana, "A slave is one who is in the power of a master to whom he belongs. The master may sell him, dispose of his person, his industry, and his labour; he can do nothing, possess nothing, nor acquire anything but what must belong to his master"... In South Carolina it is expressed in the following language: — "Slaves shall be deemed, sold, taken, reputed and judged in law to be *chattels personal* in the hands of their owners and possessors, and their executors, administrators, and assigns, *to all intents, constructions, and purposes whatsoever*" ... The Constitution of Georgia has the following ... "Any person who shall maliciously dismember or deprive a slave of life, shall suffer such punishment as would be inflicted in case the like offence had been committed on a free white person, and on the like proof, except in case of insurrection of such slave, and unless SUCH DEATH SHOULD HAPPEN BY ACCIDENT IN GIVING SUCH SLAVE MODERATE CORRECTION" [*Running a Thousand Miles* 13–14; emphasis in original].

In his 1842 *Narrative by Lewis G. Clarke*, Lewis G. Clarke contended:

> Kentucky is the best of slave States, in respect to the laws, but the masters manage to fix things pretty much to their own liking. The law don't allow 'em to brand a slave, or cut off his ear; but if they happen to switch it off with a cow-hide, nobody says anything about it. Though the laws are better than in other States, they ain't anyways equal" [*Narrative* 393].

In the *Narrative of the Life and Adventures of Henry Bibb, An American Slave, Written by Himself*, Henry Bibb argued against a 1770 law enacted by the state of Georgia, which stated:

> That is shall not be lawful for any number of free negroes, molattoes or mestinos,[7] or even slaves in company with white persons, to meet together for the purpose of mental instruction, either before the rising of the sun or after the going down of the same.... Similar laws exist in most of the slave States, and patrols are sent out after night and on the Sabbath day to enforce them. They go through their respective towns to prevent slaves from meeting for religious worship or mental instruction [*Narrative* 31–32].

It is actions like these that led Bibb to lament that without "the regulation and law of American Slavery" that was "sanctioned by the Government of the United States," America would not exist. He also concluded that "almost the whole moral, political, and religious power of the nation are in favor of slavery and aggression, and against liberty and justice" (*Narrative* 32). Bibb would agree with Clarke that Kentucky had the most lenient laws regarding punishment of slaves:

> The laws of Kentucky, my native State, with Maryland and Virginia, which are said to be the mildest slave States in the Union, noted for their humanity, Christianity

and democracy, declare that "Any slave, for rambling in the night, or riding horseback without leave, or running away, may be punished by whipping, cropping, and branding in the cheek, or otherwise, not rendering, him unfit for labor." "Any slave convicted of petty larceny, murder, or wilfully [sic] burning of dwelling houses, may be sentenced to have his right hand cut off; to be hanged in the usual manner, or the head severed from the body, the body divided into four quarters, and head and quarters stuck up in the most public place in the county, where such act was committed" [*Narrative* 35].

However, after Bibb's second attempt at freedom was spoiled by the "imfamous [sic] laws of the Commonwealth of Ohio," he later revealed that "for the awful crime of stealing a jackass" and "running away" was met with "death by the law when committed by a negro." Bibb lamented the fact that he was "regarded as property, and so was the ass." In his reasoning, however, Bibb suggested that he "thought if one piece of property took off another, there could be no law violated in the act; no more sin committed in this, than if one jackass had rode off another." Bibb suffered "the penalty of a slaveholder's broken law" (*Narrative* 62, 122, 130). When juxtaposed against the nineteenth-century rhetoric of human freedom and equality, the "broken law[s]" that Bibb, the Crafts, and Clarke exposed, illustrated the hypocrisy of common antebellum notions of "race, class, and gender" (Butterfield 29). The governing laws of the land should be concerned with the oppressed, not curtailing the rights of the oppressor. The Crafts, Clarke, and Bibb promptly realized that they could use the jeremiad to speak to African American torment and dehumanization with an authoritative voice by exposing America's democratic ideologies that were used to justify their dehumanization. By filtering such injustices through this powerful Euro-American socio-political lens, African Americans gained strategic control over their own destiny. The African American jeremiad helped to alter society's socio-political and moral positions on the unjust treatments of blacks in hopes that it would help create a socio-economic venue for blacks to elevate and take their rightful place in society.

The African American Jeremiad Advocated Temperance

The African American jeremiad developed in numerous avenues to curtail black oppression. During the 1830s, the temperance movement was viewed by Black abolitionist Jeremiahs in the framework of moral improvement. They believed that by refraining from consuming intoxicating beverages, blacks would achieve the admiration of whites and thereby prejudice and discrimination would eventually fade. Temperance was an "essential component of moral reform." Sobriety, argued Black abolitionist Jeremiahs, would characterize "black moral advancement" (*BAP III* 17). "We shall advocate temperance in all things," encouraged William Whipper, Alfred Niger, and Augustus Price, "and total abstinence from all alcoholic liquors" ("Address by William Whipper, Alfred Niger, and Augustus Price" 149). Temperance, they believed, was an essential vehicle to elevate the masses to a consciousness concerning oppression. To rid black communities of this evil, William Whipper utilized the jeremiad to warn his black audience against falling victim to the "*tyrant* intemperance — a *demon* more ferocious" in its "character and despotic" in its "cruelty of" "infliction and the destructiveness of" its influence. In his "Speech by William Whipper Delivered before the Colored Temperance Society of Philadelphia," Whipper attacked white racism and discrimination by suggesting that for the injustices inflicted on blacks through slavery and intemperance, whites "derserve[s] the condign punishment of an insulted Providence, and the just execration of the wise and good." Whipper continued, "Even Negro slavery, horrible as it is, painted in its most ignominious colors, and ferreted out in all its degrading consequences, is but a concomitant." Intemperance, the "still greater tyrant reigns," he believed ("Speech by William Whipper" 122, 119, 120).

Even if a slave was able to acquire his freedom — either through manumission or by fleeing his master's whip — intemperance would only "revel in his guilt, and fan[s] the flames of his destruction." Whipper suggested that after a slave acquired his freedom from his master, he became slave to another. "The subject of intemperance finds that *his* master is almost omnipresent ... he finds that the omniscient eye of his master is upon him." Whipper offered his brethren a way out by beckoning them to support temperance by the "improvement of their moral condition." They were "morally, politically, and religiously bound," Whipper said, "to support the cause of temperance, as advocated and supported in the country." By doing so, he suggested, they would be "exercising the highest order of legislation" ("Speech by William Whipper"119, 120, 123) and forging for themselves the same enduring dedication to moral and temperance reform as he had done.

The Black temperance movement mirrored broader transformations in the mindset of Black abolitionist Jeremiahs. Jacob C. White, Jr., suggested that if the monies blacks spent on alcohol were "employed for the purpose of elevating our people and promoting the cause of education among them," America would "see a marked difference in the Colored People." By eradicating this evil and channeling "energies for the purpose of having the youth trained in such a manner that they will be fitted for usefulness" when they became adults, White prophesized, blacks would be placed in greater "political and social point of view" ("Essay by Jacob C. White, Jr." 210–211). By the 1850s, however, Black abolitionist Jeremiahs turned their attention toward another aspect of the temperance movement. They placed the alcohol question in an unequivocal antislavery structure and suggested to their constituents that by refusing alcoholic beverages, blacks would reveal their dedication to the slave and the endurance of the northern black populace (*BAP IV* 210).

Pamphlets of Expression: The African American Jeremiad Fueled by Racial Prejudice

As the African American jeremiad lamented the evils of American racism as the cause of blacks' degradation, it found expression in the African American pamphlet tradition. Throughout the 1830s, Robert Purvis, born on August 4, 1810, in Charleston, South Carolina to a wealthy cotton broker, sought to eliminate the problems that blacks faced in Pennsylvania. In 1837, he drafted the "Appeal of Forty Thousand Citizens Threatened with Disfranchisement to the People of Pennsylvania," which supported the abolition of a new state statute that prevented African Americans' right to vote. As with many Black abolitionist Jeremiahs, Purvis' staunchness to aide in the restoration of the black community was fueled by the racial prejudice produced by slavery (Ripley et al. 81). Purvis beckoned his "fellow citizens" "in the name of fair dealing, to look again at the just and noble charter" of the state of Pennsylvania, which he pleaded with them "to narrow down to the lines of caste and color" ("Appeal of Forty Thousand Citizens" 135).

Other Black abolitionist Jeremiahs followed Purvis' model. In June 1839, Daniel A. Payne, the sixth Bishop of the African Methodist Episcopal Church, delivered his "Slavery Brutalizes Man" speech in Fordsboro, New York, at his ordination by the Franckean Synod of the Lutheran Church (Foner and Branham 173). Payne's speech later appeared in the *Lutheran Herald and Journal of the Fort Plain* on 1 August 1839. In his lamentation, Payne supported the abolition of slavery. At the onset of his speech, Payne sets the tone by vehemently criticizing the moral principles of slavery, "*American Slavery brutalizes man — destroys his moral agency, and subverts that moral government of God.*" Payne utilized the jeremiad to deliberately chastise the American institution which he believed "tramples the laws of the living God under its unhallowed feet — weakens and destroys the influence which those laws are calculated to exert over the mind of man, and constrains the oppressed to blaspheme the name of the Almighty." Slavery, Payne bemoaned, "fetter[s] or obstruct[s] the will of man." This impediment constituted the "code of laws" that are meant to "regulate moral actions." By enslaving their fellow man, Americans defied not only the natural laws of man, but also every Christian concept. As long as blacks were slaves, there can be no elevation; Payne continued, "Slavery never legislates for the religious instruction of slaves, but, on the contrary, legislates to perpetuate their ignorance." Slaves were, as Payne suggested, aware of the religious hypocrisy practiced by slaveholders and they "know that oppression and slavery are inconsistent with the Christian religion." To validate his claims, Payne told his audience that "I speak not of what others have told me, but of what *I have seen and heard from the slaves themselves.*" Payne's culmination of the jeremiad furthered his moralizing analysis with a radical call to arms. "O, Brethren ...

awake! Awake to the battle and hurl the hottest thunders of divine truth at the head of this cruel monster, until he shall fall to rise no more, and the groans of the enslaved are converted into the songs of the free!!" ("Slavery Brutalizes Man" 174–177; emphasis in original). For Payne, the jeremiad did, in effect, condemn the racial and political ideologies of the status quo by bringing forth greater awareness from whites concerning American slavery.

In his pervasive pamphlet "Series of Letters by a Man of Colour," James Forten, Sr., mounted a personal campaign against the early republic for not following its own creed that "all men are created equal." Written to eliminate the "evils arising from the bill before the Legislature" that were "so fatal to the rights of freemen" and so typical "of European despotism," Forten's purpose was "to convince every unprejudiced mind, of its unjust, degrading, underserved tendency" ("Series of Letters by a Man of Colour" 69, 71). Through his jeremiadic rhetoric, Forten attempted to reconstruct what he felt the government attempted to destroy: self-determination among blacks who were unwavering in their efforts to leave the Southern plantocracy behind. Russell Parrott, a proletarian reader for the African Church of St. Thomas and a protégé of Forten (Newman, Rael, and Lapsansky 73), who argued that freedom and civil liberties for every man was required if America was to become a great nation, believed that "if the security of a country should rest within her bosom, then it is necessary that each citizen should be a freeman." In his 1814 pamphlet "An Oration on the Abolition of the Slave Trade; Delivered on the First of January, 1814. At the African Church of St. Thomas," Parrott further suggested that:

> The abolition of the slave trade, is one of the greatest events that mark the present age. It was a sacrifice that virtue compelled avarice to make, at the shrine of justice, as her first oblation. And, when to this is added the emancipation of those already in bondage, the name of slave, and heavens first, best gift, be universally enjoyed. That freedom is the natural inheritance of man, is a truth that neither sophistry-nor interest can shake; and the being that exists from under her benign rays, can neither by exhilarated by the influence of learning, nor warmed into a proper knowledge of himself, by religion ["An Oration" 78].

Freedom from slavery, Parrott argued, did not lie "in the influence of learning" or of religion: the "violators of the rights of man" should aid in the erasing the "narrow-minded prejudice" ("An Oration" 78–79). In his economic jeremiad, Parrott exercised the history of the slave trade as a tool to attack the insidious design, and to celebrate its finale.

While utilizing the jeremiad in his 1837 pamphlet "New York Committee of Vigilance for the Year 1837, together with Important Facts Relative to Their Proceedings," David Ruggles, secretary of the New York Vigilance Committee which was formed to aid in black emancipation, confronted the "innumerable evils continually springing up to embitter the lot of the colored man" who were "kept in ignorance." According to Ruggles, it was generally known that blacks— free and fugitives—were often kidnapped from free territory and remanded to slavery. However, he continued, the "practice" was "so extensive that no colored man is safe, be his age or condition in life what it may — by sear and land, in slave states, or in those where colored men are considered free, in all the varied occupations of life, they are exposed to the horrors of slavery" ("New York Committee of Vigilance" 147). His pamphlet laid the foundation of "organized black self-defense groups during the antebellum era" (Newman, Rael and Lapsanky 144). To prove and distinguish themselves as "practical abolitionists" ("New York Committee of Vigilance" 149), Ruggles, and his brethren, established a "Committee of Vigilance for the Protection of the People of Color" which set out to aid in destroying the "innumerable evils" and other "prominent evils" of the state of Pennsylvania and the slaveholding South. Seeking to eliminate "the foundation on which the social fabric rests," Ruggles revealed that the previous groundwork laid by the American Anti-Slavery Society did nothing to better African Americans' "civil and religious liberty and social welfare"; it only offered them "hope deferred." Ruggles suggested, however, that free black communities had the capability to oppose the countless ills of prejudiced whites and the "ruffian kidnapper" ("New York Committee of Vigilance" 147, 148, 155). In his pamphlet "A Dialogue between a Virginian and an African Minister," Daniel Coker chose to continually refer to biblical text to help illustrate his moral argument against slavery. In the dialogue, the minister offered "scriptures to be of Divine authority":

> "For they are my servants, which I brought forth out of the land of Egypt: they shall not be sold as bondmen. And if he be not redeemed in these years, then he shall go out in the year of Jubilee, both he, and his children with them." The passage of scripture under consideration was so far from authorizing the Israelites to make slaves of their servants children, they evidently forbid it; and therefore, are so far from proving the lawfulness of your enslaving the children of the Africans, that they clearly condemn the practice as criminal ["A Dialogue" 58].

Providing a hypothetical discussion between a minister and slaveholder, Coker, a "free yellow man," developed an appeal for equality and justice for African Americans. While employing the jeremiad, African American pamphlets such as Coker's were situated not only as a jeremiadic tool of protest, but also as the protocol of "moral uplift" (Newman, Rael and Lapsanky 33). These pamphlets were decidedly aimed at assuring their black audience that, as Absalom Jones and Richard Allen suggested, "The Lord was pleased to strengthen us, and removed all fear from us, and disposed our hearts to be as useful as possible" (*A Narrative* 40).

The Political Discourse of the African American Jeremiad in the Age of Abolitionism, 1845–1850

To understand the African American jeremiad as political discourse, it is imperative to first discuss the framework of the ideologies of America's antebellum years toward its black populace. The story of black political participation, wrote Frederick D. Wright was "one of a constant Black struggle" to contribute to a "political system; depending upon the time, place, and nature of the Black efforts, this struggle was met with either resistance, co-optation, or cooperation by whites" ("The History of Black Political Participation" 9). Given Wright's analysis, antebellum America saw many changes in government and public policy, and issues concerning the enslavement of blacks were oftentimes at the forefront of the debates. In March of 1845, for example, *The Baltimore American* reported the senseless shooting death of a slave by "a young man, named Matthews, a nephew of General Matthews" "whose father, it is believed, holds an office in Washington."[8] Pressured by residents of Maryland's Montgomery and Prince George counties, the District of Columbia initiated a peculiar law to prohibit blacks from settling in those areas. Five years later, the Fugitive Slave Act of 1850 gave Southern slave holders the justification to claim their escaped property in any Northern territory. By the early 1850s, slavery's "peculiar institution" was readily connecting the South to the Pacific Ocean as many slaves moved westward to work for their masters in the California gold mines. Optimistic that this "manifest destiny" would afford them equal citizenship, many slaves learned that they could not escape the dark cloud of American prejudice. Working for "13 months for [Dr. Bassett] in California," Alvin Coffey, a former slave born in 1822 in Madison County, Kentucky, who later moved to Missouri with his master's family, was able to save nearly $6,000 in gold dust for his master and nearly $700 of his "own money." Coffey was deceived by his master into thinking that he could obtain his freedom. "He kept my money, and when we got up to Missouri, he sold me for a thousand more" (qtd. in Johnson and Smith 387).[9] Abner H. Francis, in a letter published in *Frederick Douglass' Paper*, lamented the ills of the Oregon Territory's new settlement law:

> Even in the so-called *free* territory of Oregon, the colored American citizen, thought he may possess all the qualities and qualifications which make a man a good citizen, is driven out like a beast in the forest, made to sacrifice every interest dear to him, and forbidden the privilege to take the portion of the soil which the government says every citizen shall enjoy ["Black Laws in the West" 104; emphasis in original].

Francis concluded with a prophetic quote borrowed from Thomas Jefferson's *Notes on the State of Virginia* (1785). "Ah! When I see and experience such treatment, the words of that departed patriot come before me, '*I tremble for my country when I remember that God is just, and that his justice will not always sleep*'" ("Black Laws in the West" 104; emphasis in original). Yet, as Coffey illustrated, some Black abolitionist Jeremiahs were optimistic about progress for blacks in the West. Writing under the pseudonym NUBIA, William H. Newby, the first editor of the San Francisco weekly the *Mirror of the Times*,[10] wrote that blacks were "steadily progressing in all that pertains to our welfare" in San Francisco including the establishment of "one public school of color" with approximately "fifty children" and the establishment of one "Literary Association — the 'San Francisco Athenaeum,'" which required its constituents "to be moral and intelligent." Even though blacks in San Francisco were progressing in some areas, Newby wrote, they still suffered "many deprivations" such as being "debarred from the polls." "The Legislature," he lamented "refused to accept our petition for the right to testify in courts of justice against whites" ("William H. Newby to Frederick Douglass" 234, 235).

What would begin, however, as religious exegesis to provide blacks with vital organizational resources for socio-political mobilization during antebellum America was progressively finding its footing in the political consciousness of African Americans. Frederick Douglass, for example, gradually began shedding his original Garrisonian belief that moral suasion could end slavery (Howard-Pitney 39–40) became increasingly dogmatic in his thinking. By the 1850s, Douglass had become a "full-fledge political abolitionist" (Howard-Pitney 41), and in his 1852 "What to the Slave is the Fourth of July?" speech delivered in Rochester, New York, he took the time to reveal the obvious paradoxes he saw as a "political abolitionist" between American's professed Christian ideologies, its "shouts of liberty and equality ... prayers and hymns ... sermons and thanksgivings, with all [your] religious parade, and solemnity," and its real manifestation. His hope, Douglass explained to his audience, was to "pour out a fiery stream of biting ridicule, blasting reproach, withering sarcasm, and stern rebuke" on Americans for their injustices. Douglass chided the "gross injustice and cruelty" of a "nation of savages" of which the slave was "the constant victim" ("What to the Slave is the Fourth of July?" 124). Poignantly charging that slavery was given authority by the religion of the republic, Douglass suggested that white Christianity:

> Favors the rich against the poor; which exalts the proud above the humble; which divides mankind into two classes, tyrants and slaves; which says to the man in chains, *stay there*; and to the oppressor, *oppress on*; it is a religion which may be professed and enjoyed by all the robbers and enslavers of mankind; it makes God a respecter of persons, denies his fatherhood of the race, and tramples in the dust the great truth of the brotherhood of man ["What to the Slave is the Fourth of July?" 124; emphasis in original].

An important consequence of understanding Douglass' attack on America's form of Christianity — not "Christianity proper" — lay in his belief that concrete actions by whites of his day were responsible for their own downfall. Slavery, he lamented, violated "the first principles of Protestantism, democracy, and free enterprise" (Howard-Pitney 38). Douglass' scathing attack on America's so-called Christian ideologies stood at the forefront of the African American jeremiad's political development as a driving force in the shaping of politics of America's pre–Civil War years. "Go where you may," Douglass instructed his audience, and "search where you will, roam through all the monarchies and despotisms of the old world, travel through South America" in search of a nation whose cruelty will match America's. "And when you have found the last," he deplored them, "lay your facts by the side of the everyday practices of this nation, and you will say with me, that, for revolting barbarity and shameless hypocrisy, America reigns without a rival" ("What to the Slave is the Fourth of July?" 124). Douglass was urging such a conception of rhetoric in an era when America was still recovering from the wave of religious fervor of the Second Great Awakening (1820–1830s). Implicit in his theory of socio-political discourse, more importantly, was his belief that white politics must yield to the demands of his rhetorical position.

Because the core of political activity in Douglass' America was steeped in the rhetoric of American slaveholders, and because politicians who were slaveholders built treaties amongst themselves since they were not in a position to speak out against their injustices, any rhetoric — jeremiadic, nationalistic — of the period was presumed to be political in nature and in the best interests of Americans. The question must be, which Americans? For Douglass, the advancement of politics should rest in the interests of those Americans of African extraction, not in those who profited from a traditionally established immorality and caused suffering and who had an ambiguous comprehension of honesty, justice, and righteousness. As illustrated in Douglass' jeremiadic discourse, the political rhetoric of the African American jeremiad called for significant reconceptualizations of American political ideologies. Improvements that changed whites' perception of black participation in the country's "national identity" needed to be examined. In response to A. C. C. Thompson's critique of his *Narrative*, published in the 12 December 1845 edition of the Wilmington *Delaware Republican*, Douglass wrote:

> Slaveholders and slave-traders never betray greater indiscretion, than when they venture to defend themselves, or their system of plunder, in any other community than a slaveholding one. Slavery has its own standards of morality, humanity, justice, and Christianity. Tried by that standard, it is a system of the greatest kindness to the slave — sanctioned by the purest morality — in perfect agreement with justice — and, of course, not inconsistent with Christianity. But, tried by any other, it is doomed to condemnation. The naked relation of master and slave is one of those monsters of darkness, to whom the light of truth is death! ["Reply" 91].

As Douglass' reply to Thompson illustrated, African American jeremiadic rhetoric sought to reinforce, yet instill sharp change in white America's ideologies based on race; therein lay its political importance. Because of issues that were leading the country to the brink of civil war, African American jeremiadic discourse became overwhelmingly and more apparently political. In doing so, the pre–Civil War African American jeremiad inadvertently sought to uncover the workings of the American political system. This, then, suggested that if blacks' pre–Civil War jeremiadic rhetoric theoretically impeded public morals and forged a political system that interfered with understanding and knowledge, then America's downfall of necessary ethical (especially religious) institutions was inevitable because of their perceived "national identity."

The rudiment of the political jeremiad which Douglass helped to solidify was furthered when it later appeared in the narratives of former slaves. Two of the most noteworthy narratives of the period of American abolitionism illustrate how the American institution of slavery corrupted the "national identity" and humanity of the country. For example, William and Ellen Craft, in *Running a Thousand Miles for Freedom; or, the Escape of William and Ellen Craft from Slavery*, utilized the jeremiad to represent the many traveling indicators of racial bigotry of Americans who practice the insidious practice of slaveholding. William achieved this by illustrating that "the practical working of slavery is worse than the odious laws by which it is governed" (*Running a Thousand Miles* 15). He concluded the story of their journey over 1,000 miles to freedom:

> In the preceding pages I have not dwelt upon the great barbarities which are practised upon the slaves; because I wish to present the system in its mildest form, and to show that the "tender mercies of the wicked are cruel." But I do now, however, most solemnly declare, that a very large majority of the American slaves are over-worked, under-fed, and frequently unmercifully flogged [*Running a Thousand Miles* 111].

In January 1849, fugitives William and Ellen arrived in Boston from Macon, Georgia's "peculiar institution." Perhaps the most extraordinary known escape from the Southern plantocracy — other than Henry "Box" Brown — William confronted America's backsliding by showing that Ellen, light complexioned enough to pass for white, had to transcend both race and gender in order to experience true *equality* of *all* men by becoming a white male slaveholder traveling North accompanied with his property.

In his condemnation on African servitude in America, William Wells Brown made some of the same claims about the institution of slavery in America as the Crafts. However, Brown's career as a Black abolitionist Jeremiah was more diverse than that of his contemporaries. Brown's authorship as the first African American to publish a novel, play, military study of his people, study of black sociology, and travel book made him a forerunner in African American arts and letters of the nineteenth century. In his *Narrative of William W. Brown, An American Slave, Written by Himself*, Brown criticized slavery to show America's backsliding by using stimulating examples to prove his claims. Brown told his readers that he was once given a note and a dollar by Mr. Walker, "though not a good master" who, according to Brown, "had not flogged a slave since [he] had been with him" (*Narrative* 52). Brown was told to take the note to a jailer so that he would be whipped for some "carelessness." Brown "took the note and started for the hotel." Upon reaching his destination, he gave the note and dollar to "a stranger whom" he "had not seen before" and asked the stranger to take it to the jailer. As far as Brown could tell, the note requested that the jailer whip him. Through his own wit, Brown was able to evade the whipping; instead, the stranger was whipped. Brown wrote:

> This incident shows how it is that slavery makes its victims lying and mean; for which vice it afterwards reproaches them, and uses them as arguments to prove that

they deserve no better fate. Had I entertained the same views of right and wrong which I now do, I am sure I should never have practiced the deception upon that poor fellow which I did. I know of no act committed by me while in slavery which I have regretted more than that; and I heartily desire that it may be at some time or other in my power to make him amends for his vicarious sufferings in my behalf [*Narrative* 56–57].

According to Brown, the pious one, slavery caused him to do the wrong he had done. No doubt that thousands, perhaps millions of other slaves felt that slavery had contaminated their souls as well. The innocent stranger received "twenty lashes" that were intended for Brown. Brown's ideologies seemed to point to the social aspects of the jeremiad as he confronted the reader with the kind of social, religious, and political construction that they supported on a daily basis. In addition, his narrative gave abolitionists fuel for their arguments. It influenced them with a certainty that each of Brown's moral values served a direct purpose that rose from his experience of being a slave. Brown criticized slavery "with its democratic whips—its Republican chains—its evangelical blood-hounds, and its religious slave-holders" (*Narrative* 56, 69). He claimed to have traveled the Mississippi River several times witnessing slave auctions along the way from New Orleans to St. Louis. It is no wonder that he was able to position his jeremiadic rhetoric so straightforwardly to America. Brown wrote that in St. Louis, it was:

Uncommon ... to pass an auction-stand, and behold a woman upon the auction-block, and hear a seller crying out, "*How much is offered for this woman? She is a good cook, good washer, a good, obedient servant. She has got religion!*" Why should this man tell the purchasers that she has religion? I answer, because in Missouri, and as far as I have any knowledge of slavery in the other states, the religious teaching consists in teaching the slave that he must never strike a white man; that God made him for a slave; and that, when whipped, he must not find fault—for the Bible says, and slave-holders find such religion very profitable to them [*Narrative* 82–83; emphasis in original].

Brown had witnessed the use of the Bible to justify American slavery. One can gather that these lines—written so mournfully in terms of the emotions Brown expressed and their compassion with the position of blacks—would have instantly initiated feelings from whites' concerning the plight of black slaves in America. Brown's passage was meant to formulate eradication of slavery based on his own conversations. His jeremiadic discourse also suggested that blacks were discontent with their social conditions. When the Fugitive Slave Act of 1850 was enacted, more blacks would publicly speak out against prejudices and injustices, thus drastically increasing black abolitionist activity.

The Fugitive Slave Act of 1850

"I don't respect this law—I don't fear it—I won't obey it! It outlaws me, and I outlaw it, and the men who attempt to enforce it on me. I place the governmental officials on the ground that they place me. I will not live a slave, and if force is employed to reenslave me, I shall make preparations to meet the crisis as becomes a man [sic]," bellowed Jermain Wesley Loguen to a crowd in Syracuse, New York, one month after the Fugitive Slave of 1850 (FSA) was enacted. Loguen, who escaped slavery from Tennessee in 1834 and became a prominent abolitionist, appealed to Syracuse residents to dishonor not only the law, but the spirit that enacted it. Refusing to return to the "Hell of slavery," he lamented, "The government having transgressed Constitutional and natural limits, you will bravely resist its aggressions, and tell its soulless agents that no slaveholder shall make your city and county a hunting field for slaves" ("I Won't Obey the Fugitive Slave Law" 226). Loguen's aggressive attack on the FSA epitomized the essence of unrest throughout the African American community in the 1850s. In 1852, Granville B. Blanks wrote to the editor of the *Syracuse Daily Journal* that the FSA "aroused in my mind and excited in me a purpose to examine for myself what would be the probably future history of my people" ("Granville B. Blanks to Editor" 131). Blanks' reprise would only chafe at the issues that would be addressed by Black abolitionist Jeremiahs. Sarah Parker Remond viewed the FSA as a "law which had disgraced America so much, and which could find no parallel in history, ancient or modern" ("Speech by Sarah P. Remond, Delivered at the Music Hall" 438). A report from the Fifteenth Annual Meeting of the Rhode Island State Anti-Slavery Society in Providence on 13 November 1850 reported Sojourner Truth revealed that although she "did not know anything about politics-could not read the newspapers" she believed because of the FSA, "the worse had come to worst; now the best must come to best" (qtd. in Fitch and Mandziuk 18).

The FSA unleashed a storm of protest and greatly impacted the development of the African American jeremiad. A part of the group of laws put forward as the "Compromise of 1850," the FSA was the "least-debated item in the Compromise of 1850, but it radicalized the North." The law pushed northerners into vigorous hostilities toward the South (Menand 10). As Martin Delany saw it, "the insufferable Fugitive Slave Law" disregarded the states' rights by reducing "the free to slave States, without a murmur from the people" ("Political Destiny of the Colored Race" 278). Delany furthered argued that blacks had no rights under the FSA:

> By the provisions of this bill, the colored people of the United States are positively degraded beneath the level of the whites — are made liable at any time, in any place, and under all circumstances, to be arrested — and upon the claim of any white person, without the privilege, even of making a defence, sent into endless bondage. Let no visionary nonsense about *habeas corpus,* or a *fair trial* deceive us; there are no such rights granted in this bill, and except where the commissioner is too ignorant to understand when reading it, or too stupid to enforce it when he does understand, there is no earthly chance — no hope under heaven for the colored person who is brought before one of these officers of the law. Any leniency that may be expected, must proceed from the whims or caprice of the magistrate — in fact, it is optional

with them; and *our* rights and liberty entirely at their disposal [*Condition, Elevation, Emigration* 200; emphasis in original].

The negotiations of the FSA, however, were advantageous for both sides of the slavery debates: California entered the Union as a free state, slave-trading was prohibited in the District of Columbia, and the South received the right to reclaim their runaway property. Passages of the law, however, plagued Black abolitionist Jeremiahs throughout the country. Section 7, for example, furthered the position of the Fugitive Slave Act of 1793 by declaring that "any person who shall knowingly and willingly obstruct, hinder, or prevent" the capture of or "shall harbor or conceal such fugitive, so as to prevent the discovery and arrest of such person," shall "be subject to a fine not exceeding one thousand dollars, and imprisonment not exceeding six months, by indictment and conviction before the District Court of the United States," "and shall moreover forfeit and pay, by way of civil damages to the party injured by such illegal conduct, the sum of one thousand dollars for each fugitive so lost as aforesaid" (The Avalon Project 2008). Charles H. Langston, a free black leader in Ohio, was charged under the FSA's guidelines for his connection in the Oberlin-Wellington Rescue, in which John Price, a fugitive slave, was arrested in Oberlin, Ohio. Rescuers took Price by force and soon carried him to Canada. In a speech delivered to the court before his sentencing, Langston revealed why the FSA further divided the country on issues concerning race and prejudice:

> The prejudices which white people have against colored men grow out of the facts that we have as a people *consented* for two hundred years to be *slaves* of the whites. We have been scourged, crushed and cruelly oppressed, and have submitted to it all tamely, meekly, peaceably — I mean as a people, and with rare individual exceptions.... The colored man is oppressed by certain universal and deeply fixed *prejudices* ["Should Colored Men" 325; emphasis in original].

Resulting in a surge of African American protest across both the North and South as blacks sought to force white America to conform to their ideologies about slavery which would recognize blacks' socio-political participation, the FSA gave Black abolitionist Jeremiahs a "weapon which they would exploit to the hilt" (Quarles 199). Black denunciation of the FSA suggested that they were investing a great deal of time and energy at changing the atmospheric structure created by the contextualizations of white America's public opinion. Samuel Ringgold Ward attacked the "bill which would attempt to make the whole North the slavecatchers of the South," and assured slaves, should they make their way to New York, his home state, that "he shall have the law of Almighty God to protect him." Ward concluded his speech with a special message to the country's "postmasters," who may feel that they "cannot *live* without playing the pander of the slave-hunters." Ward suggested that "they need not *live at all*" ("Speech by Samuel Ringgold Ward" 49, 50, 51; emphasis in original).

Ways to achieve significant victory over the FSA were assiduously studied by Black abolitionist Jeremiahs. Gradually, even the black church stepped in to voice its opinion about the law. At its 1854 conference held at Bethel African Methodist Episcopal Church in Providence, Rhode Island, the African Methodist Episcopal (AME) church condemned the prejudices encouraged by the law by providing antislavery resolutions (*BAP IV* 195). In its resolutions, the AME delegates resolved:

> That in the enactment and passage of the Fugitive Slave Law, and the more recent act, namely, the repealing of the Compromise of 1820, in the passage of the Nebraska Bill[12] — in these wicked and cruel acts are burning coals of fire, which will burn to the lowest hell. Over them all hovers the dark angel of night, covering them with the dark mantel of wickedness ["Report by the Committee on Slavery of the New England Conference" 196].

The Nebraska Bill, it seemed, along with the FSA, presented upsetting delays to the antislavery movement. The Bill was introduced into Congress in 1853 and was meant to systematize Kansas and Nebraska. It rescinded the negotiations of Missouri Compromise of 1820 and allowed settlers in those territories the right to determine if they would allow slavery within their territorial limits. As Martin Delany protested, "did not the Nebraska Bill disrespect the feelings and infringe upon the political rights of Northern *white* people." Delany maintained that adoption of the Bill "would be hailed with loud shouts of approbation, from Portland to San Francisco" ("Political Destiny of the Colored Race" 278; emphasis in original). As expected, however, southern Senators protested the bill because slavery would be prohibited in these new territories set by the new provisions. Black abolitionist Jeremiahs vacillated between hope and anguish in regards to the bill, (*BAP IV* 197, 207) and some believed, as did William J. Watkins, the bill would have a "most salutary influence in working out the salvation of the American slave" ("Effect of the Nebraska Bill" 207). On 14 October 1850, a group of militant Black abolitionist Jeremiahs met at Brick Wesley African Methodist Episcopal Church in Philadelphia to organize against the enactment of the FSA. The result of their meeting was the formulation of a committee that sought to challenge the "legality and morality of the law" (Ripley et al. 68). They opened their "Resolutions by a Committee of Philadelphia Blacks" by appropriating the language of the country's founding fathers:

> The Declaration of American Independence declares it to be a self-evident truth, "that all men are created equal, and are endowed by their Creator with certain inalienable rights, among which are life, liberty, and the pursuit of happiness"... the Constitution ... declares that "the privilege of the writ of habeas corpus shall not be suspended"... that "no person shall be deprived of life, liberty, or property, without due process of law" ["Resolutions by a Committee of Philadelphia Blacks" 68].

The FSA, they conclude, "is in clear, palpable violation of these several provisions." Therefore, several resolutions were enacted. Among them, to sanction, "to the full," the revolutionary sentiments of Patrick Henry, "Give me Liberty or give me Death" by resisting "to the death any attempt to enforce" the law upon them ("Resolutions by a Committee of Philadelphia Blacks" 68, 69, 70). William Wells Brown lamented that the FSA was "in every respect an unconstitutional measure." Brown believed that the law:

> Set[s] aside the right formerly enjoyed by the fugitive of trial by jury — it afforded to him no protection, no opportunity of proving his right to be free, and it placed every free coloured person at the mercy of any unprincipled individual who might wish to lay claim to him. That law is opposed to the principles of Christianity — foreign alike to the laws of God and man, it had converted the whole population of the free States into a band of slave-catchers, and every rood of territory is but so much hunting ground, over which they might chase the fugitive [*Three Years in Europe* 243].

"The love of freedom," Brown lamented, "is one of those natural impulses of the human breast which cannot be extinguished" (*Three Years in Europe* 236).

Martin Delany, who by 1850 knew that white behavior was already subject to whites' superior status in society, responded to the FSA in an unprecedented manner of the times. In his response, Delany positioned his rhetoric in the language of the nation's time-honored principles: the right to protect one's family and home. When he gathered before the crowd at Allegheny, Pennsylvania, Delany took the time to deride those who supported the entrapment:

> Honorable Mayor,[13] whatever ideas of liberty I may have, have been received from reading the lives of your revolutionary fathers. I have therein learned that a man has a right to defend his castle with his life, even unto the taking of life. Sir, my house is my castle; in that castle are none but my wife and my children, as free as the angels of heaven, and whose liberty is as sacred as the pillars of God. If any man approaches that house in search of a slave — I care not who he may be, whether constable, or sheriff, magistrate even judge of the Supreme Court — nay, let it be he who sanctioned this act to become a law surrounded by his cabinet as his bodyguard,[14] with the Declaration of Independence waving above his head as his banner, and the constitution of his country upon his breast as his shield, — if he crosses the threshold of my door, and I do not lay him a lifeless corpse at my feet, I hope the grave may refuse my body a resting place, and righteous Heaven my spirit a home. O, no! He cannot enter that house and we both live [qtd in Rollins 76].

Delany's response to the FSA was forced by his perceptions of white power relations. His jeremiad, to some degree, was a pivotal factor in the ongoing process solidifying black reaction to the FSA as other Black abolitionist Jeremiahs shared his nonconformity. Delany also advocated forceful violence in relation to the act, since he said that if anyone "crosses the threshold of my door, and I do not lay him a lifeless corpse at my feet, I hope the grave may refuse my body a resting place, and righteous Heaven my spirit a home." Following suit, "We must be prepared," said Frederick Douglass, speaking in Boston's Faneuil Hall, "should this law be put in operation, to see the streets of Boston running with blood." Douglass' assault on the FSA became further solidified when he argued that it defied Christianity and encouraged citizens not to help runaway slaves. It encouraged them to turn away the hungry, tired and victims of injustices. "I take this law to be one of the grossest infringements of Christian Liberty, and, if the churches and ministers of our country were not stupidly blind, or most wickedly indifferent, they, too, would so regard it" ("What to the Slave?" 122). "The only way to make the fugitive slave law dead letter," Douglass further lamented, "is to make a half a dozen or more dead kidnappers" (qtd. in Olsen). Likewise, Robert Purvis responded to the FSA by declaring that "should any wretch enter my dwelling, any pale-faced spectre among ye, to execute this law on me or mine, I'll see his life, I'll shed his blood" (qtd. in Quarles 201). "Slavery will be abolished in this land," he prophesied, "and with it, that twin relic of barbarism, prejudice against color" ("The American Government and the Negro" 339). These reactions to the law were expected since the FSA threatened the lives of both fugitive and free blacks. In his 2 June 1854 editorial published in the *Frederick Douglass' Paper*, William J. Watkins also defended bloodshed, suggesting that blacks "should certainly kill the man who would dare lay his hand on us, or on our brother, or sister, to enslave us." Watkins was writing in response to the death of a Deputy U.S. Marshal who was attempting to retrieve a fugitive, Anthony Burns, a Virginia runaway. "Slavery is the murder in the highest degree," lamented Watkins, "Every slaveholder is a murderer, a wholesale murderer" ("Who Are the Murderers?" 227, 229).

Some Black abolitionist Jeremiahs vehemently responded to the FSA and called vigilance meetings and rallies to invent ways to repeal the law. One such meeting was held 13 October 1851 at the Memorial African Methodist Episcopal Zion Church, Rochester, New York. Rochester blacks gathered that evening and made several resolutions against the "'Hunting of Men' in the valley of Genesee." Of the most prevailing of the resolutions that came out of the meeting was one that sent a sneering attack on the system of American slavery:

> That the system of American slavery — the vilest that ever saw the sun — is a violation of every sentiment of christianety [sic], and the antipodes of every dictate of humanity. The Slaveholders pretensions to property in Man are of no more weight than those of the midnight assassin or pirate on the high seas. "God made all men free — free as the birds that cleave the air or sing on the branches—free as the sunshine that gladdens the earth—free as the winds that sweep over sea and land—free at his birth—free during his whole life—free to day—this hour—this moment" ["Proceedings of a Meeting of Rochester Blacks" 99].

The committee members advanced their caution to "every colored Man, woman and child to be careful in their walks through the highways and byways of the City" ("Proceedings of a Meeting of Rochester Black" 99).

Black abolitionist Jeremiahs' understanding of the complexities of social representations of the power of white supremacy deepened with the enactment of the FSA. The jeremiad, which had been previously solidified in the political discourse of leaders such as Frederick Douglass, David Walker, and Sojourner Truth, would continue to gain maturity as a politically based construction. As

African Americans in the antebellum area began to adopt the Puritan rhetoric that would soon become the African American jeremiad, they began to bear the burden of fighting not just for justice and retribution but also for the essence of their survival in a world that did not see them as humans.

"Mrs. Stowe knows nothing about us": The Proliferation of Uncle "Tom-Mania"

With concerns like those discussed above plaguing black social life, the 1852 publication of Harriet Beecher Stowe's *Uncle Tom's Cabin, or Life Among the Lowly* was not a welcome addition to American political correctness, as far as some Black abolitionist Jeremiahs were concerned. Stowe's novel created a wave of concern about black life while at the same time set precedence — which slave narrators had previously attempted to do—for slave life in the United States. William Wells Brown and William Craft were in full support of Stowe's efforts. On his many travels, Brown was asked "again and again if certain portions of *Uncle Tom's Cabin* were not exaggeration." He revealed to his audience in Manchester, England, however, that he did not believe "anything can exaggerate [the] infamous system" of American slavery ("Speech by William Wells Brown, Delivered at the Town Hall, Manchester, England" 400). Brown praised the novel for "awakening sympathy in hearts that never before felt for the slave" ("William Wells Brown to William Lloyd Garrison" 344). After reading the novel in September 1852, Craft did not find "a single expression" which he felt was "at all an exaggeration of the enormities of American slavery" ("William Craft to the Editor" 317). *Uncle Tom's Cabin* had a powerful effect on America's political structure. In the South, the novel was labeled utter filth and even criminal charges were brought against some who possessed it. In 1857, for example, former slave Samuel Green was sentenced to serve 10 years in prison after authorities searched his home and found a copy of *Uncle Tom's Cabin* (*BAP I* 461, 7n).

Stowe's novel assisted in igniting the burning flame amongst the black abolitionist community and led Martin Delany to the conclusion that "Mrs. Stowe *knows nothing about us*—'the Free Colored People of the United States'— neither does any white person — and consequently, can contrive no successful scheme for our elevation; it must be done by ourselves." As a matter of fact, Delany fashioned his anti–Tom novella, *Blake, or the Huts of America: A Novel*, to argue against the obedient black servant presented in Stowe's text, while at the same time attempting to uplift and instill pride in the black community through his character Blake/Henry.[15] The African American novel, therefore, was not exempt from employing the jeremiad as a vehicle of uplift. Through illusions, the African American novel lamented black anguish in a more subtle tone than the black orator. In Delany's theodicy, however, Christianity as the "master's religion" must be rejected. Therefore, Blake stated that "No religion but that which brings us liberty will we know; no God but He who owns us as his children will we serve." Blake, acting in direct opposition to Uncle Tom, took it upon "himself to spread the 'germs' of insurrection by creating a sort of black Masonic network in the slave South, with himself as grand master" (Levine, *Martin Delany, Frederick Douglass* 195).

While still debating the effectiveness of a work like *Uncle Tom's Cabin*, Delany methodically attacked Stowe's representation and made his claims concerning the novel more visible in a series of letters to Frederick Douglass. Stowe, Delany believed:

> Ably, eloquently and pathetically portrayed some of the sufferings of the slave, is it any evidence that she has any sympathy for his thrice-morally crucified, semi-free brethren any where, or of the *African* race at all; when in the same world-renowned and widely circulated work, she sneers at Hayti — the only truly free and independent civilized black nation as such, or colored if you please, on the face of the earth — at the same time holding up the little dependent colonization settlement of Liberia in high estimation? I must be permitted to draw my own conclusions, when I say that I can see no other cause for this singular discrepancy in Mrs. Stowe's interest in the colored race, than that one is independent of, and the other subservient to, white men's power ["Delany and Douglass on *Uncle Tom's Cabin*" 232; emphasis in original].

Delany saw flaws in Stowe's portrayal of slave life because she was not, according to him, qualified to characterize it; therefore, he lamented Stowe's fallacious portrayal. But Delany's condemnation did not stop there. At the time he wrote his letters to Douglass, Delany had not yet read the novel, but he nonetheless evoked the authenticity and credibility of the work. "I am of the opinion, that Mrs. Stowe has draughted largely on all of the best fugitive slave narratives — at least on Douglass's, Brown's, Bibb's and perhaps Clark's, as well as the living Household of old Father Henson; but of this I am not competent to judge, not having yet *read* 'Uncle Tom's Cabin'" ("Delany and Douglass on *Uncle Tom's Cabin*" 231; emphasis in original). According to Marion Starling, Stowe infused scenes from several slave narratives into her rendering of slave life in the South:

> We have been on the Shelby plantation before — at the Lloyd plantation in Douglass's narrative, at the Campbell plantation in the Clarke brothers' story, and at the Tilghman plantation in Pennington's narrative. George Harris is a composite picture of Douglass and William Wells Brown; Legree combines Messrs. Gore and Covey; Mr. St. Clair looks like Mr. Freeland; and we met Haley and Marks and Tom Loker when we went down to New Orleans with Henson. Clarke's sister Delia looks out from Cassy's eyes; Eliza is Henson's Charlotte; Little Evas run through dozens of slave testimonials telling of the loyalty and affection of the children of the Big House, who would openly defy the scorn of older members of their family to dress the wounds of a favorite slave beaten dreadfully for some trifle or other and run the risk of punishment themselves of slipping off to teach slave children the rudiments of learning denied them. Mrs. Stowe's New England need not be looked to as the only possible source of Ophelia and St. Clair's Yankee brother; New Englanders appear on a number of the plantations, in the narrative of the slavers [*The Slave Narrative* 301].[16]

Another of the inherent problems Delany saw with the novel, however, was Stowe's use of language. "The 'negro language,' attributed to Uncle Tom," he insisted, "makes the character more natural for a slave; but I would barely state, that Father Josiah Henson makes use of as good language, as any one in a thousand Americans." Douglass, in contrast, could not comprehend why anyone would oppose "the efforts of Mrs. Stowe, or any one else, who is moved to anything on our behalf" ("Delany and Douglass on *Uncle Tom's Cabin*" 225, 231, 226). Douglass regarded Stowe as "a fellow believer in the importance of black elevation" (Levine "*Uncle Tom's Cabin* in Frederick Douglass' Paper" 78). He believed that Stowe's antislavery novel would "unlock the slave prisons to millions" ("A Nation in the Midst of a Nation" 435).

Uncle Tom's Cabin stirred mixed emotions in Great Britain from Black abolitionist Jeremiahs. After its publication, "Tom-mania," the "extraordinary public interests the book ... aroused on both sides of the Atlantic" swept England (Meer 1). In the October 1852 edition of the *Southern Literary Messenger* (Richmond, VA), an anonymous reviewer wrote that "Tom-mania" "crossed the water to Great Britain, filling the minds of all who" knew "nothing of slavery with hatred for that institution and those who uphold it" ("*Uncle Tom's Cabin*" 638). Douglass believed that nothing in Stowe's "reception abroad" indicated "a declension of interest in the great subject which" she had "done so much to unfold and illustrate" ("A Nation in the Midst of a Nation" 436). By 1853, Samuel Ringgold Ward's reputation as a formidable Black abolitionist Jeremiah had intensified. He was sent to England by the Anti-Slavery Society of Canada because "his strong arm," lamented William J. Wilson to Frederick Douglass, "may hoe the good seed sown there by *Uncle Tom's Cabin*, and otherwise culture the stock and the blade till the full ear comes" ("William J. Wilson to Frederick Douglass" 142). Ward explained why Stowe's novel was so popular in England:

> *Uncle Tom's Cabin* had so impressed the antislavery people of the aristocratic classes, as to lead to the celebrated address of English women to the women of America, in behalf of the enslaved. This, with its powerful effect, was the theme of universal discussion when Mrs. Stowe arrived in England. The book from the one side of the Atlantic, the address from the other side, and the arrival of her whose gifted pen had been the occasion of the one and the origin of the other, awakened more attention to the antislavery cause in England, in 1853, than had existed since the agitation of the emancipation question in 1832 [*Autobiography* 248–249].

In their travels abroad, other Black abolitionist Jeremiahs disclosed their beliefs that Stowe's portrayal of black life was either superficial or inclusive of slavery's atrocities. William G. Allen's ambivalence toward the novel was revealed within his description of Stowe's inventiveness. Stowe had "never suffered martyrdom, and however much others may honor her, she has too much sense and piety" to justly "covet honors which more properly belong to those who have led on in the fore-front of this battle" ("William G. Allen to William Lloyd Garrison" 357). Later, however, Allen felt that the novel was a welcome addition to the growing mound of antislavery literature. Stowe, he lamented, gave the institution of slavery a "blow" with the publication of *Uncle Tom's Cabin*. "Oh! What a book was that! Every page was that of genius on the fire of truth. She had sprung a mine, out of which would issue prayers and sympathies for the coloured race." Allen further applauded Stowe's efforts, "Now has the start of our hope arisen above the horizon" and praised her "wonder of wonders" ("Speech by William G. Allen" 370).

Robert Purvis felt that the novel was a "portraiture of the infernal system" of American slavery. Purvis' "excited feelings" carried him "with accelerated pulse through the thrilling incidents" of the novel. He argued that "by its reading, slavery would be cursed of all men, and that a speedy and mighty change in the nation's sentiment toward the cause of freedom and the rights of man would be effected" ("Robert Purvis to Oliver Johnson" 124). However, eight years prior to revealing the incidents of her life as a slave girl, Harriet Jacobs lamented that Stowe had "not told the half" of slavery's inhumanity. "Would that I had one spark from her storehouse of genius and talent," she bemoaned, "I would tell [you] of my sufferings—I would tell you of wrongs ... that England never dreamed of" ("Harriet A. Jacobs to Horace Greeley" 167). Black abolitionist Jeremiahs clearly debated the importance of *Uncle Tom's Cabin* as a vehicle of uplift for the black community. One of the most widely read and extremely powerful books of the nineteenth century, the novel's antislavery message goaded extraordinary levels of critical debate throughout the Northern and Southern United States as well as Great Britain.

The Dred Scott Decision and John Brown's Raid

The *Dred Scott v. Sanford*[17] case had deeply influenced the African American jeremiad. Black abolitionist Jeremiahs became further convinced that slavery would not be abolished by governmental procedures. A "devastating blow to hopes of racial progress" (*BAP IV* 362), the U.S. Supreme Court ruled that people of African extraction brought into the United States and held as slaves (or their descendants) were not protected by the Constitution and could never become citizens. The decision was handed down by Chief Justice Roger B. Taney on 6 March 1857, just two days after James Buchanan's (1857–1861) inauguration as America's fifteenth president. Two months after the decision was passed, Frederick Douglass lamented:

> This infamous decision of the Slaveholding wing of the Supreme Court maintains that slaves are, within the contemplation of the Constitution of the United States, property; that slaves are property in the same sense that horses, sheep, and swine are property; that the old doctrine that slavery is a creature of local law is false; that the right of the slaveholder to his slave does not depend upon the local law, but is secured wherever the Constitution of the United States ex-tends; that Congress has no right to prohibit slavery anywhere; that slavery may go in safety anywhere under

the star-spangled banner; that colored persons of African descent have no rights that white men are bound to respect; that colored men of African descent are not and cannot be citizens of the United States.... To decide against this right in the person of Dred Scott, or the humblest and most whip-scarred bondman [slave], is to decide against God ["The Dred Scott Decision" 163, 165].

Robert Purvis, with "resentment, anger, and despair," delivered a speech at New York's City Assembly Rooms in retaliation to the decision. Purvis, now convinced that the Constitution was "a proslavery document to which blacks owed no allegiance" (*BAP IV* 362), bellowed:

> Mr. Chairman, look at the facts—here, in a country with a sublimity of impudence that knows no parallel, setting itself up before the world as *a free country*, a land of *liberty!*, "the land *of the free*, and the *home of the brave*," the "*freest country in all the world*"! Gracious God! and yet here are millions of men and women groaning under a bondage the like of which the world has never seen—bought and sold, whipped, manacled, killed all the day long. Yet this is a *free country!* The people have the assurance to talk of their *free institutions*. How can I speak of such a country and use language of moderation? How can I, who, every day, feel the grinding hoof of this despotism, and who am myself identified with its victims ["Speech by Robert Purvis, Delivered at the City Assembly Rooms" 363; emphasis in original].

Purvis examined the dichotomy of the United States espousing freedom, yet remaining involved in the most grossly and inhumane practice of human history. Echoing Douglass' sentiments, Purvis maintained:

> Sir, have we not self-respect? Are we to clank the chains that have been made for us, and praise the men who did the deed? Are we to be kicked and scouted, trampled upon and judicially declared to "*have no rights which white men are bound to respect*" and then turn round and glorify and magnify the laws under which all this is done? ... I will never ... disgrace myself by eulogizing a government that tramples me and all that are dear to me in the dust ["Speech by Robert Purvis, Delivered at the City Assembly Rooms" 364; emphasis in original].

Black abolitionist Jeremiahs assiduously sought to combat the Dred Scott decision. Sarah P. Remond lamented that the American church aided in making judgments like the aforementioned possible:

> The American churches were responsible for many of the worst features that existed in regard to the slavery of the African population. When that infamous [Dred Scott] decision was given ... the church did not set their face against it, but tamely said with the pro-slavery party at the north, "we must obey the law. It is necessary for the public safety that we should obey the law." But if there was an attempt made to pass a law in favour of the negro, there was no movement on their parts, or sympathy shown towards it. Thus the laws of America stood condemned—for they were insincere and inconsistent ["Speech by Sarah P. Remond, Delivered in the Music Hall" 436].

The moral fiber of Black abolitionist Jeremiahs' responses to the decision not only "reflected black vulnerability in the face of federal tyranny" but also "revealed seething militancy and growing unity" (*BAP IV* 391). In the southern black community, "secret abolition movements" were established that enabled slaves to "escape from the prison house of slavery" ("Resolutions by William Lambert" 51). Countless meetings were held across the North and resolutions determined in protest of the decision. On 16 June 1858, Lloyd H. Brooks delivered such decrees before an assembly at the Third Christian Church in Bedford, Massachusetts. The congregation adopted Brooks' resolution "that the infamous 'Dred Scott' decision is a palpably vain, arrogant assumption, unsustained by history, justice, reason or common sense, and merits the execration of the world as a consummate villainy" ("Resolutions by Lloyd H. Brooks" 392). Resolutions like these aided in solidifying Black abolitionist Jeremiahs' commitment to battling the Dred Scott decision on every front.

Enthusiastic that slavery would eventually end through legislative actions, some Black abolitionist Jeremiahs revealed that — because of the Dred Scott decision — more severe measures were needed. If freedom was to be valued, it was worth the battle. H. Ford Douglas supported an absolute defeat of slavery through utilizing measures similar to those that John Brown[18] had previously employed. "More than any other white person ... [Brown] forged close friendships with blacks, live with them, [and] established an interracial army" (McCarthy and Stauffer xxix) through his relations with the black community. "Yes! We must do as John Brown did," Douglas lamented, "not necessarily in the *way* he did it, but we must labor with the sure determination to effect, in some way, the complete overthrow of slavery." Brown's 16 October 1859 raid on Harpers Ferry, Virginia (now West Virginia) shocked the nation. "If [George] Washington and his associates of the Revolution were right, so was John Brown," Douglas maintained, "If our Revolutionary fathers had failed, would they ... have been the greatest of criminals?" ("Speech by H. Ford Douglas, Delivered at the Town Hall" 89, 92; emphasis in original). Douglas furthered that if Abraham Lincoln's[19] bid for the presidency was supported, slavery would continue to thrive. Revealing that Lincoln was an enemy of the black man, Douglas said:

> Yet Abraham Lincoln will carry out the fugitive slave law, and you will carry him into office! He will be the bloodhound to catch the slave and send him back to his hard life of toil, and you by sustaining him, will make yourselves as guilty as he. I want to see the day when no slaveholders will dare to come here for his slave. But that day cannot come so long as you are willing to exalt to the presidency men who endorse the Dred Scott decision ["Speech by H. Ford Douglas, Delivered at the Town Hall" 92].

Exigency was at an all time high in the northern black communities in the weeks following Brown's raid. Black abolitionist Jeremiahs "were more comfortable with Brown's violent legacy; the Harper's Ferry affair had given a new vitality to the movement to bear arms. Blacks not only accepted but truly venerated Brown's martyrdom" (Finkelman 60). Robert Purvis displayed the utmost respect for Brown, "He believed that the black man was a man," he lamented, "and he laid down his life to secure for him the rights of man" ("The American

Government and the Negro" 339). In his resolutions presented at the Second Baptist Church in Detroit, Michigan, William Lambert immortalized Brown's efforts in a spectacular display:

> [H]aving become personally acquainted with the life and character of our much beloved and highly esteemed friend, Old Capt. John Brown, and his band of valiant men, who, at Harpers Ferry ... demonstrated to the world his sympathy and fidelity to the cause of the suffering slaves of this country by bearding the hydra-headed monster, Tyranny, in his den, and by his bold, effective, timely blow is now causing the whole South to tremble with a moral earthquake, as he boldly and freely delivered up his life today as a ransom for our enslaved race; and thereby, "solitary and alone," he has put a liberty ball in motion which shall continue to roll and gather strength until the last vestige of human slavery within this nation shall have been crushed beneath its ponderous weight.... We hold the name of Old Capt. John Brown in the most sacred remembrance as the first disinterested martyr for our liberty, who, upon the true Christian principle of his Divine Lord and Master, has freely delivered up his life for the liberty of our race in this country. Therefore will we ever vindicate his character throughout all coming time as our temporal redeemer, whose name shall never die ["Resolutions by William Lambert" 51–52].

Declarations like Lambert's appeared throughout the black community. Thomas Hamilton lamented that Brown "had and held possession of [Virginia's] Ancient Dominion and the terror-stricken chivalry, chattels, and all, and might have continued possession but for the interference of Uncle Sam's troops" ("Editorial by Thomas Hamilton" 41). He warned the South of future insurrections while at the same time called those who would take revolutionary action against slavery to arms:

> [T]he future John Browns who make take it into their heads to again break into the State of Presidents, or some other of her sister States, it is now proposed that the whole South wheel out of the Union, and build a strong barrier against future inroads, and set up for itself. Out of what materials this barrier is to be erected, does not matter ["Editorial by Thomas Hamilton" 42].

Advocating insurrection against slavery's inhumane treatment of blacks, George Lawrence, Jr., audaciously declared in his 27 April 1861 editorial published in the *Weekly Anglo-African*, "We want Nat Turner — not speeches; Denmark Vesey — not resolutions; John Brown — not meetings" ("Editorials by George Lawrence, Jr." 112).

Conclusion

At some point in their careers, Black abolitionist Jeremiahs were likely to have delivered messages that their audience did not want to accept and was, therefore, unlikely to react to optimistically — an audience with strong reservations. It was truly a time when the message required powerful persuasion. Perhaps Frederick Douglass' powerful jeremiadic discourse was able to change the public's behavior; this does not mean, however, that he was able to change the public's underlying attitude toward blacks. In order for the Black abolitionist Jeremiahs to get the job done, their audience must have *really* paid attention to their messages and modified its behavior accordingly. Unfortunately, however, the public often does not *really listen* when the issue is controversial. Why not? Henry Highland Garnet's concern that slaves have the benefit of religious training was based on his belief that it was necessary to building discipline, strength, character and political representation. Viewing religion as something that could serve humanity, he meant to employ it as a vehicle for self-expression and uplift. Devotion to God was equated to devotion to the struggle. Imagine listening to Garnet's or reading David Walker's addresses while they used Christianity as a vehicle of struggle, exhorting slaves to revolt in order to eradicate slavery. No doubt slaveholders would contrive schemes to remind slaves of the meekness of their abilities to change the system in any progressive manner. After all, it is natural to feel threatened by change or aggression, particularly in the conservative South. These typical reactions block comprehension and create resistance. But in whose mind? The slave's? The slaveholder's? After all, Black abolitionist Jeremiahs like Garnet and Walker recommended to slaves that resistance was their obligation to God, and without it, freedom would not happen. The role of the African American jeremiad in the abolitionist movement has not received its credit as a driving force in the process of self-worth and self-definition among its constituents in either the United States or abroad. This chapter seeks to bridge the transformational gap between the American abolitionism movement and the African American jeremiad and ends much in the same way it begins: with the conceptualization of freedom and retribution throughout the African American consciousness. Consider Robert Purvis' speech delivered at the Anti-Slavery Society in Philadelphia in 1860 in which he held the United States' government responsible for "destroy[ing] the coloured man, as a man":

> What is the attitude of your boasting, braggart republic toward the 600,000 free people of colour who swell its population and add to its wealth? I have already alluded to the dictum of Judge Taney in the notorious Dred Scott decision. The dictum reveals the animus of the whole government; it is a fair example of the cowardly and malignant spirit that pervades the entire policy of the country. The end of the policy is, undoubtedly, to destroy the coloured man, as a man. With this view, it says a coloured man shall not sue and recover his lawful property; he shall not bear arms and train in the militia; he shall not be a commander of a vessel, not even of the meanest craft that creeps along the creeks and bays of your Southern coast; he shall not carry a mailbag, or serve as a porter in a post-office ["The American Government and the Negro" 332].

7

The Transatlantic African American Jeremiad

> When I came to this country, two of my fellow passengers were slaveholders, one a Briton, and the other an Irishman. The latter told me more than once that he knew his slaves in Kentucky had more to waste than his friends in Ireland have to live upon. (Laughter.) I appeal to the audience, never at the peril of liberty to countenance the idea that we are to have perpetual slavery. I wish to make known today, before heaven and earth, that if you are to have perpetual slavery, you cannot have the black man for a perpetual slave. (Immense cheers.) I am prepared to abide by this position. I say it advisedly, that our servitude, which has been a submissive and a bloody one, is nearly out.
>
> —J. W. C. Pennington,
> "Speech by J. W. C. Pennington, Delivered at Exeter Hall,"
> London, England, 21 June 1843

Oftentimes Black abolitionist Jeremiahs delivered their jeremiads to audiences in Europe, Africa and Great Britain. Either as fugitive slaves or abolitionists, they traveled to foreign countries for a variety of reasons. J. W. C. Pennington, born a slave in 1809 and later became a blacksmith until he escaped to Pennsylvania in his early 20s, demanded his 1843 British audience to consider their role in America's antislavery campaign. "If slavery is to be perpetual, the question comes," he raised, "who are to be the slaves? Who shall settle this question? Will the British Government, the British nation, or any other government or nation, undertake the settlement of this question?" Pennington's appeal to his audience sought to engage their morality concerning American slavery. He emphasized that slavery in the United States was not just an African American problem, but a problem for humanity. "Would anyone be prepared to stand up and assign a reason why I should be ... [a] slave?" he questioned. Pennington felt that his achievements would better the lot of all blacks regardless of locale. "I am the representative of [American slaves], and what I gain anywhere and everywhere, I gain for every manacled slave in America, and for every benighted African in the world" ("Speech by J. W. C. Pennington, Delivered at Exeter Hall" 131). While informing his British audience that some Amer-

7. The Transatlantic African American Jeremiad   161

ican whites questioned black involvement in their own elevation, Pennington revealed that some hastily believed that the black man "is still a nigger." "Pardon me," he beckoned, "if I recur to an American 'Jim Crow' definition for illustration — Do what you will, / The nigger will be a nigger still." He commented on the refinement of free blacks in America by using white Europeans' civility as a point of comparison, "If, by civilization, is meant in general pursuing the same conduct, and following the same avocations that white persons of European descent do, then it must be answered, that they are civilized so far as circumstance and means will permit" ("Speech by J. W. C. Pennington, Delivered at Freemasons' Hall" 106, 104). The transatlantic jeremiads of Black abolitionist Jeremiahs such as Pennington were demonstrative of the horrors and cruelties of American slavery and offered audiences abroad pervasive descriptions of America's "peculiar institution."

Evading the crisis of the Fugitive Slave Act of 1850 (FSA), expanding the antislavery agenda, or raising funds to purchase their freedoms or to support the building of separate communities in the United States or Canada, many Black abolitionist Jeremiahs saw foreign countries as a place where they could spread "the antislavery gospel" and support the "transatlantic antislavery network" (Ripley et al., 3). Traveling abroad held particular significance for those who traversed the Atlantic Ocean. The socio-political movement of the transatlantic African American jeremiad served an important purpose for black activism in the United States: it stretched across the Atlantic — the same ocean that had previously engulfed millions of African souls — to give its architects the apparatus needed to destabilize precisely the repressive laws in the United States to a foreign audience; it gave Black abolitionist Jeremiahs the tools needed to call their foreign audiences to aide in the restructuring of the United States' democracy beyond the restraints of her shores. "Perhaps it is not generally known that in the United States of America — that land of freedom and equality," lamented Nathaniel Paul in his 1883 address to a crowd in London, "the laws are so exceedingly liberal that they give to man the liberty of purchasing as many negroes as he can find means to pay for (hear, hear) and also the liberty to sell them again" ("Speech by Nathaniel Paul, Delivered at Exeter Hall" 45).

Although Canada was a vital part of the American antislavery movement, the country could not provide Black abolitionist Jeremiahs the necessary forums in which to garner support for the cause in the United States partly due to the neighboring counties' close proximity and because the antislavery sentiments of both countries were closely aligned. New approaches were needed. As Samuel Ringgold Ward lamented, "Canada and the United States are too closely allied in feeling as well as in geographical position to make the cause of the black man otherwise than *one*, on both sides of the line." Therefore, when Black abolitionist Jeremiahs took their messages overseas, they were able to "vindicate [the] race, and repel the vile, foul slanders by which that race has been — by the baser half of the Anglo Saxon race — aspersed" on both sides of the Atlantic

("Modern Negro No. 1" 412; emphasis in original). Ward believed that black abolitionists had a sustained role to play in the uplift of blacks globally:

> Let us ... do what we can, by the elevation, improvements and evangelization of the native or adopted British Negro; by adding our quota to the swelling tide of universal public sentiment against slavery; by holding up Yankee character in the light of its facts; to hasten the day when, peacefully, if possible, but if not peaceably, by what cause or causes soever, American Slavery shall be overthrown, and then the despotism of no country can long survive ["Samuel Ringgold Ward to the Readers" 392].

Thousands lectured to audiences as large as 2,000. As the African American jeremiad positioned its appeal to a transatlantic audience, towns such as London, Birmingham, Plymouth, Glasgow, Dublin, and Paris, including many smaller villages, became hotbeds for antislavery activity and offered many avenues, platforms and publications in which to spread messages. Shaped by the political, economic, or social events that were occurring in the United States at that time, Black abolitionist Jeremiahs' messages scraped at the influence and deception of a nation that asserted "democratic principles" while allowing racial subjugation and the continued enslavement of their people (*BAP IV* 256). Therefore, with sound, defined goals, Black abolitionist Jeremiahs felt it a necessity to enlist the aid and financial support of foreign countries like Great Britain.

Black abolitionist Jeremiahs' involvement in the antislavery movements abroad was not, however, constant throughout the antebellum era. Although they established the magnitude of the black presence abroad, by the late 1850s, abolitionists' participation in Great Britain weakened (Ripley et al. 3). This sporadic change was in response to circumstances in the United States. After the passing of the FSA, however, Black abolitionists' participation in antislavery activities in Great Britain increased significantly. The FSA, in Alexander Crummell's opinion, had sought to "retard the advancement of the cause of freedom" ("Speech by Alexander Crummell" 276). However, Black abolitionist Jeremiahs did not engage in the "politics of the American antislavery movement to define their British mission" (*BAP I* 345). As Ward lamented, "In the British Empire, we have not to devise means, and adopt measures to be free or to regain lost or withholden rights. What we need now to learn, is how to use our liberty, and to make it serviceable to the crushed millions of our native land" (Samuel Ringgold Ward to the Readers" 392–393). To his British audience William J. Watkins lamented that America "is ruled by a horde of despots, who would, if possible, hurl the Eternal from his throne, in order to get at the heart's blood of the negro. The influence of the American Government abroad is only an influence of evil" ("Our Influence Abroad" 257).

Black abolitionist Jeremiahs expressed their views on the American Colonization Society (ACS). Nathaniel Paul felt that because he was a black man, he had the right to criticize ACS more so than other detractors, "As a colored man, and as a citizen of the United States, it necessarily follows that I must feel more deeply interested in its operation.... I know not which is the most

7. The Transatlantic African American Jeremiad

detestable in my view — its CRUELTY or its HYPOCRISY. Both of these are characteristics of its whole operation" ("Speech by Nathaniel Paul, Delivered at Exeter Hall" 46; emphasis in original). Paul, a minister from Albany, New York, identified a number of reasons why ACS further degraded blacks in the United States:

> I brand it as a *cruel* institution, and one of the most cruel that has ever been brought into existence by the ingenuity of man ... [ACS] seek[s]to expel [blacks] ... because the God of heaven has given them a different complexion from [whites] ... I say it is a *cruel* institution, because it seeks to rob the colored men in [the United States] of every right civil, political, or religious, to which they are entitled by the American Declaration of Independence.... I say it is a *cruel* institution, because ... it has also been the means of having laws enacted which prevents [blacks] from meeting together to pay homage to their Creator, and worship God who made them. I might go on enumerating instances of cruelty, and show ... that even combinations have been formed in what are called the free States, under the influence of this Society, not to give the colored man employment, but to rob him of the means of gain his livelihood, that he may thereby be compelled to leave the land of his nativity, and go to Africa ["Speech by Nathaniel Paul, Delivered at Exeter Hall" 46–47; emphasis in original].

When Charles Lenox Remond traveled abroad and lectured on the "subject of anti-slavery" on that "side of the Atlantic," his transatlantic Jeremiads criticized sexism and colonization. Upon his arrival in London in June 1840, Remond "learned with much sorrow of the rejection of the female delegation" at the World's Anti-Slavery Convention. He wrote to Charles B. Ray, "In the name of heaven, and in the name of the bleeding dying slave, I ask if I shall scruple in the propriety of female action." After hearing Daniel O'Connell speak in Exeter Hall, Remond was "moved to think, and feel, and speak." O'Connell's "soul-stirring eloquence and burning sarcasm" moved "every fibre" [*sic*] of his heart toward his antislavery mission ("Charles Lenox Remond to Charles B. Ray" 71, 73). Remond charged that in the United States, the "non-slaveholding" states aided in allowing slavery to flourish there:

> [Slavery] exercises its authority by assisting in the kidnapping the innocent and free at the capitol, disfranchises the citizens of Pennsylvania, proscribes the colored man in Rhode Island, abuses and gives him no resting place as a man in New Hampshire, which murders in Illinois, cries out amalgamation in Maine, mobs him in New York, and stones him in Connecticut. I say this hydra headed personage, thanks be to God, has but few advocates in [England], if any ["Charles Lenox Remond to Charles B. Ray" 73].

Some Black abolitionist Jeremiahs discovered that Scotland would offer them avenues to implore their audiences to resist racial prejudice in America. When James McCune Smith traveled to Glasgow to study medicine, he was elated to find the Scottish "more generally engaged in the cause of Emancipation" ("Remarks by James McCune Smith" 65) than he had imagined. Joining the Glasgow Emancipation Society in 1833, McCune beckoned his Scottish audience to continue their antislavery efforts. Free blacks, he assured them, would endure any antislavery scheme in America:

> If at this moment any warlike armament were to invade the United States, even for the purpose of liberating the victims of prejudice and of Slavery, the men who would strike first, and would struggle longest in defence [sic] of the American coast, would be the 800,000 free people of colour, who are Americans by birth, Americans in principle, and have proved themselves in many a field of fight, as well as by present suffering ... the most ardent lovers of the American soil ["Remarks by James McCune Smith" 66].

Although a free man, Smith was well aware of the challenges that blacks faced in America and devoted his time to eradicating racism and prejudice through establishing institutions and organizations for black self-empowerment. He lamented:

> Let me entreat you ... never to forget these circumstances ... forget not incessantly to exercise that influence for the benefit of the helpless Slave.... I will go back to the land whence I came, happy in the thought that at a day not very distant, it may be my privilege once more to appear before you — no longer an outcast from the land of the free — no longer the victim of a cruel prejudice — no longer debarred from seats of learning, for a physical accident, no fault of mine — no longer deprived of any of the privileges of an American citizen — but that it will be my lot to tell you that AMERICA IS FREE! (Cheers). And who knows ... but that there may come with me an American Slave, whose chains shall have been broken; and American Slave-holder, whose whip shall have been destroyed; and an American Christian, whose prejudices shall have been annihilated by the means you are now using to attain these ends. (Tremendous cheering.) And we will come, not only to thank you for what you have done, but to entreat you to re-engage your eloquent and devoted agent in those labours, which, I trust, will never cease until Slavery be banished from the face of the earth. (Cheers.) ["Remarks by James McCune Smith" 66–67].

Many Black abolitionist Jeremiahs would find that "an Irish tour could rejuvenate a flagging British antislavery mission" (*BAP I* 332). Edmund Kelly was one such activist. Traveling abroad to raise funds to purchase his family's freedom, Kelly, whose father was Irish, reminded his audience that slave holding in America was in "open violation of the letter and spirit of the Declaration of Independence." Lamenting the "sad account of the wretched condition of the slaves in the southern states of America," Kelly reminded all Christians that they had to duty to "sympathize with and advocate the cause of all who were suffering in slavery" ("Speech by Edmund Kelly" 333). When he traveled to Ireland, Frederick Douglass urged his listeners "neither to apologize for nor give countenance to Christian slave owners" (N. Brown, "Send Back the Money," 4). Said he:

> We want to awaken the slave holder to a sense of the iniquity of his position, and to draw him from his nefarious habits. We want to encircle America with a girdle of Anti-slavery fire, that will reflect light upon the darkness of the slave institutions, and alarm their guilty upholders—(great applause). It must also be stated that the American pulpit is on the side of slavery, and the Bible is blasphemously quoted in support of it.... Slavery with all its bloody paraphernalia is upheld by the church of the country. We want them to have the Methodists of Ireland speak to those of America, and say, "While your hands are red with blood, while the thumb screws and gags

7. The Transatlantic African American Jeremiad 165

and whips are wrapped up in the pontifical robes of your Church, we will have no fellowship with you, or acknowledge you (as) Christians" ["I Am Here to Spread Light on American Slavery" 43–44].

Douglass interweaved his "forceful arguments with the poignancy of actual slave experiences" (N. Brown, "Send Back the Money," 4) when he revealed "The natural elasticity of the human soul repels the slightest attempt to enslave it. Black slaves of America were not wholly without that elasticity; they are men, and, being so, they do not submit readily to the yoke" ("I Am Here to Spread Light on American Slavery" 44). William G. Allen, lecturer and educator born in Virginia in 1820, the son of a free mulatto mother and a Welsh father, spoke "authoritatively about the close connection between slavery and northern racial prejudice" in Leeds, England (*BAP I* 367). In 1850, Allen escaped American prejudice and fled to Europe because he asked Mary King, daughter of the Reverend Lyndon King, a white abolitionist, to marry him. Public opposition to the relationship intensified, forcing Allen to flee the country. While in England, Allen had a difficult time securing work as a lecturer (Garner, "William G. Allen") but was able to author two memoirs, *The American Prejudice Against Color: An Authentic Narrative, Showing How Easily the Nation Got into An Uproar* (1853) and *A Personal Narrative* (1860). In 1852, Allen was invited by the Leeds Anti-Slavery to deliver a series of speeches at the Stock Exchange. In the speeches, Allen dealt out "indiscriminate abuse of America and her institutions." Allen informed his audience that he had no wishes to "indulge in fulsome flattery" concerning American slavery, but had every intention of condemning the country's "abomination of abominations" ("Speech by William G. Allen" 367). Since Allen had been educated at the Oneida Institute, "a progressive interracial school in upstate New York" (Garner, "William G. Allen"), he carefully called his audience's attention to the relationship between blacks' education in the United States and prejudice. "No coloured man in America could afford to write poetry or become an artist," he lamented, "when all the powers of that mighty people were combined together to keep him in the dust." Allen pleaded with his audience to do all they could to "break down" the "iniquitous system of slavery, by protesting against it, and shaming the people of American out of it" ("Speech by William G. Allen" 367, 368, 369, 370). Charles Lenox Remond would also realize that an Irish tour would support his antislavery agenda. Visiting some "six or seven important cities & towns in Ireland" and holding "Anti American Slavery meetings" in all of them, Remond announced that "never in my life have I seen deeper interest Exhibited in proportion as the Irish people become Enlightened" ("Charles Lenox Remond to Nathaniel P. Rogers" 97).

Paris also served as a place where Black abolitionist Jeremiahs could find a receptive audience for their transatlantic jeremiads and an opportunity to turn "a variety of reform meetings into antislavery forums" (*BAP I* 155). William Wells Brown and J. W. C. Pennington attended the Second General Peace Congress held in Paris 22–24 August 1849. Brown, who had been a slave for 20 years, revealed that Paris offered greater freedoms than the United States. "I can utter my sentiments with perfect freedom in Paris," he lamented, "but if I were to do so in the United States, my life would be in danger." Brown evaluated slavery as "war against blacks. It is impossible to maintain slavery without maintaining war," he lamented. "If therefore we can obtain the abolition of war, we shall at the same time proclaim liberty throughout the world, break in pieces every yoke of bondage, and let all the oppressed go free" ("Speeches by William Wells Brown and J. W. C. Pennington" 155). Pennington agreed with Brown's comparison of slavery and "war against blacks." Slavery was "the cause of discord, strife, and ill will among men," he mourned. Pennington's declaration of peace involved abolishing the system of slavery so that "universal peace" could exist. To illustrate this idea further, Pennington told the audience "we are wronged, but we do not wrong others. In our character," he added, "you will find an element of *Peace*" ("Speech by J. W. C. Pennington" 158; emphasis in original). Pennington furthered assured his "pacifist listeners" (*BAP I* 155) that all nations had the responsibility to accept the role of eliminating the "war against blacks." "It seems to me," he lamented, "that those nations claiming to be Christian and civilized, lie under a weight of responsibility in reference to the interests of the peace cause" ("Speech by J. W. C. Pennington" 158).

Traveling abroad or sometimes becoming an expatriate of their native America by escaping the oppressive laws enacted to further subjugate them, Black abolitionist Jeremiahs delivered jeremiads to foreign spectators that were, for the most part, well received and were meant to build momentum for their antislavery cause in the United States.

Opposition to American Prejudice: The Transatlantic Jeremiads of William Wells Brown and Frederick Douglass

At 8 P.M. on Wednesday, 5 September 1849, William Wells Brown found himself facing his "first English audience" as an "enthusiastic" assembly welcomed him to Croydon, England (*The American Fugitive in Europe* 128). Reaching beyond America's borders while advocating the cause of the American slave, Brown protested against American slavery because he felt it "enslaved man, and brought the human being down from the high position which God intended him to occupy, and placed him upon a lower level than the best of the field" ("Speech by William Wells Brown Delivered at the Lecture Hall, Croydon, England" 170). Brown left Croydon "with a good impression of the English," (*The American Fugitive in Europe*, 128) and during his five-year mid-nineteenth-century (1849–1854) lecture tour of Europe, he often concluded his lengthy

7. The Transatlantic African American Jeremiad 167

and "eloquent" rhetorical jeremiads "amdist loud applause" ("Speech by William Wells Brown Delivered at the Lecture Hall, Croydon, England" 170). As a spokesperson for what he called America's "domestic institution" ("Speech by William Wells Brown, Delivered at the Concert Rooms" 176), Brown became a world citizen, "in spite of, or perhaps because of the fact that in the U.S. he was not a citizen, but rather a fugitive slave" ("'Unbecoming' to Become American").

Lecturing for support of the American abolitionist's causes abroad, Brown used his speeches to attack America's idea of democracy and the hypocrisy of using religion to ensure the docility of slaves. As he condemned the language of the founding fathers, Brown informed his British audience:

> In their *Declaration of Independence*, the Americans declare that "all men are created equal; that they are endowed by their Creator with certain inalienable rights; that among these are life, liberty, and the pursuit of happiness." Yet one-sixth of the inhabitants of the great Republic are slaves. Thus they give the lie to their own professions. No one forfeits his or her character or standing in society by being engaged in holding, buying or selling a slave; the details of which, in all their horror, can scarcely be told. Although the holding of slaves is confined to fifteen of the thirty-one States, yet we hold that the non-slave-holding States are equally guilty with the slave-holding. If any proof is needed on this point, it will be found in the passage of the inhuman Fugitive Slave Law, by Congress; a law which could never have been enacted without the votes of a portion of the representatives from the free States, and which is now being enforced, in many of the States, with the utmost alacrity [*Three Years in Europe* 247–48].

Brown's denunciation of America's democratic principles put forth in the Declaration of Independence and the FSA suggested that in order for the newly formed republic to become a true democracy, the "non-slave-holding States" should aide in the normative freedom and cultural establishment of African Americans. Brown continued his criticism of the Declaration of Independence and the FSA throughout his exile abroad. Brown lamented:

> Slavery was introduced into the constitution by allowing the African slave trade to be continued for twenty years, making it lawful and constitutional, which it had never been before; and then the slaveowner was allowed representation for this slave property, and every man that would go to the Coast of Africa, and steal five negroes and bring them to the United States, was allowed by the constitution, then, three votes for the five slaves. And it is carried down to the present time, as the American congress has more than twenty-five representatives based upon this slave representation. And that is one of the reasons why in the national congress the slaveowners have the power of carrying so many of their measures, and the twenty-five ... ["Speech by William Wells Brown, Delivered at the Town Hall" 399].

Emphasizing the paradox of a country founded on freedom yet continuing to depend on and support slave labor, the nucleus of Brown's transatlantic jeremiads suggested to his audience that American "persecution was a domineering and tyrannical structure that impeded every echelon of black life in America. "The act of the British people which struck off the fetters of their own slaves,"

Brown lamented, "was a *prima facie* evidence that they held that" the slave had that right ("American Slavery"; emphasis in original). Politically, economically, and religiously, American prejudice regarded blacks as less than second-rate to everyone else within the American social order. Opposition to American prejudice, Brown felt, was an ongoing struggle.

> America is called a free and independent country, and yet there is not a single foot of soil over which the stars and the stripes wave upon which *I* could stand and be protected by law. (Sensation.) There is not a foot of soil in the United States upon which I could stand where the constitution would give me any protection; and let me return to the United States, I am liable to be seized at any moment and conveyed in chains to the southern states, and there handed over to a man who claims me as his property, and to be worked up as he may think fit ["Speech by William Wells Brown, Delivered at the Town Hall" 399; emphasis in original].

Brown's transatlantic jeremiads advocated the rights of man. As he understood God's natural law, every human being was born into the world with the right to life, the right to liberty, and the right to the pursuit of happiness. He lamented:

> When the American colonies separated from the mother country in 1776, and adopted the constitution for themselves, and formed a government upon their own plan, they engrafted in the constitution of that country certain provisions, giving certain rights to the slave-holding people of the colonies — rights of property in their fellow man — the right of carrying on the African slave trade for a period of twenty years — the right of chasing a runaway slave, not only in the free states, and recapturing him if they could find him, and taking him back to the prison house he had left, to fasten the chains upon his limbs; but it was required that they should bind themselves to put down any insurrection — any effort on the part of the blacks of the slave states to regain their liberties — by physical force. These were certain parts of the American constitution, which had become the law of the land ["Slavery in America"].

His transatlantic jeremiad sought to raise the laboring classes of America — people of whom he was connected to by skin color and stripes — because, as he bemoaned in his rhetoric, he believed American blacks were the very "bone and sinew" of the United States. However, the system of American slavery left blacks no right to participate in the budding governmental processes. After lecturing abroad for five years, Brown informed his British audience that he would return to America:

> Conscious that I may safely give to the free coloured people of the north, and to the abolitionists of the United States, the assurance that something is being done here for their cause, and that the English people only want to know what they can do, and they will act about it and do it ["Speech by William Wells Brown, Delivered at the Town Hall" 404].

However, he assured them that the facts of slavery in the United States ought to be known throughout England:

> Now, go to the United States, and you will see, that acts as cruel as ever were done in England, in that age, are done in America now-done every day in the southern

7. The Transatlantic African American Jeremiad 169

states, and done almost every week in the northern states; you will see there judges who sit on the bench, giving their sentence in favour of slavery, and condemning freedom; judges who knew, too, that the persons whom their sentence orders thus to be seized and carried back into the southern states, will be cruelly tortured there. It was asserted not long since in Boston ... that one of those slaves, who had been seized in the north, and carried back to slavery, had been flogged to death, or nearly to death; and such will be the fate of many of them. Then, ought not facts like those to be known throughout this country? ["Speech by William Wells Brown, Delivered at the Town Hall" 402].

Brown's speech chimed with echoes of jeremiadic discourse: his critique of American slavery; his mourning for his people; and his optimism for the future aid of the British in eradicating American prejudice:

I hope [this meeting] will do something to instruct the people here, and to maintain the anti-slavery principles, so that Englishmen, when they visit the United States, may not do henceforth, as many of their countrymen have done, give their influence to the side of the oppressor, instead of the oppressed ["Speech by William Wells Brown, Delivered at the Town Hall" 402].

Brown furthered forewarned that "if therefore we can obtain the abolition of war, we shall at the same time proclaim liberty throughout the world, break in pieces every yoke of bondage, and let all the oppressed go free" ("Speech by William Wells Brown, Delivered at the Town Hall" 402).

Frederick Douglass enjoyed delivering speeches abroad, informing audiences about the trials and tribulations of slaves in the United States. As his transatlantic jeremiads reached their apex at Paisley, Scotland, 17 March 1846, Douglass assured his audiences that he was qualified to "impart accurate information respecting the workings of American slavery" and informed them that his purpose was to reveal slavery's "outrages upon its victims, by exposing it to the gaze and indignation of the Christian world." If slavery existed in England as it did in America, Douglass assured his audience, "I will do all in my power to crush it, but I utterly deny you have the least shadow of it." Douglass then turned his attention to defining the system of slavery in order to gain understanding of it existence. "What is slavery?" he posited ("International Moral Force Can Destroy Slavery" 183):

There seems to be a great want of information regarding it. It is not a system whereby a man is compelled to work, it is not slavery to have one peculiar right struck down; if it is, all women all minors, are slaves. I protest against the use of the term slavery being applied in such a manner — it is an awful misnomer. Slavery must be regarded as something different; it must be regarded as one man holding property in another, subjected to the destroying of all the higher qualities of his nature, deprived of his own body, his own soul. A slave is one who is to all intents and purposes a marketable commodity — common goods and chattels ["International Moral Force Can Destroy Slavery" 183].

Douglass further lamented that slavery in the United States had grown to such epic proportions that "one nation is not fit to cope with it." Slavery was:

> A system so deeply imbedded in the constitution of America, so firmly rooted in her churches, so entwined about the hearts of the whole people that it requires a moral force from without as well as within. I am anxious to have a remonstrance from Britain. America may boast of her abilities to build forts to stand the fire of the enemy, but she shall never be able to drive back that moral force which shall send slavery tottering to its grave ["International Moral Force Can Destroy Slavery" 183].

While delivering another speech at Paisley, Scotland, on 17 April 1846, Douglass utilized the jeremiad to yield a "reproachful British opinion" concerning American slavery (Blassingame 215). "I believe that slavery is such an enormous system of fraud and wrong," he told his audience, "that if once we get the people to see it they will exert themselves for its removal." Douglass believed, however, that it was the influence of British writers that would help further the day of liberation for blacks in America, "If we wish to call attention to anything we may point at Britain. We learn what is the mind of Britain by reading the writings of such men as Dickens."[1] Douglass conceived that Dickens' "calling attention to the subject" would aid in the destruction of "slavery in the United States" ("British Influence on the Abolition Movement in America" 220). Douglass lamented, however, that slavery in the United States:

> Would have been long since removed if the honest people had been prevailed on to discuss the matter. I trust we shall now soon succeed in awakening them from their indolence — in arousing them to get the weight thrown off which bears down their moral energies. We have not yet been able to get them to see it — to get them to concentrate their attention upon it ["British Influence on the Abolition Movement in America" 219].

Douglass voiced his opinions about how the abolitionist crusade affected whites in the United States. He told his audience that even though he detested the "American institution" of slavery, he believed in "the Declaration of Independence" because he understood that "it contains a true doctrine — 'that all men are treated equal.'" It was because Americans did not "carry out this principle" that Douglass attempted to "appeal to the people of Britain — to people everywhere" and draw their attention to the "indignant eye of ... slavery" ("British Influence on the Abolition Movement in America" 220–221). Douglass informed listeners in London that "amidst obstacles and difficulties of various kinds, mobs, and so on" in the United States, he was still "very well known" ("Emancipation is an Individual" 250). In his 12 May 1846 "Reception Speech," delivered at Finsbury Chapel, Moorfields, England, Douglass continued to examine "the inquiry, what is American slavery?":

> Slavery in the United States is the granting of that power by which one man exercises and enforces a right of property in the body and soul of another. The condition of a slave is simply that of the brute beast. He is a piece of property — a marketable commodity, in the language of the law, to be bought or sold at the will and caprice of the master who claims him to be his property; he is spoken of, thought of, and treated as property. His own good, his conscience, his intellect, his affections, are all set aside by the master. The will and the wishes of the master are the law of the

slave. He is as much a piece of property as a horse. If he is fed, he is fed because he is property. If he is clothed, it is with a view to the increase of his value as property. Whatever of comfort is necessary to him for his body or soul that is inconsistent with his being property, is carefully wrested from him, not only by public opinion, but by the law of the country. He is carefully deprived of everything that tends in the slightest degree to detract from his value as property. He is deprived of education. God has given him an intellect; the slaveholder declares it shall not be cultivated. If his moral perception leads him in a course contrary to his value as property, the slaveholder declares he shall not exercise it. The marriage institution cannot exist among slaves, and one-sixth of the population of democratic America is denied its privileges by the law of the land ["Reception Speech" 408–09]

Douglass' transatlantic jeremiad embraced universal humanistic ethics about the affects slavery had on those who were victims of its tyranny. His lamentation on the dregs of American slavery no doubt had a lasting effect on his British audience. Douglass helped to restructure the definition of Black abolitionist Jeremiahs because he influenced the expectation of British audiences.

The Transatlantic Jeremiads of Alexander Crummell and Martin R. Delany

While touring Great Britain to raise funds to build a church for his New York congregation, Alexander Crummell took the time to give "an account of the civil and spiritual condition of the negro race" in America. Crummell's appeal to his British audience was one already familiar among black abolitionists. He reminded his audience of the "integral relationship between southern slavery and northern racial prejudice" (*BAP I* 349). "It might be supposed that in the United States a free man would be a free man," he pronounced, "but unfortunately it was not so if he happened to have a black face." Crummell remained steadfast in his efforts to aid in black uplift. He felt it imperative that this uplift take place in America. "Anxious to remain" with "his brethren in the United States, and help to rebuild them," Crummell was ready to "make any sacrifices" needed to become "one of the humblest agents" in the education of his brethren by "raising them above degradation, and breaking down the barriers of hindrance, which now prevented their temporal and spiritual progress" ("Speech by Alexander Crummell, Delivered at the Lower Hall" 349, 350, 351).

Born to a former slave in 1819 in New York City, Crummell, accompanied by his wife and four children, eventually moved to England in 1847. Two years after making England his home, Crummell introduced a resolution which beckoned his audience at the annual British and Foreign Anti-Slavery Society to abstain "as far as practicable, from the use of slave-labour produce." Crummell felt that if the English accepted his resolution, the result would be a "powerful means for securing the universal abolition of slavery." He reminded his audience that in order to "put down the slave-trade ... the whole system must be destroyed" ("Remarks of Alexander Crummell" 149–150). Crummell went so far as to remind Great Britain that its denizens had a role to play in the continuation of America's "peculiar institution." Said he:

> The simple fact is, that Great Britain is still the great supporter of slavery, by her immense consumption of the slave-grown produce. You use two-thirds of the whole American cotton crops. Let your Lancashire mills stop working, let your Manchester factory people be standing still, and the effect on the American cotton-growers is wonderful. But let your markets be active, let the price of cotton rise here, and, immediately it is known across the Atlantic, the price of slaves rises, droves of human beings are sent up to our slave-markets, men in their strength, women in their prime, are sold and separated, and sent to Baltimore or Kentucky. Tell the planters that you will no longer, by buying the produce of their slaves, suffer them to get rich by the sweat, and agony, and blood of your fellow-creatures—that you will reduce them from affluence to poverty and bankruptcy, and immediately the system will come to an end. The sugar of Brazil and Cuba is also chiefly used in Great Britain. You have extensive possessions for the production of those commodities; and thus you could benefit yourselves, while you destroy an accursed system, and liberate millions of your fellow-creatures. I trust the subject will be thought of and acted upon a most sacred duty ["Remarks of Alexander Crummell" 150].

Crummell's "commercial jeremiad" to Great Britain was simple: the system of slavery continued to thrive because of their greed. But Crummell did not stop there. He continued to attack the system of slavery and the many problems it caused on a global scale. "The liberties of mankind have as much, if not more," he revealed, "to fear from the democracy of the United States, than from the autocracy of Russia." Crummell wished to elicit the support of the "friends of freedom in England" to aid in the gradual advancement of blacks in America ("Speech by Alexander Crummell" 276, 278).

While seeking a viable solution to the oppressive reality of blacks in America, the rhetoric of the transatlantic jeremiad reached the West coast of Africa. In the late 1850s, the discourse of Martin Delany's transatlantic jeremiad illustrated that he supported emigration to Africa instead of Central and South America. In 1859, Delany was able to obtain financial support from the American Colonization Society and the African Civilization Society to travel to Liberia (Levine 332). Supporting emigration to Africa in order to "establish a distinct nationality" for his oppressed brethren within the walls of America's "peculiar institution," Delany traveled to Liberia to seek "rapprochement with the nation's leaders and populace." Speaking on the subject of "political condition and destiny of the African race," Delany described blacks' state of being in the United States as "stationary, for the reason ... that two opposite forces of nearly equal power are brought to bear upon them, Abolitionism and Colonization." It was these two impositions, Delany believed, that aided in the degradation of blacks in the United States because they were "operating in contrary directions." Therefore, he believed, the black man in the United States must "hurl his fulminations at his brethren in Liberia" to gain support for the abolitionists' cause. Delany believed that emigration was "the best and only hope of the colored people in the United States." Because the black populace in America "could never wield a great influence," no matter how "highly favored they might become," Delany advocated "emigration ... to Africa," where he believed blacks would "join the one hundred and sixty millions of their degraded brethren [and] assist to elevate them." If this happened, Delany prophesized, "the reflex influence upon America" would be felt and "be powerful, in behalf of the slaves" ("Martin R. Delany in Liberia" 332, 333, 334, 335).

"Liberty or death": Sarah Parker Remond's Transatlantic Jeremiads

A powerful and persuasive speaker, Sarah Parker Remond delivered her jeremiads to enthusiastic crowds in cities throughout England, Scotland and Ireland. Having "more invitations tha[n]" she could fill ("Sarah P. Remond to Maria Weston Chapman" 462), Remond, the younger sister of Charles Lenox Remond, based her transatlantic jeremiads on "unquestionable facts" instead of "personal statements" ("Speech by Sarah P. Remond, Delivered at the Red Lion Hotel" 445). Remond's approach to relay the facts of slavery, to establish them in an unquestionable manner, affirmed that these specific details did not in any way alter the status of her representation. Her mission was to ignite compassion for those whose complexion was darker than "the majority of American citizens." "A common sympathy," she lamented, "should unite all." By 1859, she revealed to her British audience that "in America politics were corrupt. It would be uninteresting to [them] to state the mass of corruptions that underlaid the whole system of American government." Therefore, Remond did not intend on spending a "moment of the precious time" occupying an endeavor "to prove that slavery was a sin." That, she revealed, would be "an insult to their hearts." When she toured Great Britain to raise funds for American antislavery, Remond maintained that she was there, representative of "a race that was stripped of every right and debarred from every privilege — a race which was deprived of the protection of the law, and the glorious influences of religion, and all the strong ties and influences of social life." Her heavily feminists transatlantic jeremiads honored the heroic efforts of women who fought against America's "iron despotism." Remond commemorated the actions of Margaret Garner[2] as a means to galvanize Britons, "The courts decided that Margaret Garner must be returned to slavery under the Fugitive Slave Law," she lamented. But after Garner's counsel revealed to Remond "that he could have raised 10,000 dollars" to aid in rescuing her from "the hands of the tyrant," Garner's owner "said there was not enough money in Cincinnati to purchase his chattel!" To enhance the effect, Remond lamented, "She was a thing! (Deep sensation.) Yes, every slave below Mason and Dixon's line was a thing" ("Slave Life in America" 435, 436, 437). "Women are the worst victims of the slave power," she lamented ("Speech by Sarah P. Remond, Delivered at the Athenaeum" 459). Parker stressed the sexual exploitation of black women under slavery and argued:

> Above all sufferers in America, American women who were slaves lived in the most pitiable condition. They could not protect themselves from the licentiousness which met them on every hand — they could not protect their honour from the tyrant.... Yes, I can tell you English men and women, that women are sold into slavery with cheeks like the lily and the rose, as well as those that might compare with the wing of the raven ["Slave Life in America" 437, 438].

Her transatlantic jeremiads overflowed with the miseries and disgraces which her sisters suffered in America. "The fearful amount of licentiousness which everywhere pervaded the Southern States," she lamented, was evident in the fact that "there were 800,000 mulattoes" in the South alone. This fact brought:

> Nothing but desolation in the hearts of the mother who bore them, and it ought to have brought shame to the fathers; but there was no respect for morality while the ministers of the gospel and statesmen of the south did not set an example with even their slaves could follow ["Speech by Sarah P. Remond, Delivered at the Red Lion Hotel" 445].

Speaking out against both slavery and racial discrimination, Remond revealed:

> Black men and women were treated worse than criminals for no other reason that because they were black. "Liberty or death" was the motto of the American slaves; and there were from 30,000 to 40,000 who had escaped into Canada in spite of the overwhelming obstacles that present themselves ["Slave Life in America" 438].

According to Remond, the end result of American slavery was inevitable. "The great American republic was destined to be sundered," she prophesied and thanked "God for it":

> [The American government] would be severed, and no power could save it unless a sentiment could be created in the northern mind which would override the antagonism of the south. The work would go on. God, love, and the truth would prevail ["Slave Life in America" 440].

Although Remond did not ask her British audiences for "political interference," she beckoned them to aid heightening "the moral public opinion until its voice" reached "the American shores." She beseeched them to aid in the fight of American prejudice "until the shackles of the American slave melt like dew before the morning sun." Identifying herself as an "Ultra-abolitionists," Remond made palpable distinctions between social life in the North and South:

> In the north, democracy, not what the Americans call democracy, but the true principle of equal rights, prevails — I speak of the white population, mind — wealth is abundant; the country, in every material sense, flourishes. In the south, aristocratic feelings prevail, labour is dishonourable, and five millions of poor whites live in the most degrading ignorance and destitution.... The five millions poor whites are most

of them in as gross state of ignorance as Mrs. Stowe's "Topsey," in *Uncle Tom's Cabin*. The free colored people of the northern states are, for no crime but the fact of complexion, deprived of all political and social rights ["Speech by Sarah P. Remond, Delivered at the Athenaeum" 457–458].

Remond took the time, however, to chastise Great Britain for allowing an "internal slave trade" to manifest in the United States. "The whole power of the country is in the hands of the slaveholders," she lamented, "For more than thirty years we have had a slaveholding President, and the slave power has been dominant." The result of "slave power" was a "series of encroachments" with the reopening of the slave trade. Since British ships had no "'right of search'" on American ships (*BAP I* 460, 2n), "slavers ply on the seas which were previously guarded" by British ships ("Speech by Sarah P. Remond, Delivered at the Athenaeum" 458). If the British would heightened their presence on the Atlantic Ocean, slavery would no doubt suffer a severe blow.

Remond felt that the blame for the growth and development of slavery in America "rests on the Constitution of the country." Believing that the very heart of England beats for the antislavery cause in the United States, Remond told listeners:

> The first settlers began by enslaving the Indians; then they brought over the Africans, and slavery was firmly established long before the [States] confederated, and the proclamation of the Declaration of Independence made no difference. The first compromise of liberty was made then, and every successive change and development of the so-called democratic republic has been a fresh compromise with slavery.... America has always been a slave-holding nation, and never more so than at the present time ["American Slavery and African Colonisation"].

Although slavery did not exist in "the northern states" of America, it was "upheld almost universally by the Church, the press, and the laws." No politician, Remond lamented, "would advocate immediate abolition on the floor of Congress" because the best political leaders:

> Stand outside of politics, and disclaim all connexion with a democracy with, while professing to believe in the Fatherhood of God and the brotherhood of man, cancels its own professions by every act of its political life ... the north has as much to do with slavery as the south ["American Slavery and African Colonisation"].

Throughout her transatlantic jeremiads, Remond remained steadfast in supporting poor blacks in the American South. Remond played a crucial role in appealing to British sensibilities and drew their attention to the hindrances women suffered throughout the United States.

Conclusion

Illustrative of the ills of slavery in the United States, the transatlantic jeremiad beckoned its foreign audience to aid in the abolition of slavery in America either through direct intervention or by aiding in the emigration efforts posed by Black Nationalists. Black abolitionist Jeremiahs who delivered their jeremiads to such audiences saw no need to beseech them to change their philosophies but rather to recruit them to join the bandwagon of American abolitionism. As William Wells Brown informed his British audience on 5 August 1854, "We do not ask you to take up arms; we do not ask you to do any act, or utter any language, unbecoming Christians; but we ask you to learn the facts and the truth of this matter, and honestly and strongly to speak out upon it" ("Speech by William Wells Brown, Delivered at the Town Hall" 401). Black abolitionist Jeremiahs addressed their international audiences on a personal level encouraging their aid in the liberation of African Americans on all fronts in America. Their transatlantic jeremiads sought to condemn slavery while demonstrating to its foreign audiences how slavery had corrupted every institution — religious, political, social, economic, and commercial — in the United States.

8

The Black Canadian Jeremiad

> We, who have escaped from your toils, can perceive that the traffic in the flesh and blood of our brethren must have a speedy termination — that you must adopt one of the many proposed schemes which the benevolent have put forth for our emancipation — or take the consequences of your blind obstinacy, which can only result in confusion and ruin to yourselves.
> Henry Bibb, "To Our Old Masters," 1851

When former slaves, such as Henry Bibb, sought to free themselves of the persecution of America's so-called democracy, many took to Canada their rhetoric that sought to further support the growing antislavery movement in the United States and formed a unique discourse outside the realm of the country's politics. When he used his Canadian residency as a means to garner the support needed to assail American racial prejudice and criticized Canadian discrimination, Bibb voiced his opinions in the *Voices of the Fugitive*, the first black newspaper, of his own design, published in Canada from 1851–1853. Bibb lamented the hardships of American slavery by attacking the notion of slaves' supposedly inherent inferiority. "It is contented by many of you," he mourned, "that our enslavement is just." He informed Southern slaveholders that "every negro in the South" was discerning enough "to know that he is placed in a false position" and knew that "his master robs him of his liberty." Bibb used his voice to further his position that American slaveholders were "the descendants of men who were placed much in the same position as" blacks, "namely, fugitive slaves" ("A Letter to My Old Master" 122, 121). Concerned that America's racial indifference, "Capt. *Slavery*" he coined it, would influence Canada's standing as a safe haven in black America's consciousness, Bibb proclaimed "this most obnoxious and fatal disease has made its way into" Canadian provinces where "it is destined to make havoc among the ignorant and vicious if a speedy remedy is not applied" ("Color-Phobia in Canada" 136; emphasis in original). Unlike its African American precursor, the rhetoric of the Black Canadian jeremiad was situated, then, in the context of two evolving debates: the degradation of 1) American slavery and 2) Canadian prejudice.

No doubt a jeremiadic discourse previously existed in Black Canada's social protest rhetoric. Embedded in rhetoric of Black Canadian Jeremiahs who crossed the American-Canadian border in search of true freedoms not offered to them in the United States, however, was the maturing discourse of the African American jeremiad. Given that their jeremiads were delivered and written while they resided within Canadian borders, their rhetoric was shaped by American prejudice and the practical circumstances of their residence in Canada. There are, however, three major characteristics that distinguish the Black Canadian jeremiad from its African American predecessor. First, because of their experience with American prejudice, blacks who fled to Canada held more significant positions in the Canadian antislavery movement than they had in the United States. Second, as they dominated the Canadian antislavery movement, they were incessantly aware of the antislavery potential of the black experience in Canada. Black Canadian Jeremiahs believed that when they supported refugees who where beginning new lives in Canada, their actions were fundamental to the struggle in the United States. They viewed black prosperity as an antislavery tool that revealed indisputable proof of their self-reliance and accomplishment. Finally, Black Canadian Jeremiahs sought to connect black struggles both north and south of the American-Canadian border in the common cause of self-elevation and determination through intellectual and social activities. In the hands of Black Canadians, a determined rhetoric, critical of "republican oppression" that categorized America as the land of "whips and chains," developed and was supported by both fugitive slaves and free blacks (Cooper 136) throughout western Canadian provinces.

While a corpus of research exists on the rhetoric and social implications of both the American and African American jeremiad, a study on the centrality of jeremiadic discourse Black Canadians employed does not. Black Canadian jeremiads made considerable contributions to the antislavery cause because they were more "conspicuous in the mainstream Canadian antislavery movement" than they had been in the United States (*BAP II* 20). As Samuel Ringgold Ward lamented, "there is no country in the world so much hated by slaveholders, as Canada; nor is there any country so much beloved and sought for, by the slaves" (*Autobiography of a Fugitive Negro* 158). Black Canadian Jeremiahs fashioned their jeremiads to assail not only Canadian prejudice, but also to overcome the injustices that their brethren endured in the United States. In order to strengthen their Canadian presence, Ward believed:

> What we do here [in Canada] must exert a most powerful influence upon our cause in the United States. Indeed I believe that should our improvement, here, go on regularly, steadily, progressively, two results would follow which our friends in the States are very backward in seeing and acknowledging. In the first place, all the boasted influence for good flowing from Liberia,[1] would be realizing more at home, and with it must go down for ever the old, oft refuted lie, of our incapacity for social equality with the Anglo-Saxons. In the second place, persecution must cease in the North, and the more rigorous features of slavery in the South, for our enemies will feel unwilling to do anything that will even indirectly tend to driving us where we can be freemen to the fullest extent ["Samuel Ringgold Ward to Henry Bibb" 182].

Ward argued that if blacks were able to "ameliorate the condition of the free black," they would surely "injure slavery. Diminish the rigors of slavery, in respect to the slave himself," he continued, and "you both feed the flame of liberty in his bosom, and increase his facilities for running away" ("Samuel Ringgold Ward to Henry Bibb" 182).

Often referred to as "Canaan," Canada's standing as the "land of freedom" materialized from its antislavery legislation, from the unwillingness of Canadian courts to return fugitive slaves to America, and from its nonracial political and legal system (*BAP II* 4). To deliver their jeremiads to Canadian audiences and seek support and acceptance, then, Black Canadian Jeremiahs utilized every means at their disposal, including newspapers, lectures, societies and other organizations, and especially the Anti-Slavery Society of Canada (ASC). Found in 1851, ASC, in part, owed its birth to the racial tensions in the United States. Canadian blacks had previously attempted to establish an antislavery organization but had failed. When ASC was established, its purpose was solely to assist slaves who escaped into British territory from the United States and to bring about abolition in America. Because of the Fugitive Slave Act of 1850, Canadian blacks now had the fuel needed to accept that responsibility. Although ASC eventually lost its momentum, Black Canadian Jeremiahs pressed on.

The Fugitive Slave Act of 1850: A "notoriously wicked and cruel enactment"

The Black Canadian jeremiad came to its maturity and reached its apex during the 1850s. The Fugitive Slave Act (FSA) had a profound impact on this development. Forced to flee to Canada, Jermain Wesley Loguen was "shaken by the passage of the horrible Fugitive Slave enactment." "The notoriously wicked and cruel enactment," lamented Loguen, caused him to "abandon the cause" of his "suffering brethren, and forsake" his "native country" ("Jermain Wesley Loguen to Washington Hunt" 194). Haunted by the FSA, banned from obtaining educational advancement, and restricted to the most unskilled jobs, life in Canada offered the promise of liberty and opportunity to all black Americans, free and fugitive alike. According to one estimate, within a few months after the enactment of the FSA, approximately 3,000 fugitives found liberty on Canadian soil (Hite 272). "There are hundreds of slaves coming here daily" ("Mary E. Bibb to Gerrit Smith" 108), wrote Mary E. Bibb, the wife of Henry Bibb. Three years after the FSA was approved, Samuel Ringgold Ward revealed the difficultly in "ascertain[ing] the numbers of fugitive slaves in Canada"; however, with the passing of the FSA, Ward lamented that the numbers "increases at the rate of ten per day, or three thousands per annum. There had been ten thousand," he reported, "since September 1850" ("Fugitive Slaves in Canada").

Black Canadian condemnation of the FSA suggested that Black Canadians were engaging in the process of eliminating racial prejudice on both sides of the border. "Fugitives were fleing [sic] to Canada in such vast numbers," Bibb wrote, that he was "induced by friends of humanity" to set in motion an "organ through which their wants & conditions might be made known to our friends in the States, & which should be devoted to the elevation of the condition of our people generally" ("Henry Bibb to the Executive Committee" 114). Bibb, who was a vital campaigner for Canadian refuge and emigration (*BAP II* 143), revealed that his intentions were to bring before the public facts "relative to the rapid influx and actual condition of our refugee brethren in Canada since the enactment of the notorious Fugitive Slave Law." Bibb sought to inform all that there was no safeguard for a "refugee slave in America, until the Canadian line is drawn between him and his pursuer" ("The American Refugees Home" 143, 144). As Bibb's invectives indicated, Black Canadian Jeremiahs' understanding of the complexities of social representations and the power of white supremacy deepened with the enactment of the FSA.

Because they felt the FSA was "an insult to God, and an outrage upon humanity," members of the North American Convention, convened at St. Lawrence Hall in Toronto from 11–13 September 1851, resolved in their "Proceedings of the North American Convention" that the "infamous fugitive slave enactment of the American Government — whether constitutional or unconstitutional ... [was] not to be endured by any people." The conventioneers, therefore, "entreat" their brethren to "come out from under the jurisdiction of those wicked laws—from the power of a Government whose tender mercies, towards the colored people, are cruel" ("Proceedings of the North American Convention" 152). As the jeremiad continued to gain maturity as a politically-based construction in Black Canadian consciousnesses, Black Canadian Jeremiahs began to bear the burden of fighting not just for justice and retribution in the United States, but also for the essence of their survival in Canada.

"Thanks be to God that I am elected to Canada": Black Canadian Jeremiahs Advocate Social, Political, and Educational Development

When he sought not to "deal in intangible abstractions, but concrete realities," William J. Watkins lamented the condition of blacks in both the United States and Canada. As an agent for James Redpath's Haitian Emigration Bureau who crisscrossed Canada West recruiting emigrants (*BAP II* 446), Watkins, as did William Wells Brown, took advantage of the opportunity to lecture to audiences concerning race relations in both neighboring countries. In his

"Meeting of the Colored Education Institute" oration, Watkins suggested that because blacks did "not fully realize and appreciate the responsibilities which rest upon them, and which must be discharged by them," they were held in inferior positions in both countries. The movement to "rise superior to the crushing circumstances which affect" blacks, had previously intended "upon projecting new theories than in reducing old ones to practice" ("Meeting of the Colored Education Institute"). Therefore, Watkins advocated a new all-encompassing approach that would be more involved in "the circle of human activities" and which would "crystallize into practical life." He believed that the oppressed must be the ones responsible for forging social change. "They must look upward, not downward, forward not backward," he advocated, "They alone can refute the allegation of inherent inferiority which is constantly paraded against them" ("Public Meeting of the Colored Citizens"). Watkins maintained that each black person, whether in the United States or Canada, must be accountable for his or her own social, political, and educational development:

> Be intelligent, industrious, economical [sic]. Aspire daily to something higher. Show your appreciation of the blessings of liberty. Be self-reliant. God helps those who help themselves. Stand up where the sunlight can flash upon and fertilize your energies; where you can drink the invigorating dews of heaven. Never despair, for God sits upon the throne, and amid the clash of contending armies, he cannot and will not forget you, for the very hairs of your head are numbered ["Emancipation Day at Drummondville"].

Even though Canada was free soil, slaveholders and their agents still found ways to capture fugitive slaves and remand them back into American bondage. In their treachery, slaveholders and agents lured fugitives from Canadian provinces with pledges of money, secure jobs, and other creative ventures. This required, however, that they cross the border into Canada in order to carry out their nefarious designs. It did not take long for blacks in Canada to notice this suspicious activity. In 1843, Henry Gouins, a Chatman fugitive who had been a slave on plantations in Virginia, North Carolina, Tennessee, Alabama, and Mississippi, was enticed under some frivolous circumstance by a fellow black man to return to Ohio. When Gouins arrived in Ohio, he was arrested by slave catchers but was soon rescued by two local white sympathizers (*BAP II* 99). When he returned to Canada, Gouins cautioned his Canadian brethren against "the impropriety of placing too much confidence in any person, particularly those of color, who can thus be guilty of such nefarious conduct to his own people, on a mere superficial acquaintance" ("Circular by Henry Goiuns" 99). American slaveholders, however, soon found other means of reclaiming what they considered to be their rightful property. Charles L. Reason warned blacks against writing letters "on matters touching fugitives who have made good their escape." Reason was well aware that mobs often ransacked post offices in search of antislavery literature. "*Fugitive friends have no letters written South*," (emphasis in original) he warned. In his 1 March 1854 published editorial, Reason informed friends of the slave that their "thoughtless act" may break up families forever and let slave catchers know not only their whereabouts, but also the secrets to their escape ("To the Fugitive Slaves and Their Friends" 205–206).

Renowned former and fugitive slaves such as Frederick Douglass, Jermain W. Loguen, and Samuel Ringgold Ward amazed Canadian audiences with their jeremiads. Lesser known fugitives inexperienced in the rhetoric of the abolitionists, however, left their mark on crowds in Canada as well. Although not as polished as antislavery lecturers in the Northern United States, these Black Canadian Jeremiahs took their show on the road. Lewis Richardson, who escaped from Senator Henry Clay's[2] "peculiar institution," attracted large crowds that rivaled Douglass' audiences. In his discourse, Richardson revealed that Clay was a benevolent slave owner. His "slaves had rather live with him than be free." Richardson, however, assured them that being a slave was not a fate for any man. He emotionally revealed, "I had rather this day, have a millstone tied to my neck, and be sunk to the bottom of the Detroit river [sic], than to go back to Ashland [Kentucky] and be his slave for life." Richardson's jeremiad further chastised Clay for his treatment of his slaves. "He has said publicly his slaves were 'fat and slick!' But I say if they are, it is not because they are so well used by him. They have nothing but coarse bread and meat to eat, and not enough of that." When Richardson escaped from Clay's plantation in Lexington, Kentucky, in 1845, he left behind his wife and child. "I can truly say," he told his audience, "that I have only one thing to lament over, and that is my bereft wife who is yet in bondage" ("Speech by Lewis Richardson" 101). After he revealed that he regretted leaving his family behind, Richardson then drew parallels between himself and his former owner to show the inhumanity of slavery's design:

> Thanks be to Heaven that I have got here at last: on yonder side of Detroit river [sic], I was recognized as property; but on this side I am on free soil. Hail, Brittania! Shame, America! (Cheers.) A Republican despotism, holding three millions of our fellow men in slavery. Oh what a contrast between slavery and liberty! Here I stand erect, without a chain upon my limbs. (Cheers.) Redeemed, emancipated, by the generosity of Great Britain. (Cheers.) I now feel as independent as ever Henry Clay felt when he was running for the White House.... He has been defeated four or five times, and I but once. But he was running for slavery, and I for liberty.... Thanks be to God that I am elected to Canada, and if I don't live but one night, I am determined to die on free soil. Let my days be few or many, let me die sooner or later, my grave shall be made in free soil ["Speech by Lewis Richardson" 101–102].

Richardson made it clear that being on "British soil," regardless of how Canadians viewed blacks, was very much a privilege to be acknowledged since the Canadian government recognized him "as a man" ("Speech by Lewis Richardson" 101).

Colorphobia, Canadian Negrophobia and "The deep-rooted hatred of the negro"

In the consciousnesses of blacks in the United States, free and enslaved, Canada represented a place promising freedom and opportunity. In reality, those who did manage to make the treacherous escape to Canada faced new obstacles. It was certain that the ex-slave, black émigré and abolitionist alike did not always find Canadian hospitality to be the "land of freedom" they might have expected. Once there they still had to battled racism. Although holding liminal citizenships in both neighboring countries, their passage across American-Canadian borders symbolized what Afua Cooper identified as a "new social identity in the land of their freedom." Crossing the border signified that they were "no longer slaves but free persons [who] ... took on new national and political identities." The American-Canadian border, "as a creator of new identities," provided those who "crossed and transgressed it ... a heightened sense of self" (134–135). With this newly found self-determination, Black Canadian Jeremiahs made every effort to contest all racial stereotypes that white Canadians embraced about blacks. Some reported that they enjoyed the right to play a part in the social, economic, and political affairs of their newfound homeland. On 13 January 1838, a group of Black Canadian Jeremiahs convened at the residence of William Osborne, a white abolitionist of Toronto, to reflect on a series of motions that contested American proslavery customs, to applaud Britain for eradicating slavery in the British West Indies, and to exalt Canada as a land of liberty and possibility (*BAP II* 68). In their "Proceedings of a Meeting of Toronto Blacks," the participants adopted several resolutions, one of which articulated their grief over the treatment of blacks in both Canada and America:

> We express the universal feeling of our coloured brethren throughout this Province when we state our perfect contentment with our political condition, living, as we do, under the influence of free and equal laws, which recognize no distinction of colour in the protection which they afford and the privileges which they confer; and that we distinctly contradict all statements to the contrary which have been industriously circulated in the States, by slaveholders and others of the kindred spirit, for the purpose of creating a belief that coloured people are unprepared for freedom, and that our emigration to this country has effected no real improvement in our circumstances ["Proceedings of a Meeting of Toronto Blacks" 67].

Canadian law allowed blacks citizenship; however, even that residency, some acknowledged, came with its price. When he arrived in Toronto on 1 August 1839, the Rev. Jehu Jones, as did many blacks, rejoiced that he did not find racial prejudice in Canadian politics:

> Under the blessings of Divine Providence, I enjoy good health, and what are the impressions that was first made upon my feelings, which have been actively engaged for seven years in the States, carefully looking out for a home, but without success, to more favorable prospects under the crown of Great Britain ... my soul was absorbed

in rejoicing, prayer and thanksgiving to the Author of all good gifts, that he has given me courage, through so many difficulties that I have experienced faithfully to pursue an object dear to my heart and to find a place where I am protected by law — besides that I can enjoy my peculiar Religious opinions, without giving offence to my neighbors.... On my arrival, I received a polite invitation from one of the Marshals of the day ["Jehu Jones to Charles B. Ray" 76].

Although the American-Canadian border "stood as the ultimate symbol between slavery and freedom" (Cooper 142), not all former American blacks found liberty in Canada. Some American émigrés were torn between their perceptions and ideas of racial discrimination and prejudice as far as Canadian politics were concerned and used their voice to criticize Canadian democracy because they saw many similarities to prejudice in the Northern United States. Black Canadian Jeremiahs, then, had the unique opportunity to argue that as desirous as freedom was, it was not the end to the "race problem" that had previously plagued them in the United States. Canadian racism, they discovered, was fueled by several episodes: the growth of fugitive slaves, the influx of new immigrant groups, and the increase of blacks in urban areas. Victimized by "verbal abuse, by public criticism, and by race-baiting politicians," they quickly discovered "de facto discrimination and racism" were not easily purged in Canada (*BAP II* 7). The prejudice they suffered in Canada illustrated that freedom did not eliminate racial hatred; their jeremiads, then, gave concrete evidence that political and legal transformations did not bring about attitudinal changes from the white majority. As the numbers of blacks grew in Canada, so did "Negrophobia on the part of white Canadians" (Silverman 103).

Black Canadian Jeremiahs found a harmonious voice when they lamented the ills of Canadian prejudice. Henry Bibb observed that "Color-Phobia" manifested in Canadian consciousnesses when he lamented, "In Canada, it gets hold of the very dregs of society. It makes them [Canadians] shudder at the idea of 'negro settlement' 'they will ruin the country.'" The thought, Bibb lamented, of Black Canadians having "negro lawyers, doctors, judges &c" excites white Canadians' "imagination so much that they become alarmed about amalgamation":

> The white girls are all going to make choice of black men, and white gents will be left without wives, and what then? Don't be alarmed friends, you shall not be hurt. All this is the workings of a diseased imagination, of which you must be cured, or it will destroy your souls and bodies both ["Color-Phobia in Canada" 137].

When he further expressed his concerns that "Color-phobia" was a "contagious disease," Bibb's contextualization revealed that "Color-phobia" was "more destructive to the mind than to the body." Its predecessor in the United States, he proclaimed, "Is not satisfied with what has been accomplished in the states; but is now striving to get a foot-hold in Canada where many of the objects of his prey have settled under the protection of Her Majesty's law" ("Color-Phobia in Canada" 136). As illustrated in Bibb's discourse, Black Canadian Jeremiahs were troubled by the mounting racist behavior that followed the sudden increase of the Canadian black population during the 1850s (*BAP II* 136). Therefore, Bibb advised, "Anti-Slavery is the very best remedy for [colorphobia]. It will cure you of prejudice and hatred, and prepare you for a happier state of existence" ("Color-Phobia in Canada" 137).

When he arrived in Canada, Samuel Ringgold Ward, the self-proclaimed "stranger from the backwoods of Canada" ("Fugitive Slaves in Canada"), echoed Bibb's sentiments concerning Canadian racism when he revealed that "there was certainly a prejudice in Canada, but it was of a very different character to that which existed in the United States." Ward's Canadian jeremiads lamented the threats, complexities, deprivations, and cruel hardships of American slavery. At the same time, Ward recognized that Canadian prejudice was deep-rooted throughout the western Canadian provinces and he "poured forth a torrent of natural, and therefore burning eloquence, which roused the enthusiasm" of his Canadian audiences and "electrified those who had not heard him before, and were therefore unprepared for such a speech[es] from such as '*chattel.*'" Slaves who escaped the clutches of America's "peculiar institution," he bemoaned, "did not escape merely from the United States, but from the dominion of one of the most oppressive and wicked systems of tyranny which could possibly exist" ("Fugitive Slaves in Canada," emphasis in original) and even in Canada, there was very little protection because the "natives of the United States ... brought their pro-slaveryism with them" ("Relations of Canada to American Slavery" 230). He lamented that since the American Anti-Slavery Society, and other friends of blacks in the United States, did not appreciate Canada as a place to foster black uplift, many would not financially support the Black Canadian movement (*BAP II* 183n):

> Our friends in the United States are not so clear sighted as our enemies. They would not really like to abandon the fugitives here, but they very greatly undervalue this field. If it be not the great moral lighthouse for the black people, free and enslaved, on this continent, I am altogether mistaken. This seemed so to me, long before I came here; every day confirms me in the opinion. Our enemies see it, know it, deplore it, hate it. Still, every letter I get, remonstrates against my remaining here, and demands my return! ["Samuel Ringgold Ward to Henry Bibb" 182].

Ward, born a slave in 1817 in Maryland, wrote at length about Canadian racism. Upon his "*entrée* into Canada, as a resident and a fugitive" at Montreal in October 1851, Ward initially discovered Canada was not "free from negrophobia" (*Autobiography of a Fugitive Slave* 133, 177). Ward's analysis of Canadian racism was "less tenacious, less ingrained than that which existed in the United States" (Rhodes 144). Ward wrote that in America, blacks were "slaves, and but demi-freemen, if not all slaves"; in Canada, however, blacks "stand on a legal and political equality." They were "as free as the whites" and enjoyed many benefits from of the "immunities and privileges of an Englishman." He urged blacks to live as respectable citizens to illustrate that they were not a degraded, sinful people as they had been represented by whites. By 1853, however, Ward's interpretation of Canadian racism radically transformed as he revealed "some facts showing how [racism] operates in Canada" and pointed out some of the "differences from the negro hate of the United States." As he resented the entire system of racial prejudice, "Canadian Negro Hate," Ward contextualized, was "incomparably MEANER than" racism in the Northern United States. Canadian racism was "NOT ORIGINAL," for its "copied aped deviltry is always meaner than the original diabolism." When he compared "Canadian Negro Hate" to racism in the Northern United States, Ward further believed, however, that "Canadian Negro Hate" did not possess the "religion [or] civil law, to uphold it" that American racism possessed. He prophesized, however, the end of "Canadian Negro Hate"; it "can not be eternal" ("Canadian Negro Hate" 226, 224, 225, 226; emphasis in original), he declared:

> The labors of the anti-slavery society, the improvement, progress, and good demeanor of the black people will, in a very short time, undermine and destroy this abomination, unless, certain things, to which I shall presently refer, exert an unhappy influence. Having law, religion, and British example at headquarters against it, Canadian negrophobia, cannot long abide. When publicly attacked, it hides its head from the indignant gaze of a condemning community ["Canadian Negro Hate" 227].

Ward admitted, however, that "Canadian Negro-Haters" were, as a rule, "the lowest, the least educated, of all the white population" and possessed "next to nothing, of what are liberal enlightened views and genteel behavior" ("Fugitive Slaves in Canada" 143). He further revealed his belief that the United States' social and economic influences gravely affected "Canadian Negro-Haters":

> Canadians travel extensively in the States, as do the people of the States in Canada. Thus the spread of slaveholding predilections is both favoured and facilitated; and, what is more, there is abundant evidence that some Americans industriously use these opportunities for the purpose of giving currency to their own notions [*Autobiography of a Fugitive Negro* 138].

Additionally, he felt that some Black Canadians were partially to blame for the increase of "Canadian Negro Hate." "I do well to be angry," Ward expressed, "with any black man who throws discredit upon our people" (*Autobiography of a Fugitive Negro* 197). Some blacks, he believed, strengthened racist attitudes when they developed their own institutions and organizations, disregarded Victorian social customs, and neglected their part in the antislavery movement once they were safe on Canadian grounds (*BAP II* 24). "There is only one thing to be feared," he lamented, "some of the black people will act in such a manner as to increase, rather than diminish the prejudice against us" ("Canadian Negro Hate," 224). "Rum and Negro hate," he lamented, "the two great public evils of our adopted land, shall receive unyielding fight from me during my life" ("Samuel Ringgold Ward to Henry Bibb" 179). Nevertheless, Ward felt "unspeakably thankful to God that Canada existed" ("Canadian Negro Hate," 224).

By the time William Wells Brown made his trek through Canada West in

1861, touring the country to gain support for the Haitian immigration movement and lecturing in black communities from Toronto to Windsor, he, too, found that racism was very much a part of the democratic principles of the country (*BAP II* 58). When he arrived in Canada as an agent for James Redpath's Haitian Emigration Bureau, he lamented, "I was not prepared to meet the prejudice against colored persons which manifests itself wherever a member of that injured race makes his appearance." Brown's witnessing racism in Canada led him to conclude that in none of "the States, not even in Pennsylvania, is the partition wall between the blacks so high as in Canada." His description of Canadian prejudice was comparable to the "separate and *un*equal" doctrines of Jim Crow which later plagued the Southern United States. Of Canadian racism, he wrote:

> The equality meted out to colored persons in the hotels of New England, are unknown in Canada. No where here, are our people treated with any kind of respect in the hotels; they are usually put off into inferior rooms by themselves, fed at separate tables from the whites, and not permitted to enter the common sitting rooms of the inn. Most of the towns have excluded the colored children from the common schools ["The Colored People of Canada" 467].

These acts of racial discrimination that Brown witnessed in Canada led him to lament "the more I see of Canada, the more I am convinced of the deep-rooted hatred of the negro." Notwithstanding the "prejudice" that prevented blacks from obtaining "the more profitable employments," Brown wrote, "they are ... thrifty, and doing well" ("The Colored People of Canada" 469, 479).

Henry Bibb's Black Canadian Jeremiad

As they drew on their sense of black responsibility and agency, Black Canadian Jeremiahs made palpable contributions to antislavery fashions in the United States on every front. Many took immediate and prescribed action to free their brethren and believed, as Henry Bibb revealed, that slavery in the United States "would be abolished in even less than a single day, were it not that the strong arm of the whole American Government is under a pledge to Keep the slave in his chains" ("Address by Henry Bibb, John T. Fisher and James D. Tinsely" 170). Bibb, the preeminent Black Canadian Jeremiah, visited Chatham during the summer of 1852 "to advocate the cause of the bleeding slave" (Winks 254). Education, he lamented, would work wonders for elevating the race:

> We regard the education of colored people in North America as being one of the most important measures connected with the destiny of our race. By it we can be strengthened and elevated — without it we shall be ignorant, weak, and degraded. By it we shall be clothed with a power which will enable us to arise from degradation and command respect from the whole civilized world: without it, we shall never be imposed upon, oppressed and enslaved; not that we are more stupid than others

would be under the same circumstances, indeed very few races of men have the corporal ability to survive, under the same physical and mental depression that the colored race have to endure, and still retain their manhood ["Education" 119].

Bibb advocated education as one of the most important components to slavery and racial prejudice. Bibb's jeremiads were hailed by "continued cheers" and prompted Chatham blacks to form an antislavery organization for the purpose of sketching out their beliefs, and to consign themselves to antislavery efforts (Winks 254). Born in Shelby County, Kentucky, on 10 May 1815 to state Senator James Bibb and Mildred Jackson, a slave who worked on the plantation owned by Willard Gatewood, Bibb loathed the American institution and believed that condemning white slaveholders was paramount to achieving social status for American blacks. Throughout his Canadian residency, Bibb helped establish schools, churches and antislavery societies in various regions of Canada and found a biweekly newspaper, the *Voice of the Fugitive*. Bibb used *Voice* as an organizational tool for the abolitionist movement, as a vehicle to aid other Black Americans' immigration to Canada, "as a mouthpiece for the cross-border communities" (Cooper 39), and as the primary vehicle for propagating his separatist philosophy (Hite 273) and jeremiadic discourse.

Bibb's separatist ideologies, however, embroiled him in a public discord with Mary Ann Shadd Cary, who supported racial integration. Cary strongly disagreed with Bibb's crusade to accept government sponsorship for public schools for blacks because she believed that such support would impede building self-reliant communities (Yee "Finding a Place"). For Cary, the most important impediment that blacks faced was "lack of unity and common purpose, a condition she attributed to the lingering effects of slavery" on many of the blacks who had settled in Canada (*BAP II* 360). Their conflicts over approach lead Bibb to attack Cary's character in *Voice*, which led Cary and Samuel Ringgold Ward to establish *The Provincial Freeman* newspaper in 1853. The Bibb-Cary dispute revealed the important role gender played in the development of Black Canadian jeremiadic discourse. Cary clearly understood the gender dynamics in the antislavery movement (Yee "Finding a Place") and believed that separate institutions for Canadian blacks would eventually weaken the quest for freedom. She promoted equality and integration for Canadian blacks, and publicly addressed issues of abolition and other reforms. Bibb continued, however, to voice his antislavery politics.

After the passing of the FSA, Bibb immediately turned his attention to the prospect of creating a black community in Canada by acquiring the necessary land from the Canadian government so that fugitives would establish permanent agencies "of *self support* and of *Educating their children*." Bibb believed that in order to improve "the moral, mental and political condition" of "stricken and degraded people," they must possess and control the land where they live ("Henry Bibb to the Executive Committee" 115; emphasis in original). As he envisioned the political polarization that ultimately resulted from federal implementation of the FSA, Bibb joined forces with another former slave, Josiah Henson, to demonstrate blacks' readiness for independence. When Henson, who was born 15 June 1789 in Charles County, Maryland, first arrived in Canada, he settled, as did many blacks, "on the first spot in Canada" he reached. According to Henson's assessment, several hundred "coloured persons" had settled in "the neighbourhood, and, in the first joy of their deliverance, they were living in a way, which ... led to little or no progress in improvement" (*An Autobiography* 103). Henson noticed that the inhabitants of this community were "generally working for hire upon the lands of others, and had not yet dreamed of becoming independent proprietors themselves. It soon became my great object to awaken them to a sense of the advantages which were within their grasp (*An Autobiography*, 103–104). He lamented "the degraded and hopeless condition of a slave can never be properly felt by him while he remains in such a position." After he tasted "the blessings of freedom," Henson "reverted to those" who were "groaning in captivity" and proceeded to take immediate measures to free as many as he could. In his Black Canadian jeremiad, Henson took on the role of Jeremiah when he sought to "impress upon [blacks] the importance of the obligations they were under; first, to God, for their deliverance; and then, secondly," he sermonized, "to their fellow-men, to do all that was in their power to bring others out of bondage" (*An Autobiography* 107). Bibb and Henson's actions illustrated that "black men should continue their abolitionist activities, but should also encourage free blacks to separate from the land of their oppressor." They envisioned a "'promised land' where blacks might assert a powerful national identity and cultivate their talents unfettered by white racism" (Hite 270). Therefore, in January 1851, Bibb and Henson established the Refugee Home Society (RHS), which provided the disadvantaged fugitives with land along the Detroit frontier in Canada West (*BAP II* 12; Cooper 139). The purpose of the society was to "improve the moral, mental and political condition of a poverty stricken and degraded people." They must, Bibb encouraged, "become owners and tillers of the soil — and PRODUCE WHAT THEY CONSUME." It was Bibb's jeremiadic discourse that fervently supported the future of blacks in Canada; "Such an enterprise commenced," he proclaimed, would be one of the "greatest temeral [sic] blessings that could be conferred" on his people. Bibb lamented that "Ignorance, dissipation and pauperism" were the "landmarks of slavery, and the great aim and object," therefore, ought to be to allow blacks to "arise above it by their own industry" ("The American Refugees Home" 115, 144; emphasis in original). In response to Bibb's RHS, subsequently published in the *Voice of the Fugitive*, James Theodore Holly, born in 1829 in Washington, DC, to the descendent of freed slaves, exhibited elements of the jeremiad when he wrote:

> Therefore we should vigorously pursue this project, and swarm in a ceaseless tide to Canada West, and hang like an ominous *black cloud* over this guilty nation, until the precipitated occurrence of providential circumstances— the terrible thunderbolts

of Omnipotent judgment hurled from the hand of Jehovah, shall scale the Alleghany summits, and reverberate through the valley of the Mississippi, breaking every chain and letting the oppressed free ["Voice from the 'Green Mountains'" 139; emphasis in original].

An advocate of Haitian emigration, Holly warned the United States of God's judgment to come. His scathing rhetoric illustrated that Black Canadian jeremiadic discourse sought to challenge and instill sharp change in white America's ideologies based on race.

In his "To Our Old Master" series of essays, however, Bibb continued to illustrate the tenor of jeremiadic protest rhetoric. "We have not taken up the pen to write on our own position at present," he informed his audience. Instead Bibb used his jeremiads to draw parallels between the oppression of blacks in America to that of the oppression Britons had previously encountered in Europe:

> We mean to show that you are the most inconsistent race of slaveholders that the world has yet produced; that your practice is entirely at variance with your preaching; that in prosperity you have repudiated the doctrines which in adversity you Promulgated; in fact that you are now inflicting upon us a tyranny similar to that under which your forefathers groaned, and against which rebelled ["To Our Old Master" 122].

He reminded them that their forefathers, "though savages, had the spirit of liberty strongly implanted in their breast" ("To Our Old Master" 122). Bibb could not comprehend, then, why white America could not offer blacks the same privilege. Bibb warned his intended audience of the atrocities to come when his prophetic visions shined in the public letters he wrote to his former master, Albert G. Sibley. Often slaves wrote these letters, and they served specific purposes within the antislavery crusade: these letters illustrated that with freedom came intellectual advancement, they opposed black inferiority, and they presented a public forum for addressing explicit antislavery concerns (*BAP II* 217). In the first of two letters, written in September 1852, Bibb assailed the "ungodly relation of master and slave" when he warned Sibley that if he continued to practice slaveholding in such an "unhallowed course of conduct ... the Lord, will turn his face away, in disgust, and will not hear or look upon" his prayers and "solemn fasts and ordinances." In the second letter, written 7 October 1852, Bibb's prophetic vision became more defined, and he sought to inform Sibley of "the great danger to which you are exposed while standing in the attitude of an incorrigible slaveholder" ("A Letter to My Old Master" 217, 218). His prophetic rhetoric was profoundly influenced by the traditional African American jeremiad, though it was radical in its engagement of what he saw as divine law:

> I mean that you shall know that there is a just God in heaven, who cannot harmonise human slavery with the Christian religion: I mean that you shall know that there is a law which is more binding upon the consciences of slaves than that of Congress,

or any other human enactment—and I mean that you shall know that all of your slaves have escaped to Canada, where they are just as free as yourself, and that we have not forgotten the cruel treatment which we received at your hands while in a state of slavery ["A Letter to My Old Master" 219].

Bibb fully accepted his role as the preeminent Black Canadian Jeremiah when he lamented that the "despotic laws [such as the FSA] can never have permanent existence among free people" ("The Proclamation" 131). Bibb's jeremiads critiqued the proslavery attitudes that blacks were slaves because they were intrinsically inferior and pleased with this fate. The fundamental thematic concern in Bibb's jeremiads, however, was the failure of white America to confront the paradox of slave holding while decreeing that "all men are created equal," and their hypocrisy in refusing blacks equality.

Mary Ann Shadd Cary's Black Canadian Jeremiad

Because the abolitionist movement in American had already struggled with concerns of racial equality, which created an environment crying out for discussions concerning equal opportunity between the sexes, some Black Canadian women activists found refuge in Canada and used their voices to critique the divisions in American reform. Even those who had never been slaves recognized the abolition of slavery as a symbol for their rights as well. Because of this undertaking toward slavery, women, such as Mary Ann Shadd Cary, made noteworthy strides in the development of the Black Canadian jeremiad. In her view, Canadian blacks would become educated, self-reliant citizens of the British Empire (*BAP II* 360). Cary believed, however, that blacks were in part to blame for their own degradation. Since they had arrived in Canada, their failure to attain a "consensus had opened the way for three decades of incompetent leadership and demeaning begging operations" (*BAP II* 360):

> When viewed in the light of an ordinary transaction for the exact extent of the censure to be attached to the colored people themselves is not quite clear, we are convinced however, that the fault is not all one side, but that to them belongs a fair share of the blame. We make these remarks with no intention to shield with men from merited blame at all, but that the colored people may not take to themselves complete exemption from rebuke for their great indifference to their interests ["Obstacles to Progress of Colored Canadians" 360].

Born to free blacks in Wilmington, Delaware, Cary and her brother, Isaac, migrated to Windsor, Ontario, after the FSA was passed in 1850. Cary's jeremiads sought to regain a community identity that existed apart from the dominate culture. "America," she bemoaned, was "wanted for those whom Sojourner Truth delights in calling the 'Shaxon [sic] race'" ("The Humbug of Reform" 286). Cary's support for black emigration to Canada and the development of a Black Canadian identity demonstrated two crucial elements for the antislavery cause: the role gender played in the emigration movement and the conceptualization of black national identity and, how "Canada emerged as a problematic site for the formation of identity and community during this period" (Yee "Finding a Place"). She cautioned blacks, however, that not all of Canada was a land of milk and honey. "Many in coming to Canada, have but fled from the sting, the bitterness of the dose, the direct result of the relation of master and slave, but not at all from these other evils with are as clearly concomitants of the relation" ("Obstacles to the Progress of Colored Canadians" 361). When she arrived in Canada, Cary immediately revealed her intentions. "We wish to help create a sentiment in Canada, and out of Canada, that shall tell against Slavery; and to point out, so far as we can see it, the course that people in this country should pursue that end" ("Anti-Slavery Relations" 284). She quickly gained the respect of Black Canadians (Yee, *Black Women Abolitionists* 70) and used her jeremiads to criticize American democracy and other abolitionists who did not, as she saw it, continue the crusade collectively:

> We have ... the exhumed relics of the past; the fact that instead of unrelenting Democrats and heartless slaveholders, to push forward this new crusade against the best interests of the free colored man of the North, we have Republican abolitionists, and fugitive-slaves, who "once upon a time" fought bravely against the dogma, and when its now cherished arguments were the pet theme of the fierce negro-hater and the great conservators of slave property. ["Editor of the *Anglo-African*" 452].

Through it all, though, Cary instilled hope in blacks that their day of tranquility would come. "There is a surplus of affectionate consideration for the black brother," she lamented, "wondrous things are to be done for him, and that in the twinkling of an eye" ("The Humbug of Reform" 286).

In her Canadian jeremiads, Cary employed both feminine and masculine discourse when she revealed the subtle forms of racism that existed in the anti-slavery movement. Although she lamented that the crusade to end slavery in America "must be a moral one," her level of education, comparative economic security and family advocacy did not bespeak of the trials and tribulations that slaves endured. When she hoped to "lead the growing liberal sentiment of the people" ("Anti-Slavery Relations" 284, 285), Cary lamented that the "'humbug' connected with abolition reform" was one that would make even a "worm-eating New Hollander hide his head from very disgust." She furthered bemoaned that every "colored man should live in America" among his neighbors. "He must have his rights," she proclaimed ("The Humbug of Reform" 287). Cary believed, however, that some would not accept the "term man in a generic sense" ("Sermon," 388). By the 1850s, she began to deliver her jeremiads in feminist terms. She understood that emancipation for the slave and equality for women should be treated with equal significance (*BAP II* 388). In a Sunday evening sermon delivered before a Chatham audience on 6 April 1858, Cary lamented:

> The oppress [sic], or nominally free woman of every nation or clime in whose Soul is as Evident by the image of God as in her more fortunate contemporary of the male

sex has a claim upon us by virtue or that irrevocable command Equally as urgent. We cannot successfully Evade duty because the Suffering fellow woman is only a woman! ["Sermon" 388–389].

Since Cary believed that the Sabbath was "made for man and *woman*," she further sermonized that "the spirit of true philanthropy knows *no sex*," that women were afforded the same rights to speak out against a system that had placed them "in the pit figurat[ively]" ("Sermon" 389; emphasis in original).

Throughout her Canadian jeremiads, Cary attempted to fashion the United States and Canada as "moral and political opposites" to promote black achievement (Yee, *Black Women Abolitionists* 73). She encouraged blacks in the United States to participate in any effort to achieving political rights. "Determine to remove to a country or to countries," she implored, "where you may have equal political rights, and thus be *elevated at once*" ("The Emigration Convention" 341; emphasis in original). In the 1850s, however, the United States was divided on issues concerning the abolition of slavery. Optimism was at its apex when James Buchanan took office; some believed that he would be the one to avoid national catastrophe. Miserably, Buchanan disappointed the American public. During his leadership, the country separated, and his administration ended with civil war eminent. Mournful about America's new leadership, Cary displayed the prophetic visions of the jeremiad in her essay "The Presidential Election in the United States." Written only a few weeks after Buchanan was elected president, Cary lamented "a fearful thing is the result of that last Presidential election!" For Cary, Buchanan's triumph destroyed optimism of peaceful liberation for slaves (*BAP II* 349). "But into the future who can bear to look without a shudder at what must be," she lamented, "judging from the decided and demon-like attitude of the South, and her past history and present aggression?" Now that Buchanan had taken office, Cary foresaw the contemplation of "a great but gory struggle" ("The Presidential Election" 350). Her prophecy seemingly came true. The "gory struggle" she alluded to intensified with the Dred Scott Decision in 1857; John Brown's 1859 raid on Harper's Ferry; the accumulation of "Bleeding Kansas"; and, ultimately, the Civil War (*BAP II* 349). Eventually, however, she moved back to America in 1863 and promoted Black Nationalism when she served as a recruiting officer for the Union Army during the Civil War. Her mounting cynicism with the "Canadian Canaan" and the optimism for a victorious Union were significant incentives (Yee, "Finding a Place") in the development of the Black Canadian jeremiad.

Canadian Emigrationist Sentiments and Black Canadian Jeremiadic Discourse

As emigrationists actively engaged in the most "sustained black speaking" engagements of the Canadian provinces (*BAP II* 458), the Black Canadian jeremiad both opposed and advocated emigration from the North American continent. Some Black Canadian Jeremiahs felt that emigration to Haiti or Africa was a viable solution to escape the racial prejudice that blacks faced. William J. Watkins believed that emigration from North America was unproductive to the cause unless blacks "emigrate from the gross faults which have characterised" them. To leave the continent for Haiti and escape the racial inequities in America and Canada, he thought, was not the answer. "Those who have been like driftwood washed down stream," he grieved, "will be a valuable acquisition nowhere." Those who intended on aiding Haiti, Watkins' jeremiad stressed, should "go thither to develop the resources of the country, and thus conduce to its prosperity, and the government and the people will receive them with open arms." Watkins understood that the fight against the ills of race prejudice could not be fought from another continent. Therefore, he suggested, blacks should remain in Canada "in close proximity with our oppressed brethren, who may yet summon us from the hand of the pine and the palm to help strike down" race prejudice ("Meeting of the Colored Education Institute").

Canadian emigrationist sentiments increased in the early 1850s, however, under the tutelage of Henry Bibb and Joseph C. Holly. Emigration to Canada became more than just an intellectual discussion; it became a means of critically assessing American society and a call for definite action. Bibb envisioned Canada West as a "showplace that would demonstrate blacks' readiness for freedom" (*BAP II* 143). Bibb used *Voice* to spread his sentiments that blacks should leave the United States. In his 3 December 1851 "Emigration to Canada and Jamaica" editorial, Bibb revealed that the British government clearly offered "certain fields of enterprise ... which will enable us to do far more for the abolition of slavery, and the elevation of the colored population in North America." Bibb assured readers that his emigrationist plan was "not a scheme of colonization." To further his belief in emigration to Canada and Jamaica, Bibb painted appealing portraits of both countries. Canada, he lamented, "is known to be one of the best agricultural countries on this continent, or at least a large portion of it" while Jamaica "is now owned and governed chiefly by the colored population." Free labor, which was becoming an accepted substitute to the moral suasionists ideologies, was his selling point for both countries. "We believe that the time has now fully come when the watchword of every colored American should be FREE LABOR FOR FREE MEN," he maintained ("Emigration to Canada and Jamaica" 200, 201; emphasis in original).

Because American prejudice degraded blacks, Bibb lamented that thousands had "been compelled to take refuge in Canada under the British flag, which protects them in the enjoyment of that liberty which the American government has so earnestly sought to take from unoffending people" ("The American Refugees Home" 143). Holly, an early proponent of emigration to Canada, saw the country as "'a *beacon of hope* to the slave and a *rock of terror* to the oppressor.'" When he supported the "'regenerative power'" of emigration to

Canada, Holly urged blacks in both neighboring countries to "'facilitate the *escape* and comfortable settlement of more refugees in Canada'" (qtd. in Ripley et al. 33; emphasis in original). Holly supported Bibb's emigrationist scheme and believed the entire free colored population of the United States was obligated "to support [emigration] as the most practical [scheme] ever presented for their consideration, and the most available for the speedy emancipation of our enslaved brethren" ("Editorial by Henry Bibb" 138). Bibb and Holly worked to create a convention where emigrationist ideas could be discussed and would ultimately fashion a Canadian organization that would be devoted to managing the destiny of North American blacks. As a result, the North American Convention met in September 1851 in Toronto (*BAP II* 33).

Conclusion

The success of the Black Canadian jeremiad in the arena of social change and activism depended on its architects' ability to deliver persuasive rhetoric to their audiences within the context of black struggle. This call arrived in a number of implicit ways coded within the architects' language as a doctrine that connected them with their audience. Samuel Ringgold Ward, for example, lamented "the most painful of all to reflect" was that slavery was "so perseveringly upheld by a nation which is constantly affirming, in the plainest possible language, that perfect freedom is God's birthright to his creatures" ("Escaped Slaves From the 'Land of Freedom'"). The mastery of the oppressor's language helped Black Canadian Jeremiahs conceptualize the problems American blacks faced and offered their audiences — whether black or white — alternative methods of achieving their perceived "national identity" while it sought to engage Canadians in the process of liberating American slaves. American democracy, as Black Canadian Jeremiahs saw it, was facing a crisis. Consider Henry Bibb's actions when he attempted to create a safe haven for escaped slaves in Canada. "You are now in Canada," he lamented, "free from American slavery; yes, the very moment you stept [sic] upon these shores you were changed from articles of property to human beings. You are entitled to all the privileges and immunities of citizens of Canada so long as you obey her laws" ("Interesting Arrival in Canada"). The jeremiad offered Black Canadian Jeremiahs numerous ways to critique America's pledge of freedom and liberty, while they advocated and promoted Canada as a place where freedom could be obtained.

Conclusion
The Great Tradition of Black Protest Continues

Whether in the United States, Canada or Europe, African Americans' consistent use of jeremiadic rhetoric revealed not only a fervent attachment to their cultural legacy, but also an extraordinary determination to abolish the evils of slavery and all forms of oppression. Early African American activists sought complete citizenship for blacks. The forerunners of the Puritan jeremiad did not seek citizenship, but sought acceptance from their God. Blacks, then, cultivated the jeremiad to support their call for their civil liberties. Fighting not with the British, but with those who were responsible for withholding the God-given privileges every man had the right to attain in no way apes the American employment of the jeremiad. African American jeremiadic discourse was a foundation from which modern black social protest and blacks' humanity and identity derived and existed in America. What I have attempted to identify in the preceding pages was that the development of the African American jeremiad—its thoughts and attitudes—were based upon racism and racial prejudice that developed throughout the history of slavery in America. As the jeremiad has had an evolving influence on American cultural synthesis, the African American jeremiad has sought to promote a successful moral revolution amongst black constituents.

The African American Jeremiad and the Formulation of a More Perfect Union

As the republic began to form a *more* perfect union, the African American jeremiad began to represent a stronger commitment to solving the country's cultural baggage problem: the abolition of slavery. As African Americans saw it, the newly formed republic could not progressively move forward until it resolved its dichotomy of slaveholding while upholding its credence that "all men are created equal." If all men were *truly* equally created, Americans could not justify slaveholding with biblical arguments anymore; more persuasive action would have to occur. It seems, therefore, that when their biblical arguments began to falter, the slaveholding class would turn to the only other option it felt it had: the law. As laws began to augment the rights of the slaveholding classes by limiting the rights of African Americans, a stronger sense of a restored community began to embody those who rallied for equal rights. The works of Phyllis Wheatley and Jupiter Hammon began to abstractly reflect this sociopolitical struggle as it was for slaves in eighteenth-century America. Wheatley and Hammon did not abandon attacking the social politics of the early republic; they concentrated on the agonizing socio-political issues of slavery and thus marked not only the evolution of an African American literary tradition, but also the beginning of a form of social protest that would have a sustaining effect on the development of the African American arts and letters.

Although it may be difficult to measure how much of an impact early activist such as Wheatley and Hammon had on eradicating the system of slavery, it is certain that they played a vital role in inspiring resistance among blacks through their use of the African American jeremiad. In this sense, the jeremiad would also serve as a way of building a conceptual community, which in turn offered early African American activists a sense of self-worth. As they drew their rhetoric from their understanding of the issues that surrounded their culture and their enslavement, the jeremiad would later shape race and class ideologies that subsequently formed the action of its architects. In this manner, the African American jeremiad challenged the social and political order of the day and formed a critical part of eighteenth- and nineteenth-century black protest and resistance that, until recently, had not received its place in the African American literary development of the antebellum period.

To what extent, then, did the architects of the African American jeremiad have a lasting effect on African American leaders today? The jeremiad has played a vital role in black consciousness, empowerment, and activism. The jeremiad certainly contributed to the establishment of the African American literary tradition. In their individual attempts, African American activists were able to reveal a genuine plea for religious, social, economic, and political reform by reaching all cultural groups of their audiences. Absorbing jeremiadic discourse, early African American activists attempted to establish their own freedom against white domination as they simultaneously evolved and claimed their own cultural, religious, and socio-political values as people who were deserving of equal rights.

Although African Americans only chafed at the authoritarian regimen of a white institution in an era when they shared the nameless values of community and equality, they still depended on their understanding of liberation and for their imprimatur as they contributed to the African American literary canon. Their jeremiadic verse called for a new socio-politicized African American as their ideologies called for an elimination of some, if not all, of the racial constraints that plagued African Americans since the first Africans set foot on New World soil. When other African Americans later answered the call, victories against these racial inequalities would be won all over the land. Indeed, their voices were heard. The jobs of these nineteenth-century activists as persuasive Jeremiahs were to overcome resistance so that effective communication could occur. Therefore, they had to keep their goal within its conservative limitations. Most important, they have had an everlasting impact on twentieth-century jeremiadic discourse of leaders such as W. E. B. DuBois, Ida B. Wells, Malcolm X, Martin Luther King, Jr., Al Sharpton, bell hooks, Tavis Smiley, Angela Davis, Jesse Jackson, Alan Keyes, and Louis Farrakhan (just to name a few), which is proof that their writings and activism still speak to an attuned audience today.

The construction of the black consciousness embedded in African American jeremiadic discourse deserves further investigation and synthesis. As this study examines the various ways the architects of the African American jeremiad became pioneers of a distinctive African American discourse that encapsulated the essence of their fight for equality, it is hoped it will goad interest in the reconceptualizations of the complexities that shroud the African American jeremiad and set in motion an excavation of African American jeremiadic rhetoric with greater interest. As William J. Wilson lamented in 1853:

> We must begin to tell our own story, write our own lecture, paint our own picture, chisel our own bust (I demand not caricatures but correct emanations), acknowledge and love our own peculiarities if we have any. Ever so little done in these directions is worth more than all we have ever done, assimilative of the whites since creation, or can do till the end of time. The encouragement and self-reliance it will inspire will do more to push us forward than all the speculations about our "manifest destiny" ... Now is the time to begin to cultivate among us both a taste for the arts and sciences themselves, before we become more deeply immersed in the rougher affairs of life. Our present peculiar situation well calculates us for their highest perfection ["William J. Wilson to Frederick Douglass" 142].

It was precisely statements like these that goaded not only the development of the African American jeremiad but also cultivated the black self amongst the hostile and racial waters of nineteenth-century America.

Chapter Notes

Introduction

1. In an earlier lecture, "Speech by William Wells Brown, Delivered at the Horticultural Hall, West Chester, Pennsylvania," 23 October 1854, Brown also charged the North for allowing slavery to continue. The speech was reprinted in *BAP IV*, pp. 245–255 (see Chap. 3, n. 4).
2. Throughout this text, I use the terms "African American" and "black" interchangeably.
3. In his revised and expanded edition of *The Afro-American Jeremiad: Appeals for Justice in America* (Philadelphia: Temple University Press, 1990), in 2005 David Howard-Pitney defined the American jeremiad as "a rhetoric of indignation expressing deep dissatisfaction and challenging the notion to reform" (xii). Howard-Pitney expanded his work to include an updated section on Jesse Jackson and a new section on Alan Keyes. In doing so, Howard-Pitney titled his text *The African American Jeremiad: Appeals for Justice in America*. This is evidence that African American jeremiads have an unwavering effect on the American political system. In this more "inclusive" revised edition, Howard-Pitney added a continuous examination of "the thought and rhetoric of a major Black Nationalist," Malcolm X (xii). I quote, however, from the 1990 edition.

Chapter 1

1. Spelling is consistent with Winthrop's own.
2. For more on the Mashpee Revolt of 1833, see Donald M. Nielsen's "The Mashpee Revolt of 1833," *New England Quarterly* 58. 3 (1985): 400–420; Theresa Strouth Gaul's "Dialouge and Public Discourse in William Apess's *Indian Nullification*," *The American Transcendental Quarterly* 15.3 (2001): 276–92; James Clifford's *The Predicament of Culture: Twentieth-Century Ethnography, Literature, and Art* (Cambridge: Harvard University Press, 1988); and Jack Campisi's *The Mashpee Indians: Tribe on Trial* (Syracuse: Syracuse University Press, 1991).
3. According to Luke 16:19–31:

> There was a rich man who was dressed in purple and fine linen and lived in luxury every day. At his gate was laid a beggar named Lazarus, covered with sores and longing to eat what fell from the rich man's table. Even the dogs came and licked his sores.
> The time came when the beggar died and the angels carried him to Abraham's side. The rich man also died and was buried. In hell, where he was in torment, he looked up and saw Abraham far away, with Lazarus by his side. So he called to him, "Father Abraham, have pity on me and send Lazarus to dip the tip of his finger in water and cool my tongue, because I am in agony in this fire."
> But Abraham replied, "Son, remember that in your lifetime you received your good things, while Lazarus received bad things, but now he is comforted here and you are in agony. And

besides all this, between us and you a great chasm has been fixed, so that those who want to go from here to you cannot, nor can anyone cross over from there to us."

He answered, "Then I beg you, father, send Lazarus to my father's house, for I have five brothers. Let him warn them, so that they will not also come to this place of torment."

Abraham replied, "They have Moses and the Prophets; let them listen to them."

"No, father Abraham," he said, "but if someone from the dead goes to them, they will repent."

He said to him, "If they do not listen to Moses and the Prophets, they will not be convinced even if someone rises from the dead."

Ward symbolically used Dives, the name properly given to the rich man in the parable of "Lazarus and the Rich Man," although not revealed in the biblical verse, as the inevitable judgment for whites who continue the nefarious design of racial prejudice.

4. Smith was paraphrasing a quote from the Duke of Wellington at the battle of Waterloo (1815). As the 3rd Regiment of Chasseurs approached the ridge opposite Maitland's Brigade of Foot Guards (2nd and 3rd Battalions of the 1st Foot Guards), Wellington reportedly called to the brigade commander "Now, Maitland. Now's your time." One authority reported him as saying, "Up, guard, and at them again!"

5. Spelling is consistent with Johnstone's own.

6. Also, see chapter two of John W. Blassingame's *The Slave Community: Plantations Life in the Antebellum South* (New York: Oxford University Press, 1972) for his discussion of European enslavement by the Arabs, Turks, and West Africans. Johnstone was probably alluding to this period of European enslavement as well.

7. All emphasis in original. Haynes was referencing *The Sedition Act of 1798*, sometimes referred to as *The Alien and Sedition Acts of 1798*, which sought to punish those who "shall unlawfully combine or conspire together, with intent to oppose any measure or measures of the government of the United States." Haynes suggested that acts like these would undermine government as it existed in the Bible. Therefore, it would be difficult for the government and religion to coexist without conflicting ideologies about, for example, oppression.

8. The full title of Haynes' document, "Liberty Further Extended: Or Free thoughts on the illegality of Slave-keeping; Wherin those arguments that Are used in its vindication Are plainly confuted. Together with an humble Address to such as are Concearned in the practise," will be referred to as "Liberty Further Extended." The work is grounded in Haynes' ideologies that the liberty enjoyed by white America should be "further extended" to black America. I will be quoting from Ruth Bogin's work "'Liberty Further Extended': A 1776 Antislavery Manuscript by Lemuel Haynes," *The William and Mary Quarterly* 40.1 (1983): 85–105. As Bogin notes, the spelling in the document is consistent with Haynes' own.

Chapter 2

1. *The Collected Works of Phyllis Wheatley*, ed. John C. Shields (New York: Oxford University Press, 1988) will henceforth be referred to as *CW* when parenthetically cited within the text.

2. Even though Henderson was writing in 1973 about "New Black Poetry, Black Speech and Black Music as Poetic References," his theory can be applied to the early poets of the republic. Although the idea of blackness does not surface in much of Wheatley's verse, its representation in "On Being Brought from AFRICA to AMERICA" was visible.

3. C.C. Martindale defines pagan as any "religions other than the true one revealed by God, and, in a narrower sense, all except Christianity, Judaism, and Mohammedanism." The term, Martindale continued, "is also used as the equivalent of polytheism (q.v.). It is derived from the Latin *pagus*, whence *pagani* (i.e., those who live in the country), a name given to the country folk who remained heathen after the cities had become Christian ("Pagan," http://www.ourladyswarriors.org/dissent/defpagan.htm). If Africans were already heathen when Europeans arrived, then, Europeans are acknowledging that Chris-

tianity existed in Africa before they arrived. In other words, according to the enlightenment of the times, Africans were pagans because they discarded Christianity. Also, this suggested that there were numerous pagans, white and black, in America who did not convert during the revivalism of the Great Awakenings.

4. Sondra O'Neale's *Jupiter Hammon and the Biblical Beginnings of African-American Literature* (Metuchen, NJ: The American Theological Library Association and The Scarecrow Press, 1993), will henceforth be referred to as *JH* when parenthetically cited within the text.

5. The phrase "stand still," however, is seen throughout African American forms of social protest. Its earliest appearance as a tool of jeremiadic discourse, however, is seen here in Hammon's essay. In *Martin Delany, Frederick Douglass, and the Politics of Representative Identity*, Robert Levine wrote that the phrase "stand still" was frequently proscribed by preachers who advocated slavery to support slave conformity (194). It came from Exodus 14:13:

> And Moses said to the people, "Do not be afraid. Stand still, and see the salvation of the LORD, which He will accomplish for you today. For the Egyptians whom you see today, you shall see again no more forever. The LORD will fight for you, and you shall hold your peace."

6. Spelling is consistent with Bustill's own.

7. See Chapter 6, "The Religious Teacher," of Brown's *Clotel, or the President's Daughter* (Armonk: M. E. Sharpe, 1996), pp. 33–46, for his interpretation of forced slave catechism by white owners.

8. See John C. Shields' preface to *The Collected Works of Phyllis Wheatley* (New York: Oxford University Press, 1988), p. xxvii; Carla Willard's "Wheatley's Turns of Praise: Heroic Entrapment and the Paradox of the Revolution," *American Literature* 67.2 (1995): 234; and Robert Kendrick's "Re-membering America: Phyllis Wheatley's Intertextual Epic," *African American Review* 30.1 (1996): 72.

9. See Henry Louis Gates, Jr., *The Trials of Phyllis Wheatley: America's First Black Poet and Her Encounters with the Founding Fathers* (New York: Basic Books, 2003). Fifteen prominent Massachusetts citizens, including Reverend Moorhead, pastor of the Church of the Presbyterian Strangers, signed a testimonial that prefaced Wheatley's collection. For more on Wheatley's "trial," see Mary McAleer Balkun's "Phyllis Wehatley's Construction of Otherness and the Rhetoric of Performed Ideology," *African American Review* 36.1 (2002): 121–136.

10. According to Robert Kendrick, Scipio Moorhead, a slave artist, produced the portrait of Wheatley that appeared adjacent to the title page of her 1773 *Poems on Various Subjects, Religious and Moral*. See Kendrick's "Other Questions: Phyllis Wheatley and the Ethics of Interpretation," *Cultural Critique* 38 (1997–98): 39–64. Moorhead was the slave of the Reverend John Moorhead, a friend of the Wheatley family.

11. Emphasis in original. Taken from "Extract From Weld's American Slavery As It Is," printed in the appendix to Henry Watson's *Narrative of Henry Watson, A Fugitive Slave: Written By Himself* (1848), p. 43.

Chapter 3

1. Brown is referencing the three-fifths clause of the *Constitution*.
2. Spelling is consistent with Cuffe's own.
3. In three of her poems, "To the KING's Most Excellent Majesty. 1768," "On the Death of the Rev. Mr. GEORGE WHITEFIELD. 1770," and "To the Right Honorable William, Early of Dartmouth, His Majesty's Principal Secretary of State for North America, Etc.," Phyllis Wheatley advocated a similar belief that the mistreatment of people of African extraction would diminish when certain political leaders came into power.
4. *The Black Abolitionist Papers*, 5 vols., ed. C. Peter Ripley et al. (Chapel Hill: The

University of North Carolina Press, 1985, 1986, 1991, 1992), when referenced within the text, will be referenced as *BAP*. When I cite "Ripley et al.," I am referring to the volumes' general "Introduction."

Chapter 4

1. Established in 1775, Hall's African Lodge of the Honorable Society of Free and Accepted Masons of Boston was the first lodge of Black Freemasons in the world. Receiving a permanent charter from the Grand Lodge of England in 1784, the secret organization, which still exists today, promoted brotherly love and social, political, and economic improvement for its members. Actually, the very establishment of Hall's lodge also pointed to the connections of Black Nationalism — having a lodge void of white involvement — and the African American jeremiad — the lodge was dedicated black uplift.

2. See Moses' *The Golden Age of Black Nationalism, 1850–1925* (New York: Oxford University Press, 1978), pp. 15–31.

3. Still was referencing the National Council of Colored People which was assembled "for the purpose of improving the character, developing the intelligence, maintaining the rights, and organizing a Union of the colored people of the free States" (qtd. in Smith, "The Anniversaries. National Council of the Colored People").

4. According to Judith Butler, Marxist philosopher Louis Pierre Althusser suggested that when an oppressed group masters the language of the oppressors, they are in effect assimilating into the oppressor's culture. Althusser wrote: "The production of labor power requires not only a reproduction of (the laborer's) skills, but also, at the same time, a reproduction of its submission to the rules of the established order" (qtd. in Butler 116). With this in mind, one has to take into account why the oppressed masters the oppressors' language. For Africans in this country, mastering the oppressors' language was not an act of assimilationism, rather an act of overpowering the reality of their oppression and searching for their place within the confines of the oppressors' language. Employing the jeremiad in their rhetoric, for example, did not suggest that blacks assimilated. When Fredrick Douglass, for example, mastered the oppressor's language, it was to better understand the "dark and mysterious" regions to the "white's man power to enslave the black man" (*Narrative* 29).

5. In *The Philadelphia Negro*, W.E.B. DuBois would later write that the founding of FAS "was the first wavering step of a people toward organized social life" (19).

6. It is important to note here that Forten, a supporter of emigration, would later become embittered with the American Colonization Society and segregation and Nationalism altogether (Moses, *Classical Black Nationalism* 50).

7. In 1843, Delany began publishing the antislavery newspaper *The Mystery*. After serving as editor of the paper for four years, Delany joined Frederick Douglass on the *North Star*. The paper was based in Pittsburgh and was the first black newspaper west of the Alleghenies. *The Mystery* was respected by blacks in Pennsylvania, but it never was economically solvent. One year after Delany left the paper to work with Douglass on the *North Star*, it began to fold without his leadership. In 1848, *The Mystery* was purchased by the American Methodist Episcopal Church (AME) and moved to Philadelphia where it became known as *The Christian Recorder*.

Chapter 5

1. After her marriage on 10 August 1826 to James W. Stewart, Maria Miller "adopted at her husband's request his middle initial, 'W.,'" as part of her surname. Sometimes, however, James Stewart was "called Steward by mistake." She recorded her name as "Mrs. Maria W. Steward [*sic*]" as the author of her 1831 *Religion and the Sure Principles of Morality, the Sure Foundation on which We Must Build*. In the "Introduction" to her pamphlet, Stewart

recorded her husband's name as "James W. Stewart." Her name was also spelled "Stuart" in an advertisement that announced her farewell speech. She signed the speech as "MARIA S. STEWART." See Marilyn Richardson's *Maria W. Stewart, America's First Black Woman Political Writer* (Bloomington: Indiana University Press, 1987), pp. 4, 28–29, 65, 74, 122.

2. Ampadu briefly discusses Stewart's employment of the African American jeremiad in her essay "Maria W. Stewart and the Rhetoric of Black Preaching: Perspective on Womanism and Black Nationalism," in *Black Women's Intellectual Traditions: Speaking Their Minds* (Burlington: University of Vermont Press, 2007), pp. 38–54. Also, in the same volume, see Ebony Utley's discussion in "A Woman Made of Words: The Rhetorical Invention of Maria W. Stewart," pp. 55–71. Others who have discussed Stewart's rhetoric in terms of feminist thought include Marilyn Richardson, *Maria W. Stewart, America's First Black Woman Political Writer*; Susan Roberson, "Maria Stewart and the Rhetoric of Mobility," *Journal of International Women's Studies* 4.3 (2003): 56–61; and Dianne Bartlow, "Maria W. Stewart as a Forerunner of Black Feminist Thought," *Black Women's Intellectual Traditions: Speaking Their Minds* (Burlington: University of Vermont Press, 2007), pp. 72–88.

3. The full passage of Jeremiah 29:18 reads: "I will pursue them with the sword, with famine and with pestilence; and I will make them a terror to all the kingdoms of the earth, to be a curse and a horror and a hissing, and a reproach among all the nations where I have driven them."

4. Revelation 6:16 reads: "Hide us from the face of him that sitteth on the throne, and from the wrath of the Lamb: for the great day of their wrath is come; and who is able to stand?"

5. The full version of the phrase reads: "Oh, that my head were a spring of water and my eyes a fountain of tears I would weep day and night for the slain of my people" (Jeremiah 9:1).

6. Roman emperor Justinian is known for his reorganization of the government of the Roman Empire and his codification of the laws, the *Codex Justinianus* ("Institutes of Justinian") in A.D. 534.

7. Richardson believed that the date 18 September 1833 was probably incorrect. Stewart recalled the date of the address a year after it was delivered. The speech was published, however, in *The Liberator* on 28 September 1833 (*Maria M. Stewart* 64, 128).

8. In antebellum America, several Northern states passed laws that would further prohibit black communities from establishing within their borders. Illinois (1848), Indiana (1851), and Oregon (1857) incorporated black exclusion provision in their constitutions. In 1860, Minnesota considered enacting such a provision, but defeated a measure that would have barred blacks from entering the state. However, the Minnesota legislature did required registration of those free blacks already residing there (*BAP V* 56).

Chapter 6

1. See Orlando Patterson's *Slavery and Social Death: A Comparative Study* (Cambridge: Harvard University Press, 1982) for his discussion on this subject.

2. See Section 6 of *Cohens v. Virginia*.

3. See Garrison's "The Insurrection," *The Liberator*, 3 September 1831. Garrison's prophecy appears in the following poetic form:

> Wo if it come with storm, and blood, and fire,
> When midnight darkness veils the earth and sky!
> Wo to the innocent babe—the guilty siare—
> Mother and daughter—friends of kindred tie!
> Stranger and citizen alike shall die!
> Red-handed Slaughter his revenge shall feed,
> And Havoc yell his ominous death-cry,
> And wild Despair in vain for mercy plead—
> While hell itself shall shrink and sicken at the deed!

Of his prophetic verse, Garrison wrote that "What was poetry — imagination — in January, is now a bloody reality. Wo to the innocent babe — to mother and daughter! Is it not true? Turn again to the record of slaughter! Whole families have been cut off — not a mother, not a daughter, not a babe left. Dreadful retaliation!"

4. Douglass' speech memorialized the anniversary of the liberation of the British West Indian slaves in 1834 (Blassingame 183).

5. Douglass was referencing Lord Byron's *Childe Harold's Pilgrimage* (1812). In canto 2, stanza 76, Byron wrote:

> Hereditary bondsmen! know ye not
> Who would be free themselves must strike the blow?
> By their right arms the conquest must be wrought?

Douglass, as did countless African Americans, understood too, that blacks would have to rise up against their oppression if freedom was to be obtained. When that day came, Douglass believed, blacks "shall be more abundant in labors, according to their measure of our ability, than ourselves" (309).

6. Garnet's reference was to Daniel O'Connell, the Irish politician who believed in ensuring Irish freedom through political measures rather than violence. Known as "The Liberator," O'Connell (b. 6 August 1776; d. 15 May 1847) was Ireland's foremost politician in the first half of the nineteenth century. An opponent of violent insurrection in Ireland, O'Connell fervently believed that the freedom of the Irish from the British was not worth the spilling of blood. He supported parliamentary and populist methods of forging change. Also see Noel Ignatiev's *How the Irish Became White* (Routledge: New York, 1995) for his discussion on the racial consciousness of the Irish Americans. On 20 February 1895, Douglass would employ O'Connell's philosophy when he opened a women's suffrage meeting by exhorting them to "Agitate, agitate, agitate!" for their rightful place in racial prejudice.

7. Bibb was sold to a tribe of the Cherokee Indians. A mestino (or today spelled "mestizo") was a person of mixed racial ancestry, the offspring of an Indian or an African and an European or person of European ancestry. Bibb wrote that his owner possessed "a large plantation and quite a number of slaves" (152).

8. Quoted in William Lloyd Garrison's preface to Frederick Douglass' 1845 *Narrative of the Life of Frederick Douglass, an American Slave, Written by Himself*, eds. William L. Andrews and William S. McFeely (New York: W. W. Norton & Company, 1997), p. 9.

9. For more on Coffey's perilous journey, see Sue Bailey Thurman's *Pioneers of Negro Origin in California* (San Francisco: ACME Publishing Company, 1949), pp. 11–17.

10. The *Mirror of the Times*, published 1857–1862, attracted a small community of African Americans in the San Francisco Bay Area. Founded by two African American businessmen, Mifflin W. Gibbs and James Townsend, the weekly newspaper gained national attention with its staff of over 30 corresponding editors and subscription agents.

11. Douglass' reply to Thompson's critique was published in the 27 February 1846 edition of the *Liberator*. Thompson was the neighbor of Thomas Auld. In his critique of Douglass' *Narrative*, Thompson wrote that he was giving "true representations of the persons connected with the aforesaid Narrative, and I respectfully submit the facts to the judgment of an impartial public" (90–91). Thompson's critique was reprinted in the *Narrative of the Life of Frederick Douglass, an American Slave, Written By Himself* (1845), eds. William L. Andrews and William S. McFeely (New York: W. W. Norton & Company, 1997), pp. 88–91. Douglass responded to Thompson's allegations by saying that "I am sure I have recorded in my narrative, nothing so revoltingly cruel, murderous, and infernal, as may be found in your own statue book" (95).

12. In January 1854, the Nebraska Bill was introduced by Senator Stephen A. Douglas, the Illinois senator who largely responsible for the Compromise of 1850 that apparently settled slavery issues (*BAP IV* 197). On 30 May 1854, the Kansas–Nebraska Bill created the

Kansas Territory and the Nebraska Territory, divided by the Parallel 40 degrees North. The territorial capital of Nebraska was Omaha.

13. Pittsburgh Mayor Hugh S. Fleming, 1850–1852.

14. Millard Fillmore, serving from 1850–1853, became America's 13th president. Known as the "compromise" president, Fillmore supported the Missouri Compromise, including its provision for the return of runaway slaves, and brought about the sudden ascension of his presidency.

15. Delany's text (chapters 1–23 and 29–31) appeared serially in *The Anglo-African Magazine*, January to July, 1859. Delany reprinted some parts of his story in *The Weekly Anglo-African*, November 1861 to May 1862. In 1970, Floyd J. Miller collected most of the chapters and published the novel with Beacon Press. Many other anti–Tom novels were published in the South. Some include: *Antifanaticism: A Tale of the South* by Martha Haines Butt; *The Ebony Idol* by Mrs. G.M. Flanders; *Liberia; or, Mr. Peyton's Experiments* by Sarah Josepha Hale; *Frank Freeman's Barber Shop* by the Rev. Baynard R. Hall; and *The Planter's Northern Bride* by Caroline Lee Hentz.

16. According to Marion Wilson Starling, *Uncle Tom's Cabin* fused two types of the slave narrative: "the raw material of the slave's account and the sentimental material of the imagined account" (*The Slave Narrative* 301). *Uncle Tom's Cabin* combined elements of five narratives published in the 1840s (*Narrative of the Life of Frederick Douglass, An American Slave, Written by Himself*, 1845; *Narrative of the Sufferings of Lewis Clarke, During a Captivity of More Than Twenty-Five Years, Among the Algerines of Kentucky, One of the So Called Christian States of America. Dictated by Himself*, 1845; *Narrative of William W. Brown, A Fugitive Slave. Written by Himself*, 1847; *The Life of Josiah Henson, Formerly a Slave, Now an Inhabitant of Canada, as Narrated by Himself*, 1849; and *The Fugitive Blacksmith; or, Events in the History of James W. C. Pennington, Pastor of a Presbyterian Church, New York, Formerly a Slave in the State of Maryland, United States*, 1849).

17. A Missouri slave, Dred Scott was sold to John Emerson, an Army surgeon, in St. Louis in 1834 and taken to Illinois, a free state, and on to the free Wisconsin Territory before returning to Missouri. When Emerson died in 1846, Scott filed suit in the Missouri state courts against Emerson's widow, arguing that since he had lived in free territory, he too was free. After defeat in state courts, Scott sued in a local federal court. Eleven years after Scott's initial suit, the case came before the U.S. Supreme Court. The Supreme Court decided 7–2 in favor of the slave owner. Each judge submitted an individual opinion; however, Taney's was the most influential. According to Taney, African Americans, even free, were not citizens of the United States. Because he was a slave, moreover, Scott was considered property, and, therefore, had no right to bring suit against anyone in federal courts. "In regard to the issue of Scott's becoming free when he moved to the free State of Illinois," Taney wrote, "the laws of the State in which the petitioner was currently resident, namely the slave State of Missouri, should apply" (*"Dred Scott v. Sandford*, 1857").

18. Brown was the radical abolitionist who encouraged armed revolution as a means to completely abolish slavery. Along with a group of abolitionists, Brown led the Pottawatomie Massacre in 1856 in Bleeding Kansas, which claimed the lives of five settlers north of Pottawatomie Creek in Franklin County, Kansas. Brown continued his revolutionary tactics by leading the raid at Harpers Ferry in 1859.

19. In spirit Lincoln had given up politics after an unhappy term in Illinois Congress in the late 1840s. He returned to the political arena in 1858, however, when he opposed Senator Stephen A. Douglas of Illinois. Although Lincoln lost the seat on the Senate, he went on to win the Republican Party's nomination for president two years later.

Chapter 7

1. Charles Dickens began a tour of America in January 1842. This tour culminated in the publication of his travel book *American Notes*. In Chapter 17, Dickens wrote discursively

about American slavery. "Slavery is not a whit the more endurable because some hearts are to be found which can partially resist its hardening influences; nor can the indignant tide of honest wrath stand still, because in its onward course it overwhelms a few who are comparatively innocent, among a host of guilty" (210).

2. After escaping slavery in Kentucky in January 1856, Margaret Garner killed her own daughter rather than allow the child to be returned to slavery. To contest the FSA, Garner's attorney moved to have her trial in Ohio, a free state. For more on Garner, see Steven Weisenburger's *Modern Medea: A Family Story of Slavery and Child Murder from the Old South* (New York: Hill and Wang, 1998).

Chapter 8

1. The colonization of Liberia by the free blacks of the United States.

2. Clay was a leading nineteenth-century politician and orator who represented Kentucky in both the House of Representatives and Senate. Known as "The Great Compromiser" and "The Great Pacifier" for his ability to bring others to agreement, he was the founder and leader of the Whig Party and a leading advocate of programs for modernizing the economy. See Clement Eaton, *Henry Clay and the Art of American Politics* (Boston: Little, Brown and Company, 1957).

Works Cited

Adams, Francis D., and Barry Sanders. *Alienable Rights: The Exclusion of African Americans in a White Man's Land, 1619–2000*. New York: Perennial, 2003.

———. *Three Black Writers in Eighteenth Century England*. Belmont, CA: Wads-worth Publishing Company, Inc., 1971.

Allen, Richard. *The Life, Experience, and Gospel Labours of the Rt. Rev. Richard Allen. To Which is Annexed the Rise and Progress of the African Methodist Episcopal Church in the United States of America. Containing a Narrative of the Yellow Fever in the Year of Our Lord 1793: With an Address to the People of Colour in the United States*. 1833. Electronic Edition. *University of North Carolina — Chapel Hill Academic Affairs Library*, 11 September 2004. Web. 15 April 2005. <http://docsouth.unc.edu/>.

Allen, Theodore W. *The Invention of the White Race, Volume One: Racial Oppression and Social Change*. London: Verso, 1994.

Allen, William G. "Speech by William G. Allen, Delivered at the Stock Exchange, Leeds, England." 29 November 1853. *The Black Abolitionist Papers, Volume II, Canada 1830–1865*. Ed. C. Peter Ripley et al. Chapel Hill: The University of North Carolina Press, 1986, pp. 367–371.

———. "William G. Allen to William Lloyd Garrison." *The Black Abolitionist Papers, Volume II, Canada 1830–1865*. Ed. C. Peter Ripley et al. Chapel Hill: The University of North Carolina Press, 1986, pp. 355–361.

Alexander, E. Curtis. *Richard Allen: The First Exemplar of African American Education*. New York: ECA Associates, 1985.

"An American Citizen." 26 September 1787. *The Debate on the Constitution: Federalist and Antifederalist Speeches, Articles, and Letters During the Struggle Over Ratification, Part One*. Ed. Bernard Bailyn. New York: The Library of America, 1993, pp. 20–24.

Ampadu, Lena. "Maria W. Stewart and the Rhetoric of Black Preaching: Perspectives on Womanism and Black Nationalism." *Black Women's Intellectual Traditions: Speaking Their Minds*. Eds. Kristin Waters and Carol B. Conaway. Burlington: University of Vermont Press, 2007, pp. 38–54.

———. "Modeling Orality: African American Rhetorical Practices and the Teaching of Writing." *African American Rhetoric(s): Interdisciplinary Perspectives*. Eds. Elaine B. Richardson and Ronald L. Jackson, II. Carbondale: Southern Illinois University Press, 2004, pp. 136–54.

Andrews, William, ed. Introduction. *The Oxford Frederick Douglass Reader*. New York: Oxford University Press, 1996.

Apess, William. *A Son of the Forest*. 1831. Rptd. in *On Our Own Ground: The Complete Writings of William Apess, A Pequot*. Ed. Barry O'Connell. Amherst: The University of Massachusetts Press, 1992, pp. 1–97.

Aptheker, Herbert. *American Negro Slave Revolts*. New York: International Publishers, 1963.

The Avalon Project: Fugitive Slave Act 1850. 2008. Yale Law School. Web. 13 June 2007. <http://www.yale.edu/lawweb/avalon/fugitive.htm>.
Bacon, Jacqueline. *The Humblest May Stand Forth: Rhetoric, Empowerment, and Abolition.* Columbia: University of South Carolina Press, 2002.
Baker, Houston A. *The Journey Back: Issues in Black Literature and Literary Criticism.* Chicago: University of Chicago Press, 1980.
Balkun, Mary McAleer. "Phyllis Wheatley's Construction of Otherness and the Rhetoric of Performed Ideology." *African American Review* 36.1 (2002): 121–136.
Barksdale, Richard and Keneth Kinnamon. *Black Writers of America: A Comprehensive Anthology.* New York: Prentice Hall, 1997.
Barry, Brian. *Culture and Equality: An Egalitarian Critique of Multiculturalism.* Cambridge: Harvard University Press, 2001.
Bartlow, Dianne. "Maria W. Stewart as a Forerunner of Black Feminist Thought." *Black Women's Intellectual Traditions: Speaking Their Minds.* Eds. Kristin Waters and Carol B. Conaway. Burlington: University of Vermont Press, 2007, pp. 72–88.
Bassard, Katherine Clay. *Spiritual Interrogations: Culture, Gender, and Community in Early African American Women's Writing.* Princeton: Princeton University Press, 1999.
Bercovitch, Sacvan. *The American Jeremiad.* Madison: University of Wisconsin Press, 1978.
Berlin, Ira. *Many Thousands Gone: The First Two Centuries of Slavery in North America.* Cambridge: Harvard University Press, 1998.
Bibb, Henry. "The American Refugees Home." 18 June 1851. *The Black Abolitionist Papers, Volume II, Canada 1830–1865.* Ed. C. Peter Ripley et al. Chapel Hill: The University of North Carolina Press, 1986, pp. 143–148.
_____. "Color-Phobia in Canada." 21 May 1851. *The Black Abolitionist Papers, Volume II, Canada 1830–1865.* Ed. C. Peter Ripley et al. Chapel Hill: The University of North Carolina Press, 1986, pp. 136–137.
_____. "Editorial by Henry Bibb." 21 May 1851. *The Black Abolitionist Papers, Volume II, Canada* Ed. C. Peter Ripley et al. Chapel Hill: The University of North Carolina Press, 1986, pp. 136–137.
_____. "Education." *The Black Abolitionist Papers, Volume II, Canada 1830–1865.* Ed. C. Peter Ripley et al. Chapel Hill: The University of North Carolina Press, 1986, pp. 119–120.
_____. "Emigration to Canada and Jamaica." 3 December 1851. *The Black Abolitionist Papers, Volume II, Canada 1830–1865.* Ed. C. Peter Ripley et al. Chapel Hill: The University of North Carolina Press, 1986, pp. 200–203.
_____. "Henry Bibb to the Executive Committee of the American Missionary Association." 14 December 1850/14 April 1851. *The Black Abolitionist Papers, Volume II, Canada 1830–1865.* Ed. C. Peter Ripley et al. Chapel Hill: The University of North Carolina Press, 1986, pp. 113–118.
_____. "Interesting Arrival in Canada." 1847. *Black Abolitionist Archives*, University of Detroit–Mercy. Doc. No. 08570. Web. 26 May 2007. <http://research.udmercy.edu/>.
_____. "A Letter to My Old Master." 23 September 1852/7 October 1852. *The Black Abolitionist Papers, Volume II, Canada 1830–1865.* Ed. C. Peter Ripley et al. Chapel Hill: The University of North Carolina Press, 1986, pp. 217–221.
_____. *Narrative of the Life and Adventures of Henry Bibb, An American Slave, Written by Himself.* 1849. Electronic Edition. University of North Carolina — Chapel Hill Academic Affairs Library. Web. 30 September 2000. <http://docsouth.unc.edu/>.
_____. "The Proclamation." 26 February 1851. *The Black Abolitionist Papers, Volume II, Canada 1830–1865.* Ed. C. Peter Ripley et al. Chapel Hill: The University of North Carolina Press, 1986, pp. 130–132.
_____. "To Our Old Masters." January–February 1851. *The Black Abolitionist Papers, Volume II, Canada 1830–1865.* Ed. C. Peter Ripley et al. Chapel Hill: The University of North Carolina Press, 1986, pp. 121–129.

Bibb, Henry, John T. Fisher, and James D. Tinsely. 1851. "Address by Henry Bibb, John T. Fisher, and James D. Tinsley." *The Black Abolitionist Papers, Volume II, Canada 1830–1865*. Ed. C. Peter Ripley et al. Chapel Hill: The University of North Carolina Press, 1986, pp. 170–176.

Bibb, Mary E. "Mary E. Bibb to Gerrit Smith." 8 November 1850. *The Black Abolitionist Papers, Volume II, Canada 1830–1865*. Ed. C. Peter Ripley et al. Chapel Hill: The University of North Carolina Press, 1986, pp. 108–112.

Blanks, Granville B. "Granville B. Blanks to Editor, *Syracuse Daily Journal*." 18 August 1852. *The Black Abolitionist Papers, Volume IV, The United States, 1847–1858*. Ed. C. Peter Ripley et al. Chapel Hill: The University of North Carolina Press, 1991, pp. 131–136.

Blassingame, John W., ed. *The Frederick Douglass Papers: Series One; Speeches, Debates, and Interviews*, vols. 1, 2, & 3. New Haven: Yale University Press, 1979.

———. *The Slave Community: Plantation Life in the Antebellum South*. New York: Oxford University Press, 1972.

———, ed. *Slavery Testimony: Two Centuries of Letters, Speeches, Interviews, and Autobiographies*. Baton Rouge: Louisiana State University Press, 1977.

Bogin, Ruth. "'Liberty Further Extended': A 1776 Manuscript by Lemuel Haynes." *The William and Mary Quarterly*. 40.1 (1983): 85–105.

Bracey, John H., Jr., August Meier, and Elliot Rudwick. *Black Nationalism in America*. Indianapolis: The Bobbs-Merrill Company, Inc., 1970.

Brooks, Lloyd H. "Resolutions by Lloyd H. Brooks, Delivered at the Third Christian Church, New Bedford, Massachusetts." 16 June 1858. *The Black Abolitionist Papers, Volume IV, The United States, 1847–1858*. Ed. C. Peter Ripley et al. Chapel Hill: The University of North Carolina Press, 1991, pp. 391–394.

Brown, David. *Contemporary Nationalism: Civic, Ethnocultural and Multicultural Politics*. New York: Routledge, 2000.

Brown, Nikki. "'Send back the money!' Frederick Douglass's Anti-Slavery Speeches in Scotland and the Emergence of African American Internationalism." *STAR (Scotland's Transatlantic Relations) Project Archive*, 2004, pp. 1–10.

Brown, William Wells. *The American Fugitive in Europe. Sketches of Places and People Abroad*. University of North Carolina–Chapel Hill Academic Affairs Library. 30 September 2000. <http://docsouth.unc.edu/>.

———. "American Slavery." 13 April 1850. *Black Abolitionist Archives*, University of Detroit-Mercy. Doc. No.10602. Web. 26 May 2007.

———. *Clotel, or the President's Daughter*. 1853. Armonk: M. E. Sharpe, 1996.

———. "The Colored People of Canada." 1861. *The Black Abolitionist Papers, Volume II, Canada 1830–1865*. Ed. C. Peter Ripley et al. Chapel Hill: The University of North Carolina Press, 1986, pp. 461–498.

———. "The History of the Haitian Revolution." *Pamphlets of Protest: An Anthology of Early African American Protest Literature, 1760–1860*. New York: Routledge, 2001, pp. 240–253.

———. "A Lecture Delivered Before the Female Anti-Slavery Society of Salem." 14 November 1847. *Black Abolitionists Archive*. University of Detroit–Mercy. Doc. No. 20202. Web. 4 May 2007.

———. *Narrative of William W. Brown, An American Slave. Written by Himself*. London. 1849. Electronic Edition. *University of North Carolina–Chapel Hill Academic Affairs Library*. Web. 30 September 2000. <http://docsouth.unc.edu/>.

———. "Slavery in America." 10 May 1851. *Black Abolitionist Archives*, University of Detroit-Mercy. Doc. No. 11543. Web. 26 May 2007.

———. "Speech by William Wells Brown, Delivered at the Concert Rooms, Store Street, London, England." 27 September 1849. *The Black Abolitionist Papers, Volume I, The British Isles,1830–1865*. Ed. C. Peter et al. Chapel Hill: The University of North Carolina Press, 1985, pp. 176–181.

---. "Speech by William Wells Brown, Delivered at the Horticultural Hall, West Chester, Pennsylvania." 23 October 1854. *The Black Abolitionist Papers, Volume IV, The United States, 1847–1858.* Ed. C. Peter Ripley, et al. Chapel Hill: The University of North Carolina Press, 1991, pp. 245–255.

---. "Speech by William Wells Brown, Delivered at the Lecture Hall, Croydon, England." 5 September 1849. *The Black Abolitionist Papers, Volume I, The British Isles,1830–1865*.Ed. C. Peter Ripley, et al. Chapel Hill: The University of North Carolina Press, 1985, pp. 168–175.

---. "Speech by William Wells Brown, Delivered at the Town Hall, Manchester, England." 1 August 1854. *The Black Abolitionist Papers, Volume I, The British Isles, 1830–1865.* Ed. C. Peter et al. Chapel Hill: The University of North Carolina Press, 1985, pp. 398–406.

---. "Speeches by William Wells Brown and J. W. C. Pennington." 24 August 1849. *The Black Abolitionist Papers, Volume I, The British Isles, 1830–1865.* Ed. C. Peter Ripley et al. Chapel Hill: The University of North Carolina Press, 1985, p. 155–160.

---. *Three Years in Europe: or, Places I Have Seen and People I Have Met.* Edinburgh, London: Oliver and Boyd, 1852. *University of North Carolina–Chapel Hill Academic Affairs Library.* Web. 30 September 2000. <http://docsouth.unc.edu/>.

---. "Unbecoming to Become American." 27 April 1850. Black Abolitionist Archives, University of Detroit–Mercy. Doc. No.10605. 26 May 2007.

---. "William Wells Brown to William Lloyd Garrison." 17 May 1853. *The Black Abolitionist Papers, Volume I, The British Isles, 1830–1865.* Ed. C. Peter Ripley et al. Chapel Hill: The University of North Carolina Press, 1985, pp. 344–348.

Bruce, Dickson D., Jr. *The Origins of African American Literature, 1680–1865.* Charlottesville: University of Virginia Press, 2002.

Bustill, Cyrus. "I Speak to Those Who are in Slavery." *Lift Every Voice: African American Oratory, 1787–1900.* Eds. Philip S. Foner and Robert Branham. Tuscaloosa: The University of Alabama Press, 1998, pp. 20–25.

Butler, Judith. *The Psychic Life of Power: Theories in Subjection.* Stanford, CT: Stanford University Press, 1997.

Butterfield, Stephen. *Black Autobiography in America.* Amherst: University of Massachusetts Press, 1974.

Cambridge History of American Literature, Vol. 1. New York: Cambridge University Press, 1944.

Campisi, Jack. *The Mashpee Indians: Tribe on Trial.* Syracuse, NY: Syracuse University Press, 1991.

Carmichael, Stokely, and Charles V. Hamilton. *Black Power: The Politics of Liberation.* New York: Vintage Books, 1967.

Carretta, Vincent. Introduction. *Phillis Wheatley, Complete Writings.* New York: Penguin Classics, 2001, pp. ix–xxiv.

---. Introduction. *Thoughts and Sentiments on the Evil of Slavery: And Other Writings.* By Quobna Ottabah Cugoano. 1787. New York: Penguin, 1995, pp. ix–xxiv.

Cary, Mary Ann Shadd. "Anti-Slavery Relations." 25 March 1854. *The Black Abolitionist Papers, Volume II, Canada 1830–1865.* Ed. C. Peter Ripley et al. Chapel Hill: The University of North Carolina Press, 1986, pp. 283–285.

---. "Editor of the *Anglo-African.*" 17 September 1861. *The Black Abolitionist Papers, Volume II, Canada 1830–1865.* Ed. C. Peter Ripley et al. Chapel Hill: The University of North Carolina Press, 1986, pp. 452–457.

---. "The Emigration Convention." 5 July 1856. *The Black Abolitionist Papers, Volume II, Canada 1830–1865.* Ed. C. Peter Ripley et al. Chapel Hill: The University of North Carolina Press, 1986, pp. 339–342.

---. "The Humbug of Reform." 27 May 1854. *The Black Abolitionist Papers, Volume II, Canada 1830–1865.* Ed. C. Peter Ripley et al. Chapel Hill: The University of North Carolina Press, 1986, pp. 285–288.

———. "Mary Ann Shadd Cary to Robert Hamilton." 17 September 1861. *The Black Abolitionist Papers, Volume II, Canada 1830–1865.* Ed. C. Peter Ripley et al. Chapel Hill: The University of North Carolina Press, 1986, pp. 452–457.
———. "Obstacles to the Progress of Colored Canadians." 31 January 1857. *The Black Abolitionist Papers, Volume II, Canada 1830–1865.* Ed. C. Peter Ripley et al. Chapel Hill: The University of North Carolina Press, 1986, pp. 360–363.
———. "The Presidential Election in the United States." 6 December 1856. *The Black Abolitionist Papers, Volume II, Canada 1830–1865.* Ed. C. Peter Ripley et al. Chapel Hill: The University of North Carolina Press, 1986, pp. 349–351.
———. "Sermon by Mary Ann Shadd Cary." 1856. *The Black Abolitionist Papers, Volume II, Canada 1830–1865.* Ed. C. Peter Ripley et al. Chapel Hill: The University of North Carolina Press, 1986, pp. 388–391.
Clarke, Lewis G. *Narrative by Lewis G. Clarke.* 1842. *The Black Abolitionist Papers, Volume II, Canada 1830–1865.* Ed. C. Peter Ripley et al. Chapel Hill: The University of North Carolina Press, 1986, pp. 393–397.
Clifford, James. *The Predicament of Culture: Twentieth-Century Ethnography, Literature, and Art.* Cambridge: Harvard University Press, 1988.
Coker, Daniel. "A Dialogue Between a Virginian and an African Minister." 1810. *Pamphlets of Protest: An Anthology of Early African American Protest Literature, 1760–1860.* Eds. Richard Newman, Patrick Rael, and Phillip Lapsansky. New York: Routledge, 2001, pp. 54–65.
A Colored Female of Philadelphia. "Emigration to Mexico." 2 January 1832. *Early Negro Writing, 1760–1837.* Ed. Dorothy Porter. Baltimore: Black Classics Press, 1995, pp. 293–294.
Cooper, Afua. "The Fluid Frontier: Blacks and the Detroit River Region. A Focus on Henry Bibb." *Canadian Review of American Studies.* 30.2 (2000): 129–149.
Cottman, Martha L., and Richard W. Cottman. *Nationalism and Politics: The Political Behavior of Nation States.* Boulder: Lynne Rienner Publishers, 2001.
Craft, William. "William Craft to Editor, London *Morning Advertiser.*" September 1852. *The Black Abolitionist Papers, Volume I, The British Isles, 1830–1865.* Ed. C. Peter Ripley et al. Chapel Hill: The University of North Carolina Press, 1985, pp. 316–326.
———, and Ellen Craft. *Running a Thousand Miles for Freedom; or, the Escape of William and Ellen Craft from Slavery.* London: William Tweedie, 1860. Electronic Edition. University of North Carolina–Chapel Hill Academic Affairs Library. Web. 30 September 2000. <http://docsouth.unc.edu/>.
Crew, Louie. "Charles Dickens as a Critic of the United States." *Midwest Quarterly* 16.1 (1974): 42–50.
Crummell, Alexander. "Remarks of Alexander Crummell." 21 May 1849. *The Black Abolitionist Papers, Volume I, The British Isles, 1830–1865.* Ed. C. Peter Ripley et al. Chapel Hill: The University of North Carolina Press, 1985, pp. 149–151.
———. "Speech by Alexander Crummell." 19 May 1851. *The Black Abolitionist Papers, Volume I, The British Isles, 1830–1865.* Ed. C. Peter Ripley et al. Chapel Hill: The University of North Carolina Press, 1985, pp. 276–282.
———. "Speech by Alexander Crummell, Delivered at the Lower Hall, Exeter Hall, London, England." 26 May 1853. *The Black Abolitionist Papers, Volume I, The British Isles, 1830–1865.* Ed. C. Peter Ripley et al. Chapel Hill: The University of North Carolina Press, 1985, pp. 349–354.
Cugoano, Quobna Ottobah. *Narrative of the Enslavement of Ottobah Cugoano, a Native of Africa; Published by Himself, in the Year 1787.* Electronic Edition. University of North Carolina–Chapel Hill Academic Affairs Library. Web. 30 September 2000. <http://docsouth.unc.edu/>.
———. *Thoughts and Sentiments on the Evil and Wicked Traffic of the Commerce of the Human Species.* 1787. Ed. Vincent Carretta. New York: Penguin, 1995.

Darsey, James. *The Prophetic Tradition and Radical Rhetoric in America*. New York: New York University Press, 1997.
Day, William Howard. "Exchange between H. Ford Douglas and William Howard Day." 16 January 1851. *The Black Abolitionist Papers, Volume IV, The United States, 1847–1858*. Ed. C. Peter Ripley et al. Chapel Hill: The University of North Carolina Press, 1991, pp. 73–80.
Delany, Martin R. *Blake, or the Huts of American: A Novel*. 1861–1862. Boston: Beacon Press, 1970.
_____. "Call for a National Emigration Convention of Colored Men to Be Held in Cleveland, Ohio, on the 24th, 25th and 26th of August." 1854. *Martin Delany: A Documentary Reader*. Ed. Robert S. Levine. Chapel Hill: The University of North Carolina Press, 2003, pp. 240–242.
_____. *The Condition, Elevation, Emigration, and Destiny of The Colored People of the United States* and *Official Report of the Niger Valley Exploring Party*. 1852; 1861. New York: Humanity Books, 2004.
_____. "Delany and Douglass on *Uncle Tom's Cabin*." *Martin Delany: A Documentary Reader*. Ed. Robert S. Levine. Chapel Hill: The University of North Carolina Press, 2003, pp. 224–237.
_____. "Letter to James McCune Smith." *Martin R. Delany: A Documentary Reader*. Ed. Robert S. Levine. Chapel Hill: The University of North Carolina Press, 2003, pp. 370–371.
_____. "Martin R. Delany in Liberia." 1859. *Martin R. Delany: A Documentary Reader*. Ed. Robert S. Levine. Chapel Hill: The University of North Carolina Press, 2003, pp. 332–335.
_____. "Martin R. Delany to Frederick Douglass." 10 July 1852. *The Black Abolitionist Papers, Volume IV, The United States, 1847–1858*. Ed. C. Peter Ripley et al. Chapel Hill: The University of North Carolina Press, 1991, pp. 221–223.
_____. "Not Fair." 20 October 1843. *Martin Delany: A Documentary Reader*. Ed. Robert S. Levine. Chapel Hill: The University of North Carolina Press, 2003, pp. 32–33.
_____. "Political Destiny of the Colored Race on the American Continent." 1854. *Martin R. Delany: A Documentary Reader*. Ed. Robert S. Levine. Chapel Hill: The University of North Carolina Press, 2003, pp. 245–279.
_____. "Self-Elevation Tract Society." 16 December 1846. *Martin Delany: A Documentary Reader*. Ed. Robert S. Levine. Chapel Hill: The University of North Carolina Press, 2003, pp. 36–37.
Dickens, Charles. *American Notes*. 1842. New York: St. Martin's Press, 1985.
Douglas, H. Ford. "Exchange between H. Ford Douglas and William Howard Day." 16 January 1851. *The Black Abolitionist Papers, Volume IV, The United States, 1847–1858*. Ed. C. Peter et al. Chapel Hill: The University of North Carolina Press, 1991, pp. 73–80.
_____. "Speech by H. Ford Douglas, Delivered at the Town Hall." 23 September 1860. *The Black Abolitionist Papers, Volume V, The United States, 1859–1865*. Ed. C. Peter Ripley et al. Chapel Hill: The University of North Carolina Press, 1991, pp. 88–96.
Douglass, Frederick. "British Influence on the Abolition Movement in America: An Address Delivered in Paisley, Scotland." 17 April 1846. *The Frederick Douglass Papers: Series One — Speeches, Debates, and Interviews, Vol. I*. Eds. John Blassingame et al. New Haven: Yale University Press, 1979, pp. 215–217.
_____. "The Church and Prejudice." *Life and Writings of Frederick Douglass, Volume I*. Ed. Philip S. Foner. New York: International Publishers, 1975, pp. 103–105.
_____. "Comments on Gerrit Smith's Address." 30 March 1849. *Frederick Douglass: Selected Speeches and Writings*. Ed. Philip S. Foner. Chicago: Lawrence Hill Books, 1975, pp. 137–141.
_____. "Country, Conscience, and the Anti-Slavery Cause: An Address Delivered in New York, New York." 11 May 1847 *The Frederick Douglass Papers, Series One, Speeches, Debates, and Interviews, Vol. II, 1847–54*. Eds. John Blassingame et al. New Haven: Yale University Press, 1982, pp. 57–68.
_____. "The Dred Scott Decision: An Address Delivered, in Part, in New York, New York."

11 May 1857. *The Frederick Douglass Papers: Series One, Speeches, Debates, and Interviews, Vol. III, 1855–63.* Eds. John Blassingame et al. New Haven: Yale University Press, 1979, pp. 163–183.

———. "Emancipation is an Individual, A National, and an International Responsibility: An Address Delivered in London, England, on 18 May 1846." *The Frederick Douglass Papers: Series One; Speeches, Debates, and Interviews, Vol. I, 1841–46.* Eds. John Blassingame et al. New Haven: Yale University Press, 1979, pp. 249–261.

———. "I Am Here to Spread Light on American Slavery: An address Delivered in Cork, Ireland, on 14 October 1845." *The Frederick Douglass Papers: Series One— Speeches, Debates, and Interviews, Vol. I.* Eds. John Blassingame et al. New Haven: Yale University Press, 1979, pp. 39–45.

———. "I Have Come To Tell You Something About Slavery: An Address Delivered in Lynn, Massachusetts." October 1841. *The Frederick Douglass Papers: Series One; Speeches, Debates, and Interviews.* Eds. John Blassingame et al. New Haven: Yale University Press, 1979, pp. 3–5.

———. "If There Is No Struggle There Is No Progress." *Lift Every Voice: African American Oratory, 1787–1900.* Eds. Philip S. Foner and Robert James Branham. Tuscaloosa: The University of Alabama Press, 1998, pp. 308–312.

———. "International Moral Force Can Destroy Slavery: An Address Delivered in Paisley, Scotland." 17 March 1846. *The Frederick Douglass Papers: Series One— Speeches, Debates, and Interviews, Vol. I.* Eds. John Blassingame et al. New Haven: Yale University Press, 1979, pp. 183–185.

———. *Narrative of the Life of Frederick Douglass, an American Slave, Written By Himself.* 1845. Eds. William L. Andrews and William S. McFeely. New York: W. W. Norton & Company, 1997.

———. "A Nation in the Midst of the Nation: An Address Delivered in New York, New York." 11 May 1853. *The Frederick Douglass Papers: Series One; Speeches, Debates, and Interviews, Vol. II, 1847–54.* Eds. John Blassingame et al. New Haven: Yale University Press, 1979, pp. 423–440.

———. "Reception Speech At Finsbury Chapel, Moorfields, England." 12 May 1846. *University of North Carolina–Chapel Hill Academic Affairs Library.* Web. 15 July 2006. <http://docsouth.unc.edu/>.

———. "Reply to Thompson's Letter." *Narrative of the Life of Frederick Douglass, an American Slave, Written By Himself.* 1845. Eds. William L. Andrews and William S. McFeely. New York: W. W. Norton & Company, 1997, pp. 91–96.

———. "The Significance of Emancipation in the West Indies: An Address Delivered in Canandaigua, New York." 3 August 1857. *The Frederick Douglass Papers: Series One, Speeches, Debates, and Interviews, Vol. III, 1855–63.* Eds. John Blassingame et al. New Haven: Yale University Press, 1979, pp. 183–208.

———. "The Slaves' Right to Revolt: An Address Delivered in Boston, Massachusetts." 20 May 1848. *The Frederick Douglass Papers: Series One: Speeches, Debates, and Interviews. Vol. II, 1847–54.* Eds. John Blassingame et al. New Haven: Yale University Press, 1982, pp. 130–132.

———. "What to the Slave is the Fourth of July?" *The Oxford Frederick Douglass Reader.* Ed. William L. Andrews. New York: Oxford University Press, 1996, pp. 108–130.

Douglass, Sarah M. "Speech by Sarah M. Douglass Delivered before the Female Literary Society of Philadelphia, Philadelphia, Pennsylvania." *The Black Abolitionist Papers, Volume III, The United States, 1830–1846.* Ed. C. Peter Ripley et al. Chapel Hill: The University of North Carolina Press, 1991, pp. 116–118.

"Dred Scott v. Sandford, 1857." Web. 12 December 2010. <http://www.graves.k12.ky.us/schools/GCHS/bleonard/HTML/sc/dred.htm>.

DuBois, W.E.B. *The Philadelphia Negro: A Social Study.* 1896. Philadelphia: The University of Pennsylvania Press, 1995.

Easton, Hosea. "An Address: Delivered Before the Coloured Population, of Providence Rhode Island on Thanksgiving Day." 27 November 1828. *Preaching with Sacred Fire: An Anthology of African American Sermons, 1750 to the Present*. Eds. Martha Simmons and Frank A. Thomas. New York: W. W. Norton & Company, 2010, pp. 45–56.

"Editorial." 27 August 1831. *Black Abolitionist Archives*, University of Detroit–Mercy. Doc. No. 00201. Web. 30 May 2007. <http://research.udmercy.edu>.

Elliott, Emory. "New England Puritan Literature." *Cambridge History of American Literature, Volume 1*. Ed. Sacvan Bercovitch. Cambridge, MA: Cambridge University Press, 1997.

Equiano, Olaudah. *The Interesting Narrative of the Life of Olaudah Equiano, or Gustavus Vassas, the African. Written by Himself.* 1789. Electronic Edition. *University of North Carolina–Chapel Hill Academic Affairs Library*. Web. 15 July 1999. <http://docsouth.unc.edu/>.

"Essay by 'A Colored Woman.'" *The Black Abolitionist Papers, Volume III, The United States, 1830–1846*. Ed. C. Peter Ripley et al. Chapel Hill: The University of North Carolina Press, 1991, pp. 326–327.

Finkelman, Paul. "Manufacturing Martyrdom: The Antislavery Response to John Brown's Raid." *His Soul Goes Marching On: Responses to John Brown and the Harpers Ferry Raid*. Ed. Paul Finkelman. Virginia: University of Virginia Press, 1995, pp. 41–66.

Fitch, Suzanne Pullon, and Roseann M. Mandziuk. *Sojourner Truth as Orator: Wit, Story, and Song*. Westport, CT: Greenwood Press, 1997.

Foner, Philip S., and Robert James Branham. *Lift Every Voice: African American Oratory 1787–1900*. Tuscaloosa: The University of Alabama Press, 1998.

Forten, James, Sr., "Letter to Paul Cuffee." 1817. *Classical Black Nationalism: From the American Revolution to Marcus Garvey*. Ed. Wilson Jeremiah Moses. New York: New York University Press, 1996, pp. 50–52.

_____. "Series of Letters by a Man of Colour." 1813. *Pamphlets of Protest: An Anthology of Early African American Protest Literature, 1760–1860*. Eds. Richard Newman, Patrick Rael, and Phillip Lapsansky. New York: Routledge, 2001, pp. 66–72.

_____, and Russell Parrott. "To the Human and Benevolent Inhabitants of the City and County of Philadelphia." 1817. *Early Negro Writing, 1760–1837*. Ed. Dorothy Porter. Baltimore: Black Classic Press, 1995.

Francis, Abner H. "'Black Laws in the West,' Petition of California Blacks to the California State Legislature." October 1851. *The Black Abolitionist Papers, Volume IV, The United States, 1847–1858*. Ed. C. Peter Ripley et al. Chapel Hill: The University of North Carolina Press, 1991, pp. 102–107.

Franklin, John Hope. *From Slavery to Freedom: A History of African Americans*. 7th ed. New York: McGraw-Hill, Inc. 1994.

Freire, Paulo. *Pedagogy of the Oppressed*. New York: Continuum, 1970.

Gardell, Mattias. *In the Name of Elijah Muhammad: Louis Farrakhan and the Nation of Islam*. Durham: Duke University Press, 1996.

Gardner, Charles. W. "Speech by Charles W. Gardner, Delivered at the Broadway Tabernacle, New York, New York." 9 May 1837. *The Black Abolitionist Papers, Volume III, The United States, 1830–1846*. Ed. C. Peter Ripley et al. Chapel Hill: The University of North Carolina Press, 1991, pp. 206–215.

Garner, Carla W. "William G. Allen." *An Online Reference Guide to African American History*. BlackPast.org. Web. 4 April 2010. <http://www.blackpast.org/?q=aah/allen-william-g-1820>.

Garnet, Henry Highland. "An Address to the Slaves of the United States of America." 1843. *Walker's Appeal and Garnet's Address to the Slaves of the United States of America*. Nashville: James C. Winston Publishing Company, Inc., 1994, pp. 89–96.

_____. "Debate over Garnet's 'Address to the Slaves of the United State of America.'" 1843. *Pamphlets of Protest: An Anthology of Early African American Protest Literature, 1760–1860*.

Eds. Richard Newman, Patrick Rael, and Phillip Lapsansky. New York: Routledge, 2001, pp. 157–159.

———. "Essay by 'Sidney.'" February 1841. *The Black Abolitionist Papers, Volume III, The United States, 1830–1846.* Ed. C. Peter Ripley et al. Chapel Hill: The University of North Carolina Press, 1991, pp. 356–361.

———. "Henry Highland Garnet to Simeon S. Jocelyn." 14 September 1859. *The Black Abolitionist Papers, Volume V, The United States, 1859–1865.* Ed. C. Peter Ripley et al. Chapel Hill: The University of North Carolina Press, 1992, pp. 35–37.

———. "The Past and the Present Condition, and the Destiny, or The Colored Race: A Discourse Delivered at the Fifteenth Anniversary of the Female Benevolent Society of Troy, N.Y." 14 February 1848. Miami: Mnemosyne Publishing Inc., 1969.

———. "Speech by Henry Highland Garnet, Delivered at the Music Hall, Birmingham, England." 15 October 1861. *The Black Abolitionist Papers, Volume I, The British Isles, 1830–1865.* Ed. C. Peter Ripley et al. Chapel Hill: The University of North Carolina Press, 1991, pp. 515–518.

Garrison, William Lloyd. "The Insurrection." *The Liberator.* 3 September 1831. Web. 24 August 2009. <http://fair-use.org/the-liberator/1831/09/03/the-insurrection>.

Gates, Henry Louis, Jr. *The Trials of Phyllis Wheatley: America's First Black Poet and Encounters with the Founding Fathers.* New York: Basic Civitas Books, 2003.

Gaul, Theresa Strouth. "Dialogue and Public Discourse in William Apess's *Indian Nullification*." *The American Transcendental Quarterly* 15.3 (2001): 276–92.

Gilyard, Keith, and Anissa Wardi, eds. *African American Literature.* New York: Pearson Longman Press, 2004.

Gordon, Dexter B. *Black Identity: Rhetoric, Ideology, and Nineteenth-Century Black Nationalism.* Carbondale: Southern Illinois University Press, 2003.

Gouins, Henry. "Circular by Henry Gouins." *The Black Abolitionist Papers, Volume I, The United States, 1830–1846.* Ed. C. Peter Ripley et al. Chapel Hill: The University of North Carolina Press, 1985, pp. 98–99.

Gould, Philip. *Barbaric Traffic: Commerce and Antislavery in the Eighteenth-Century Atlantic World.* Cambridge: Harvard University Press, 2003.

Gronniosaw, James Albert Ukawsaw. *A Narrative of the Most Remarkable Particulars in the Life of James Albert Ukawsaw Gronniosaw, An African Prince, As Related By Himself.* 1770. Electronic Edition. *University of North Carolina–Chapel Hill Academic Affairs Library.* Web. 30 September 2000. <http://docsouth.unc.edu/>.

Hahn, Steven. *A Nation Under Our Feet: Black Political Struggles in the Rural South From Slavery to the Great Migration.* Cambridge: The Belknap Press of Harvard University Press, 2003.

Hall, Prince. *A Charge.* 1797. *Pamphlets of Protest: An Anthology of Early African American Protest Literature, 1760–1860.* Eds. Richard Newman, Patrick Rael, and Phillip Lapsansky. New York: Routledge, 2001, pp. 45–50.

Hamilton, Thomas. "Editorial by Thomas Hamilton." 19 November 1859. *The Black Abolitionist Papers, Volume V, The United States, 1859–1865* Ed. C. Peter Ripley, et al. Chapel Hill: The University of North Carolina Press, 1992, pp. 41–42.

Hamilton, William. "Address to the New York African Society." *Lift Every Voice: African American Oratory, 1787–1900.* Eds. Philip S. Foner and Robert Branham. Tuscaloosa: The University of Alabama Press, 1998, pp. 80–86.

———. "An Address to the New York Society for Mutual Relief, Delivered In the Universalist Church." 2 January 1809. *Early Negro Writing, 1760–1837.* Ed. Dorothy Porter. Baltimore: Black Classics Press, 1995, pp. 33–41.

———. "An Oration Delivered in the African Zion Church, on the Fourth of July, 1827, in Commemoration of the Abolition of Domestic Slavery in This State." *Early Negro Writing, 1760–1837.* Ed. Dorothy Porter. Baltimore: Black Classic Press, 1995, pp. 96–104.

Hammon, Jupiter. "Address to the Negroes of the State of New York." 1787. *Libraries at the University of Nebraska-Lincoln: Electronic Text in American Studies.* Ed. Paul Royster. Web. 23 September 2007. <http://digitalcommons.unl.edu>.

_____. *Jupiter Hammon and the Biblical Beginnings of African-American Literature.* Metuchen, NJ: The American Theological Library Association and The Scarecrow Press, 1993.

Harding, Vincent. *There is a River: The Black Struggle for Freedom in America.* New York: Harcourt Brace Jovanovich, 1981.

Hartman, Saidiya V. *Scenes of Subjection: Terror, Slavery, and Self-Making in Nineteenth-Century America.* New York: Oxford University Press, 1997.

Harper, Frances E.W. "Circular by Frances Ellen Watkins Harper for Arkansas Free Blacks." January 1860. *The Black Abolitionist Papers, Volume V, The United States, 1859–1865.* Ed. C. Peter Ripley et al. Chapel Hill: The University of North Carolina Press, 1992, pp. 54–57.

_____. "Frances Ellen Watkins Harper to Jane E. Hitchcock Jones." 21 September 1860. *The Black Abolitionist Papers, Volume V, The United States, 1859–1865.* Ed. C. Peter Ripley et al. Chapel Hill: The University of North Carolina Press, 1992, pp. 81–83.

_____. "Liberty for Slaves." *Lift Every Voice: African American Oratory 1787–1900.* Eds. Philip S. Foner and Robert James Branham. Tuscaloosa: The University of Alabama Press, 1998, pp. 305–307.

_____. "New York City Anti-Slavery Society." 23 May 1857. *Black Abolitionists Archive.* University of Detroit–Mercy. Doc. No. 18726. Web. 23 June 2007.

_____. "Our Greatest Want." *We Are Your Sisters: Black Women in the Nineteenth Century.* Ed. Dorothy Sterling. New York: W. W. Norton and Company, 1984, p. 163.

Harris, Andrew. "Speech by Andrew Harris." 7 May 1839. *The Black Abolitionist Papers, Volume III, The United States, 183–1846.* Ed. C. Peter Ripley et al. Chapel Hill: The University of North Carolina Press, 1985, pp. 294–297.

Haynes, Lemuel. "The Important Concerns of Ministers and the People of Their Charge." 1798. *Black Preacher to White America: The Collected Writings of Lemuel Haynes, 1774–1833.* Ed. Richard Newman. Brooklyn: Carlson Publishing, Inc., 1990, pp. 55–64.

_____. "The Influence of Civil Government on Religion." 1798. *Black Preacher to White America: The Collected Writings of Lemuel Haynes, 1774–1833.* Ed. Richard Newman. Brooklyn: Carlson Publishing, Inc., 1990, pp. 65–76.

Henderson, Stephen. Introduction. "The Forms of Things Unknown." *Understanding the New Black Poetry, Black Speech and Black Music as Poetic References.* New York: William Morrow & Co., 1973, pp. 1–69.

Henson, Josiah. *An Autobiography of the Rev. Josiah Henson ("Uncle Tom"). From 1789 to 1881. With a Preface by Mrs. Harriet Beecher Stowe, and Introductory Notes by George Sturge, S. Morley, Esq., M. P., Wendell Phillips, and John G. Whittier.* Ed. John Lobb, F.R.G.S. London, Ontario: Schuyler, Smith, & Co., 1881. Revised and Enlarged. Electronic edition. *Documenting the American South.* Web. 23 May 2006.

Hinks, Peter P. *To Awaken My Afflicted Brethren: David Walker and the Problem of Antebellum Slave Resistance.* University Park: The Pennsylvania State University Press, 1997.

Hirschfeld, Fritz. *George Washington and Slavery: A Documentary Portrayal.* Columbia: University of Missouri Press, 1997.

Hite, Roger W. "Voice of a Fugitive: Henry Bibb and Ante-Bellum Black Separatism." *Journal of Black Studies* 4.3 (1974): 269–284.

Holly, Joseph C. "American Slavery — Its Effect Upon the Rights and Interests of the North." 17 April 1848. *The Black Abolitionist Papers, Volume IV, The United States, 1847–1858.* Ed. C. Peter Ripley et al. Chapel Hill: The University of North Carolina Press, 1991, pp. 18–26.

_____. "Voice from the 'Green Mountains.'" May 1851. *The Black Abolitionist Papers, Volume II, Canada 1830–1865.* Ed. C. Peter Ripley et al. Chapel Hill: The University of North Carolina Press, 1986, pp. 138–142.

Hord, Fred Lee. *Reconstructing Memory: Black Literary Criticism.* Chicago: Third World Press, 1991.

Horton, James Oliver. "Weevils in the Wheat: Free Blacks and the Constitution, 1787–1860." Web. 23 May 2009. <http://www.apsanet.org/imgtest/FreeBlacksConstitution.pdf>.
Howard-Pitney, David. *The Afro-American Jeremiad: Appeals for Justice in America.* Philadelphia: Temple University Press, 1990.
Ignatiev, Noel. *How the Irish Became White.* New York: Routledge, 1995.
Jackson, Ronald L., and Elaine B. Richardson, eds. *Understanding African American Rhetoric: Classic Origins to Contemporary Innovations.* New York: Routledge, 2003.
Jacobs, Harriet A. "Harriet A. Jacobs to Horace Greeley." 19 June 1853. *The Black Abolitionist Papers, Volume IV, The United States, 1847–1858.* Ed. C. Peter Ripley et al. Chapel Hill: The University of North Carolina Press, 1991, pp. 164–169.
James, Elisabeth. *All Black Voices Count.* Jackson: Town Square Books, Inc., 1998.
Jamison, Angelene. "Analysis of Selected Poetry of Phyllis Wheatley." *Journal of Negro Education.* 43.3 (1974): 408–416.
Jefferson, Thomas. *Notes on the State of Virginia.* Electronic Text Center, University of Virginia Library. Web. 6 June 2005. <http://etext.lib.virginia.edu/toc/modeng/public/JefVirg.html>.
Johnson, Charles, and Patricia Smith. *Africans in America: America's Journey Through Slavery.* New York: Harcourt Brace and Company, 1998.
Johnstone, Abraham. "The Address of Abraham Johnstone, a Black Man, Who Was Hanged at Woodbury, in the County of Glocester, and State of New Jersey, on Saturday the 8th Day of July Last; To the People of Colour. To Which Is Added His Dying Confession or Declaration. Also, a Copy of a Letter to His Wife, Written the Day Previous to His Execution." 1797. Electronic Edition. Web. 31 October 2004. *University of North Carolina–Chapel Hill Academic Affairs Library* <http://docsouth.unc.edu/>.
Jones, Absalom, and Richard Allen. "A Narrative of the Proceedings of the Black People During the Late Awful Calamity in Philadelphia." 1794. *Pamphlets of Protest: An Anthology of Early African American Protest Literature, 1760–1860.* Eds. Richard Newman, Patrick Rael, and Phillip Lapsansky. New York: Routledge, 2001, pp. 33–42.
Jones, Jehu. "Jehu Jones to Charles B. Ray." 8 August 1839. *The Black Abolitionist Papers, Volume III, The United States, 1830–1846.* Ed. C. Peter Ripley et al. Chapel Hill: The University of North Carolina Press, 1991, pp. 76–83.
Jones, Thomas. *The Experience of Thomas H. Jones, Who Was A Slave for Forty-Three Years.* Boston: Bazin & Chandler, 1862. Electronic Edition. *University of North Carolina–Chapel Hill Academic Affairs Library.* Web. 30 August 1999. <http://docsouth.unc.edu/jones/menu.html>.
Jordan, Winthrop D. *White Over Black: American Attitudes Toward the Negro, 1550–1812.* Chapel Hill: The University of North Carolina Press, 1968.
Kaplan, Sidney, and Emma Nogrady Kaplan. *The Black Presence in the Era of the American Revolution.* Boston: University of Massachusetts Press, 1989.
Karenga, Maulana. *Introduction to Black Studies.* 2nd ed. Los Angeles: The University of Sankore Press,1993.
Katz, William Loren. *Black Indians: A Hidden Heritage.* New York: Simon Pulse, 1986.
Kellas, James G. *The Politics of Nationalism and Ethnicity.* New York: St. Martin's Press, 1991.
Kelly, Edmund. "Speech by Edmund Kelly, Delivered at Baptist Chapel, Dublin, Ireland." 7 April 1853. *The Black Abolitionist Papers, Volume I, The British Isles, 1830–1865.* Ed. C. Peter Ripley et al. Chapel Hill: The University of North Carolina Press, 1985, pp. 332–334.
Kendrick, Robert. "Other Questions: Phyllis Wheatley and the Ethics of Interpretation." *Cultural Critique,* 38 (1997–98): 39–64.
———. "Re-membering America: Phyllis Wheatley's Intertextual Epic." *African American Review,* 30.1 (1996): 71–88.
Kohn, Hans. *The Idea of Nationalism: A Study in Its Origins and Background.* New York: The Macmillan Company, 1944.

Lambert, William. "Resolutions by William Lambert, Presented at the Second Baptist Church, Detroit, Michigan." 2 December 1859. *The Black Abolitionist Papers, Volume V, The United States, 1859–1865*. Ed. C. Peter Ripley et al. Chapel Hill: The University of North Carolina Press, 1991, pp. 51–53.

Langston, Charles H. "Should Colored Men be Subject to the Penalties of the Fugitive Slave Law?" June 1859. *Lift Every Voice: African American Oratory, 1787–1900*. Eds. Philip S. Foner and Robert James Branham. Tuscaloosa: The University of Alabama Press, 1998, pp. 322–328.

Lauter, Paul, ed. *The Heath Anthology of American Literature*. New York: Houghton Mifflin, 2002.

Lawrence, George, Jr. "A Carbonari Wanted." 13 April 1861. *The Black Abolitionist Papers, Volume V, The United States, 1859–1865*. Ed. C. Peter Ripley et al. Chapel Hill: The University of North Carolina Press, 1991, pp. 110–111.

———. "Editorials by George Lawrence, Jr." 27 April 1861. *The Black Abolitionist Papers, Volume V, The United States, 1859–1865*. Ed. C. Peter Ripley et al. Chapel Hill: The University of North Carolina Press, 1991, pp. 111–112.

Lee, Jarena. *Religious Experience and Journal of Mrs. Jarena Lee, Giving An Account of Her Call to Preach the Gospel*. 1849. *Spiritual Narratives*. Ed. Henry Louis Gates, Jr. New York: Oxford University Press, 1988, pp. 3–32.

Levine, Robert S., ed. *Martin Delany: A Documentary Reader*. Chapel Hill: The University of North Carolina Press, 2003.

———. *Martin Delany, Frederick Douglass and the Politics of Representative Identity*. Chapel Hill: The University of North Carolina Press, 1997.

———. "*Uncle Tom's Cabin* in Frederick Douglass' Paper: An Analysis of Reception." *American Literature* 64.1 (1992): 71–93.

Lincoln, C. Eric. "The Development of Black Religion in America." *African American Religious Studies: An Interdisciplinary Anthology*. Ed. Gayraud S. Wilmore. Durham: Duke University Press, 1989, pp. 5–21.

Loguen, Jermain Wesley. "I Won't Obey the Fugitive Slave Law." 4 October 1850. *Lift Every Voice: African American Oratory 1787–1900*. Eds. Philip S. Foner and Robert James Branham. Tuscaloosa: The University of Alabama Press, 1998, pp. 223–226.

———. "Jermain Wesley Loguen to Washington Hunt." 2 December 1851. *The Black Abolitionist Papers, Volume II, Canada, 1830–1865*. Ed. C. Peter Ripley et al. Chapel Hill: The University of North Carolina Press, 1986, pp. 193–199.

Lowance, Mason. *Against Slavery: An Abolitionist Reader*. New York: Penguin, 2000.

Marable, Manning. "Religion and Black Protest Thought in African American History." *African American Religious Studies: An Interdisciplinary Anthology*. Ed. Gayraud S. Wilmore. Durham: Duke University Press, 1989, pp. 318–339.

McCarthy, Timothy Patrick, and John Stauffer, eds. Introduction. *Prophets of Protest: Reconsidering the History of American Abolitionism*. New York: The New Press, 2006, pp. xiii–xxxiii.

McFeely, William. *Frederick Douglass*. New York: W.W. Norton & Company, 1991.

Meer, Sarah. *Uncle Tom Mania: Slavery, Minstrelsy, and Transatlantic Culture in the 1850s*. Athens: University of Georgia Press, 2005.

Menand, Louis. *The Metaphysical Club: A Story of Ideas in America*. New York: Farrar, Straus and Giroux, 2001.

Meyer, Michael. Introduction. *Frederick Douglass: The Narrative and Selected Writings*. New York: The Modern Library, 1984, pp. ix–xxx.

Milan, Anne, and Kelly Tran. "Blacks in Canada: A Long History." *Canadian Social Trends* (2004): 2–7.

Miller, Perry. *Errand into the Wilderness*. Cambridge: Harvard University Press, 1956.

———. *The New England Mind: From Colony to Province*. Cambridge: Harvard University Press, 1953.

Works Cited

Moses, Wilson Jeremiah. *Black Messiahs and Uncle Toms: Social and Literary Manipulations of Religious Myth*. University Park: The Pennsylvania State University Press, 1982.
_____. *Classical Black Nationalism: From the American Revolution to Marcus Garvey*. New York: New York University Press, 1996.
_____. *The Golden Age of Black Nationalism, 1850–1925*. New York: Oxford University Press, 1978.
Nash, Gary B. "New Light on Richard Allen: The Early Years of Freedom." *The William and Mary Quarterly*. 46.2 (1989): 332–340.
New American Standard Bible. BibleGateway.com. Web. 13 August 2007. <http://www.biblegateway.com>.
Newby, William. H. "William H. Newby to Frederick Douglass." 10 August 1854. *The Black Abolitionist Papers, Volume IV, The United States, 1847–1858*. Ed. C. Peter Ripley et al. Chapel Hill: The University of North Carolina Press, 1991, pp. 234–241.
Newman, Richard. *Lemuel Haynes: A Bio-Bibliography*. New York: Lambeth Press, 1984.
_____, Patrick Rael, and Phillip Lapsansky, eds. *Pamphlets of Protest: An Anthology of Early African American Protest Literature, 1760–1860*. New York: Routledge, 2001.
Nielsen, Donald M. "The Mashpee Revolt of 1833." *New England Quarterly* 58.3 (1985): 400–420.
Northup, Solomon. *Twelve Years a Slave: Narrative of Solomon Northup, a Citizen of New-York, Kidnapped in Washington City in 1841, and Rescued in 1853*. London: Sampson Low, Son & Company. Electronic Edition. *University of North Carolina — Chapel Hill Academic Affairs Library*. Web. 30 September 2000. <http://docsouth.unc.edu/>.
O'Connell, Barry. Introduction. *On Our Own Ground: The Complete Writings of William Apess, A Pequot*. Amherst: The University of Massachusetts Press, 1992, pp. xiii–lxxviii.
O'Connor, Lillian. *Pioneer Women Orators*. New York: Columbia University Press, 1972.
Olsen, Ted. Editorial. *Christian History*. 1999. Web. 23 February 2001. <http://www.christianitytoday.com/ch/62h/62h020.html>.
Olwell, Robert. *Masters, Slaves, and Subjects: The Culture of Power in the South Carolina Low Country, 1740–1790*. Ithaca: Cornell University Press, 1998.
O'Neale, Sondra. "Challenge to Wheatley's Critics: 'There Was No Other "Game" in Town.'" *Journal of Negro Education*, 54.4 (1985): 500–511.
Patterson, Orlando. *Jupiter Hammon and the Biblical Beginnings of African-American Literature*. Metuchen: American Theological Library Association and Scarecrow Press, 1993.
_____. *Slavery and Social Death: A Comparative Study*. Cambridge: Harvard University Press, 1982.
Parrott, Russell. "An Oration on the Abolition of the Slave Trade; Delivered on the First of January, 1814. At the African Church of St. Thomas." 1814. *Pamphlets of Protest: An Anthology of Early African American Protest Literature, 1760–1860*. Eds. Richard Newman, Patrick Rael, and Phillip Lapsansky. New York: Routledge, 2001, pp. 74–79.
Paul, Nathaniel. "An Address on the Occasion of the Abolition of Slavery in New-York." 5 July 1827. *Preaching with Sacred Fire: An Anthology of African American Sermons, 1750 to the Present*. Eds. Martha Simmons and Frank A. Thomas. New York: W. W. Norton & Company, 2010, pp. 181–189.
_____. "Speech by Nathaniel Paul, Delivered at Exeter Hall, London, England." 13 July 1833. *The Black Abolitionist Papers, Volume I, The British Isles, 1830–1865*. Ed. C. Peter Ripley et al. Chapel Hill: The University of North Carolina Press, 1985, pp. 44–52.
Payne, Daniel Alexander. "First Annual Address of the Philadelphia Annual Conference of the A.M.E. Church." 16 May 1853. Philadelphia: C. Sherman, Printer. *Sermons and Addresses, 1853–1891: Bishop Daniel A. Payne*. Ed. Charles Killian. New York: Arno Press, 1972, pp. 1–23.
_____. "Slavery Brutalizes Man." *Lift Every Voice: African American Oratory 1787–1900*. Eds. Philip S. Foner and Robert James Branham. Tuscaloosa: The University of Alabama Press, 1998, pp. 173–177.

Pennington, J. W. C. "Speech by J. W. C. Pennington." 24 August 1849. *The Black Abolitionist Papers, Volume I, The British Isles, 1830–1865*. Ed. C. Peter Ripley et al. Chapel Hill: The University of North Carolina Press, 1985, pp. 157–160.

———. "Speech by J. W. C. Pennington, Delivered at Exeter Hall, London, England." 21 June 1843. *The Black Abolitionist Papers, Volume I, The British Isles, 1830–1865*. Ed. C. Peter Ripley et al. Chapel Hill: The University of North Carolina Press, 1985, pp. 129–133.

———. "Speech by J. W. C. Pennington, Delivered at Freemasons' Hall, London, England." 14 June 1843. *The Black Abolitionist Papers, Volume I, The British, 1830–1865*. Ed. C. Peter Ripley et al. Chapel Hill: The University of North Carolina Press, 1985, pp. 104–128.

Pinckney, Charles Cotesworth. "Debates in the Legislature and in the Convention of the State of South Carolina, on the Adoption of the Federal Constitution." 1898. *Debates on the Adoption of the Federal Constitution Vol. 4*. Ed. Jonathan Elliot. New York: Ayer Publishing, 1987, pp. 253–317.

Pipes, William H. *Say Amen, Brother!: Old-Time Negro Preaching : A Study in American Frustration*. Detroit: Wayne State University Press, 1992.

Porter, Dorothy, ed. *Early Negro Writing, 1760–1837*. Baltimore: Black Classics Press, 1995.

Powell, William P. "William P. Powell to William Lloyd Garrison." 10 July 1839. *The Black Abolitionist Papers, Volume III, The United States, 1830–1846*. Ed. C. Peter Ripley et al. Chapel Hill: The University of North Carolina Press, 1985, pp. 298–300.

"Proceedings of a Meeting of Rochester Blacks." 13 October 1851. *The Black Abolitionist Papers, Volume IV, The United States, 1847–1858*. Ed. C. Peter Ripley et al. Chapel Hill: The University of North Carolina Press, 1991, pp. 98–101.

"Proceedings of a Meeting of Toronto Blacks." 13 January 1838. *The Black Abolitionist Papers, Volume II, Canada, 1830–1846*. Ed. C. Peter Ripley et al. Chapel Hill: The University of North Carolina Press, 1986, pp. 68–75.

"Proceedings of the North American Convention." 1851. *The Black Abolitionist Papers, Volume II, Canada 1830–1865*. Ed. C. Peter Ripley et al. Chapel Hill: The University of North Carolina Press, 1986, pp. 149–169.

Purvis, Robert. "The American Government and the Negro." 18 May 1860. *Lift Every Voice: African-American Oratory, 1787–1900*. Eds. Philip S. Foner and Robert James Branham. Tuscaloosa: University of Alabama Press, 1997, pp. 331–339.

———. "Appeal of Forty Thousand Citizens Threatened with Disfranchisement, to the People of Pennsylvania." 1837. *Pamphlets of Protest: An Anthology of Early African American Protest Literature, 1760–1860*. Eds. Richard Newman, Patrick Rael, and Phillip Lapsansky. New York: Routledge, 2001, pp. 133–142.

———. "Robert Purvis to Oliver Johnson." 24 April 1852. *The Black Abolitionist Papers, Volume IV, The United States, 1847–1858*. Ed. C. Peter Ripley et al. Chapel Hill: The University of North Carolina Press, 1991, pp. 124–125.

———. "Speech by Robert Purvis, Delivered at the City Assembly Rooms, New York, New York." 12 May 1857. *The Black Abolitionist Papers, Volume IV, The United States, 1847–1858*.

Quarles, Benjamin. *Black Abolitionists*. Oxford: Oxford University Press, 1969.

Raboteau, Albert J. *Slave Religion: The "Invisible Institution" in the Antebellum South*. Oxford: Oxford University Press, 1978.

Rael, Patrick. *Black Identity and Black Protest in the Antebellum North*. Chapel Hill: The University of North Carolina Press, 2002.

———. "Black Theodicy: African Americans and Nationalism in the Antebellum North." *The North Star: A Journal of African American Religious History*. 2.3 (2000). Web. 14 September 2004. <http://northstar.vassar.edu>.

Rakove, Jack N. *Original Meanings: Politics and Ideas in the Making of the Constitution*. New York: Vintage Books, 1997.

Reason, Charles L. "To Fugitive Slaves and Their Friends." 1 March 1854. *The Black Abolitionist Papers, Volume IV, The United States, 1847–1858*. Ed. C. Peter Ripley et al. Chapel Hill: The University of North Carolina Press, 1991, pp. 204–206.

Reising, Russell. *Loose Ends: Closure & Crisis in American Social Text*. Durham, NC: Duke University Press, 1996.

Remond, Charles Lenox. "Cazenovia Anti-Slavery Convention." 25 March 1947. *Black Abolitionists Archive*. University of Detroit–Mercy. Doc. No. 08465. Web. 4 May 2008.

———. "Charles Lenox Remond to Charles B. Ray." 30 June 1840. *The Black Abolitionist Papers, Volume I, The British Isles, 1830–1865*. Ed. C. Peter Ripley et al. Chapel Hill: The University of North Carolina Press, 1991, pp. 71–79.

———. "Charles Lenox Remond to Nathaniel P. Rogers." 2 October 1841. *The Black Abolitionist Papers, Volume I, The British Isles, 1830–1865*. Ed. C. Peter Ripley et al. Chapel Hill: The University of North Carolina Press, 1991, pp. 97–99.

———. "Report of the New England Convention." 18 July 1844. *Black Abolitionists Archive*. University of Detroit–Mercy. Doc. No. 07522. Web. 4 May 2008.

———. "Speech by Charles Lenox Remond, Delivered at Marlboro Chapel, Boston, Massachusetts." 29 May 1844. *The Black Abolitionist Papers, Volume III, The United States, 1830–1846*. Ed. C. Peter Ripley, et al. Chapel Hill: The University of North Carolina Press, 1991, pp. 442–445.

———. "Speech by Charles Lenox Remond Delivered at Mozart Hall, New York, New York." 13 May 1858. *The Black Abolitionist Papers, Volume IV, The United States, 1830–1846*. Ed. C. Peter Ripley et al. Chapel Hill: The University of North Carolina Press, 1991, pp. 382–390.

———. "Wednesday Afternoon — Fifth Session." 8 August 1844. *Black Abolitionists Archive*. University of Detroit–Mercy. Doc. No. 07537. Web. 4 May 2008.

Remond, Sarah P. "Slave Life in America." 10 May 1851. Black Abolitionist Archives. University of Detroit–Mercy. Web. Doc. No. 11543. 26 May 2007.

———. "Speech by Sarah P. Remond, Delivered at the Athenaeum, Manchester, England." 14 September 1859. *The Black Abolitionist Papers, Volume I, The British Isles, 1830–1865*. Ed. C. Peter Ripley et al. Chapel Hill: The University of North Carolina Press, 1985, pp. 457–461.

———. "Speech by Sarah P. Remond, Delivered at the Music Hall." 24 January 1859. *The Black Abolitionist Papers, Volume I, The British Isles, 1830–1865*. Ed. C. Peter Ripley, et al. Chapel Hill: The University of North Carolina Press, 1985, pp. 435–444.

———. "Speech by Sarah P. Remond, Delivered at the Red Lion Hotel, Warrington, England." 2 February 1859. *The Black Abolitionist Papers, Volume I, The British Isles, 1830–1865*. Ed. C. Peter Ripley et al. Chapel Hill: The University of North Carolina Press, 1985, pp. 445–446.

Remond, Sarah Parker. "American Slavery and African Colonisation," 1 November 1859. *Black Abolitionists Archive*. University of Detroit–Mercy. Doc. No. 21295. Web. 7 May 2007.

———. "Lecture on American Slavery by a Coloured Lady." 24 January 1859. *The Black Abolitionist Papers, Volume I, The British Isles, 1830–1865*. Ed. C. Peter Ripley et al. Chapel Hill: The University of North Carolina Press, 1985, pp. 435–444.

———. "Sarah P. Remond to Maria Weston Chapman." 6 October 1859. *The Black Abolitionist Papers, Volume I, The British Isles, 1830–1865*. Ed. C. Peter Ripley et al. Chapel Hill: The University of North Carolina Press, 1985, pp. 462–463.

"Report by the Committee on Slavery of the New England Conference of the African Methodist Episcopal Church." *The Black Abolitionist Papers, Volume IV, The United States, 1847–1858*. Ed. C. Peter Ripley et al. Chapel Hill: The University of North Carolina Press, 1991, pp. 195–199.

"Resolutions by a Committee of Philadelphia Blacks, Presented at the Brick Wesley African Methodist Episcopal Church, Philadelphia, Pennsylvania." 14 October 1850. *The Black Abolitionist Papers, Volume IV, The United States, 1847–1858*. Ed. C. Peter Ripley et al. Chapel Hill: The University of North Carolina Press, 1991, pp. 68–72.

Rex, John. *Race Relations in Sociological Theory*. New York: Schocken Books, 1970.

Rhodes, Jane. *Mary Ann Shadd Cary: The Black Press and Protest in the Nineteenth-Century*. Bloomington: Indiana University Press, 1988.

Richardson, Lewis. "Speech by Lewis Richardson." *The Black Abolitionist Papers, Volume*

III, The United States, 1830–1846. Ed. C. Peter Ripley et al. Chapel Hill: The University of North Carolina Press, 1991, pp. 101–103.
Richardson, Marilyn, ed. *Maria W. Stewart: America's First Black Woman Political Writer.* Bloomington: Indiana University Press, 1987.
Ripley, C. Peter, et al., eds. *The Black Abolitionist Papers, 5 vols.* Chapel Hill: The University of North Carolina Press, 1985, 1986, 1991, 1992.
Roberson, Susan. "Maria Stewart and the Rhetoric of Mobility." *Journal of International Women's Studies.* 4.3 (2003): 56–61.
Robinson, Dean E. *Black Nationalism in American Politics and Thought.* Cambridge: Cambridge University Press, 2001.
Rollins, Frank L. *Life and Public Services of Martin R. Delany, Sub-Assistant Commissioner Bureau Relief of Refugees Freedmen, and of Abandoned Lands, and Late Major 104th U.S. Colored Troops.* Boston: Lee and Shepard, 1883.
Ruggles, David. "New York Committee of Vigilance for the Year 1837, together with Important Facts Relative to Their Proceedings." 1837. *Pamphlets of Protest: An Anthology of Early African American Protest Literature, 1760–1860.* Eds. Richard Newman, Patrick Rael, and Phillip Lapsansky. New York: Routledge, 2001, pp. 145–155.
Ryan, Barbara. "Maria W. Stewart." *African American Authors, 1745–1945: A Bio-Bibliographical Critical Sourcebook.* Ed. Emmanuel S. Nelson. Westport, CT: Greenwood Press, 2000, pp. 375–378.
Saunders, Prince. "A Memoir Presented to The American Convention for Promoting the Abolition of Slavery, and Improving the Condition of the African race." 11 December 1818. *Early Negro Writing, 1760–1837.* Ed. Dorothy Porter. Baltimore: Black Classic Press, 1995, pp. 269–278.
Shadd, Abraham D., Peter Spencer and William S. Thomas. "Address by Abraham D. Shadd, Peter Spencer, and William S. Thomas." 12 July 1831. *The Black Abolitionist Papers, Volume III, The United States, 1830–1846.* Ed. C. Peter Ripley et al. Chapel Hill: The University of North Carolina Press, 1991, pp. 102–108.
Sharp, Carolyn J. "The Call of Jeremiah and Diaspora Politics." *Journal of Biblical Literature,* 119.3 (2000): 421–438.
Shields, John C., ed. *The Collected Works of Phyllis Wheatley.* New York: Oxford University Press, 1988.
Shirley, Walter. Preface. *A Narrative of the Most Remarkable Particulars in the Life of James Albert Ukawsaw Gronniosaw, An African Prince, As Related By Himself.* 1770. Electronic Edition. *University of North Carolina–Chapel Hill Academic Affairs Library.* Web. 30 September 2000. <http://docsouth.unc.edu/>.
Shortell, Timothy. "The Rhetoric of Black Abolitionism: An Exploratory Analysis of Anti-Slavery Newspapers in New York State." *Social Science History,* 28.1 (2004): 75–109.
Silverman, Jason H. "Mary Ann Shadd and the Search for Equality." *A Nation of Immigrants: Women, Workers, and Communities in Canadian History.* Eds. Franca Iacovetta and Robert Ventresca. Toronto: University of Toronto Press, 1998, pp. 101–115.
Simons, Peter Paul. "Speech by Peter Paul Simons, Delivered before the African Clarkson Association, New York, New York." 23 April 1839. *The Black Abolitionist Papers, Volume III, The United States, 1830–1846.* Ed. C. Peter Ripley et al. Chapel Hill: The University of North Carolina Press, 1991, pp. 288–293.
Sinha, Manisha. "Coming of Age: The Historiography of Black Abolitionism." *Prophets of Protest: Reconsidering the History of American Abolitionism.* Ed. Timothy Patrick McCarthy and John Stauffer. New York: The New Press, 2006, pp. 23–38.
Smith, James McCune. "The Anniversaries. National Council of the Colored People." 1856. Web. 24 July 1007. <http://jamesmccunesmith.com/?page_id=12>.
_____. "James McCune Smith to Frederick Douglass." *The Black Abolitionist Papers, Volume IV, The United States, 1847–1858.* Ed. C. Peter Ripley et al. Chapel Hill: The University of North Carolina Press, 1991, pp. 220–226.

_____. "Remarks by James McCune Smith." 15 March 1837. *The Black Abolitionist Papers, Volume I, The British Isles, 1830–1865.* Ed. C. Peter Ripley et al. Chapel Hill: The University of North Carolina Press, 1985, pp. 65–67.
"The Sons of Africans: An Essay on Freedom. With Observations on the Origin of Slavery. By A member of the African Society in Boston. 1808. *Early Negro Writing, 1760–1837.* Ed. Dorothy Porter. Baltimore: Black Classic Press, 1995, pp. 13–27.
Stanton, Elizabeth Cady, et al. *History of Woman Suffrage.* New York: Fowler & Wells, 1881.
Starling, Marion Wilson. *The Slave Narrative: Its Place in American History.* 2nd ed. Washington, DC: Howard University Press, 1988.
Starobin, Robert S. *Denmark Vesey: The Slave Conspiracy of 1822.* Englewood Cliffs, NJ: Prentice-Hall, 1970.
Sterling, Dorothy. ed. *We Are Your Sisters: Black Women in the Nineteenth Century.* New York: W. W. Norton and Company, 1984.
Steward, Barbara Ann. "Barbara Ann Steward to Frederick Douglass." 29 May 1855. *The Black Abolitionist Papers, Volume IV, The United States, 1847–1858.* Ed. C. Peter Ripley et al. Chapel Hill: The University of North Carolina Press, 1991, pp. 295–297.
Stewart, Maria Miller. "An Address Delivered At the African Masonic Hall." *Maria W. Stewart: America's First Black Woman Political Writer.* Ed. Marilyn Richardson. Bloomington: Indiana University Press, 1987, pp. 56–64.
_____. "An Address Delivered Before the Afric-American Female Intelligence Society of America." *Maria W. Stewart: America's First Black Woman Political Writer.* Ed. Marilyn Richardson. Bloomington: Indiana University Press, 1987, pp. 50–55.
_____. "Cause for Encouragement." *Maria W. Stewart: America's First Black Woman Political Writer.* Ed. Marilyn Richardson. Bloomington: Indiana University Press, 1987, pp. 43–44.
_____. "Lecture Delivered at the Franklin Hall." *Maria W. Stewart: America's First Black Woman Political Writer.* Ed. Marilyn Richardson. Bloomington: Indiana University Press, 1987, pp. 45–49.
_____. "Mrs. Stewart's Farewell Address to Her Friends in the City of Boston." *Maria W. Stewart: America's First Black Woman Political Writer.* Ed. Marilyn Richardson. Bloomington: Indiana University Press, 1987, pp. 65–74.
_____. "Religion and the Pure Principles of Morality, the Sure Foundation of Which we must Build." *Maria W. Stewart: America's First Black Woman Political Writer.* Ed. Marilyn Richardson. Bloomington: Indiana University Press, 1987, pp. 43–44.
Still, John N. "John N. Still to Frederick Douglass." *The Black Abolitionist Papers, Volume IV, The United States, 1847–1858.* Ed. C. Peter Ripley et al. Chapel Hill: The University of North Carolina Press, 1991, pp. 214–219.
Thomas, Helen. *Romanticism and Slave Narratives: Transatlantic Testimonies.* Cambridge: Cambridge University Press, 2000.
Truth, Sojourner. "New York City Anti-Slavery Society." *Sojourner Truth as Orator: Wit, Story, and Song.* Eds. Suzanne Pullon Fitch and Roseann M. Mandziuk. Westport, CT: Greenwood Press, 1997, pp. 109–110.
_____. "Specimens of Religious Talk to Second Adventists." *Sojourner Truth as Orator: Wit, Story, and Song.* Eds. Suzanne Pullon Fitch and Roseann M. Mandziuk. Westport, CT: Greenwood Press, 1997, pp. 101–102.
_____. "Women's Right Convention." *Sojourner Truth as Orator: Wit, Story, and Song.* Eds. Suzanne Pullon Fitch and Roseann M. Mandziuk. Westport, CT: Greenwood Press, 1997, pp. 111–112.
_____, and Olive Gilbert. *Narrative of Sojourner Truth, a Northern Slave, Emancipated from Bodily Servitude by the State of New York, in 1828.* Boston: J. B. Yerrinton and Son, Printers. Electronic Edition. *University of North Carolina–Chapel Hill Academic Affairs Library.* Web. 30 September 2000. <http://docsouth.unc.edu/>.
Turner, Nat. *The Confessions of Nat Turner, the Leader of the Late Insurrection in South Hampton, Va.* Published By Thomas R. Gray. Baltimore: Lucas & Deaver, 1831. Electronic

Edition. University of North Carolina–Chapel Hill Academic Affairs Library Web. 30 September 2000. <http://docsouth.unc.edu/>.
200 Years of United Methodism: An Illustrated History. 4 April 2008. Web. 23 September 2009. <http://depts.drew.edu/lib/books/200Years/200UM/homepage.htm>.
Ullman, Victor. *Martin Delany: The Beginnings of Black Nationalism*. Boston: Beacon Press, 1971.
"Uncle Tom's Cabin." *Southern Literary Messenger* (October 1852): 630–638.
Utley, Ebony. "A Woman Made of Words: The Rhetorical Invention of Maria W. Stewart." *Black Women's Intellectual Traditions: Speaking Their Minds*. Eds. Kristin Waters and Carol B. Conaway. Burlington: University of Vermont Press, 2007, pp. 55–71.
Van Deburg, William L. *Modern Black Nationalism: From Marcus Garvey to Louis Farrakhan*. New York: New York University Press, 1997.
Walker, David. *Appeal, in Four Articles, Together With A Preamble, to the Colored Citizens of the World, But in Particular, and Very Expressly to those of the United States of America*. Boston. 1829. *Walker's Appeal and Garnet's Address to the Slaves of the United States of America*. Nashville: James C. Winston Publishing Company, Inc., 1994, pp. 9–88.
Walters, Ronald W. *Pan Africanism in the African Diaspora: An Analysis of Modern Afrocentric Political Movements*. Detroit: Wayne State University Press, 1993.
Ward, Samuel Ringgold. "Aid for Fugitive Slaves in Canada." *Black Abolitionist Archives*. University of Detroit–Mercy. Doc. No. 14259. Web. 16 August 2007.
_____. *Autobiography of a Fugitive Negro: His Anti-Slavery Labours in the United States, Canada, & England*. 1855. Electronic Edition. *University of North Carolina–Chapel Hill Academic Affairs Library*. Web. 30 September 2000. <http://docsouth.unc.edu/>.
_____. "Canadian Negro Hate." October 1852. *The Black Abolitionist Papers, Volume II, Canada 1830–1865*. Ed. C. Peter Ripley et al. Chapel Hill: The University of North Carolina Press, 1986, pp. 224–237.
_____. "Escaped Slaves from the 'Land of Freedom.'" *Black Abolitionist Archives*. University of Detroit–Mercy. Doc. No. 14612. Web. 17 August 2006.
_____. "Fugitive Slaves. Public Meeting at Crosby Hall." *Black Abolitionist Archives*. University of Detroit–Mercy. Doc. No. 16479. Web. 29 July 2007.
_____. "Fugitive Slaves in Canada." 22 March 1855. *Black Abolitionist Archives*. University of Detroit–Mercy. Doc. No. 14934. Web. 23 March 2007.
_____. "Modern Negro. No. 1" January 1855. *The Black Abolitionist Papers, Volume I, The British Isles, 1830–1865*. Ed. C. Peter Ripley et al. Chapel Hill: The University of North Carolina Press, 1985, pp. 412–416.
_____. "Modern Negro. No. 2" March 1855. *The Black Abolitionist Papers, Volume I, The British Isles, 1830–1865*. Ed. C. Peter Ripley et al. Chapel Hill: The University of North Carolina Press, 1985, pp. 417–422.
_____. "Relations of Canada to American Slavery." 24 March 1853. *The Black Abolitionist Papers, Volume II, Canada, 1830–1865*. Ed. C. Peter Ripley et al. Chapel Hill: The University of North Carolina Press, 1986, pp. 228–237.
_____. "Samuel Ringgold Ward to Henry Bibb." 6 November 1851. *The Black Abolitionist Papers, Volume II, Canada, 1830–1865*. Ed. C. Peter Ripley et al. Chapel Hill: The University of North Carolina Press, 1986, pp. 182–183.
_____. "Samuel Ringgold Ward to the Readers of the *Provincial Freeman*." 27 April 1854. *The Black Abolitionist Papers, Volume I, The British Isles, 1830–1865*. Ed. C. Peter Ripley et al. Chapel Hill: The University of North Carolina Press, 1986, pp. 391–394.
_____. "Speech by Samuel Ringgold Ward, Delivered at Faneuil Hall, Boston, Massachusetts." 25 March 1850. *The Black Abolitionist Papers, Volume IV, The United States, 1847–1858*. Ed. C. Peter Ripley et al. Chapel Hill: The University of North Carolina Press, 1991, pp. 48–52.
Waters, Kristin. "Some Core Themes of Nineteenth-Century Black Feminism." *Black*

Women's Intellectual Traditions: Speaking Their Minds. Eds. Kristin Waters and Carol B. Conaway. Burlington: University of Vermont Press, 2007, pp. 365–392.

Watkins, William J. "Anti-Slavery Celebration at Abington, July Fourth." 15 July 1853. *Black Abolitionists Archive.* University of Detroit–Mercy. Doc. No. 14334. Web. 13 April 2006.

———. "Effect of the Nebraska Bill." 3 March 1854. *The Black Abolitionist Papers, Volume IV, The United States, 1847–1858.* Ed. C. Peter Ripley et al. Chapel Hill: The University of North Carolina Press, 1991, pp. 207–209.

———. "Emancipation Day at Drummondville, Canada West." 23 August 1861. *Black Abolitionist Archives.* University of Detroit–Mercy. Doc. No. 24325. Web. 23 May 2008.

———. "Meeting of the Colored Education Institute." *Black Abolitionist Archives*, University of Detroit–Mercy. Web. Doc. No. 24337. 26 May 2007.

———. "One Thing Thou Lackest." 10 February 1854. *The Black Abolitionist Papers, Volume IV, The United States, 1847–1858.* Ed. C. Peter Ripley et al. Chapel Hill: The University of North Carolina Press, 1991, pp. 200–203.

———. "Our Influence Abroad." 22 December 1854. *The Black Abolitionist Papers, Volume IV, The United States, 1847–1858.* Ed. C. Peter Ripley et al. Chapel Hill: The University of North Carolina Press, 1991, pp. 256–258.

———. "Public Meeting of Colored Citizens." *Black Abolitionist Archives*, University of Detroit–Mercy. Doc. No. 24111. Web. 26 May 2007.

———. "Who are the Murderers?" 2 June 1854. *The Black Abolitionist Papers, Volume IV, The United States, 1847–1858.* Ed. C. Peter Ripley et al. Chapel Hill: The University of North Carolina Press, 1991, pp. 227–229.

———. "William Watkins to William Lloyd Garrison," 12 February 1831. *The Black Abolitionist Papers, Volume III, The United States, 1830–1846.* Ed. C. Peter Ripley et al. Chapel Hill: The University of North Carolina Press, 1991, pp. 92–97.

Watkins, William, Jacob M. Moore, and Jacob C. White, Sr. "To the Colored Churches in the Free States." November 1836. *The Black Abolitionist Papers, Volume III, The United States, 1830–1846.* Ed. C. Peter Ripley et al. Chapel Hill: The University of North Carolina Press, 1991, pp. 189–200.

Watson, Henry. *Narrative of Henry Watson, A Fugitive Slave: Written By Himself.* 1848. Electronic Edition. University of North Carolina–Chapel Hill Academic Affairs Library. Web. 30 September 2000. <http://docsouth.unc.edu/>.

Weisenburger, Steven. *Modern Medea: A Family Story of Slavery and Child Murder from the Old South.* New York: Hill and Wang, 1998.

Wesley, Charles H. *Richard Allen: An Apostle of Freedom.* Trenton: Africa World Press, 2002.

Wheatley, Phillis. *The Collected Works of Phillis Wheatley.* Ed. John C. Shields. New York: Oxford University Press, 1988.

Whipper, William. "Speech by William Whipper Delivered at the First African Presbyterian Church Philadelphia, Pennsylvania." 16 August 1837. *The Black Abolitionist Papers, Volume III, The United States, 1830–1846.* Ed. C. Peter Ripley et al. Chapel Hill: The University of North Carolina Press, 1991, pp. 238–251.

———. "Speech by William Whipper Delivered before the Colored Temperance Society of Philadelphia." *The Black Abolitionist Papers, Volume III, The United States, 1830–1846.* Ed. C. Peter Ripley et al. Chapel Hill: The University of North Carolina Press, 1991, pp. 119–131.

———. "William Whipper to Frederick Douglass." October 1854. *The Black Abolitionist Papers, Volume IV, The United States, 1847–1858.* Ed. C. Peter Ripley et al. Chapel Hill: The University of North Carolina Press, 1991, pp. 242–244.

———, Alfred Niger, and August Price. "Address by William Whipper, Alfred Niger, and August Price." 3 June 1835. *The Black Abolitionist Papers, Volume III, The United States, 1830–1846.* Ed. C. Peter Ripley et al. Chapel Hill: The University of North Carolina Press, 1991, pp. 146–153.

White, Jacob C., Jr. "Essay by Jacob C. White, Jr." *The Black Abolitionist Papers, Volume IV, The United States, 1847–1858.* Ed. C. Peter Ripley et al. Chapel Hill: The University of North Carolina Press, 1991, pp. 210–211.

Willard, Carla. "Wheatley's Turns of Praise: Heroic Entrapment and the Paradox of the Revolution." *American Literature* 67.2 (1995): 233–256.

Williams, George Washington. *History of the Negro Race in America from 1619 to 1880.* New York: G. P. Putnam's Sons, 1885.

Williams, Peter. "A Discourse Delivered in St. Phillip's Church, for the Benefit of the Coloured Community of Wilberforce, in Upper Canada." 4 July 1830. *Early Negro Writing, 1760–1837.* Ed. Dorothy Porter. Baltimore: Black Classics Press, 1995, pp. 294–307.

Wilson, William J. "William J. Wilson to Frederick Douglass." 5 March 1853. *The Black Abolitionist Papers, Volume IV, The United States, 1847–1858.* Ed. C. Peter Ripley et al. Chapel Hill: The University of North Carolina Press, 1991, pp. 140–145.

Winch, Julie. *A Gentleman of Color: The Life of James Forten.* Oxford: Oxford University Press, 2002.

Winks, Robin W. *Blacks in Canada.* New Haven: Yale University Press, 1971.

Winthrop, John. "A Modell of Christian Charity." 1630. *Collections of the Massachusetts Historical Society, 3rd Series 7.* Boston: Massachusetts Historical Society, 1838, p. 31–48.

Wright, Donald R. *African Americans in the Early Republic, 1798–1831.* Wheeling: Harlan Davidson, Inc., 1993.

Wright, Frederick D. "The History of Black Political Participation to 1965." *Blacks in Southern Politics.* Eds. Laurence W. Moreland, Robert P. Steed, and Todd A. Baker. New York: Praeger, 1987, pp. 9–30.

Wright, Richard L. "The Word at Work: Ideological and Epistemological Dynamics in African American Rhetoric." *Understanding African American Rhetoric: Classical Origins to Contemporary Innovations.* Eds. Ronald L. Jackson II and Elaine B. Richardson. New York: Routledge, 2003, pp. 85–98.

Wright, Theodore S. "Prejudice Against the Colored Man." 8 July 1837. *Black Abolitionists Archive.* University of Detroit–Mercy. Doc. No. 02086. Web. 5 January 2006.

Yee, Shirley. *Black Women Abolitionists: A Study in Activism, 1828–1860.* Knoxville: The University of Tennessee Press, 1992.

_____. "Finding a Place: Mary Ann Shadd Cary and the Dilemmas of Black Migration to Canada, 1850–1870." *Frontiers: A Journal of Women Studies.* 18.3 (1997). Web. 3 July 2009. <http://findarticles.com/p/articles/mi_qa3687/is_199701/ai_n8750717>.

Zafar, Rafia. *We Wear the Mask: African Americans Write American Literature, 1760–1870.* New York: Columbia University Press, 1997.

Index

abolitionism 115–159; *see also* Black abolitionist Jeremiahs
African American jeremiad: advocated temperance 137–138; components 16; constructivist principles 63–64; definition 9–10; differences from American jeremiad 15, 25–26; phases 34; purposes 10, 25–30, 61; recognizable stages 34–35; religious piety and foundations 38; three types 30–33 (*see also* economic jeremiad; political jeremiad; religious jeremiad); Transatlantic jeremiads 160–176
African American rhetoric 6
African Lodge of the Honorable Society of the Free and Accepted Masons of Boston 73, 83
African Methodist Church 19
Alexander, E. Curtis 79
Allen, Richard 9, 19, 54, 79, 104, 141; *see also* Free African Society (FAS)
Allen, William G. 154–155, 165
"An American Citizen" 63
American Colonization Society (ACS) 79, 86, 162
The American Industrial School 124; *see also* The National Council for the Colored People
American jeremiad 13–14, 25, 26
American Revolution 18, 21
Amistad Trial 92
Ampadu, Lena 104
anamnesis 105, 107, 108; *see also* Stewart, Maria Miller
Anti-Colonization Jeremiad 97–99; *see also* Stewart, Maria Miller
Anti-Constitution Jeremiad 69–71; *see also* Remond, Charles Lenox
anti–jeremiad 69–70; *see also* Sacvan Bercovitch

Anti-Slavery Society of Canada (ASC) 179
Apess, William 16–17

"Back-to-Africa" movement 79; *see also* Colonization Movement
Baker, Houston A. 120–121
The Baltimore American 142
Barry, Brian 33, 63, 66
Bercovitch, Sacvan 13–14, 17, 25, 26, 69, 70, 82, 102; *see also* anti-jeremiad
Bethel African Methodist Episcopal Church 149
Bibb, Henry 2, 136–137, 177, 179–180, 184–185, 187–191, 194–195; *see also* *Voices of the Fugitive*
Bibb, Sen. James 188
Bibb, Mary 179
black abolitionist Jeremiahs 115–159; *see also* abolitionism
black Canadian jeremiad 177–195; differences from African American jeremiad 177–178, gender 188; *see also* Cary, Mary Ann Shadd
black jeremiad 1, 9
black Jeremiah Nationalists 73–92
Black Nationalism 73–92
black women Jeremiahs: development 94–95
Blake, or the Huts of America 152–153; *see also* Delany, Martin
Blanks, Granville B. 61, 82, 147
Brick Wesley African Methodist Episcopal Church 149
Brooks, Lloyd H. 157
Brown, Henry "Box" 145
Brown, John 112, 157–158, 193; *see also* Harpers Ferry
Brown, William Wells 5, 7, 58, 61, 116–

117, 127, 145–146, 150, 152, 165–169, 176, 180, 186–187
Buchanan, Pres. James 155, 193
Burns, Anthony 151
Bustill, Cyrus 44
Butler, Judith 68

Calvinism 41
Carmichael, Stokley 81
Cary, Mary Ann Shadd 119, 188, 191–193, 191; feminist discourse 192
Clarke, Lewis G. 135
Clay, Sen. Henry 182
Coffey, Alvin 142
Coker, Daniel 141
Colonization Movement 98
"A Colored Baltimorean" 65; see also Watkins, William J.
"A Colored Woman" 95
commercial jeremiad 32–33, 172
Committee of Vigilance for the Protection of the People of Color 141
Compromise of 1850 147; see also Fugitive Slave Act of 1850
Constitutional Convention 1787 22, 60, 64
Convention of the People of Colour 128
Cooper, Afua 183
Cottman, Martha L. 75
Cottman, Richard W. 75
Craft, Ellen 135, 145
Craft, William 135, 145, 152
Crummell, Alexander 162, 171–172
Cuffee, Paul 64–65, 79, 85
Cugoano, Quobna Ottabah 32–33, 56–58

Darsey, James 16, 100
Day, William Howard 65–66
Delany, Martin 58, 66, 88–91, 104, 122–123, 132, 147–148, 150, 152–154, 172–173; see also *Blake, or the Huts of America*
Delondes, Charles 29
Dickens, Charles 170
Dickson, Bruce D., Jr. 42
Douglas, H. Ford 65, 66, 157
Douglass, Frederick 11, 19, 29, 58, 60, 66, 89, 115–116, 117–118, 121–122, 124, 129, 130–131, 143–145, 150–151, 153–154, 155–156, 158, 164–165, 169–171, 182
Douglass, Sarah M. 28
Dred Scott Decision 66, 92, 155–157, 193

early slave narrators 52–58
Easton, Hosea 27, 45, 64, 82
economic jeremiad 32–33, 140; see also commercial jeremiad
Elliot, Emory 10
emigration 88–91; to Africa 172, 194; to Canada 89, 193–195; to Haiti 87, 187, 194; to Jamaica 194; to Liberia 88, 134; to Mexico 87
Enlightenment ideology 36, 39
Ephesians 6: 5–9 31
Equiano, Olaudah 28, 54–56
Ethiopianism 90; see also Stewart, Maria Miller
European jeremiad 25

feminism 95–97, 107–108, 113; see also Harper, Frances Ellen; Stewart, Maria Miller
feminists transatlantic jeremiad 173–174
First African Baptist Church 23
First Great Awakening 38; see also Great Awakenings
Forten, James, Sr. 32, 63, 67–69, 84–85, 86, 125, 139
Francis, Abner H. 142
Franklin Hall (Boston) 93
Free African Society (FAS) 79; see also Allen, Richard
Free African Society of Newport 79
"A Free Female of Philadelphia" 87
Freire, Paulo 80–81
Fugitive Slave Act of 1793 22, 34, 148
Fugitive Slave Act of 1850 19, 82, 91, 142, 146–152, 161, 179–180; see also Compromise of 1850

Gardell, Mattias 75–76
Gardner, Charles W. 20, 23, 116
Garnet, Henry Highland 17, 19, 29, 45, 78, 81, 127, 128, 131–135, 159; see also "Sidney"
Garrison, William Lloyd 104, 116, 118, 119, 120, 128, 130
Garrisonians 118–119
Gilyard, Keith 9, 104
Gordon, Dexter, B. 6, 74
Gouins, Henry 181
Gould, Philip 32
Gray, Thomas 128
Great Awakenings 7, 38, 41, 52, 54, 58
Green, Samuel 152
Gronniosaw, James Albert Ukawsaw 54

Index

Hahn, Steven 8
Haitian Emigration Society 79, 85
Hall, Prince 73, 83–82, 103
Hamilton, Charles V. 81
Hamilton, Thomas 158
Hamilton, William 51, 65, 122
Hammond, Jupiter 9, 24, 36–39, 43–48, 52, 54, 59, 122, 125, 127, 197
Harper, Frances Ellen 23, 25, 112–114, moral reform 113; *see also* feminism
Harpers Ferry 112; *see also* Brown, John
Harris, Andrew 22, 86–87
Hartman, Saidiya V. 26
Haynes, Lemuel 9, 24–25, 30–31
Henderson, Stephen 40
Henry, Patrick 149
Henson, Josiah 189
Holly, James Theodore 189–190
Holly, Joseph C. 78, 80, 194–195
Hord, Fred Lee 76
Howard-Pitney, David 1, 8, 10, 118

indentured servitude 20–21
Independent Gazetteer 63

James, Elisabeth 40
James Redpath's Haitian Emigration Bureau 180, 187
Jefferson, Thomas 142
Jehu, Jones 183
jeremiad, defined 7
Jim Crow 187
Johnstone, Abraham 21–22
Jones, Absalom 9, 104, 141
Jones, Thomas 53
Jordan, Winthrop D. 10

Karenga, Maulana 76
Katz, William Loren 29
Kellas, James G. 76
Kelly, Edmund 164
King, Martin Luther, Jr. 20
King George III 50–51

Lambert, William 158
Langston, Charles H. 148
Lawrence, George, Jr. 85–86, 92, 158
Lee, Jarena 54
Liberator 76, 104, 116, 128
Lincoln, Abraham 157
Loguen, Jermain Wesley 147, 179, 182

manifest destiny 18, 77, 90, 91, 142, 143

Mashpee Revolt of 1833 16
"A Member of the African Society in Boston" 62–63; *see also* "The Sons of Africans"
Memorial African Methodist Episcopal Zion Church 151
Methodism 43
Miller, Perry 24, 25, 26, 27
Mississippi (black codes) 128
Missouri Compromise of 1820 149
Moore, Jacob 33
Moorehead, Scipio 51–52
moral reform 113, 120, 127
moral suasion 43, 70, 116, 125, 127, 131, 194
Moses, Wilson Jeremiah 1, 9, 74, 75, 90, 104

The National Council for the Colored People 124; *see also* The American Industrial School
national identity 14, 22, 38, 60, 77, 78, 144, 145, 195
Native American Declaration of Independence 16
Native American jeremiad 16
Nebraska Bill 149
New York Vigilance Committee 140
Newby, William H. 142–143; *see also* NUBIA
Niger, Alfred 28, 124–125
North American Convention 180, 195; *see also* "Proceedings of the North American Convention"
Northup, Solomon 29
NUBIA 142–143; *see also* Newby, William H.

Oberlin-Wellington Rescue 148
Occom, Samson 38
O'Connell, Daniel 134–135, 163
O'Neale, Sondra 118
Oneida Institute 165
Osborne, William 183

paganism 42
pamphlets 139–141
Parrott, Russell 86, 139
Paul, Nathaniel 23, 34, 161, 162–163
Payne, Daniel A. 22, 35, 139–140
Peck, John 124
Pennington, J.W.C. 160–161, 165–166
Pennsylvania's constitution 1838 67
Pennsylvania's Emancipation Act 22

Pinckney, Charles Cotesworth 63
"political abolitionist" 143
political jeremiad 31–32
Powell, William P. 119–120
"practical abolitionists" 141
Pre–Civil War jeremiad 144
Price, Augustus 28, 124–125, 138
Price, John 148
"Proceedings of a Meeting of Toronto Blacks" 183
"Proceedings of the North American Convention" 180; *see also* North American Convention
Prosser, Gabriel 29
The Provincial Freeman (Canada) 188
Puritan jeremiad 24, 27, 196
Puritan Nationalism 82
Purvis, Robert 139, 151, 156, 157–158, 159

Quakers 118; *see also* The Society of Friends (SOF)

Rael, Patrick 9, 74
Rakove, Jack N. 64
Ray, Charles 163
Read, Thomas 21
Reason, Charles L. 181–182
Refugee Home Soceity (RHS) 189
Reising, Russell 39
religious jeremiad 30–31
Remond, Charles Lenox 64, 70–71, 128, 147, 163, 165, 173; *see also* Anti-Constitution Jeremiad
Remond, Sarah P. 156, 173–175; *see also* feminists transatlantic jeremiad
"Resolutions by a Committee of Philadelphia Blacks" 149–150
Rex, John 8
Richardson, Lewis 182
Richardson, Marilyn 103
Roberson, Susan 100
Ruggles, David 28, 140–141

Saunders, Prince 87
"Second Annual Convention of the People of Color" 104
Second Great Awakening 53, 122, 127, 144
Self-Elevation Tract Society 89
Seven Years' War 18
Shadd, Abraham D. 90, 91, 104
Shirley, Walter 54
"Sidney" 81
Simons, Peter Paul 62, 120

Smith, James McCune 19, 124, 163
The Society of Friends (SOF) 118; *see also* Quakers
"The Sons of Africans" 18, 62–63; *see also* "A Member of the African Society in Boston"
Southern Literary Messenger (Richmond, VA) 154
Spencer, Peter 90, 91, 104
Starling, Marion 153
Steward, Austin 124
Steward, Barbara Ann 124
Stewart, Maria Miller 93–94, 95–109; anamnesis 105, 107, 108; Anti-Colonization Jeremiad 97–99; criticized black manhood 97; Ethiopianism 103–106; feminism 95–97, 107–108; prophetic jeremiads 100–103
Still, John N. 79
Stowe, Harriet Beecher 152–155; *see also Uncle Tom's Cabin*

Taney, Roger B. 155
Third Christian Church (Bedford, MA) 157
Thomas, William S. 90, 91, 104
Thompson, A.C.C. 144
three-fifth clause 64
"Tom-mania" 154; *see also Uncle Tom's Cabin*
Truth, Sojourner 109–112, 147, 151
Turner, Nat 29–30, 91, 127–129, 132

ultra-abolitionists 116, 174
Uncle Tom's Cabin 152–155; *see also* Stowe, Harriet Beecher; "Tom-mania"

Van Deburg, William L. 75
Vesey, Denmark 29, 128
Voice of the Fugitive 177, 188; *see also* Bibb, Henry

Walker, David 17, 28, 29, 45, 69, 83, 125–127, 129, 151, 159
Walters, Ronald W 8
Ward, Samuel Ringgold 18, 19, 23, 118–119, 148, 154, 161–162, 178–179, 182, 185–186, 188, 195
Wardi, Anissa 9, 104
Washington DC 128, 142
Watkins, William J. 33, 61, 65, 122, 124, 149, 151, 162, 180–181, 194; *see also* "A Colored Baltimorean"

Wesley, John 118
Wheatley, Phyllis 9, 24, 36–43, 48–52, 54, 59, 122, 125, 197
Whipper, William 15, 28, 81, 117–118, 123–124, 124–125, 138
White, Jacob C., Sr. 33, 138
White American Nationalism 77

Whitefield, George 38, 49, 50, 54, 118
Williams, Peter 17, 87–88, 121
Wilson, William J. 154, 198
Winthrop, John 13
Wright, Frederick D. 142
Wright, Richard L. 26
Wright, Theodore S. 117–118

www.ingramcontent.com/pod-product-compliance
Lightning Source LLC
Chambersburg PA
CBHW032049300426
44116CB00007B/667